Fanatical

fanatical

Fanatical

Everpresent since 1968. An incredible journey.

Gary Edwards and Andy Starmore

Foreword by Brian McDermott

First published by Pitch Publishing, 2014

Pitch Publishing
A2 Yeoman Gate
Yeoman Way
Durrington
BN13 3QZ
www.pitchpublishing.co.uk

A CIP catalogue record is available for this book
from the British Library.

ISBN 978 1-90962-637-9

Typesetting and origination by Pitch Publishing

Printed in Spain by GraphyCems

Contents

This is the story of an extraordinary supporter. Leeds United fan Gary Edwards has missed just one game (a friendly) anywhere in the world since January 1968. Gary's epic journey began in 1966 when he was ten years old and is brilliantly captured here by Andy Starmore who has painstakingly sewn together every single match that Gary has been to from all four corners of the earth. Leeds United have conceivably the most loyal fan base anywhere in the world and this superb book is the recollections of just two of those amazing supporters.

Mike O'Grady
A prominent member of Don Revie's elite squad in the 1960s

Dedications

From Gary:
Wub, for her continued support in my quest –
and also for her contribution to the cover.

From Andy:
Malena, Ben, Russell, Harry, Alison and Barry
Starmore – and Mum
   And Granddad, Henry (Harry) James
Huddart (ever present at Elland Road from
1930 to 1939)
      Love you all
      We're all Marching On Together

Prologue

ETCH Field, the home of Swansea Town, was the scene in 1962 where Don Revie introduced a crop of youngsters as part of his plan to make the struggling Second Division side Leeds United into a top team, one of the best in Europe.

Gary Sprake was a 16-year-old apprentice goalkeeper when Revie had given him his first-team debut the season before and now here against Swansea (where Sprake was born) Revie was ready to play him again.

Alongside Sprake that day, Revie gave three more promising youngsters their debuts – Rod Johnson (who scored), Paul Reaney and Norman Hunter. All three were 17 years old. Leeds won 2-0 with another youngster called Billy Bremner getting the second.

The resurgence of Leeds United had begun.

Gary Edwards's journey would begin four years later.

Introduction

THIS is the story of Gary Edwards, who hasn't missed a competitive Leeds United match anywhere in the world since January 1968. That's 46 years of incredible loyalty. In fact he's only missed one friendly and that was through no fault of his own. An air traffic control strike prevented him from boarding a flight to Toronto – he had a match ticket and a flight ticket.

Brian Clough lasted 44 days. Jock Stein lasted 44 days. Another 19 managers have come and gone (20 if you include Eddie Gray twice – although he's far from gone, given his role as commentator on Yorkshire Radio with the brilliant Thom Kirwin, hospitality stuff and complete and utter devotion to Leeds United) and Brian McDermott is the latest man to depart Elland Road. Hundreds of players have been and gone and, since Gary began his mammoth run there have been 11 chairmen taking over the reins at Elland Road.

Players, managers, chairmen, members of the board, coaches and staff will always be bypassing as their football careers go in different directions but what about the football fan? From the moment you are hooked as a small boy, kicking a tennis ball around in the playground, as I can remember, to the maturity of retirement days, the football fan is a loyal-to-the-bitter-end beast. Through thick and thin, ups and downs, highs and lows, the football fan will never change. Once it's in your blood that's it.

How often do you see grown men with beer bellies big enough to take up two seats sobbing into their hops at the end of a season when their side has been relegated? How often have you seen supposedly mature men, who have very responsible jobs, returning to the office on the Monday in their smart suits and gleaming shoes, turning into some kind of demented kid at a friend's party, jumping around like Zebedee on the Saturday just gone when your team has won a trophy – or beaten manchester united? It's all part and parcel of a game that is electrifying because of the fans. The fans make the game.

If you take out the war years, when no competitive football was played, Gary Edwards has seen over half of the entire history of Leeds United's matches. I would be absolutely amazed if anyone in the world could beat that. Gary is not only the biggest supporter in the world (probably), he also possesses a true Yorkshire wit, which will certainly make you chuckle.

'We all love Leeds, we all love Leeds...' 'You're only here to watch the Leeds...' 'Marching on Together.' Yes, Leeds fans are both noisy and loyal.

Gary's first ever Leeds game came on 26 March 1966, two days prior to his 11th birthday. It was a First Division fixture against Blackpool at Elland Road. With all the excitement and the incredible atmosphere, Gary left Elland Road that day thinking that Leeds had won the match 1-0. Unfortunately Blackpool emerged as 2-1 winners. You could forgive Gary for thinking the way he did though, as when Blackpool had scored the only noises coming from the terraces were still Leeds supporters. The atmosphere alone had Gary hooked for life.

Prior to getting on to the non-stop run of matches Gary has attended, he had already been to many games for two years.

West Ham United and Sunderland spring to Gary's mind as he explains, 'I remember seeing West Ham for the very first time in 1967. It was at Elland Road on the last day of November. England had won the World Cup the year before and there had been a trio of West Ham players in the team. And, although Bobby Moore, Geoff Hurst and Martin Peters were warmly applauded that day, a lot of Leeds fans wanted Leeds to "knock the stuffing out of 'em," as the bloke stood next to me and my dad shouted, along with a mouthful of chewed up crisps that ended up on the shoulder of the lad who was about my age and was stood at the side of me at the wall in front of the open kop.

'The reason for this outburst from that bloke and many other Leeds fans was down to the fact that just three weeks before, West Ham had beaten Leeds 7-0 in the League Cup at Upton Park. Ouch!

'Leeds won that day 2-1, after going a goal down, Johnny Giles and good old Albert Johanneson doing the honours. I thought afterwards, "That should make that bloke happy." I have no idea where it came from, but I had visions of him going home if Leeds had lost, and his poor wife (if indeed he had one) sat there at the table with all of the bloke's tea all over her face as he ranted about another defeat.

'Funnily enough, my first ever Leeds game against Sunderland was an FA Cup tie in the 1966/67 fifth round. In front of a hostile crowd Jack Charlton scored to earn Leeds a 1-1 draw and a replay at Elland Road just four days later.

'There wasn't enough time to make the replay all-ticket and this caused more problems than anyone could have imagined. About half an hour before kick-off, the gates were closed, leaving thousands of fans outside. Several of them scaled the exterior walls and clambered on to the roof of the Scratching Shed to watch the game. I remember looking at them and thinking that one day I'm going to go up there. Alas, I never did.

'Meanwhile there were around 5,000 too many spectators inside the ground and during the match one of the steel and concrete crush barriers in the Lowfields Road stand gave way under the pressure. Dad and me were stood in our usual spot on the halfway line and could see people spilling out on to the pitch, some were laid out receiving medical treatment from some of the Leeds and Sunderland medical staff and the St John's Ambulance brigade until a fleet of ambulances arrived to take 32 people to hospital. Fortunately, no one was seriously hurt, but it was so close to becoming a major disaster.

'The game was held up for about 20 minutes but once resumed it still ended in another 1-1 draw, courtesy of Johnny Giles, forcing a second replay five days later. The attendance that evening at Elland Road of 57,892 is still a record home gate.

'After much dispute between the two teams, Boothferry Park, Hull, was chosen for the replay and, within ten minutes Leeds had taken the lead through Rod Belfitt. Belfitt was one of Don Revie's so-called 'Shadow Squad'. These were a group of around half a dozen players who weren't quite first-team regulars, but despite being sought after by almost every other First Division team, they chose to stay with Revie and Leeds United. A large squad was invaluable to Revie.

'This second replay was played on 20 March and just two days later, Leeds were to play Bologna in the fourth round of the Fairs Cup in Italy. Leeds had asked Bologna to postpone the game until 5 April but the Italians had refused. Even worse, if the game against Sunderland was drawn again, the third replay would be on 22 March, the same night as the game in Italy!

'The prospect of two cup ties on the same evening left Don Revie with a dilemma, but he remained undeterred and said, "I am taking with me to Hull 22 or 24 players just in case, and as yet I have still not made up my mind on the exact composition of the party. If the worst should happen, I will send the reserves to Italy, you never know with our reserves, we might still have a chance in the second leg at Elland Road."

'Whatever the outcome of the game at Hull, Leeds would still have a busy few days ahead. Unable to get a hotel in Hull, they were based at Bridlington and would have to be up at 5am the next day to fly from Humberside Airport to Luton, then from there they would fly to Forti in Italy, before embarking on an hour's drive to Bologna. After the game they would have to ensure that they returned in time for Saturday's league match at Blackpool and two more Easter fixtures over the next four days. All in all, Leeds would play five games in nine days. Leeds lost the first leg to Bologna 1-0, but won the return leg at Elland Road by the same score and went through on the toss of a disc.

'There had been bad blood between Leeds and Sunderland on the pitch going back six or seven years and that evening at Hull, it would spill out like never before in front of a capacity crowd of 40,000. I'd gone to the game with my dad and uncle John and right up to kick-off and beyond, fights had broken out between both sets of supporters all over the ground. This fighting intensified after we had taken that early lead. Meanwhile tempers frayed once again on the pitch and the referee had trouble maintaining order.

'With about ten minutes remaining Sunderland equalised to make the score 1-1 yet again. The game looked to be heading for a second replay when within minutes of the final whistle Leeds were awarded a dramatic penalty when Jimmy Greenhoff was brought down inside the box. Johnny Giles ignored all of the furore going on around him and coolly slotted the spot-kick past Jim Montgomery. This prompted irate Sunderland fans to invade the pitch, but order was soon restored when a policeman dived and rugby-tackled one of the Sunderland fans and the rest retreated back over the wall on to the terraces.

'Billy Bremner said afterwards, "That copper could have waltzed into the Leeds rugby league side." Tempers then reached fever pitch in the closing moments as Sunderland had two players, George Herd and George Mulhall, sent off.'

※ ※ ※ ※ ※

'Villa Park is probably one of the most famous football grounds in the world. Aston Villa are one of the founder members of the Football League and Tom Hanks is reputed to be a Villa fan, for the simple reason that, as he says, "Aston Villa has got to be the best name ever for a soccer club. I'm big on Aston Villa because the name is so sweet, it sounds like a lovely spa."

'I first experienced this famous ground when Leeds lost the FA Cup semi-final against Chelsea there in April 1967. Leeds were consigned to a bitter 1-0 defeat by a ruthless, determined and brutal display, not from Chelsea, but from referee Ken Burns of Stourbridge. I was 11 years old back then and people still talk today about Peter Lorimer's goal being disallowed because Chelsea's defensive wall was not ready. TV footage clearly shows Burns indicating to Giles to take the kick and the Leeds man then rolls the ball inside to Lorimer, who unleashes an unstoppable screamer past Chelsea keeper Peter Bonetti followed by wild celebrations from Leeds players and fans. I was right behind that goal and I can still picture the ball nestling in the back of the net as if it belonged there.

'Within seconds, Bonetti pulled the ball from the net and threw it back to Lorimer. The goal had been disallowed by Mr Burns because Chelsea weren't ready and the kick had to be retaken, resulting in a goal kick. Tony Hateley's goal for Chelsea earlier was enough to take them to Wembley, where they were beaten by Tottenham Hotspur 2-1.'

%% %% %% %% %%

'I remember my first trip to Doncaster Rovers, it was for a friendly. I think it was the summer of either 1966 or 1967 and Doncaster were in either the Third or Fourth Division but, the thing I can remember clearly is how we got there. We travelled down the old A1 in my dad's trusty white Sunbeam Rapier, a convertible! Don't get me wrong, it wasn't brand new or anything like that, maybe ten years old but, there we were, father, son and my new Leeds woollen scarf heading for Belle Vue in style with the top down.

'It wasn't much of a ground really, but the local blokes that stood around us were giving me a bit of a history lesson. "Largest pitch in t'country that old cock," one said proudly, nodding to the early-season lush green turf. Then another joined in by saying, "See them floodleets? Tallest in t'country them." "You know why? Eh?" I felt my dad dig me as if to shut me up, but I'd already asked, "Why?" "Well," he said, puffing on his pipe. "Thuz an airfield ovver theyah an t'stop planes fleein in t'leets, thuv put more leets on top o'floodleets so that planes can see 'em affore the flee into 'em. It's all clever stuff tha knos." All these years on I can still remember that bloke at Donny.

'One of Leeds's and indeed football's most famous players is Jack Charlton, who made his Leeds debut against Donny in April 1953. A famous player for Donny at that time was comedian Charlie Williams. The great John Charles once said, "He [Charlie] is without doubt the hardest player I ever played against."

'Doncaster have yo-yoed up and down the lower divisions throughout their long history and in 1995 under the ownership of chairman Ken Richardson, they tumbled out of the Football League and into the Conference. Also in 1995 Belle Vue's main stand suffered extensive fire damage but, that's not the end of the unhappy events. Nine months after the fire, Richardson was found guilty of conspiracy to arson and sentenced to four years in prison. It transpired that he had employed three men to set fire to the stadium in order to pay off the club's debts with the insurance money.'

※ ※ ※ ※ ※

'It was Leeds Road, Huddersfield, where my dad took me to try and curb my enthusiasm for Leeds United. It was around 1967/68 that my dad saw my enthusiasm turning into an obsession. I never saw that however – and I still don't. I feel that it is quite normal to want to follow your football team to the ends of the earth and back again.

'Anyway, dad's plan was to take me to Elland Road one week and then, when Leeds were away the following week, he'd take me to watch Huddersfield Town. This little arrangement lasted for ten days. After watching Huddersfield draw 1-1 with Everton one Saturday and then beat someone else during the week, I said to my dad that if I couldn't watch Leeds play away then could we go to watch the reserve team – and this is just what we did. Inevitably though the Leeds away games began to kick in and the rest, as they say, is history.

'I remember a neighbour we used to have living across the street from us at number 15 called Mrs Cheeseborough and she had a nephew who played for Huddersfield Town called Geoff Hutt. On Tuesdays and Thursdays my mam would be late home from work and Mrs Cheeseborough would give me and my sister Julie our tea in her kitchen, or scullery as she called it. She would give us banana sandwiches. With sugar sprinkled on – yuk!

'She obviously knew that I was a Leeds fan and she would tell me about this Geoff Hutt as if he was the best footballer on the planet. She would say things like, "I like to see Leeds win, but not when our Geoff is playing against them."

'We only played at Huddersfield twice in the league in the 1970s – in April and September 1971 when Town were promoted to the First Division before being relegated two seasons later. We didn't win either of these encounters and in fact in the second one we lost 2-1 – while playing in red!

'Huddersfield really only had one player who was worthy of note and that was their captain Trevor Cherry, so Don Revie bought him for £100,000 in 1972, but only on the undertaking that we also took Town's dodgy centre-half Roy Ellam for £35,000. Revie gave him back to Huddersfield not long after on a free transfer.

'It was at Leeds Road where I met and shook hands with a very limp-wristed Brian Clough, who was our manager there for a friendly in August 1974. It was the first and only time I ever met Clough.'

※ ※ ※ ※ ※

Let's get on to Gary's non-stop story. On this journey we're not only going to visit every ground in Britain Leeds have visited in the last 46 years, we're also popping across to our European neighbours for some quite astonishing tales. Yorkshire ay – not only just the wit, the stories, a massive dose of loyalty, the friendliness but, more gold medals in the 2012 London Olympics than Australia – now that's summit to be proud of int it! I think you're going to enjoy this.

Andy Starmore

Acknowledgements

A MASSIVE thank you to Pitch Publishing for allowing these words to be printed. Thank you also to Paul Dews for bringing Brian McDermott on board. Thank you Brian as well. Thanks to every Leeds fan around the globe and, indeed, every rival football fan. A massive thank-you to Derek Hammond who I introduced the idea to and he pulled Gary and I in the right direction. Thanks to Neil Jeffries, who introduced me to Derek. Thanks to Paul Camillin for providing a London lunch when Gary and I discussed the idea and for Paul accepting the idea. Thanks to Mike O'Grady, a terrific player under the legend Don Revie. Thanks to Steve Riding for providing the photo of Gary in the Kop trying to keep his balance. A massive thank-you to Ken Radcliffe for the front and back covers. Finally thanks to Gary – a great friend and a true Yorkshireman.

Andy Starmore

Foreword

WHEN I was asked to write this foreword, I had to think about what I could actually say about Leeds United fans that I haven't said before. Then I looked through the pages, and realised that this book says it all. It encapsulates the loyalty, the dedication, the passion for the cause, and of course, the humour, sometimes from the gallows, that all forms a part of following this club to all corners of the globe.

Gary Edwards has dedicated his life to following Leeds United, and this is a fantastic story, not only about his exploits following the club, but it also provides a great snapshot of the history of Leeds United through the eyes of someone who has seen it all from the terraces, and the stands.

Like any football man, you like to think you know about Leeds United, the club's history, the players, and the fans, but it's not only until you actually join and become a part of it, that you actually realise how big this club is. Most of you reading this book will know that, and that's what makes Leeds United a truly special club.

Brian McDermott – Leeds United manager,
April 2013 to May 2014

1

Welcome To
Leeds United

T HE Beatles were number one and number three in the charts with 'Hello, Goodbye' and the EP 'Magical Mystery Tour' respectively. Sandwiched in between them at number two was Georgie Fame with 'The Ballad of Bonnie and Clyde'. *Planet of the Apes* had just been released in the cinema, as had the sci-fi film *2001: A Space Odyssey*.

The 'I'm Backing Britain' campaign had just been endorsed by the British Prime Minister Harold Wilson with the idea of working an extra half an hour each day for no pay. The average price of a house was £2,530 and a loaf of bread was just five pence.

In the football world Manchester City were heading towards the old First Division title. Little did their fans know at the time that they would be waiting another 44 years before they were next crowned champions of England. Back in the 1967/68 campaign Leeds were also having a great season. On 17 January 1968 the mighty Leeds, as they most certainly were in those days, travelled a relatively short distance down to Derby County. There was never any love lost between these two rival clubs who had two managers that would be destined to loathe the sight of each other – Leeds's Don Revie and Derby's Brian Clough.

The rivalry inspired writer David Peace to produce *The Damned United*, an excellent book which ended up in the cinema, although I have to add that the film didn't really portray Revie in a good light, which was disappointing.

Leeds had already established themselves in the top flight by this time, having finished second, second and fourth in their first three seasons after promotion in 1964. They had just thumped

Southampton 5-0 in a league match at Elland Road and were now on their way to the Baseball Ground for a League Cup semi-final first-leg showdown.

Of the 31,904 fans packed inside Derby's home there was one fan who couldn't make it on this particular day, and for me I haven't been able to say that about any other Leeds match in the last 46 years. This was to be the start of a journey that has had more ups and downs than a roller coaster stretching from Scarborough to Blackpool – and back!

I was just 11 years old. I travelled to Derby for the first time for this League Cup tie. It was my first experience of the infamous 'corrugated alley' that used to run adjacent to the away end at the Baseball Ground. I had gone on the 'Football Special' train from Leeds with my dad and as we walked down that alley, the noise was deafening as fans chanted and banged and kicked the corrugated panels. We had been confronted by Derby fans all the way from the station but even though my heart was pounding I never felt scared one bit – after all, I was surrounded by thousands of Leeds fans and more importantly, I had my dad with me.

I laugh now, and sometimes shudder, when I think of going to the games with dad. Even when confronted by opposition fans, with your dad by your side you have nothing to fear have you? What I didn't realise then of course was that I was only 11 years old – but my dad would only have been about 30 himself! I still have memories of me defiantly waving my Leeds scarf in the face of mean-looking, tattooed skinheads at away grounds and then sulking when my dad would snatch it from me and put it in his pocket telling me in no uncertain terms to 'shut up'!

Leeds were sitting on the top of the First Division that day and beat Second Division Derby 2-0, but it is remembered more these days as probably the game that saw Clough develop his obsessive hatred towards Revie and Leeds.

A few weeks later came my second trip to Filbert Street, Leicester, following a prior visit in 1967, and this was a memorable encounter.

Gordon Banks was widely acknowledged as the best goalkeeper in Great Britain – he had played in the 1966 World Cup Final and I had seen him play for Leicester against us a couple of times. By the time we played them in this match Banks had been transferred from Leicester City to Stoke City and had been replaced by someone who was regarded as the greatest young goalkeeping prospect in years – Peter Shilton.

Leeds fans crammed into the away end witnessed a hard-fought 2-2 draw with our goals coming from Johnny Giles and Paul Madeley. Shilton saved a penalty in the closing stages.

%% %% %% %% %%

Saturday 2 March 1968 will go down in Leeds United's folklore as a prominent date that changed the course of the club's history. Following the brilliant promotion to the top flight in 1964 Leeds had already begun a reputation of being the bridesmaids and never the bride – until now.

In 1965 Leeds lost out to manchester united in the league on goal average. They were beaten in extra time by Liverpool in the club's first FA Cup Final. In 1966, again Leeds were runners-up in the First Division – this time to Liverpool. They were beaten by Real Zaragoza in a semi-final replay in the Inter-Cities Fairs Cup in the same year.

A year later Dynamo Zagreb broke all our hearts with a 2-0 aggregate victory in the final of the Fairs Cup and Chelsea knocked us out of the FA Cup 1-0 at the semi-final stage. At last Leeds were about to come out on top by claiming silverware and becoming 'Super Leeds'.

In only my third match away from Elland Road in this mammoth footballathon I was heading to the capital and a date with Arsenal at Wembley Stadium. An average price for a ticket that day was just £1.03.

John Hamilton was a Geordie, he was a mate and later a business partner with my dad back in the mid-1960s. He was also an avid Leeds supporter. I've never really been able to pinpoint why I became a Leeds fan. Obviously there was my dad taking me to games, but looking back, John, or Mr Hamilton as he was known to me, may just be one of the reasons I became a bit of a fanatic.

In 1965 I used to go with my dad to work at 'his' factory in the centre of Leeds at weekends and evenings. Of course it wasn't really *his* factory, he just worked there. He and Mr Hamilton used to do the cleaning and general maintenance of the three-storey clothes factory when all the workers had gone home. I would sweep a floor or something while dad would disappear and ply his trade elsewhere in the dark, old, creaking factory. We would finish our work and then go home.

Mr Hamilton would do the night shift on his return from Elland Road or an away game. On Leeds United matchdays I would look out of the canteen window, which was on the second floor. It overlooked Sovereign Street on the banks of the River Aire and it was here where Leeds fans would get on the double-decker special buses that went to Elland Road.

In the beginning, it didn't mean a right lot to me, but then Mr Hamilton started leaving me a match programme under the canteen telephone which was perched on a purpose-built small wooden shelf that jutted out from the wall near the window where I would watch the buses. A lovely old lady called Elsie Binns used to run the canteen and she would leave my programme there until I next returned to 'work'. It was pure magic moving the phone and grabbing my brand new programme, which I would read from cover to cover.

On 2 March 1968 I went to Wembley Stadium for the very first time. I had already immersed myself in the world of Leeds United and had been going to most of the games for a couple of seasons.

Mr Hamilton was taking his grey mini-van to Wembley. I climbed in the back and dad sat in the front. We travelled down the old A1 and my little old belly was making all sorts of noises. Not because of hunger or travel sickness, but just pure excitement. I lay in the back watching the sky slowly come to life and listening to my dad and Mr Hamilton talking work and football.

I will never forget that first time I arrived at Wembley Stadium. I had seen crowds at Elland Road and other grounds, but here it all seemed so spread out, so big, so special. And this was outside the stadium.

The noise inside was indescribable as the two teams came out of the famous tunnel. I couldn't believe that Leeds United were out there on the hallowed turf. I thought it would have been impossible, but the crowd got even louder as the game got under way.

The game itself has been dubbed ever since as dour and boring, but I thought it was unbelievable if a tad ill-tempered. It certainly reached fever pitch as scuffles broke out at regular intervals. Then after 20 minutes, Terry Cooper hit one from the edge of the penalty area and it flew into the back of the Arsenal net. Cue more fighting between the teams.

Arsenal claimed that their goalkeeper, Jim Furnell, had been fouled by Jack Charlton and Paul Madeley – but TV footage clearly shows that Furnell was nowhere near the ball. It is well documented that Cooper had dreamt of scoring the winning goal at Wembley for three consecutive nights prior to the game. I dreamt about it for more than three nights after the game!

The afternoon just got better and better and even though we were holding on to a slender lead, I never wanted the game to end. I just couldn't get enough of the incredible atmosphere.

When the final whistle did blow, the Leeds players and fans celebrated like never before. I saw Billy Bremner do a forward roll as Jimmy Greenhoff lifted Johnny Giles up into the air. Charlton hugged Cooper. I hugged dad and Mr Hamilton and anyone near me. And everyone was doing the same.The presentation of the trophy to Bremner and Leeds's ensuing lap of honour all melted into one glorious memory.

As we came out of the ground, Leeds fans were all jumping up and down and dancing. It never dawned on me at the time, but this was the first major trophy that Leeds United had ever won, and I had been there! As we walked back towards the van I can remember sulking because my dad wouldn't buy me a small silver (plastic) cup that was on sale at one of the vendors. It had small white silk ribbons on it. 'Don't you think you've had enough today lad?' dad said. He was right of course, but even so I looked at Mr Hamilton with my best spaniel puppy-like eyes but he just laughed. 'Come on bonnie lad,' he said. 'Leeds United have won the real thing.'

I curled up in the back of the van and read my programme and as we entered the bottom end of the A1 I fell fast asleep. I woke up just as we drove into our estate. I then heard the handbrake and Mr Hamilton opened the back doors of the van. As I climbed out I thanked him for a great day and went into the house still clutching my rolled-up programme.

A few minutes later dad followed me in and put the kettle on. He made himself a sandwich and brought me one with a cup of tea. 'Enjoyed it?' He asked. 'You what?' I said, 'Not half! Thanks dad.' With that he put a small silver cup with white ribbons in my hand. 'Here, you miserable little git!' he smiled.

I love my dad…and Leeds United.

%, %, %, %, %,

Leeds followed up their first major trophy with a 2-0 win over Bristol City in the fifth round of the FA Cup at Elland Road followed by a 1-1 draw in the First Division at home to Nottingham Forest. Nine matches in and I had still not witnessed a defeat. In fact seven out of nine were victories.

There was always something to be said for going with your dad to some of the most feared football grounds in the country – and by that I mean events off the pitch. St James' Park used to be a really dodgy ground for away fans to go to. The coach park for the away fans was a cattle market and the only entrance into it was three feet wide so if you were going through it you were a visitor, simple as that – hence the hundreds of Newcastle supporters hanging around just picking off supporters trying to get through.

When a mob of Leeds fans arrived at this entrance it was a sight to behold – the police were always virtually non-existent in those days on Tyneside so there were some colourful scuffles that took place. This was my first venture into what was known as the 'Magpies Nest' and once again I travelled by car. This time it was in uncle John's lime green Ford Anglia. Dad was sat in the front and I was in the back with my cousin Graham. Graham was sat behind my dad and I soon found out why. As we trundled up the A1, John, a very heavy pipe-smoker, would wind down his window at regular intervals and jettison huge dollops of phlegm out which would invariably splatter against my window as I ducked.

Finally we arrived at St James' Park and I refer back to my comment at the beginning about going to feared grounds with your dad. During the mid-to-late-1960s and 70s St James' Park was without doubt in the top four of the most dangerous grounds to go to. My Leeds scarf was quickly confiscated and stuffed into my dad's pocket as we left the car. Then, as we entered the ground I noticed, and so did the others, that we had inadvertently paid to go into the Leazes End – the home section. I looked at the Leeds fans in the other end and then I looked at dad.

'Howay the Lads!' rang out as we stood in silence. We still stood in silence as Newcastle went 1-0 up. The home fans sang and banged on the back of the stand and my dad looked really uncomfortable. John didn't look much better and our Graham constantly stared down at the floor – we must have stuck out like a sore thumb. I got the distinct feeling that neither dad nor John wanted Leeds to score. Then with just seconds remaining Norman Hunter unleashed an unstoppable left-footed drive straight into the top corner of the Newcastle net.

I couldn't contain myself and I leapt up and punched the air. Dad and John both immediately leapt on me and held me down with a firm arm on each of my shoulders. Three thousand pairs of eyes glared at us as I was bundled out of the ground by dad and John. For the first time I saw dad visibly shaken and John began fumbling with his pipe as we started to blend in with the crowd that was now streaming out of the ground. Usually I would fly my scarf out of the car window on the way home but it remained in dad's pocket until we reached Wetherby roundabout on the A1, eight miles from Leeds.

In March 1968 came an away game at Chelsea and there is a song that starts, 'When I was just a little boy I asked my mother what should I be. Should I be Chelsea, should I be Leeds, here's what she said to me,' and continues in a rather less than complimentary manner towards Chelsea supporters.

Leeds United and Chelsea. It's a recipe that doesn't sit well on the stomach. It's a recipe that leaves a sour, bitter taste in the mouth. It's a recipe that, in the eyes of the supporter, will always be destined never to rid itself of the animosity which exists between the two sets of fans.

Well, where do we start with this one? Dear oh dear. The rivalry between Leeds and Chelsea is fierce. So fierce that it will be talked about for hundreds of years to come on space stations and galaxy outposts all across the entire universe.

I really can't remember much about my first visit to Stamford Bridge in March 1968. I do recall thinking it was a big ground though, but not a particularly good one. It had odd stands dotted about with no real conformity. We were housed in the very large open end opposite the infamous Chelsea Shed. In our end, to our left, there was a stupid little stand perched on what looked to be unsafe stilts. Home fans were in there, and they were welcome to it too. It remained a much-talked-about fixture at Stamford Bridge for many years.

Needless to say there will be plenty more to come with this fiercest of rivalries throughout the book, as the seasons and the years roll on. Leeds followed the goalless draw at Chelsea in 1968 with a 2-0 home win over Manchester City in the league before I was to be part of a noisy and tense 80,000 crowd at Ibrox as Leeds travelled to Glasgow Rangers in the Inter-Cities Fairs Cup.

When Leeds became the first British team to win the Inter-Cities Fairs Cup (now known as the Europa League) back in 1968, they beat Scottish opposition in the three consecutive rounds up to the final; Hibernian, Rangers and Dundee.

When I travelled to Ibrox for the Rangers game two days before my 12th birthday it was the first time I had ventured outside England. I travelled north with my dad on a 'Wally Trolley' (Wallace Arnold coach) and the atmosphere at Ibrox was intimidating to say the least.

Leeds fans weren't grouped all together, but instead were dotted about in little pockets around the ground. We were in what was probably the largest group of Leeds followers in one of the corners behind the goal but Rangers supporters were all around us – very large Rangers supporters they were too!

I didn't know it at the time of course but playing for Rangers that evening was a man who I would grow to dislike intensely over the years – a young Alex Ferguson. The noise from the partisan 80,000 crowd was immense but the Leeds defence in front of keeper Gary Sprake held firm to earn a 0-0 draw. There seemed to be almost as many Rangers fans at Elland Road two weeks later as there had been at Ibrox, but Leeds won the second leg 2-0 to set up a semi-final with Dundee.

Two home games against Yorkshire rivals Sheffield United, one in an FA Cup quarter-final and a league encounter, followed the trip north of the border. Two wins were just what the Don ordered. Paul Madeley secured a narrow 1-0 victory in the cup and goals from Madeley again and two from Johnny Giles made it a more comfortable 3-0 league win. After knocking Rangers (and Alex Ferguson) out of the Inter-Cities Fairs Cup, with over 50,000 spectators crammed into Elland Road, it was time for my first trip to Tottenham on this non-stop adventure. Leeds were to go down 2-1 in front of another bumper crowd.

It wouldn't happen now but back in 1968 there wouldn't be any moans about the fact that teams sometimes played two matches in two days, and so it was off to Coventry City the day after travelling to London. Coventry had recently appointed their new manager Noel Cantwell, replacing the unmistakable character who was in charge at Highfield Road for the previous seven years – Jimmy Hill.

Terry Hibbitt was one of the unsung heroes of Don Revie's legendary squad during the late 1960s and early 70s. Hibbitt was among a group of players who were known as the 'Shadow Squad' who were never regular first-teamers but remained at the club as vital squad cover despite interest in them from elsewhere.

My first vivid memory of Hibbitt was at Highfield Road, Coventry, in April 1968. He was small in stature, no taller than Billy Bremner or Johnny Giles, and he had bow legs. My dad always called him 'Cowboy' because of those unbelievable legs. 'You could drive a bus through them,' Dad would laugh.

He also had quite a large head and big beady eyes, with black wavy hair always combed back. I realise this doesn't give the most flattering description, but it's true. Above all, however, Hibbitt was a very skilful player, and took most of the corners whenever he played. I was stood at the front with dad as he took one of these corners at

Coventry that day. He was only a couple of feet from us and I saw him look at my Leeds scarf that was wrapped around my wrist and hung over the wall as he launched the ball into the six-yard box.

The Coventry defence headed it out but only as far as Hibbitt who had moved inwards. It was like slow motion as the ball left Hibbitt's boot and soared into the top corner of Coventry's net. Then, best of all, Hibbitt ran over to where we were stood to celebrate his goal. He put his hands to the side of my face and we were all jumping about like mad. That is why I have such a vivid and detailed description of him to this day.

My first trip to Goodison Park, the home of Everton, would come in 1969 but there was soon a little matter of an FA Cup semi-final against the Toffees in 1968 to come first. It was played at Old Trafford in front of 63,000 supporters.

When I started watching Leeds in the 1960s it seemed that watching them play in an FA Cup semi-final was something that occurred every season. I had seen them cruelly robbed at Villa Park against Chelsea in April 1967 and here we were, almost a year later to the day, on our way to play Everton in another semi-final, this time at Old Trafford.

A group of us, including my sister Julie and my cousin Jean, set off on our journey with dad in his 18cwt Thames Dormobile. A neighbour, Trevor Morris, had drawn and painted some Leeds posters to stick in the windows and we left Kippax with about a dozen Leeds scarves flying proudly out of the windows.

In those days it wasn't just a quick glide across the M62. Work on the trans-Pennine part of the motorway had only just begun as we embarked on a three-hour trip across the rugged Pennines and up and over Saddleworth Moor then down into the deepest, darkest depths of Lancashire. All around us there were large excavators and diggers gouging out the tough rocky landscape to make way for the new motorway – it would be a further three years before it was completed.

As we gazed at the huge rock face being carved away, dad said, 'Those JCB's aren't strong enough for this job. I've heard that they're going to hire a load of Yorkshiremen to clear the way with their teeth.'

Eventually we found ourselves very close to the ground and in a large queue of coaches, vans and cars with Leeds scarves hanging out of the windows and blue, white and yellow flags everywhere. Then the occasion took a serious grip of us in dad's van and we immediately burst into song, 'We shall not, we shall not be moved.'

Although I was only 12 years old, I had noticed that a certain pattern had emerged for these sort of games – the opposition fans were always given the 'home' end while Leeds fans were always dumped into the away end, which in those days was always open and it was impossible to generate the same atmosphere as the opposite section that always had a roof over it. This occurred at all eight semi-finals, including replays and one FA Cup Final replay, that Leeds played between 1967 and 1977 at Villa Park (twice), Old Trafford (twice), Hillsborough (three times), Burnden Park, and Maine Road. Today was to be no exception.

Unfortunately for Leeds, another pattern also emerged from these types of games. Our goalkeeper Gary Sprake was prone to costly errors. One occurred just before half-time in this game although, admittedly, Sprake was playing with a badly damaged shoulder, which restricted his movement. Everton centre-forward Joe Royle knew this and barged into Sprake at every opportunity. There were no substitute keepers back then.

Just before the interval Sprake mis-hit a clearance and it rolled just a few yards to Everton's Jimmy Husband who instinctively pounced on the ball and took a snap-shot towards goal. Leeds full-back Paul Reaney was famous for his goal-line clearances and he seemed to have things covered behind Sprake, who was on the floor, but Jack Charlton was between Reaney and the ball and stopped it with both hands. Johnny Morrissey converted the penalty.

Reaney has said many times since, 'I had everything under control and shouted such to Jack, but he handled the ball when he simply didn't have to. To this day I've never let big Jack forget it!'

Although Leeds then took the game to Everton, Mick Jones and Terry Cooper both hitting the woodwork, they were unable to break down a resilient defence and 1-0 was enough to see the Toffees through to Wembley, where they lost the final 1-0 to underdogs West Bromwich Albion.

The journey back to Yorkshire was an absolute nightmare as we stared in silence at the huge cranes and machinery silhouetted against the darkening skies overhead. Worst of all I had an awful argument with Jean over something to do with the game – I can't quite remember what. This set everyone else off arguing with each other until dad shouted at the top of his voice for us all to be quiet and we continued the rest of the journey in absolute silence, except for the odd mutter here and there.

Every Leeds fan had seen enough Scousers for the time being but the red side of Liverpool would arrive at Elland Road a week after that heartbreaking defeat to the Toffees. More misery ensued as Liverpool ran out 2-1 winners. Sandwiched in between though was to be a second jaunt up to Scotland, this time to face Dundee.

One of the best things about supporting Leeds during the Don Revie era was that you didn't have time to dwell on a disappointing result, because there was always another game literally just days away.

This was the case after the FA Cup semi-final defeat against Everton at Old Trafford. Five days later, that particular game had been consigned to the archives and I was heading north with dad, his mate John Hamilton and the Leeds United Travel Club on a Fallas coach. We were going to Dundee in Scotland to watch Leeds in yet another semi-final, this time in the Inter-Cities Fairs Cup.

Fallas Coaches were very regal-looking vehicles, dark blue with majestic gold livery. The owner of the company was a different kettle of fish however. Fallas operated from premises on Elland Road, directly opposite the ground. A large car park accommodated the coaches at the rear and at the front was the bungalow where the owner lived, and every matchday became an ordeal for him.

To the front of his property was a wall, which unfortunately became an ideal 'seat' for fans to eat their fish and chips or hot dogs. The owner was having none of it however, and would come out wielding a baseball bat and literally whacking any fans that had dared to park their rear on his wall. Police had to constantly intervene, but this activity continued almost every week. I'm not entirely certain when they vacated the premises and ceased trading, but alas Fallas Coaches are no more, and neither is the bungalow.

When we arrived in Dundee, we were confronted with *two* grounds, one on one side of the road and one on the other. Dens Park, the home of Dundee, is very close to Tannadice Park, the home of Dundee United. In fact, the two grounds are just 200 yards apart. They even share the same car park and are the closest senior grounds in Britain. Only two stadiums in Europe are closer – MTK and BKV Elore in Budapest, whose respective homes actually back on to each other.

Dundee had only previously played in Europe back in 1963 when AC Milan beat them in the semi-final of the European Cup. This season they had beaten DWS Amsterdam, RFC de Liege and FC Zurich to reach yet another European semi-final.

Once we had established which ground to enter we took our places and feasted on a Scotch pie and broth. Leeds were at full strength with the exception of Gary Sprake, who had played against

Everton with a badly injured shoulder. Our ever-reliable reserve keeper, David Harvey, deputised.

Bremner kicked off and exerted pressure from the start, which was rewarded with a goal after 26 minutes, scored by Paul Madeley. Dundee, however, were not going to give up without a fight and within ten minutes they had drawn level through Bobby Wilson. In the second half Dundee forced Leeds back and we looked in real danger of falling behind but Harvey pulled off a couple of magnificent saves and Leeds ended up the stronger of the two sides. Mr Hamilton grabbed me just before the end as a delicate lob from Jimmy Greenhoff bounced off the top of the crossbar and to safety for the Scotsmen. 'I thought that fucker was in,' he said as he let me go.

The next morning at school I was showing Graham Hunter my match programme and then it suddenly dawned on me that I may be going to my second final of the season. All we had to do was beat Dundee at home in the second leg. There was a somewhat eerie atmosphere for that second leg at Elland Road. The large open end, known as the Spion Kop, had been demolished to make way for a brand new stand to be built during the close-season. All that remained that evening was a large mound of earth and rubble.

Once again, Dundee proved worthy opponents and it took a solitary goal by Eddie Gray to finally separate the sides and put Leeds into the final of the Inter-Cities Fairs Cup for the second consecutive season.

My love affair with Leeds also includes my love affair with the brilliant white shirts that Don Revie introduced to Elland Road shortly after his appointment as manager in March 1961, so you may gasp in horror at something I am about to reveal.

I have a hatred for the colour red because of a certain club from Old Trafford. Who can blame me for that? When I was married to my first wife in 1978 she went out and bought some pots and pans. They were red. They were also immediately thrown out of the front door. The marriage lasted barely two months.

I also attempted to paint a fire engine white once and with my painting and decorating firm I will give a discount for the removal of red paint. In fact I will do it for free. So prepare to be astonished.

I have an absolutely dreadful confession to make: I used to like Arsenal's kit. I was only nine or ten years old but I would see pictures of their distinctive red shirts with white sleeves in my copies of *Goal* and *Football Monthly* and I liked it. I never had any interest in Arsenal as a team, obviously, and the shirt thing passed very quickly.

My bedroom walls were always full of pictures of Leeds, Leeds and more Leeds. There was no comparison anywhere in the world with the glorious all-white Leeds kit. It was simply magical. Hung down the wall by the side of my bedroom door was a homemade tape measure and at the side of it I had little pieces of card at different levels. These cards depicted the height of each individual Leeds player. My bedroom was a shrine to Leeds.

The final league game of the season was to be a relatively short trip across the Pennines to Burnley. It had been an unbelievably strenuous but amazing season nonetheless. Not surprisingly the players must have been shattered, having won the League Cup, lost out narrowly to Everton in the semi-finals of the FA Cup, eventually finishing fourth in the league and while still awaiting an Inter-Cities Fairs Cup Final, which would now be taking place during the beginning of the 1968/69 season. And the players think they've got it tough nowadays! I remember that trip in 1968 to Burnley's ground. Well, half a ground.

The first time I went to Turf Moor it was poor. The second time was even worse. For the first visit, in May 1968, I arrived at a ground with only two parts open. The large side that we were in (well over half of it anyway, Burnley fans were just over the adjoining fence) and the end to our right behind the goal where most of the Burnley fans were. Opposite us was a kind of building site and a large white boarding hid the other end. We lost 3-0, and there is more on that second visit in the next chapter.

The 1967/68 season had drawn to a close, albeit with an Inter-Cities Fairs Cup Final still to play in at the beginning of the following campaign, 1968/69, which would be the first campaign that I would not miss a single game – the first of what now is 45 consecutive seasons. So then, where would my next 'new ground' be?

2

Red Is Banned!

WHEN this campaign got under way little did I know that it would be a season to remember for the rest of my life, for more than one reason. Leeds United would go on to play a total of 59 matches, plus the two games in the Inter-Cities Fairs Cup Final against Ferencvaros which were hauled over from the previous season, and I would see all 61 fixtures.

I had already ventured out of England but now this season I was about to make my debut on the terraces in mainland Europe. In fact I made five trips abroad throughout this campaign. Finally, and oh so much more importantly, I was to witness a Leeds United side becoming the champions of England for the very first time. It was indeed a season to remember.

Following the home first leg of that Fairs Cup Final on 7 August, which Leeds narrowly won 1-0 via a Mick Jones effort, it was time for the first trip of the new season. And it couldn't have been a longer one.

During my earliest supporting days Southampton was the furthest away game we played and it always seemed to take an age to get there. There was a group of about six or seven of us who used to travel together from our coal-board estate. We would be about ten or 11 years old. During the week we would buy our coach tickets from a local newsagent in Kippax High Street called Eastwood's, then on Saturday morning we would travel four miles on a bus to Castleford bus station where a couple of Wallace Arnold coaches would be waiting.

We had a pact between us that if someone overslept they would be woken up by the rest of us. This meant standing behind their house on a coal bunker, often in the early morning freezing fog, throwing pieces of coal at their bedroom window to rouse them.

Inevitably some windows were cracked or smashed altogether by pieces of coal that in hindsight were probably a bit too large.

The Dell was a quaint little ground, but none of the stands matched and it always looked to me as though it had been made on *Blue Peter* from old cereal boxes of all different sizes, painted and then glued together. They obviously got their mother's permission first before cutting up the boxes.

The 1968/69 season had started in fine fettle. A 3-1 win at Southampton was followed up by back-to-back victories on home soil, a 4-1 triumph over QPR and a 2-0 victory against Stoke City. We were next setting off down to Suffolk and a date with the Tractor Boys.

'I can't read and I can't write, but that don't really matter, cos I support the Ipswich Town, and I can drive a tractor.' Ah, the 'Tractor Boys'. Don't you just love 'em? Tucked away in their little corner of East Anglia, bothering nobody, apart from beating Leeds on occasions, they just potter about and get on with their gardening or the odd trip down to Portman Road. I don't know anyone who actually hates Ipswich. Apart from their Norfolk neighbours Norwich City and Leeds fans living in East Anglia.

There are large branches of Leeds fans in both Ipswich and Norwich and I could just picture the East Anglian Whites and the Norfolk Whites coming across each other en route to Elland Road and having a right old punch-up in an A1 services car park before resuming their journey north.

There's nothing remotely special about visiting Portman Road. Maybe the odd pint or two of Tolly Cobbold's in the adjacent pub aptly named the Sporting Farmer and that's about your lot. The train station is a fair walk from the ground as well. I remember going on the train in August 1968. I travelled with my dad and a few mates, and it was here that I witnessed my first real incident of police harassment first-hand.

Hundreds of Leeds fans got off our train at Ipswich and we were met by nearly as many police officers and dogs. One of those dogs took an instant dislike to dad and caused quite a racket. As we made our way along the platform to the exit this dog leapt up at dad and bit him on the arm. Understandably dad wasn't too happy and it didn't help that the copper on the other end of the dog had a big smirk on his bearded face.

'Get your fucking dog under control,' said dad. The copper just laughed and replied, 'And what are you gonna do about it if I don't?' I can't ever recall seeing dad as angry before or since. I laughed nervously as my mate Stan said, 'Go on Mr Edwards, chin him!' Then, as other Leeds fans joined in, the copper became agitated. 'Come on then,' he said to dad. 'Me and you – here, someone take my dog,' he added childishly. Dad laughed. 'You must think I'm fucking stupid,' he said. 'Get rid of the uniform and then we'll have a go.'

It was like being back in the school playground and then amazingly my uncle Norman entered the scene. Norman was the officer in charge of the British Transport Police and had travelled down with our train and only an hour ago we had been chatting to him as he did his rounds up and down the carriages. 'You saw that Norman,' dad said. 'What are you gonna do about it?' 'I'm sorry Arthur,' he said. 'I never saw anything.' 'Thanks a lot you pillock!' replied dad as we made our way out of the station. Dad never forgave Norman for that afternoon, and whenever they met afterwards their relationship was never the same again.

'I, Rodney Charlton Trotter...' These are just some of the legendary words at Rodney's wedding to Cassandra in *Only Fools and Horses*. 'Yes, it's my mum, she was a fan,' Del Boy replies when asked by Marlene about Rodney's middle name. 'Oh, what, Charlton Heston?' comes the follow-up. 'No,' says Del. 'Charlton Athletic!'

Personally, my first recollection of Charlton Athletic was in 1968 when they came to Elland Road for round two of the League Cup. Mick Jones scored the only goal of the game and I was feeling happy as I walked back up Elland Road towards the car afterwards. All of a sudden my woollen Leeds hat was snatched from my head and the assailant sped off into the night. I was distraught, and this unsavoury incident lived with me for a good few seasons after. I still don't know if it was a Charlton or Leeds fan, but I guess the latter is the favourite.

In my infancy on this mammoth run the nearest club to Leeds thus far has been Burnley, a mere 39.4 miles from Elland Road. The furthest – Southampton – a whopping 259 miles. In the tortoise-esque travelling days of the late 1960s 259 miles was one heck of a hike. A long old journey, and then you had to get back again, all for the sake of 90 minutes of football. But that's nothing compared to 1,273 miles and a trip to Budapest in Hungary.

I don't suppose there are many people whose first trip abroad was with his grandmother's boyfriend. But that's who I went with to the 1968 Inter-Cities Fairs Cup Final in Budapest. His name was George Dean. The final itself was a two-legged affair.

Ferencvaros were widely accepted as the best team in Europe at the time. Their centre-forward, Florian Albert, had just won the

European Player of the Year award in 1967 and two of the greatest managers of that time, Bill Shankly and Jock Stein, as well as Matt Busby, rated the Ferencvaros forward line as the most dangerous in the world. They won the Inter-Cities Cup in 1965, beating manchester united in the semi-final before beating Juventus in the final. Although they never totally fulfilled their potential in European competition Ferencvaros have won their domestic league 28 times and the cup 20 times.

The first leg at Elland Road had been a strange affair. It had been held over from the previous season and took place in August. It was the first game at Elland Road in front of the newly erected Spion Kop, aka the Gelderd End, complete with roof.

Elland Road certainly looked unfamiliar, as did the Leeds kit. Leeds played in blue shirts while Ferencvaros wore the traditional all-white of Leeds. It was a scrappy game with just a scrappy Mick Jones goal separating the two sides for the second leg in Hungary.

With 'uncle' George and I was dad's business partner John Hamilton. I had to have a one-year passport and that had been a bit of a rush because I hadn't known I was going to Budapest until about a week before. As I boarded my first aeroplane at Leeds airport, the excitement was unbelievable and I felt a little ill, but it wasn't through fear of flying. I had no idea what it was going to be like. This was a totally new experience for me and looking back I didn't really have the time or the opportunity to savour the occasion. I absolutely loved flying. I still do. The thrust of the engine as we accelerated to the end of the runway was incredible.

Mr Hamilton pointed out that the *Yorkshire Evening Post* reporter Phil Brown was sat directly opposite us. He was an oldish man with glasses, not unlike Captain Mainwaring from *Dad's Army*. Another man with glasses was on the plane and I was told this was Arthur Dunhill, Leeds United's number one supporter. He had those round, really thick glasses with his hair swept back and coated thickly in Brylcreem. I had read about him in the *Football League Review*, a publication inside every club's matchday programme in those days. It seemed like he had seen United play about two million times and I couldn't believe I was on the same plane as him. Another man wearing Brylcreem was 'Woody'. Mr Hamilton said he too was a supporter who followed Leeds everywhere. Mr Hamilton didn't know his real name, he was just called Woody because he smoked lots of Woodbine cigarettes. Keith Macklin, the TV football commentator, was also on board, signing the odd autograph for the Leeds fans on the plane.

I even liked it when the plane landed with a slight bump, although it was nothing like a 'Ryanair bump' that you get these days. They are certainly worth experiencing. I'm not surprised that the airline plays a little celebratory jingle when it lands and all the priests and nuns do a quiet crossing of themselves.

The very first thing I noticed being abroad for the first time was the smell. It was like something I had never smelt before. A strong stench, sweet almost, with a very strong whiff of tobacco. I thought to myself, 'Woody will like it here.'

Once we left the plane we travelled straight from the airport on a convoy of coaches to the ground, the Nep Stadium. It was hours before kick-off but already the ground was full – 76,000 was the official attendance. Much has been written about the game itself, suffice to say that Leeds produced one of the best defensive displays ever seen to protect their slender 1-0 lead from that goal by Jones at Elland Road to become the first British team to win the trophy.

Gary Sprake was the Leeds hero that night, pulling off some incredible saves, some of the like I have never witnessed since. We were situated almost level with the edge of the six-yard box and had the perfect view of Sprake's heroics as he turned countless shots and free kicks away from the Leeds goal. I can't explain why, but I never believed that Ferencvaros would score. It may be because in those days I very rarely saw Leeds defeated. I just knew we would be OK.

The looks on the faces of Mr Hamilton and George, however, told a different story altogether. I've seen footage of that game since and I can't believe we never conceded a goal. It was incredible. We hardly came out of our box, let alone our half.

When Billy Bremner was handed the cup, it was amazing. There weren't an awful lot of Leeds fans there that night but the great sight of Leeds scarves fluttering away all over the ground was brilliant. And that unmistakable chant of 'Leeds, Leeds, Leeds' could be heard all over. This chant was a trademark at Elland Road in those days and usually began in the West Stand Paddock. All the pictures and photographs I have seen of that night in Budapest are in black and white and strangely the whole evening in real life seemed to be in black and white. And this time it was Leeds who were in all white.

We saw literally nothing of Budapest outside of the ground and within two hours of the final whistle we were back in the air bound for West Yorkshire. I looked around the plane at the Leeds fans celebrating and I felt as though I was going to burst wide open with elation and pride. Meanwhile Phil Brown sat quietly scribbling his match report on his crumpled little notepad. I couldn't wait to see that report.

I was still only 13 years old and already I was clocking up those European miles. My first voyage across the water was next.

No sooner had Leeds United won the Fairs Cup in Budapest than they began their defence of it. One week later to be exact, and his time we were off to Belgium to face Standard Liege. Although Belgian football in general wasn't at a particularly high standard, Liege would prove to be formidable opponents.

I travelled with Mr Hamilton on the ferry and it was rowdy to say the least. Leeds fans were everywhere and although I can't recall any trouble as such, it was noisy, and quite frankly the stewards and staff were scared stiff.

As with the Fairs Cup Final a week before and my first flight, this was my first time on the high seas. The school holidays had finished, everyone had gone back to school and here I was bobbing about in the North Sea off to watch Leeds in Europe. My form tutor at Garforth Comprehensive then was Miss Yates and while she supported another team, who we won't mention, she recognised that my love for Leeds United was more than just a passing interest and gave me quite a bit of leeway in my pursuit to watch my team.

Apart from that, my attendance record at school, with the exception of Leeds midweek away matches that is, was exemplary, even though I say so myself. All Miss Yates asked was that I didn't go around telling everyone that I wasn't really ill on my 'days off', although most of my mates knew anyway.

We arrived in Zeebrugge and then had to catch a train for the rest of the journey. I was loving every minute of travelling around what I considered then 'the world'. One Leeds fan became involved in a highly charged argument over his ticket with a steward and was just about to punch him when a lad who was with him intervened and said, 'Leave it mate, we're on the wrong train.' Another steward was called and as I recall they were allowed to stay on this train provided they stay quiet. We didn't find out which train these lads were supposed to be on, but there was no more trouble from them.

There was a heavy police presence when we arrived in Liege and the first person we saw was Woody, who had been on the flight to Hungary. He was just lighting another Woodbine as he walked down the side of the train with about a dozen others. Although I hadn't even spoken to him, I felt like I knew him.

Outside the station we called into a little cafe for a drink and a sandwich. It was then that this 'foreign smell' hit me again. That strong stench seemed to be everywhere outside of England. We were told in the cafe that the ground, the Sclessin Stadium, was a fair walk from here, and we would be best getting a taxi or a tram. 'No need, bonny lad,' said Mr Hamilton in his soft Geordie accent, 'We've got plenty of time, we'll walk it.'

As we walked, we passed several little bars and cafes that had plenty of Leeds fans in them and it wasn't long before Mr Hamilton decided that he fancied a beer himself so we then found ourselves sat outside a cafe. A few minutes later a waiter brought Mr Hamilton a glass of frothy beer and I got a glass of something, I have no idea what it was, it was green and horrible. The waiter then walked away. 'Don't we have to pay for these?' I asked Mr Hamilton. He just laughed and I was told that this was how they do it abroad, 'pay later'.

Later Mr Hamilton ordered another beer and this time he handed the waiter a foreign note. I got an envelope out of my pocket. In it was some Belgian money that my ma had given me before we left. I had no idea how much there was. 'Do you want some of this?' I asked Mr Hamilton. He just told me to put it back in my pocket and 'keep an eye on it'. The envelope was untouched when I got home.

When we finally got to the stadium it wasn't much to look at really, a bit similar in style to Elland Road, but not nearly as special. I had been reading my *Charles Buchan Football Monthly* magazines before we came and finding out all about foreign star players. Standard Liege had a couple of these stars playing for them. They were all internationals including Belgians Van Moer and Semmeling, a Hungarian called Sagy and a West German called Kostedde.

Straight from the kick-off Leeds were pinned back and once again we spent much of the game defending. Gary Sprake was outstanding yet again and was definitely the main reason that Leeds came away with a valuable 0-0 draw.

We left the stadium and got a taxi back to the train station and then into the ferry terminal. Our ferry wasn't due for something like seven or eight hours so we found a quiet corner and went to sleep. Some of the other Leeds fans did the same, but most of them just spent the night drinking beer and wine.

I have been asked many times, 'What is your most memorable Leeds game?' The second leg at Elland Road against Standard Liege is right up there with the very best of them. Standard had played in red shirts in the first leg, with Leeds in all-white, but the Belgians arrived at Elland Road with an all-white kit and no second strip. In those days I used to stand at the front of the Lowfields Road stand with some mates and my dad. We used to stand opposite to the players' tunnel and we could see the teams coming out before anyone else. This particular night as 11 white shirts ran out on to the pitch, the Leeds fans began cheering. Then they quickly realised that it wasn't Leeds they were cheering, it was Standard Liege!

Leeds came out also dressed in all white. There was a lengthy and at times very heated debate between the two teams and officials. We found out later that for some bizarre reason (it had to be down to gamesmanship), Standard had arrived with just one kit, insisting, quite rightly, that the onus was on the home team to change in the event of a colour clash. Even worse was that if the home team didn't change, the tie would be awarded to the away team.

Leeds insisted that Standard play in Leeds's second strip of blue shirts, but the Belgians steadfastly refused, claiming that they wouldn't fit. Eventually Leeds left the pitch and reappeared dressed as Chelsea, in blue shirts and shorts with white socks. It is the first and only time I have heard the Kop chant the name of Chelsea, albeit very briefly.

With fog and mist swirling menacingly around Elland Road, Standard took the lead just before half-time and the alarm bells really started to ring when they added a second shortly after the break, going 2-0 up on aggregate.

Then with the famous 'Leeds, Leeds, Leeds' chant echoing around Elland Road, United began to push forward and Jack Charlton scored a header to pull one back. Eddie Gray then came on as a substitute for Terry Hibbitt and immediately began tormenting the Standard defence with some brilliant attacking play down the left wing, which on 75 minutes resulted in a free kick 25 yards out as he was brought down by a worried defender.

Peter Lorimer then made no mistake as he drove a hard low rocket shot straight through the Belgian wall and into the net. The score was now 2-2 on aggregate, but away goals meant that Standard would go through if that scoreline remained. Captain Billy Bremner, as he often did in those days, provided the winner for Leeds two minutes from time to send Elland Road delirious.

That game is etched vividly in my memory and in particular the way Paul Madeley surged forward, inspiring the players around him as they relentlessly attacked the Kop end.

Less than a fortnight after beating Liege, Leeds played manchester united. I am loath to give this club so much attention, but I can assure you that it will be all one-way traffic – trust me. I hope you enjoy it half as much as me.

We'll get the pleasant stuff out of the way first. I hate manchester united with a passion. I haven't said their name in over 40 years. I own a decorating company that will not paint red under any circumstances and we remove red paint free of charge. Guaranteed! About 25 years ago I ordered a watch via mail order. When it arrived I sent it back because the second hand was red. In the mid-1970s I used to travel to the Yorkshire border across the Pennines every Friday at 4am and paint the red rose of Lancashire white. My first visit to Old Trafford was in November 1968 for a goalless draw.

It won't escape your notice that I refuse to capitalise their name throughout the book for obvious reasons but, while writing this, there has been the constant presence of our old friend 'Spell Check'.

All the way through this totally enjoyable experience their name was been underlined with red, yes red, because I wouldn't use capital letters. On numerous occasions it would place a capital 'M' contrary to my wishes and I had to break off from my enjoyment and correct Mr Spell Check. Regardless of how many times I told it not to, it continued to hound me to the end.

But then it dawned on me, Spell Check is American-owned isn't it? Enough said. I am convinced that if I had sat here in a referee's outfit, my computer would have begun pushing me and harassing me until I used capitals!

There will be plenty more about Leeds and man u later in the book but in the meantime when you talk to the majority of English fans about their experiences of visiting any Italian club, it's usually met with the same kind of response. It's a beautiful country but when it comes to football it's simply dangerous. My first trip to Italy was quite an eye-opener.

There can't be many instances where the team has been in more danger than the fans but that is precisely what happened here. Leeds were playing Napoli in the second round of the Fairs Cup, and had already won the first leg 2-0 at Elland Road thanks to two superbly headed goals from Jack Charlton. Also Mick Jones was extremely unlucky to have two goals ruled out by very dubious offside decisions. That said, Napoli were no pushovers and would certainly provide a stiff test in this second leg.

I had gone to Naples with my mate Mick Collins and his dad, and we were ushered by police from the airport to the Sao Paulo Stadium under heavy guard. Two years previously, the Burnley team had to be escorted from this very ground under armed police escort after fans rioted. Inside the stadium it was very hostile and this was with less than 20,000 fans in attendance. Although the capacity was 85,000,

Napoli's fans had stayed away in droves because of an indifferent start to their league season.

That though, didn't detract from the intimidating atmosphere. A permanent eight-foot-wide moat surrounded the pitch and it was difficult to see the pitch at all through large metal fences around the whole ground. Leeds fans were penned into a corner by riot police and I saw a Leeds fan with blood pouring down his face, but this was nothing compared to the reception awaiting our players.

As the game got under way, rockets, flares and other missiles filled the air, and the pitch. Even the referee had to dive for cover as a rocket flew directly over his head. Leeds's club doctor Ian Adams, standing in for ill trainer Les Cocker, was a busy man. Billy Bremner was punched in the face by Panzanato, Gary Sprake had to have stitches in his hand after he was struck by a broken bottle thrown at him, Paul Madeley was knocked unconscious and the referee played on for a full minute while Madeley was laid out in his own goalmouth and, Peter Lorimer was felled in their penalty area. Although no penalty was given, the referee would not allow treatment to be given to Lorimer on the field.

Mick, his dad and I watched in disbelief as Dr Adams had to go on the pitch and drag Lorimer back over the goal line so he could treat him.

Not surprisingly, Napoli scored after just a quarter of an hour through Sala, but Leeds remained focused on the task ahead and went close to scoring twice through Mick Jones and Eddie Gray, with the legendary keeper Dino Zoff pulling off two great saves for the hosts. However, with just minutes remaining the East German referee Rudi Gloekner blew his whistle for an alleged foul by Jack Charlton. But Charlton fumed afterwards, 'It was the worst penalty decision I have ever known in my entire life. I was determined not to touch him (Sala) but he took a dive and in any case we were both outside of the box.'

This decision was made even more mystifying by the fact that throughout the entire game, Gloekner had allowed several two-footed lunges from the Italians to go unpunished as well as the aforementioned incidents involving Bremner, Madeley and Lorimer.

After extra time the aggregate score stood at 2-2 so the tie would have to be settled by the toss of a disc. The disc was the size of a small dinner plate and was coloured white on one side and red on the other. Bremner had been given the honour to call 'as a guest' and as the two captains and officials watched the disc come down, Bremner called 'red', quite surprisingly, and red it was. Bremner then burst into a series of somersaults and handstands as he was joined by the rest of his white-shirted heroes. The riot police moved tighter into the Leeds fans as we jumped up and down waving our woollen Leeds scarves high into the dark Italian air.

Don Revie, though, was still seething over the evening's hostilities. He had anticipated these beforehand and had asked for two Fairs Cup official observers to be present. But one of these observers, Fairs Cup secretary Peter Joris, reported afterwards that the 'colossal output' of fireworks, bonfires, missiles, boos and hisses was 'only about normal'. Revie refused to talk to the Italian press, but told British journalists, 'It was worse than anything I had expected. It was quite our worst experience in Europe. If that is the way they treat their guests, I hope that we never have to play Napoli here again.'

As we shuffled back on to our awaiting coaches bound for the airport, Mr Collins had an arm around each of us and said, 'That showed 'em eh?' Then, right on cue a firework went up over the stadium but quickly fizzed out and fell feebly to the floor. 'Yep,' said Mick.

Back in England, my first visit to Upton Park was not long before Christmas in 1968. Leeds were on their way to becoming league champions and every team tried to pull out all the stops to beat Revie's side, much like today really.

West Ham were known as a classy footballing team but Leeds didn't let them settle at all. Giles and Bremner completely dictated the game, and when Eddie Gray scored a sublime effort to put Leeds ahead in the first half it looked as though it would be just another day at the office. But try as they might, Leeds could not get that vital second goal.

Upton Park was not the most pleasant of grounds for an away fan to visit during the 1960s and 70s and there was constant fighting in the open end to our right. I was stood with dad down the side, under an upper tier of seats. A Leeds fan was taken away by police right in front of us and he momentarily broke away from their grasp and tried to jump over the wall into where we were stood, but another policeman who had been sat on a chair in front of us grabbed him. A big chant of 'Leeds, Leeds, Leeds' came from the open end but, with just minutes remaining, West Ham equalised to make the final score 1-1.

We moved into 1969, which would be quite some year. Led Zeppelin released their first studio album, *Led Zeppelin*, Richard Nixon became the 37th President of the United States of America,

The Beatles gave their final public performance on the rooftops of Apple Records and later released their *Abbey Road* album.

There were maiden flights for the Boeing 747 and for Concorde. The founder of the Rolling Stones, musician Brian Jones, was found drowned in a swimming pool at his home in Sussex. Australian media mogul Rupert Murdoch purchased the *News of the World* newspaper, and over 500 million people worldwide watched their television screens to witness Neil Armstrong, Buzz Aldrin and Michael Collins make history by becoming the first astronauts to walk on the surface of the moon with Apollo 11.

In the football world, or more specifically the Leeds United world, future player and manager Simon Grayson was born in this year, as were Tomas Brolin (probably a bad example as a 'player' given his dreadful performances in a Leeds shirt), Lucas Radebe (a far greater example and still a huge hero now), Robert Molenaar and the wonderfully gifted Gary Speed.

On 28 March 1969 I celebrated becoming a teenager. Rewind three months earlier to 4 January and I headed to bitter Yorkshire rivals Sheffield Wednesday as 1969 got under way.

I've been to some massive games at Hillsborough. Some games have even involved Sheffield Wednesday. In 1969 I was stood in the large open end behind the Leeds goal when Gary Sprake produced one of his infamous gaffes. It was in the third round of the FA Cup and Leeds were winning thanks to a 15th-minute penalty by Peter Lorimer.

Leeds were in complete control and had just had a goal by Paul Madeley disallowed when Wednesday, desperately seeking a way back into the game, found themselves level courtesy of Sprake. Centre-forward John Ritchie hit a speculative shot towards the Leeds goal and even the defenders had turned away and were heading up the field, such was the apparent harmlessness of the shot. But I was standing right behind Sprake's right-hand post with my dad and watched as the keeper just put his arms up as if he thought the ball was going wide.

It was going that slow that had I been able to get the words out, I could have shouted at Sprake and told him that it was going in and he would still have had time to turn round and pick it up. But the ball rolled into the net and sparked violent fighting on the terraces all around us. I just stared at the Leeds goal as it was bombarded with toilet rolls.

I had been watching Leeds for less than three years and already I had seen quite a few mistakes by Sprake, but this time I was so close to him I could literally see him blushing with embarrassment. Leeds surprisingly lost the replay at Elland Road 3-1 but I was back at Hillsborough weeks later, as Leeds began their run-in for the league championship. Although they attacked for 99 per cent of the game they had to settle for a goalless draw, but it was yet another vital point towards the title. Sheffield Wednesday were relegated that season and we didn't play them again until 1982.

In January 1969 I was about to embark on the capital for my sixth London club, Queens Park Rangers. It proved to be a happy hunting ground in the early years.

Two of the seasons I have been to watch Leeds at Loftus Road were championship-winning campaigns. The first one, and my first visit there, was this match. Leeds were tightening the screws on league leaders Liverpool. QPR, meanwhile, were at the foot of the table.

Before the kick-off Billy Bremner complained to the referee that the floodlights were only half-lit which was obvious to everyone in the ground, but the ref waved Bremner away and blew the whistle. Then, in the darkened stadium, Leeds took the lead after just two minutes. The lights were turned on to full power seconds later, but even then it was hard to distinguish who were the bottom team that night at Loftus Road as QPR piled the pressure on. Things weren't helped either by the fact that because of a colour clash, Leeds were forced to play in QPR's second strip of red shirts.

QPR hit the woodwork three times that I remember and Gary Sprake was having a blinder in goal. My dad leaned into me and said, 'We're gonna win this y'know son, you just watch.'

Rodney Marsh was one of those players who opposing fans simply hated and Leeds fans were no exception. This was enhanced when Marsh deliberately kicked the ball at Leeds full-back Terry Cooper and unbelievably the referee pointed to the penalty spot for handball. The Leeds players were incensed and the fans booed. Those boos soon turned to loud cheers, though, when Sprake saved the penalty. Marsh had declined to take the spot-kick, having missed one the previous week, but Bobby Keetch missed this one as well.

Marsh continued with his antics and once again tried to con the referee when he hit the ball against Jack Charlton's hand but this time his claim was turned down and once again he received loud barracking from the Leeds fans while big Jack had to be restrained from putting Marsh on the floor for a proper penalty.

Further heroics from Sprake, who more than made amends for his blunder at Hillsborough three weeks before with some unbelievable saves, enabled Leeds to take two points from Loftus Road. The league table now showed Liverpool on 43 points, Leeds on 42 and with a game in hand on both Liverpool and Everton, who were four points behind in third place.

Hannover 96, or to give them their full name, Hannoverscher Sportverein von 1896, were founded in 1896. Even though they have won the German League twice, in 1938 and 1954, they're not one of the most fashionable outfits in Deutschland. They've ventured into Europe on a few occasions, although they did get to the quarter-finals of the Europa League in the 2011/12 season. Back in 1969 I ventured over to Hannover for the first and only time Leeds United have played at their Niedersachsenstadion.

Throughout the early years of Leeds's emergence as one of the top sides in Europe, they were quite physical. Of that there is no doubt and they soon earned the tag of 'Dirty Leeds' from the media, other clubs' supporters and footballing authorities in general during those early- to mid-1960s. But what these puritans conveniently overlook, even today, is that Leeds weren't the only hard side in those days. Other teams, including the likes of Everton, Sunderland and Preston North End to name but a few, could dish it out just as much, if not more than this young upcoming Leeds outfit. Games in those days were stopped at an alarming rate while the teams were taken off, sometimes for up to 20 minutes, to cool down.

Leeds learned much of their 'trade' from their early forays into Europe, playing some of the hardest, dirtiest and more importantly cynical sides in the world. In their very first game in Europe in 1966, against Italian team Torino, Bobby Collins had his thigh broken. 'Leeds United,' in the words of Don Revie, 'had to grow up fast.'

Leeds soon became accomplished in the physical aspect as well as the footballing aspect of their game, and some of their finest performances were on the pitches across far-flung Europe. But Revie also had a duty to protect his team, and when Leeds were drawn against Hannover 96 in the third round of the 1969 Fairs Cup, such was the West Germans' reputation for their physical as well as cynical approach, it prompted Revie to threaten to quit the Fairs Cup if these two games developed into violence.

The first leg was at Elland Road and in the first few minutes there were some eyebrow-raising tackles and certainly the foul-rate was above normal during the early stages with two tackles by centre-forward Bandura on Bremner being particularly inflammatory, and Revie's threat to pull his team off the field looked a possibility, but thankfully Leeds had the perfect solution.

In only the fourth minute, Mike O'Grady scored for Leeds. It was said that Norman Hunter's right leg was just for standing on, or he only had it there to make up the set, or indeed he didn't possess it at all but, his goal, and Leeds's second was hit as sweet as a nut from 25 yards with his right foot. Two further goals from Lorimer and one from Jack Charlton saw Leeds take a 5-1 lead to Germany for the second leg.

On the plane to Hannover I saw who I believe was Leeds's first mascot. He was maybe in his late 50s and used to wear a top hat and tails covered in Leeds badges. He wore white gloves and would hold up a large hardboard Leeds pennant with the words 'Super Leeds! European Cup Kings' emblazoned on it. Beneath his distinguished moustache he always had a cigar sticking out of his mouth.

I'd gone once again with Mick Collins and his dad, and when we arrived at the stadium I was well impressed. The atmosphere too was really good and nothing like as hostile as the Hannover team, who began this second leg with one or two early reminders of their aggressive intent, but Leeds were in fantastic form and within 15 minutes were two up with goals from Rod Belfitt and Mick Jones to make it 7-1 on aggregate.

With jeers ringing in the Hannover players' ears from their own fans, Leeds really turned on the style and I can clearly remember the German crowd being totally won over by this very skilful team from West Yorkshire. They applauded loudly as Leeds sprayed the ball around with total superiority. There were quite a lot of British squaddies in with the Leeds fans that night and 'Ilkla' Moor bah't 'at' was sung with such gusto and emotion that it received a standing ovation from the home supporters.

Frustration crept into the Hannover players during the closing stages but surprisingly Terry Cooper was sent off for a foul on Zobel. 'It was a very harsh decision,' said Revie afterwards. To put some perspective on the pressures of European football, Leeds had four players sent off in three years in Europe, whereas previously to that they had only had three players sent off in 44 years.

Back home, my first 'full' match at the City Ground in February 1969 is listed below but, it should really have been in August 1968.

My first venture to the City Ground, Nottingham, lasted just 45 minutes. I had been told by my older mates that it was rough at Forest. 'Loads of away fans end up being chucked in the River Trent,' and so on. I'd travelled with my dad, and a mate called Stan. We parked our turquoise Ford Cortina on the main road alongside the River Trent and I had a little nervous peek at the water over the wall as my imagination ran wild with bodies being thrown into it.

This was in August 1968, Leeds's third away game of the season, and four straight wins were already on the board. There were one or two scuffles between supporters as we made our way to the open end behind the goal and the excitement began. Already I loved away matches, there was always so much going on but, I didn't expect for one minute what was about to happen that afternoon.

The teams were level at 1-1 at half-time when a huge cloud of black smoke appeared in the middle of the main stand and people started running around in all directions. Then, flames engulfed the centre block and quickly spread in both directions as everyone in the other parts of the ground looked on in disbelief. With the game abandoned and several firemen battling the blaze, the players were still stood around in their kit on the pitch. It took no time at all for the whole stand to disappear amid huge flames, leaving only a metal skeleton. There was not one single person hurt.

One story from that day that is worth repeating was about Billy Bremner. The Leeds players were listening so intently to a tactical talk from Don Revie that they didn't notice smoke billowing through the dressing room door. Gary Sprake tried to tell Billy, but he just said, 'Shut up! The boss is talking!'

My first visit to Stoke City had come in April 1968 when a 3-2 defeat proved the beginning of a blip that came at the wrong time of the season as Leeds lost their final four matches of 1967/68, eventually finishing fourth and five points behind champions Manchester City.

The Victoria Ground wasn't that kind to Leeds United during the 1960s and 1970s but one game stands out in particular for me. As Leeds went neck and neck with Liverpool for the 1969 league championship every point was vital and as we entered the final run-in Leeds travelled to Stoke in March knowing that a win at all costs was needed.

Thousands of Leeds fans arrived at Stoke train station and I can still hear the chant echoing round the tunnel as we emerged into the street, 'We're gonna win the league, We're gonna win the league, and now you're gonna believe us!' Hundreds of police had been deployed for what was always a 'tasty' encounter between the two sets of supporters. The open away end was crammed full of Leeds fans but about 100 had managed to infiltrate the home section, the large Boothen End. Fighting broke out but surrounded by a cordon of police officers, the band of Leeds fans, which suddenly doubled, remained in the Boothen End throughout the game, and what a game it was.

Leeds were on fire and slaughtered Stoke 5-1. I still have a scrapbook from that season and the press cuttings make lovely reading. 'WHOOSH! THE POWER OF BREMNER! WHOOSH! THE POWER OF LEEDS!' proclaimed the *Daily Express*. The headlines are accompanied by two dramatic pictures of Stoke keeper John Farmer, one of him in the air seemingly saving a shot and the next one of him on the floor. 'Stoke goalkeeper Farmer appears to be saving this shot from Bremner (left) but it was hit with such fearsome force that it swung Farmer round and left him flat on the ground (above)', says the caption. Another headline simply reads, 'The Untouchables thrash Stoke'.

The Stoke win was a tenth match unbeaten, an impressive start to 1969 prior to my first visit to The Hawthorns for a game against West Bromwich Albion.

It was just over a week after my 13th birthday when I first ventured inside their home. Leeds were hopeful of becoming league champions for the first time, but every team we played against was determined to overcome this powerful Leeds side, and consequently put in sterling performances.

Within four minutes of that April night, West Brom had scored and Leeds were under serious pressure. Any lesser team would have buckled. In those days of one point for a draw and only two for a win, every away point became vital and Leeds gained a valuable one at The Hawthorns thanks to a superb volley from Eddie Gray early in the second half. Having said that Leeds's overall performance in the second half certainly deserved a victory.

West Brom chairman Jimmy Gaunt was full of praise for Leeds, saying afterwards, 'You have to admire Leeds, they're the most professional side I've seen. Their workrate is fantastic. They play it hard, but fair and they are a magnificent side who thoroughly deserve the title.'

West Brom's stalwart defender John Kaye added, 'You can't afford to stop running for one minute against Leeds, for to let them get on top can be fatal. I'm sure they'll win the league and, I hope so, being a Yorkshireman.'

Everton have for so many years lived in the shadow of their far more successful neighbours Liverpool but, there's never been any doubt as to how big a club they have always been. And when I started out on his mammoth journey Leeds and Everton was as big a fixture as any. It was quite vicious in the early days as well, on and off the pitch.

Alan Ball, a terrific midfielder, and not shy of a tackle either, played for the Toffees, and there was one occasion when he was met by Andy Starmore at a football event. When Andy mentioned he supported Leeds, Ball's persona changed completely. The look he gave Andy was as if to say, 'Get out of my face.' Andy thought about some of his tackles and quickly turned round to speak to somebody else.

I had seen Everton in the flesh when I saw them beat Leeds 1-0 in the FA Cup semi-final in April 1968. Now just under a year later I was in their own backyard. Leeds had three games of the campaign left and two of those were on Merseyside. Leeds were top of the league with 63 points, Liverpool were second on 58 with a game in hand, while Everton sat in fourth place, also with a game in hand, on 53. With two points for a victory Everton could not win the league, but were in the position of being able to put their arch Merseyside rivals Liverpool in with a chance of the title.

I like Goodison Park, although it can be very intimidating and it wasn't a particularly good view either. That night I was stood in a corner of the ground with my dad and uncle John when dad said something to me as the game got under way. But the noise was so loud from the crowd that although dad was standing next to me, I couldn't hear a word he was saying. There were chances at both ends, but the game ended 0-0 and Leeds were another small step towards their goal.

After the match I remember one newspaper saying, 'Leeds United dangled the championship trophy over Merseyside last night like a tantalising bone just out of reach of the lion's claw.'

※ ※ ※ ※ ※

Liverpool have gone on to become Britain's most successful club but during the Don Revie era at Elland Road it was Leeds who became the team to beat. Revie shared a very close friendship with the legendary Liverpool manager Bill Shankly and the two of them went head to head on a very special night on 28 April 1969.

In July 1969, man landed on the Moon for the very first time. But something far more important happened in 1969 – Leeds United won the Football League championship for the very first time.

My form tutor at the time was Miss Yates. She was only about four and a half foot tall I'd say, and as well as being our form tutor she was one of the PE teachers as well. She always wore tracksuit bottoms, even in class. I was a mad keen Leeds fan even back then and it was becoming increasingly difficult to skive off school to go to away midweek games, especially those that included a flight out of the country.

There had been one time, I think it was West Brom away, when I decided that I was just going to disappear out of the playground during the afternoon break and get the bus to Leeds in time to board one of the Wallace Arnold coaches destined for the West Midlands, but fate dealt me a good hand – well sort of.

I was just stood around in the playground which was, and still is, adjacent to the main road. Talking to a few mates, one of them, 'Tab' Hunter, knew of my escape plan and he had agreed to cover for me during the last hour and a half of that school day by making excuses for my absence if the need arose. Just then I felt a crack on my head and immediately noticed people looking at me. A group of girls had been standing nearby and one of them (I found out later it was Janet Wood) had thrown a rock at someone and it had hit me instead.

As I felt a small trickle of blood fall down my face I smiled. This was unbelievable. I was taken to the first-aid room and asked to lie down on the bed while the nurse took a look at my wound. 'Do you feel faint at all?' she asked. 'Yes a bit,' I lied. There was none of this namby-pamby health and safety stuff in those days and their intention was to ship me out of school and get me home at the earliest opportunity.

Miss Yates was my guardian angel and she drove me the two miles back to my house in her car. I don't know what it is with cars and me, but I can remember it was a light blue Ford Anglia estate. Understandably, my ma was distraught when the car pulled up and a midget in dark blue tracksuit bottoms and white trainers helped me down the path.

Twenty minutes after Miss Yates left, and after explaining to ma that I was fine, I was on the upper deck of the 163 bus bound for the city centre. About half a mile from town I removed the plaster that the nurse had placed on my head.

A few weeks later, Leeds were to play Liverpool at Anfield in a crunch match that would decide the league title. It was going to be on a Monday night and once again I was forced to call upon Miss Yates for assistance.

During the week leading up to this game, it became apparent that plenty of lads were planning to go missing from school and join the thousands of Leeds fans on the journey west to Merseyside. Word was rife that scores of letters claiming that their son was sick and would be unable to attend school on Monday were about to land on the various form tutors' desks. I began to feel sick myself and asked ma if she would write me a 'sick note' for Monday. My ingenious ma went one better and wrote a letter, which asked Miss Yates outright if I could have the afternoon off to go to Anfield next Monday.

At the time I had no idea what the letter said as I handed the sealed envelope to Miss Yates on Friday morning. I had put the envelope in my jacket that morning and got it out several times during the ten-minute journey on the bus and I have to admit I was sorely tempted to open it as I heard the conversations all around me talking about their letters from their parents.

As I walked into the classroom I sheepishly handed Miss Yates my letter and went to my desk at the back of the class. I never, not for one second, took my eyes off Miss Yates as the rest of the class arrived and settled in their chairs. I then saw her open my envelope, read it and then put it to one side without so much as a blink of an eye.

She then read the register and I was about the fifth or sixth name to be read out. 'Gary Edwards?' she said. 'Here, Miss,' I said eagerly awaiting eye contact. Miss Yates never looked up. Once the register had been completed we were told to go to our lessons for the day and my last attempt at catching Miss Yates's eye failed miserably.

It was 4pm and we were leaving for home when Miss Yates asked me to stay behind. When everyone had left she athletically propelled herself backwards on to her desk and sat perched on the end with her tracksuited legs swinging five inches from the floor. She had my letter in her hand as I stood there awaiting my fate.

'This Leeds United match on Monday night Gary…' She paused as only teachers can. 'I can't let you miss school for a football match.' She paused again. 'My suggestion is that you don't come in at all on Monday. Let's just say you are ill. I know how much Leeds United mean to you,' she said to me as my lips quivered uncontrollably. 'Just don't say anything to anyone else, or we are both in big trouble, OK?'

That Monday afternoon it was sunny as dad, Andy Robinson and I set off for one of the most important games in Leeds United's history. We parked on the dual carriageway near Anfield and walked up towards the ground, turning right on to Anfield Road, the away end, and because it used to be pay at the turnstiles then, thousands of Leeds fans were already queuing up waiting for the turnstiles to open. It was only about half past three – four hours before kick-off.

An estimated 10,000 Leeds fans were there that night, crammed into the Anfield Road End and down along the tunnel side of the ground. The three of us were stood in the corner near the wall with the Anfield Road End to our left and as we were only about a yard from the pitch the players seemed like giants.

In fact the Liverpool goalkeeper *was* a giant – a fat giant. Tommy Lawrence was nicknamed 'The Flying Pig' because of his stature, but he was surprisingly agile and his bulky frame belied his talents as a top keeper. Leeds also had a talented custodian in Gary Sprake. A couple of years previously, however, Sprake had given Liverpool fans an early Christmas present when he inadvertently threw the ball into his own goal right in front of the Kop. Not to let an opportunity like that pass unnoticed, 'Careless Hands', the number one single by Des O'Connor, was played over the tannoy at half-time that day – and then repeated just in case anyone had missed it.

But there were to be no such shenanigans this evening as Sprake performed heroics behind a sterling Leeds defence. Leeds needed just one point to secure the title. Liverpool on the other hand had to win, setting the scene for a tense battle. With the gates locked hours before kick-off we had a ringside seat as we watched both teams kicking lumps out of each other as they sought to gain the upper hand. The Leeds rearguard stood up defiantly throughout the 90 minutes, even threatening to capture two points on several occasions, with dangerous attacking forays of their own from Mick Jones, Eddie Gray, Mike O'Grady and of course, the dynamic duo Billy Bremner and Johnny Giles.

The match finished 0-0 and Geoffrey Green of *The Times* wrote, 'It was a night when the red waves of the Liverpool attack crashed in vain against the white cliffs of this Leeds defence.'

Then something happened that no one present that evening would ever forget. As the Liverpool team, drained and deflated, left the field, Billy Bremner led his troops away from the delirious Leeds fans and headed towards the Kop. Unbelievably they were greeted by chants of 'Champions! Champions!' and everyone on the Kop saluted the new league champions like never before, prompting Alan Thompson of the *Daily Express* to record, 'If 20,000 of the most gracious and greatest – certainly the most knowledgeable and big-hearted crowd in the country can see the greatness of this Leeds team, let no other soured men in the land try to damn them with faint praise.'

Eddie Gray recalled, 'Being cheered by a rival crowd – any rival crowd – was a new experience for us. This in itself was as much of a turning point for Leeds as winning the title.'

Don Revie's greatest rival and friend Bill Shankly, the brilliant Liverpool manager, entered the Leeds dressing room afterwards and as he handed Revie a bottle of champagne he said, 'Your Leeds side is the greatest Don. And you thoroughly deserve to be champions.'

The Liverpool tannoy system even made amends for their 'Careless Hands' gesture of 1967 by belting out the number one single of 1968, Cliff Richard's 'Congratulations'. Meanwhile, Andy and I had vaulted the small wall and were dancing a happy jig on the famous Anfield pitch before collecting a clump of souvenir turf – just as Neil Armstrong would be collecting clumps of Moon dust exactly 11 weeks later.

For good measure, in the final game of the season Johnny Giles scored in a 1-0 victory over Nottingham Forest at Elland Road that ensured Leeds had won the league with a then-record number of 67 points.

%% %% %% %% %%

The first time I can ever remember thinking Leeds United would lose a match was when I went to Budapest in Hungary for the second leg of the fourth round of the Inter-Cities Fairs Cup against Ujpest Dozsa in May 1969. Before we set off I can still recall my dad saying, 'Bloody hell, you're drip white.' It was nothing to do with flying or anything like that. I genuinely believed Leeds would lose after witnessing the first leg against probably the best side I had ever seen Leeds play.

On a cold, early March evening at Elland Road in 1969, Ujpest ran out on to the pitch wearing Leeds's white shirts and shorts while the home side played in blue. Curiously, the same thing had happened when United met Standard Liege in the first leg.

Right from the outset Ujpest were magnificent, and the superb ball artists from Hungary put on an awesome display of football which had the 30,000 crowd mesmerised for long spells of the game. 'Fuckin' 'ell, these are a bit good,' said an oldish bloke with an extremely large nose and a brown chequered flat cap stood next to me and my dad on the Lowfields Road terrace. He had grotesquely long thick black hairs protruding from the nostrils of his oversized conk, but he was totally right in what he said.

The only apparent weakness in the Ujpest side was the goalkeeper Antal Szentmihalyi. He was the Hungarian international keeper but in his last two appearances in England he had conceded seven goals. He had also been sent home in disgrace for his failure in Hungary's

World Cup bid. But that night at Elland Road, clad in all black, he was magnificent.

Early in the second half with the score still at 0-0, Leeds were awarded a penalty. Johnny Giles's record at taking penalties was phenomenal but as he struck a seemingly perfect low kick to his left, Szentmihalyi flew across his goal and tipped the ball round the post for a corner.

Leeds went close on a number of occasions, hitting the woodwork a few times. Two of those came from centre-half Jack Charlton but the Hungarians capitalised on these costly misses and went ahead through a blistering 25-yard shot from Antal Dunai which gave Gary Sprake no chance. I can still remember all these years on the silence that befell Elland Road when that goal was scored. And I can still remember one of their players running, jumping and swinging from the crossbar dressed in our white shirt with our famous blue owl badge on the chest with the ball nestled snugly in the back of our net.

When I boarded the plane to Hungary, that goal by Dunai separated the two sides, and although Leeds were a formidable team in Europe and more than capable of rescuing the tie, deep down I feared a defeat.

The game was in the very same stadium where United had won this cup less than six months before – the Nep Stadium. The Leeds team was heavily depleted with Jack Charlton, Paul Reaney and Mike O'Grady all out with flu and Billy Bremner, Norman Hunter, Terry Cooper, Paul Madeley and Mick Jones all playing with the after-effects of flu.

It registered with me early on as we sat with around 200 Leeds fans that this Hungarian crowd weren't half as fervent as the Ferencvaros supporters had been six months ago but, that said, their team didn't need any vocal support as they took up where they left off at Elland Road. To be fair, Leeds could quite easily have scored on a couple of forays into the Hungarian half, but it wasn't to be and in the end Ujpest eased over the line with a 2-0 victory, making them the first team to beat United in both legs in a European competition.

Personally, this didn't help me one jot and I really took the defeat to heart. I sulked for the entire flight home. I was introduced to Leeds United at a time when Don Revie had a side that terrorised the whole of the Football League as well as all across Europe and I simply wasn't used to seeing Leeds lose.

I firmly believed that they were invincible but when they did lose a game, which was extremely rare in those days, I was totally inconsolable. I wouldn't eat, I felt physically sick and I would grunt at anyone who had the audacity to make conversation with me. I must have been a right prat.

Theses days of course, defeats come with much more frequency, but I still bury my head in the sand. After a defeat I will not buy a newspaper and I won't watch any TV footage of the game. Incidentally, I haven't watched *Match of the Day* since Leeds were relegated from the Premier League in 2004. After a defeat I just immerse myself into countless episodes of *Laurel and Hardy* or large dollops of *Only Fools and Horses* and anything else that takes my mind away from football altogether. However, by the time the next Leeds game arrives I have conditioned myself sufficiently to embrace the next game and I'm raring to go.

3

Blackpool Beach

TWO days before Leeds won the league championship at Anfield in 1969 there was the rather less significant matter of the FA Cup Final between Man City and Leicester City. However, certain aspects of that match would lead to certain links with Leeds United.

First, the man of the match award that afternoon went to Leicester's prolific young striker Allan Clarke, despite the Manchester side winning the cup with a 1-0 victory. Things then went from bad to worse for Leicester. They were relegated and, at 1.27pm on 24 July, Don Revie swooped on Leicester and gave them a record fee of £165,000 to whisk Allan Clarke away to Elland Road.

Secondly, Manchester City as the FA Cup holders, would meet the league champions Leeds for the traditional curtain-raiser the following season – the FA Charity Shield. So the week before 1969/70 got under way, City arrived at Elland Road in their away kit of red and black stripes. Lining up in a white shirt was our new arrival Allan Clarke.

However, I nearly didn't make it. The week before the match, I had trashed a greenhouse with my pushbike. I misjudged a bend on a main road through Kippax, which resulted in my bike hitting the kerb before flying through a short wooden fence and crashing straight into the greenhouse in a garden. This would have been bad enough but the fact that I was carrying three passengers made the situation much worse.

The surrounding lawn was soon littered with broken glass, upturned plant pots, seed trays and tomatoes – hundreds of tomatoes. Oh, and my three friends. The owner was quite distraught and the local constable was summoned. He duly arrived half an hour later on his pushbike.

As a result of all this I was disciplined by my dad, who imposed on me the only thing that he knew would have an impact. I was banned from going to the next Leeds game. This just happened to be the first match of the season – the Charity Shield.

Our circus act had occurred about a week before we faced City and I felt fairly confident that dad would change his mind before the big day arrived even though I was grounded for that week. However, as the days passed and the weekend neared I began to think that I wouldn't be going to the match after all.

Dad hadn't said one single word to me and one evening I sat at the top of the stairs and heard my ma saying that he (I) had learned his (my) lesson and that he should take me to the match, but dad wasn't budging one inch and I wasn't going to Elland Road on Saturday. Not a chance in hell. I sat on my bed and took my 1969/70 season ticket book out of my drawer and threw it across the room. 'What's the point of that?' I grumbled to myself. It stayed on its side and crumpled in the corner of my bedroom for the rest of the week. I didn't sleep a wink on the Friday night and I had given up trying to talk to my dad days ago.

I was the first up on Saturday morning and was watching *The Flintstones* on TV when I heard movement upstairs. I heard my dad doing his usual loud noises in the bathroom, like clearing his nose and other things. I got up off the settee and put on my pumps before getting my football out of the cupboard under the stairs. I can count on one hand the times my dad and I fell out and I hated every one of them. We were close, and I was very proud of him, but this was the weekend he was 'Bad Dad' in my book, even though it was entirely my fault.

I was just going out of the back door when he talked to me for the first time since Wednesday, maybe even before then. 'Where you off to?' he said. I muttered something about going to play football on the bottom green and he just said, 'Aren't you going to get ready?' For the first time I sensed a glimmer of hope and meekly asked, 'For what?' 'Well, I'm off to Elland Road, you can please yourself.' I leapt upstairs like a gazelle, and within seconds I was back downstairs and stood next to 'Good Dad' with my trusty woollen Leeds scarf hung round my neck.

Leeds beat City with a superb goal from the outside of Eddie Gray's left boot. Jack Charlton added a second when he outjumped the whole City defence to head the ball over keeper Joe Corrigan. City pulled a goal back near the end when Gary Sprake ducked as the ball came across from a corner and was headed back in for

Colin Bell to finish. But Leeds went on to win their first Charity Shield.

Debutant Allan Clarke failed to get on the scoresheet that day, but just seven days later he scored on his league debut against Tottenham Hotspur at Elland Road, and I am privileged and very grateful to be able to say that I went on to witness every one of his 151 goals for Leeds United.

Our first away game of the 1969/70 season was at Nottingham Forest. We were going there as league champions and Leeds were on fire – blowing Forest away 4-1 with an exhilarating exhibition of football that even had sections of the home fans applauding. A very rare occurrence, even in those days.

I had gone on the train to that game with those older mates of mine, and it was certainly different to travelling with your dad in a turquoise Cortina. It was sort of a fashion to wear broad leather belts with metal studs in them, usually spelling a name, or more usually 'LUFC', and it was these studs that I recall glistening in the sun as a brawl occurred with some Forest fans outside the train station with these belts being used as weapons.

There was a Leeds fan who was about my age, he had long hair, a denim jacket and denim jeans turned up at the bottom and shiny brown Doc Martin boots. His woollen Leeds scarf was looped over his belt. He was the only one I saw get arrested when a police car and a police mini-van arrived. Leeds fans ran down the road chanting, 'We are the champions!'

Early in the season I went with a few mates on the train to Everton and, because of a few scuffles outside Lime Street train station, by the time we got to the ground, the gates were locked. Some fans saw this as an opportunity to carry on fighting, which they did. I was more interested in getting into the ground. I was only 14 and I latched on to this lad called John who I imagined to be about 25. The rest of my mates were enjoying the fighting that was going on all around us.

'This way,' said John, as he grabbed my arm. We turned the corner and there was a small queue of older men, Everton fans, which we joined. 'This is their main stand, but it doesn't matter, just keep quiet, at least we'll get in,' whispered John. We did get in, but by this time Everton were winning 2-0. Then early into the second half they made it 3-0. I was distraught. I hate to see Leeds lose, even today, but when I was a kid, I used to take it real bad.

Things began to improve for Leeds as Billy Bremner and then Allan Clarke scored to pull Leeds back to within touching distance.

But the comeback had been a case of too little too late and as proud Leeds gathered momentum they ran out of time and lost 3-2. John still lives in Kippax and although he only gets to a few games these days, every time he sees me and we get chatting he'll say, 'Remember that time I got you in at Everton?'

Just like my early days with John Hamilton when he would get me a programme from the Leeds games before I ventured out there myself, John from Kippax did the same as I waited on the local green at the bottom of our estate for the older lads to arrive back from Leeds's away games and he would give me a programme from that day.

Leeds United's debut in the European Cup in 1969/70 was dramatic to say the least. This was in the good old days when only the champions of each country were eligible to compete in the tournament.

Having said that, right from the start, Lyn Oslo, the Norwegian champions, had no chance whatsoever against Leeds at Elland Road. They were an amateur side made up of teachers, joiners, postmen, maybe the odd nasty whaler and others. Leeds took the lead after only 35 seconds through Mike O'Grady and by the time the final whistle went poor Lyn had been blown away to the tune of 10-0.

I can still remember watching that night beneath the floodlights with my arms folded and my chin nestled in between them on the top of the stone wall at the front of the Lowfields Road Stand and feeling desperately sorry for the red-and-white-shirted Norwegians as Leeds ran riot but, even with the ball constantly flying past him from all directions, Lyn's keeper Sven Olsen was easily the man of the match and this despite him only arriving at Elland Road just half an hour before kick-off.

A fortnight later I was on board a smallish plane, blue and white as I recall, with propellers, flying out of Yeadon airport bound for the second leg in Oslo. To my knowledge, at the time of writing, I have been to watch Leeds play in Scandinavia 36 times – once in Finland, twice in Denmark, 14 in Sweden and 19 in Norway. Out of all those visits, only three have been in European competition and all of those have been in Norway.

Even at 14 years of age I had heard of the support that was growing for Leeds among the Vikings. I soon saw evidence of it myself. The stadium was only tiny, as you would expect, yet still I was amazed to see Leeds scarves all around the ground. I quickly realised that most of them belonged to Norwegians. Apparently it all started with dads becoming interested in Don Revie's upcoming side from the early 1960s and that fanaticism and genuine love of the club is still being passed down from father to son and daughter today.

That evening, Leeds supporters' membership in Norway grew even more as the brave amateurs from Oslo were put to the sword by a team consisting of many of Revie's shadow squad members who would prove invaluable as the club chased countless trophies for well over a decade. Two of those squad members, Terry Hibbitt and Rod Belfitt, grabbed two goals each, and further goals from Mick Jones and Peter Lorimer saw Leeds cruise to a 6-0 win, going through 16-0 on aggregate.

I can still picture goalkeeper Gary Sprake signing autographs for fans *during* the match, which was a tad cheeky I thought.

Despite playing relatively low opposition, Leeds had been meticulous in carrying out Revie's instructions to the letter. Everything seemed to have been planned to perfection. During the course of the 10-0 result, the half-time score was 5-0, and for the 6-0 game the interval total had been 3-0.

During my trips to Scandinavia I have noticed how expensive things are in comparison to the UK, and elsewhere for that matter. But for my first trip as a 14-year-old schoolboy that evening in Oslo it hadn't affected me one jot, as my guardian for the trip, Mr Hamilton, bought me a bottle of fizzy orange pop and introduced me to my first packet of moose-flavoured crisps.

The Leeds support from Scandinavia continues to grow today. The main branch is the Leeds United Supporters' Club of Scandinavia (LUSCOS) that has a membership of almost 4,500 and takes in new members every week. Another supporters' group, the Leeds United Members' Club, is another organisation which will ensure that the Viking support for Leeds United will be around for many more years to come.

My early memories of The Dell include arriving late after our coach had broken down in November 1969. We caught a service bus and thumbed a lift and got there about 20 minutes late to find the gates closed and the words 'Sell Out' pinned to the walls. We quickly found a quiet corner of the ground and one by one scaled the wall and dropped into the Leeds fans behind the goal.

At the precise moment of me, Stan, Billy and Andy announcing our arrival, Leeds were awarded a penalty. It was turning out to be not such a bad afternoon after all. But I spoke too soon. The Southampton keeper, Eric Martin, guessed the right way and saved Lorimer's kick. At least we came away with a 1-1 draw and a new Wally Arnold coach.

I can't put my finger on it really but there seems to be something very special about the year 1970. It might be just the start of a new decade, the beginning of the flamboyant and colourful music scene, or could it be the sight of probably the greatest football team ever to grace a pitch as Brazil stormed to a pulsating 4-1 triumph over Italy in the World Cup Final in Mexico City?

It's certainly a memory that will never fade. They wore their golden shirts for a golden side that struck gold with Pele being the jewel in a crown littered with gleaming bright lights. Who can forget that fourth Brazilian goal? It was pure genius and a goal widely accepted as the greatest in World Cup history. Eight Brazilian players were involved in a sweeping move that tore the Italians to shreds. At the end of it all Pele just casually rolled a perfectly weighted pass into the path of right-back and skipper Carlos Alberto, who thumped a superb shot into the bottom corner of the net. It was a football moment to cherish. And, as they became the first country to win the Jules Rimet Trophy on three occasions, their just reward was being able to keep the trophy forever as FIFA introduced a new World Cup for 1974.

Hoping to make good progress in a cup competition that year were also Don Revie's Leeds in the FA Cup. After disposing of Swansea City with a 2-1 scoreline in round three at Elland Road, it was to be a first visit, and indeed the only one to date, to non-league Sutton United. It was time to get the map out and find out exactly where Sutton was ahead of the 24 January encounter.

It was freezing cold and my feet were like blocks of ice as we shuffled up to the Leeds ticket office window at the back of the West Stand at Elland Road. My dad wasn't in a good mood. Our car hadn't started that morning and we'd had to push it halfway around our estate to get it running. At least it had stopped snowing. It was late January 1970 and although it hadn't snowed that much, I really couldn't remember when it had been so cold.

Non-league Sutton United had done remarkably well in the FA Cup and their reward for reaching the fourth round was a home tie against the FA Cup and European Cup favourites Leeds United. We had season tickets in the standing paddock of the West Stand but we still had to queue for almost four hours to ensure that we got a ticket out of the meagre 1,800 allocation that Leeds fans had been given.

Revie had raised concerns about the safety of his players having to play at a non-league ground with limited resources. 'I have a team of players worth a million pounds and I have to ensure their safety,' he had told the press. Revie, though, had watched Sutton in previous weeks and had been suitably impressed, 'We will treat this game as though we were playing at Anfield or Goodison.'

He was also concerned about the state of the pitch and arranged a practice match on a non-league ground in the Leeds area. Skelton Road, home of East End Park Working Men's Club FC, was ideal. 'One of the main things I wanted,' said Revie, 'was for the players to get used to the sky line at this sort of ground. The amount of sky behind the goals and the small stands make a very different picture to what they see week in week out at First Division grounds. Skelton Road gives them a good idea of what they will see on Saturday and what points arising about passing and shooting they should note. I am very grateful for this opportunity to play here.'

Being the fanatic I was, I was at that practice match at East End Park. A group of us went on the 163 bus straight from school. The squad was already engrossed in a tense workout when we arrived and the floodlights had attracted some local attention. Paul Madeley threw a yellow training bib over to where we were sat on a grass banking. I went over and gave him it back when they had finished, although to this day, I wish that I had kept it as a souvenir.

I can't remember if we went on the coach or the train to Sutton, but I do remember going into the wrong ground when we got there. We walked straight into the cricket ground, The Oval, which was very close by, and we weren't the only Leeds fans – or Sutton fans – to do so either.

Gander Green Lane was the home of Sutton United and the whole ground was flanked by trees, which proved to be an ideal vantage point for hundreds of fans. There were two or three small stands, but mainly it was all open. We were down the side and the only thing separating us and hundreds of fans from the pitch was a rope.

Revie's meticulous planning had been faultless and Leeds cruised to a 6-0 victory, avoiding the potential 'banana skin' that would have no doubt pleased most of the country. I'm not sure if it was just coincidence but just as when Leeds had played the Norwegian amateurs Lyn Oslo earlier that season, the half-time score was exactly half that of the final score. It could have been 6-1 though; Sutton's centre-half John Faulkner scored, but was adjudged to have fouled keeper David Harvey and their goal was promptly disallowed.

Sutton fans, however, didn't realise that the goal had been ruled out and wild scenes of elation continued all around the ground, including one lad who was stood near me. He was about my age, 14, and he was jumping up and down and screaming, totally oblivious to the fact that the goal wouldn't stand. His wooden rattle was going round that fast above his head that I wouldn't have been at all surprised if he had taken off right there and then. When he realised the goal had been disallowed he threw his yellow pom-pom hat on the floor and began jumping up and down on it.

It did turn out to be a good day for Faulkner though. Revie had been so impressed with his performance that he signed him almost there and then. I met Faulkner when he attended the unveiling of Revie's statue at Elland Road in May 2012. He told me that that meeting with Revie shortly after the Sutton v Leeds game had been a bit bizarre to say the least.

Arsenal and Tottenham were also in hot pursuit of Faulkner's signature and Revie knew this. Faulkner met Revie in a Wimpy bar just behind the Leeds team hotel. There was no massive euphoria and no press conference. In fact Faulkner said that he didn't even recognise Revie when he first walked into the Wimpy because the Leeds manager was just sat there having a coffee and was wearing a hat to avoid being seen.

Unfortunately for Faulkner he scored an own goal on his debut against Burnley a week before Leeds took on Chelsea in the 1970 FA Cup Final and played only a further three games before sustaining a knee injury which ended his short-lived Leeds career.

In late 1969 a new kid joined our class at school. I forget his name, but he was an oddball. I mean that in the nicest possible sense. He had just moved into the area with his family. He had spiky fair hair, a chubby red face, enormous ears and it looked like hundreds of teeth were trying to escape from his mouth. Although we wore a uniform, his always looked old-fashioned and his trousers were always at half-mast, revealing his woollen grey socks that must have gone up to his knees. Oh, and he supported Mansfield Town. Fair play to him, Mansfield is where he came from and Mansfield were his team.

We talked a lot about football and we hung about quite a bit. In the 1970 FA Cup, Leeds had just managed to squeeze past Third Division Swansea Town in the third round, beaten non-league Sutton 6-0 in the next round and now had drawn Mansfield at Elland Road. Leeds were at the top of the First Division while Mansfield were struggling in the Third Division. But this did not worry my school chum. 'We'll slaughter you,' he said to me after we had heard the cup draw on a lad's transistor one Monday dinner-time at school.

They didn't slaughter us, but they frightened the bloody life out of us! Roared on by around 4,000 fans, Town put up a great fight and the majority of the 48,000 crowd were relieved to hear the final whistle after a 2-0 win which was definitely much closer than the scoreline suggests.

Later in 1970 we met manchester united in the semi-final of the FA Cup. The teams had met before at this stage, Leeds winning 1-0 at Nottingham Forest after a 0-0 draw at Hillsborough. This had been in 1965 and now five years later it was back to Hillsborough. Leeds fans were in the large open end opposite the Leppings Lane End and to be honest I can't remember a great deal about the game except that it was an ill-tempered affair. The replay was at Villa Park and once again Leeds fans were put in the open end with manchester united fans being afforded the prestige of going in the large covered Holte End. Once again the full-time score was 0-0.

The second replay, just three days later, was at the home of Bolton Wanderers, Burnden Park. I had caught flu and felt awful but I was determined to go to the game. My dad, my hero, got us two stand tickets so I could sit down. Leeds fans were in the open end to our right. After less than ten minutes Billy Bremner scored and that's how it remained.

Shortly after the semi-finals we played West Ham away and drew 2-2 in a game that I remember for one moment only.

Just yards in front of us Paul Reaney went down injured. It was very rare to see Reaney go down, and it was obvious that he was hurt, but the West Ham fans barracked him incessantly. The stretcher was brought on and Reaney was carried off. It was revealed later that he had broken his leg and would miss the FA Cup Final against Chelsea as well as the Mexico World Cup with England.

%% %% %% %% %%

There's nothing quite like being in a football ground with a great atmosphere. On some occasions you can have that kind of atmosphere even if the attendance is a measly 10,000. There have been some absolutely overwhelming atmospheres at Elland Road over the years, particularly in the 1970s, but any club would be hard pressed to beat the noise generated during this match at Hampden Park. The official attendance was a massive 136,505. The two opponents? Celtic and Leeds United in the second leg of the European Cup semi-final.

In 1970 Leeds were chasing an improbable and exhaustive treble of the league championship, the FA Cup and the European Cup. This led inevitably to the fixture congestion which would be the eventual downfall in United's ambitious dream.

On 1 April Celtic beat Leeds 1-0 at Elland Road in the first leg of the semi-final with a goal scored by Jimmy Johnstone after only two minutes. Despite Leeds piling on the pressure and Eddie Gray hitting the bar, the score remained 1-0. The very next day Leeds had to travel to London for a hard-fought league game at West Ham which ended in a 2-2 draw.

Two days later Leeds beat Burnley 2-0 at Elland Road in yet another vital league game. The following weekend there was the little matter of the FA Cup Final against Chelsea at Wembley and, just four days after this, they were heading north for the second leg against Celtic at Hampden Park.

A fleet of Wallace Arnold coaches made their way from the Call Lane depot in Leeds and the coach in front of us broke down in Harehills, which is a district of Leeds only two miles from base. The fans who were getting off weren't looking too pleased either and were frantically trying to flag the other coaches down for them to get on. Our driver pulled up behind the broken-down coach to offer assistance. 'Don't be too long mate!' someone shouted from the back. 'We've got a long way to go yet.' The driver disappeared down the steps, 'Don't worry yerself old cock!' he shouted back. 'I'll get you there. You have another can.'

After a quick conversation our driver climbed back aboard, telling about half a dozen waiting at our coach that he didn't have any room for them. He then drove to a nearby telephone box to ring the depot for someone to come out to the broken-down coach. Ten minutes later we were at Wetherby roundabout and began our 200-mile journey up the old A1.

It is said that around 30 Wallace Arnold vehicles travelled that day with other Leeds coach firms Fallas and Heaps also cashing in. There were also four special trains that made the journey, but it was nothing in comparison to what the Scots had brought to Elland Road for the first leg a fortnight earlier. They had invaded Leeds and Celtic fans seemed to be everywhere looking for a drink but there was very little trouble reported, unlike when Rangers had come to Elland Road two years previously.

I have no allegiance to either one of the Old Firm and over the years I have shared many a beer with both Celtic and Rangers fans, but when Rangers came in 1968 they left a trail of destruction in the city centre, it has to be said.

As the coaches arrived at Hampden, I was glad to see that the supporters we had left behind in Harehills had made it. On arrival we were besieged by thousands of Celtic fans wanting any spare tickets. I understand the same scenario took place at Glasgow Central train station as the Leeds trains arrived there. Leeds had taken 5,000 supporters, but that was to be just a drop in the ocean inside the stadium.

The crowd was officially 136,505 but many reports claim there were many more than that inside the ground. One thing is for certain, it is still a record attendance for a European tie and is unlikely ever to be surpassed. Once we were inside there was no segregation as such and large groups of Leeds fans, who were scattered all over the stadium, became engulfed in a cauldron of deafening noise. Leeds fans had bought official tickets but they weren't all for the same part of the ground.

After almost a quarter of an hour Leeds were level on aggregate. Billy Bremner had a knack of scoring vital goals and what better stage was there to produce yet another? It was an absolute belter. He raced at the Celtic defence and from around 30 yards he let fly with a terrific right-footed shot which gave the Celtic keeper absolutely no chance.

I could see the Leeds fans all over the place going mad and waving their scarves but the scene overall was one of relative silence. I reached for my scarf that had been secreted beneath my coat under dad's instructions, and I began waving it in the air. Just then a massive hand was placed on my shoulder and I gulped. 'You enjoy it laddie,' said a gruff Scottish voice. 'It's all yer gannae get son.' I smiled nervously at this huge monster behind me, and dad, apart from a slight smile, said or did nothing. I didn't blame him one bit. The monster was right though and Bremner's goal was just a stay of execution.

Only minutes after half-time, John Hughes scored for Celtic. Gary Sprake was then clattered and injured by Hughes and had to be stretchered off. David Harvey took up his position, but just seconds later he was picking the ball out of the back of his net after Bobby Murdoch had made it 2-1 on the night and 3-1 on aggregate.

There was to be no way back for Leeds and as I tried to force myself to sleep on the coach home I began thinking about our next match – a league game against Manchester City at home three days later. We could still win the league and cup double.

Someone with a radio then said that Everton had just beaten West Brom 2-0, which meant that Leeds could no longer win the league either. It was probably one of the longest trips home that I can remember.

%. %. %. %. %.

Sandwiched in between the disappointing European Cup semi-final encounters with Celtic was the 1970 FA Cup Final against Chelsea. It would turn out to be United's solitary hope of silverware that season.

My dad had been with me to almost every game that season including three gruelling FA Cup semi-finals and then he was dealt the cruellest of blows. He had to go into hospital for an operation on his 'Johnny Giles', and it would coincide with the final at Wembley. He hid his disappointment really well and on the face of it, he didn't seem too fussed about missing the game. But one night I overheard him saying to my ma, 'I'd have liked to have seen it though.' I have to admit to shedding a tear as I drifted off to sleep that night.

My dad's spare ticket caused something of a minor family squabble and my dad's brothers John and Ernie were both in the running to accompany me to Wembley. Apparently Ernie won. Ernie worked as an inspector on British Rail so, logically, we travelled to Wembley by train. He'll hate me for saying this, but Ernie always reminded me of Sid James, he still does in fact. He's always cracking jokes and always laughing.

The biggest top hat I have ever seen with the words 'Super Leeds' emblazoned on it was the first thing I saw as we turned down Wembley Way. This was my first FA Cup Final and already I was enjoying every minute of it. This, I thought to myself, was what it's all about.

I've no idea how many times I attended the original Wembley Stadium, easily over 100, but I know for certain it had a magic like no other. Climbing those massive steps to get to your turnstile, whether it be to watch Leeds or England, was something I'll treasure forever.

Walking down Wembley Way produced a buzz all of its own. Looking back, it was nothing extraordinary and I realise I could be drowning in nostalgia, but Wembley was iconic and there will never be another one like it. Never again will we see death-defying leaps by fans jumping across from one staircase window to another 30 feet up from the ground but, those who did see it will never forget it.

One thing that was far from iconic that day in 1970 was the pitch. It was an absolute disgrace. The week before the final, the Horse of the Year Show had been held on Wembley's hallowed turf and as a consequence, the showcase of the football season was played on what Revie described as 'Blackpool Beach'.

Despite this, the 1970 FA Cup Final between Chelsea and Leeds is still regarded as one of the best seen at Wembley. Not to put too fine a point on it, Leeds absolutely murdered Chelsea that day. The opening goal came from big Jack Charlton as he outjumped the Chelsea defence in the six-yard box to head Leeds in front. Charlton headed the ball downwards but the pitch was so heavily laden with sand that the bounce expected by the Chelsea defenders stood on the line never happened and instead Charlton's effort trickled over the line under the despairing boots of John Hollins and Ron Harris. The ball didn't even hit the back of the net.

Eddie Gray was pure magic that day and dazzled everyone, supporters and players alike, with his mesmerising ball skills. Chelsea full-back David Webb never got a look-in all afternoon and it came as no surprise to anyone when Gray was awarded the prestigious man of the match award afterwards. Uncle Ernie said, 'He's bloody magic him.'

It looked to be a simple case of how many goals Leeds would score. Unfortunately Chelsea had a hero of their own. That was the Leeds goalkeeper Gary Sprake. Just before half-time Peter Houseman hit a long-range, and rather speculative, shot from around 25 yards. It was at the Leeds fans' end and we couldn't believe it when Sprake slumped over the ball in what seemed like slow motion and the ball squirmed under his body for an equaliser.

The ball was going that slowly that it only just touched the back of the net. Houseman was related to someone I knew in our neighbouring village of Great Preston, but that didn't help me none that day.

Leeds continued to dominate and went back in front with less than ten minutes to go. Mick Jones followed in from Allan Clarke hitting the post and fired past Peter Bonetti. Again it was at our end and the Leeds fans went berserk. A giant teddy bear complete with Leeds colours was launched into the air and it fell on top of me and uncle Ernie as we danced and hugged everyone around us. Then with four minutes remaining Chelsea equalised yet again with a header from Ian Hutchinson. I hate Chelsea.

It was the first time since 1912 that the FA Cup Final had ended in a draw.

I've spoken since to some of the Chelsea players from that match, and their supporters who were there, and each and every one of them has admitted that they were 'slightly' fortunate that day at Wembley.

The Wembley pitch was in such poor condition that the replay had to be switched to Old Trafford. Even worse, dad's operation wasn't without complications and he would also miss the second match. It was now my uncle John's opportunity to accompany me.

John will hate me for saying this too, but whereas Ernie is Sid James, happy-go-lucky, John is a miserable old git – but I love him.

He is a typical Yorkshireman. I have stood alongside him at countless Yorkshire County Cricket Club matches and countless horse racing meetings in Yorkshire and he loves to moan.

John picked me up from school at 4pm on 29 April in his lime green Ford Anglia and we headed to Old Trafford for the replay. Every vehicle of any description seemed to have a Leeds scarf flying from it. John puffed on his pipe, 'We've got to beat these bastards tonight y'know,' he said, through gritted teeth biting down on his pipe, 'I hate 'em.'

Leeds fans had been allocated the open Scoreboard End. Chelsea had been given the Stretford End with a nice roof over their heads. Once again it was Jones who put Leeds in front with a stunning drive past Bonetti, but yet again, Chelsea were allowed to wriggle off the hook. Peter Osgood equalised in the second half to take the tie into extra time for a second time and I can remember Chelsea's winning goal as though it was yesterday. Ian Hutchinson took a long throw that reached Leeds's box, the ball was then headed on where Webb, who had been tormented so cruelly at Wembley by Gray, headed it in at the far post past David Harvey, in for Sprake after the Wembley game. I was devastated and no one in that Leeds end moved for what seemed an age.

The walk back to the coaches afterwards was like being among thousands of zombies. Nobody spoke as they ran the game past themselves in their own heads. A couple of hours later John dropped me off at my grandma's. In those days, the last bus back to my house in Kippax was at 8.30pm, so I would regularly stay at grandma's just outside Leeds in a place called Gipton and go straight to school the next day.

When I awoke the next morning I hoped it had all been a bad dream, but of course it hadn't. As I sat on the bus going to Garforth with the early-morning sun streaming through the windows into my eyes I felt like crying as I thought what might have been. Just three weeks ago, Leeds United had been favourites to land the first treble of the league championship, the FA Cup and the European Cup. As it was, we lost in the FA Cup Final, the semi-final of the European Cup and finished as runners-up to Everton in the First Division.

Now as I trudged off the bus and in to school, my world was in tatters. I hate Chelsea.

4

Disturbing Deckchairs

I HAD to wait until August 1970 and the opening day of the 1970/71 season for my own personal glory at Old Trafford. I was now 14 years old and it was well worth the wait. I was stood in the open Scoreboard End with my dad and during the first half Mick Jones scored the only goal of the game from the edge of the penalty area with a powerful header. We were right behind the line of fire and it was a moment I will never forget.

'We took the Shoreham, easy! Easy!' was a familiar cry from the Leeds fans during the early- to mid-1970s when visiting Bramall Lane for games against Sheffield United. Whites would begin to arrive at the ground at lunchtime and one particular occasion was for an evening kick-off in September 1970, a League Cup tie. Throughout the afternoon our supporters would gather and start to queue outside the Shoreham End waiting for the turnstiles to open.

By the time the home faithful arrived the Shoreham was full of visitors, which didn't please the Blades. Not one bit. This trend continued for a couple of seasons until the police, possibly under pressure from disgruntled home fans, began to disperse Leeds supporters arriving early and forced them to go into the away end.

It was around this time that Bramall Lane only had three stands. Adjacent to the pitch was a cricket field and the TV cameras were situated way across the other side of that. It must have cost a fortune in magnifying lenses whenever the match was on television.

The away end consisted of a standing terrace covered by a very steep stand. I can't recall ever being in a stand with such a sharp incline as this and many a Leeds fan would tumble into the row in front during a wild goal celebration. Great care had to be taken if you were brave enough to occupy the first couple of rows.

By September 1970, just under a year had passed since our previous visit to Norway but as we filed through the small airport just outside Sarpsborg I quickly noticed that support for Leeds had increased greatly among the Scandinavians. This adulation grew even larger after 10,000 crammed into the tiny ground to see Leeds execute a cautious but entertaining performance to ensure a 1-0 first leg victory in the first round of the 1970/71 Inter-Cities Fairs Cup.

Peter Lorimer had scored the winning goal and only hours after the game he and his team-mates were swamped with adoring Scandinavians sporting Leeds colours, wanting autographs in the airport before the team flew back home.

Thirty-six years later, Lorimer was back in this very airport still signing autographs for the Norwegians, this time as a Leeds director and a fine ambassador for the club.

There are a number of cities I have visited over the years that are very similar in appearance to Leeds. The part of Melbourne that I stayed in for our pre-season friendly there in 2001 was one such place. Another one was Dresden in 1970. As long as I can remember, I have marvelled at the Victorian architecture that dominates the streets and skyline of my home city. Dresden had similar traits. Although we only saw it briefly through our coach window as we were driven from the airport straight to the ground, 'assisted' by a combined Russian/East German escort.

The Fairs Cup of 1970/71 brought about my first trip to East Germany. I'd gone with Mick Collins and his dad and we had to fill a lot of forms in, just as we had done when we went to Hungary in 1968. There was strict control when you travelled behind the Iron Curtain, as it was called, and some people were questioned longer than others. Both Mick and I were still at school and we were quizzed quite intensely. The procedure was much stricter than when we had travelled to Budapest in 1968, possibly because it involved a divided Germany. The TV commentator Kenneth Wolstenholme was on our plane with some journalists and of course Phil Brown from the *Yorkshire Evening Post*.

Leeds had narrowly beaten Dynamo Dresden in the first leg. I was stood at the front of the Lowfields Road side and was directly behind the line of flight of the ball as Rod Belfitt headed goalwards with the keeper stranded in no-man's-land. But just then a German full-back scrambled back to the line and punched the ball over the bar. Lorimer converted the ensuing penalty in front of the Kop.

Dresden were expected to come at Leeds in Germany, but Leeds were expected to win through nonetheless. The game however was tough and the yellow-shirted Dynamo team made Leeds work every inch of the way by winning 2-1 on the night. Mick Jones's goal was just enough to send Leeds through on the away goals rule after a 2-2 aggregate draw.

The Leeds fans were then taken back to the airport where we faced even more interrogation before we were allowed to board our plane and about four or five hours after the final whistle we touched down at Yeadon airport. I slept for a couple of hours on Mick's settee, but by 9am I was sat behind my desk in Mrs Franklin's classroom at Garforth Comprehensive School, a bit blurry eyed but ready for the rigours of the day.

The third round of the Fairs Cup proved to be much easier than the game in Dresden. Sparta Prague weren't really a poor side, but they were unfortunate to come up against a rampant Leeds team who crushed them 6-0 in the first leg at Elland Road. It was far less complicated entering Czechoslovakia than East Germany but there were still forms to fill in and one Leeds fan who was wearing a white butcher's coat with club badges sewn on it had to be restrained by Czech police when he got slightly over-exuberant as he finally passed through customs.

The game itself was nowhere near as easy as the first leg and the plucky Czechs put up a real fight but a goal each from Allan Clarke and Rod Belfitt plus one from Eddie Gray was enough to give Leeds a narrow 3-2 victory on the night, but 9-2 on aggregate.

In 1971, Apollo 14 and Apollo 15 both successfully landed on the Moon with David Scott and James Irwin in Apollo 15 becoming the first astronauts to ride in a lunar rover. Back down on Earth the early 1970s music scene saw the very first Glastonbury Festival take place in June with acts such as David Bowie, Hawkwind, Traffic and Fairport Convention all performing.

On 8 March Joe Frazier beat Muhammad Ali at Madison Square Garden, in what was to be the first of three mesmerising bouts between the two of them, to retain his world heavyweight boxing championship. John Newcombe and Evonne Goolagong made it an Australian double as they both took the Wimbledon singles titles in south London.

In the football world 1971 began in the most horrific way possible. The Ibrox Stadium tragedy took place on 2 January where 66 football fans lost their lives, crushed in a stairway during a match between Rangers and Celtic. Over 200 other fans were also injured.

Arsenal went on to become only the second English side in the 20th century to win the league and FA Cup double after Tottenham became the first to achieve this back in 1961. Ironically the League Cup winners in 1971 were Tottenham, making it a north London domestic clean-sweep, as they beat Aston Villa 2-0 at Wembley.

In Europe, Dutch side Ajax began their domination with the first of three European Cup triumphs in a row after a 2-0 victory over Greek outfit Panathinaikos at Wembley.

Back in Yorkshire, on 11 January, I was heading for a short trip south of Leeds to Rotherham for my first venture to Millmoor for a 0-0 draw against the Third Division side and to be honest we had been lucky to get out of there with a replay.

A few days later, dad parked the car on Elland Road and you couldn't see your hand in front of your face because of thick, dense fog. What's more, you couldn't see anyone else either. That wasn't because of the fog though. It was because the game had been called off. We were the only ones in the whole of Yorkshire (with the exception of about a dozen other thickos) who didn't know about the postponement. When the replay finally took place, Leeds crept through by the skin of their teeth with a 3-2 victory.

On 13 February 1971 Leeds United were lying second in the First Division. Twenty days previously, the draw for the fifth round of the FA Cup had pitted them away to Colchester United, who were lying eighth in the Fourth Division.

As my dad and I stepped off the Wallace Arnold coach outside the Layer Road ground, there was an uneasy atmosphere. It was nothing to do with trouble among supporters. There was just something not right. I know that it's easy to say now, in light of what happened that afternoon, but there was definitely apprehension among Leeds fans. It became apparent afterwards that the Leeds team and manager Don Revie felt the same.

Leeds had injuries to key players. Billy Bremner was ruled out. So too was Eddie Gray, and Jack Charlton was just back from a broken nose. Allan Clarke played on the insistence of Revie after an injection but he too clearly was a long way from being fully fit. As a precaution, Revie arranged for reserve striker Rod Belfitt to be brought down from Leeds in a taxi.

Yes, the Leeds team was depleted, but with players such as Paul Reaney, Terry Cooper, Jack Charlton, Norman Hunter, Peter Lorimer, Clarke, Mick Jones, Johnny Giles and Paul Madeley, they should have beaten Colchester standing on their heads. It was revealed later that Clarke had pleurisy.

It was sunny but cold and windy as the game got under way. We were stood in front of the rickety old TV gantry situated on the halfway line and there were around 4,000 Leeds fans in the sell-out crowd of 16,000, most of them behind the goal to our right. It was this goal that was to see most of the action.

By half-time Leeds were two goals down after a 34-year-old bloke called Ray Crawford had run the Leeds defence ragged and bagged himself a brace and then only ten minutes into the second half Leeds incredibly found themselves three down. Shock waves reverberated around the country as news filtered into every football ground and household in Great Britain of the unbelievable scoreline coming through from Colchester.

The Leeds defence was in tatters. One Leeds fan in front of us was shouting abuse at Gary Sprake, but to be fair, apart from Norman Hunter, the entire defence was abysmal. It was Hunter in fact who sparked some sort of a comeback. He surged up front and literally forced the ball over the line from a corner. Not long after that, Giles scored a second for Leeds and with about 20 minutes still to play, the mood from both sets of fans changed dramatically. But it wasn't to be Leeds's day and Colchester went into the record books on what is still regarded as one of the blackest days in the history of Leeds United.

'Leeds fans have been pouring into Blackpool all day. "LUFC" was written in the sand of this world famous beach as early as eight o'clock this morning. And some of those holidaymakers bracing the early Easter climate were tipped out of their deckchairs before police officers quickly intervened to prevent further escalation.'

This was Barry Davies introducing Saturday night's *Match of the Day* on 13 March 1971. We were watching it on the lounge TV in a hotel on Blackpool seafront. Peter Lorimer had scored for Leeds in an uneventful 1-1 draw. It was to be the last time these teams faced each other for many years.

I have always had a soft spot for Blackpool Football Club, for no other reason than it was the first team that I saw Leeds United play in 1966. We also used to spend a lot of family holidays in Blackpool, including the illuminations and Christmas. The Mayfair Hotel was our home from home many times during the late 1960s and early 70s. The owners were called Charlie and Ivy Needham and Charlie would summon guests down for meals by banging a gong that was in the reception area.

One Christmas Day we were having dinner in the Mayfair's dining room and my dad said to me, 'Blackpool are at home tomorrow if you fancy?' He knew as well as me that Leeds were at Hillsborough. 'Dad, you said that we were going to watch Leeds.' Looking back, my dad must have hated me at times.

The following morning we set off for Sheffield from Blackpool in my dad's Cortina. Motorways were very much in their infancy then and it took several hours to get there and back. But even though my dad obviously wasn't quite as pleased as me, we won 1-0 thanks to a Johnny Giles penalty. Merry Christmas.

In March 1971 it was the quarter-final against the Portuguese side Vitoria Setubal that got Leeds fans, including me, thinking that we could actually win the Inter-Cities Fairs Cup for the second time in three years. It had been over 12 weeks since Leeds had disposed of Sparta Prague but Setubal proved to be quite formidable opponents. Leeds squeezed out a narrow 2-1 victory at Elland Road in the first leg thanks to a goal from Peter Lorimer and a priceless penalty from Giles.

Twice as many Leeds fans made the journey to Portugal than had gone to Prague and police were on high alert at Yeadon airport as hundreds of boisterous but overall well behaved Leeds fans almost lifted the roof off with rousing renditions of old Leeds classics such as 'We shall not be moved' and 'We're gonna win the cup!' Mick and I chuckled as his dad got carried away by the occasion and quickly stopped singing when he noticed us looking at him.

Lorimer scored again to earn Leeds a 1-1 draw in Portugal that was enough to put them into the semi-final. Once more I bedded down in Mick's living room and as his dad opened the curtains the next morning, Mick's black labrador came running in with a Leeds United rosette pinned to his collar and his tail wagging furiously. The four remaining teams left in the competition were Leeds, Juventus, FC Koln and Liverpool.

The following afternoon at Garforth Comprehensive, about a dozen of us gathered in the toilet on the top floor of the main block. We were in between lessons and were listening to a small transistor radio for the draw for the semi-finals. For some reason the draw was delayed and we were all late for our next lesson, but quite frankly we didn't give a toss. Leeds had drawn Liverpool and we all started racing up and down the corridors going berserk.

The fact that Liverpool were a fantastic team had completely gone over our heads. The bollocking we got for missing 20 minutes of our lesson mattered not one jot. The funniest thing about this was that one lad, John Appleyard, was in the toilet with us. He wasn't a football fan at all, he'd only come in with us for a smoke and he was the only one who got detention.

For the first leg at Anfield, Leeds fans filled the entire Anfield Road end but I was sat with my dad down the side with the famous Kop just a couple of yards to our left. Leeds and Liverpool were the two best sides in Britain at this time and Liverpool had gone 30 consecutive games without defeat at home.

As predicted by many, Leeds were under pressure for much of the first half, but they gradually got into their stride as Bremner, returning from injury, regained his fitness with every passing minute. After a goalless first half and what Liverpool defender Tommy Smith later described as a 'severe ear-bashing' from manager Bill Shankly, Liverpool continued to push Leeds back but the Whites' defence was magnificent.

'They won't get past us tonight son,' dad said quietly to me. I couldn't speak to him. I was so nervous. I just thought to myself 'I hope you're right' as Gary Sprake tipped another one over the bar. Then with under half an hour to go, Leeds got a free kick. It was right in front of my dad and me as Giles put the ball down. Then, as so often happened, the uncanny telepathy between Bremner and Giles produced a goal of the highest order. It would separate the sides over both legs.

Giles floated the ball delicately into the Liverpool six-yard box where Bremner came from nowhere and was completely unchallenged as he launched himself into the air to head it past the outstretched arms of Ray Clemence, stunning the Kop into complete silence. This was Leeds's 100th goal in this competition and their 50th appearance in this competition in just five seasons.

The return leg at Elland Road was another watertight affair that ended in a goalless draw, thus presenting Leeds with a cup final appointment against Italian giants Juventus.

Before then, in May 1971, Leeds were playing Hull City in Chris Chilton's testimonial but a much more important game was taking place the same evening over 200 miles away. Leeds had one hand on the 1971 championship, but Arsenal needed a win or a 0-0 draw to pip them in their last game of the season at bitter rivals Tottenham Hotspur.

The game at Hull finished 7-6 to City but Leeds fans all over the ground were preoccupied, huddled together listening to the London derby on small crackling transistor radios. I'll never forget that huge collective moan at Boothferry Park when Ray Kennedy scored for Arsenal with what proved to be the winner and Arsenal became champions. We had travelled to Hull in a minibus from the White Swan in Kippax, but on the way home we discussed the disappointment of missing out on winning the league.

We then dusted ourselves down and prepared for the next game. As the minibus dropped us off at Crosshills in Kippax, we shouted to the driver, 'Don't be late in the morning!' We were using the same mode of transport the following day to travel west this time and to Liverpool docks where we caught a ferry to Belfast for the Esso Ulster 71 Festival which Leeds lost 3-1 to Glentoran.

%% %% %% %% %%

Our arrival at Turin airport on the morning of Tuesday 26 May 1971 was met with sun and showers. By the time we arrived at our hotel, the sun had disappeared and the showers had become heavy, really heavy. As with most continental hotels the floors were mainly marble.

This created a problem almost immediately as pools of water brought in by us new arrivals appeared everywhere. Rosetta Stone wasn't around then so we had no idea what the Italian porters were saying to us as we stood there, quite gormless if the truth is known, with small lakes forming all around us.

We were despatched to our rooms as quickly as possible and a few hours later we were staring out of the main windows in the reception as the rain continued to pour down relentlessly. There was talk about the game not going ahead, but according to a couple of Italians who were in the reception and could speak perfect English, the game would definitely go ahead. 'But,' one of them added, 'it weel be very wet.'

The game did take place but the rain continued with no sign of letting up. The whole of the terracing and stands was a huge blanket of thousands and thousands of black umbrellas. Everyone on the Juve bench was wearing hoods but I noticed that Don Revie and his trusty trainer, Les Cocker, braved the torrential elements full on, with not so much as a small hanky atop their drenched heads.

As the rain continued to pour down throughout the first half I hoped that it would wash the colour out of the Leeds shirts. The *red* Leeds shirts. To my reckoning, Leeds only wore red around ten or 11 times under Revie in 13 years. Not very often in *all* red, but sometimes with red socks or red shorts. Anyway, that night in Turin, the red shirts and red socks remained wet but unfortunately intact. Not that it mattered.

About ten minutes into the second half the referee succumbed to the conditions and the game was abandoned at 0-0. He had no choice really, the ball would not travel more than a couple of feet along the floor before being stopped in a puddle or the mud, but despite this, Juventus hit our post and we hit their bar.

Back at the hotel there was utter confusion. We had no idea if or when the game would be played. There was talk about it being played the following night, or even, someone said, they were discussing playing both legs at Elland Road. The truth was that nobody knew what was happening.

We were supposed to fly back home the following day, as were most of the other Leeds fans we spoke to. I was on school holiday but the problem was going to be rearranging flights and accommodation. I remember there being some really heated arguments between supporters and our travel organisers, 4S Sports, who initially said we had to return as scheduled but in fairness, the organisers sorted everything out and we were all still there two days later when the game eventually got under way again.

It had been sunny most of the day and although the pitch was still quite soggy it was easily playable and thankfully Leeds got a great result. This was despite falling behind to a goal from Bettega, which was cancelled out by Paul Madeley. Then the Italians went back in front after a certain midfielder called Fabio Capello hit the ball on the volley past Gary Sprake. Mick Jones was then injured and replaced by Mick Bates who within a minute of coming on had levelled the tie yet again. It finished 2-2.

Late flights had been arranged back to England and within a matter of hours we were back in Blighty. One thing we had all noticed during our stay in Turin were the pictures and photographs everywhere of John Charles. His face was in cafes, bars, and hotels and even in the airport. 'The Gentle Giant', or *Il Gigante Buono*, became an absolute legend in Italy when he was transferred to Juventus from Leeds in 1957 for a British record fee of £65,000. During his five-year spell at Juve, Charles was the Italian Footballer of the Year, he scored 108 goals and won three Serie A championships and two Coppa Italias. Despite returning to Britain in 1963 he was worshipped and adored by hundreds of thousands of Italians right up until his sad death in 2004.

The second leg, a week later at Elland Road, saw Allan Clarke fire Leeds into an early lead after just 12 minutes. But only minutes later, Anastasi equalised. It looked like it was going to be like Turin all over again. The score, however, remained 1-1, meaning that Leeds had won the cup on the away goals rule after the tie finished 3-3 on aggregate.

Leeds were the last winners of the Inter-Cities Fairs Cup before it was replaced by the UEFA Cup for the following season.

%% %% %% %% %%

In the summer of 1971, Alan Ball signed for Arsenal. He was a player who Leeds fans hated with a passion. Don Revie, however, tried to sign him on a number of occasions. The first time was when he was a youngster at Blackpool. Wealthy Everton pipped Revie and Ball moved to Merseyside.

Revie desperately wanted Ball to become part of a three-man midfield alongside Billy Bremner and Johnny Giles and constantly tried to persuade Everton to part with their man. It wasn't to be and by the time Ball had moved to Arsenal, Revie's Leeds were as near as damn it to perfection, and the manager's so-called infatuation with taking Ball to Elland Road had long since gone.

Leeds fans, though, still hated Ball, and my bedroom in 1971 had a new addition: a two-foot effigy of Ball hung from a mock hangman's scaffold dressed in his Arsenal shirt. He hung there for about six months before I gave him to our dog, Kim, and from there he lasted about six seconds.

Alan Ball, bless him, seemed to have a fetish with the FA Cup and there is a remarkable piece of trivia surrounding this.

When Ball left Blackpool in 1966 he joined Everton – who had just won the FA Cup. When he left Everton in 1971 he joined Arsenal – who had just won the FA Cup. When he left Arsenal in 1976 he joined Southampton – who had just won the FA Cup.

Throughout Ball's undoubtedly successful career, he never won the FA Cup. If he had played for Leeds instead of Arsenal in the FA Cup Final in 1972 he would have got his medal.

5

A Year Never To Forget

THE opening day of the new season saw Leeds visiting Manchester City and coming away with a 1-0 win thanks to a Peter Lorimer goal.

There is no way of disguising the fact that Maine Road was a hostile place to visit for away fans, particularly in the 1960s and 70s but I have countless other memories of Moss Side that didn't involve a brawl.

This was one of them as it was the same day as my cousin Jean's wedding and I wasn't flavour of the month with our large extended family for opting to travel by train to Maine Road to support Leeds instead of going to a church.

Jean was a big Leeds fan and I could never understand any supporter getting married during a football season. I still can't. However, I won't pretend that missing special events that clash with Leeds games doesn't have its problems, even now.

Two weeks after that match we went to Ipswich Town and I again travelled down on the train. Dad wasn't with me this time but I was sat in a carriage with two right hooligans. They were both girls from my own village of Kippax.

Linda and Audrey were dressed in matching black Crombie coats, white shirts, white trousers held up with braces and sporting the shiniest Doc Martin boots I have ever seen. A silk Leeds scarf hanging through a belt loop completed the outfit. The day before at school they had been wearing pale blue cotton school uniform summer dresses.

For the record, Leeds won the game 2-0 thanks to goals from Lorimer again and Rod Belfitt.

In the 1971/72 season I went to Hillsborough twice with Leeds and one of those games was in the league. Before it becomes a brilliant pub quiz question, the reason was simple. It was down to a referee.

Ray Tinkler was responsible for one of the most talked about injustices in British football ever. He allowed a blatant offside goal to enable West Brom to beat Leeds 2-1 in a league game at Elland Road in April 1971. Leeds lost the title by a single point that year.

The incident of course has been much debated and analysed, but because around half a dozen Leeds fans invaded the pitch, plus Don Revie himself, Leeds received an unprecedented ban from the FA. The first four home games of the following season had to be played away from Elland Road.

The final game of this punishment was at Hillsborough against Newcastle United and Leeds slaughtered the Geordies 5-1. I was sat in the cantilever stand that night, with my dad and my uncle Ernie, opposite the tunnel, and I remember thinking, 'This is weird, Leeds are playing at home, in a different ground, 30 miles away, and we're still winning.'

Soon after that we were at Highbury and it was the first time I had seen trouble there. I had gone down on the train with a few mates, and Gary Noble and I found ourselves behind the North Bank at about 2pm. Arsenal fans were all over the place and we stuck out like two sore thumbs.

Cloth badges with clubs names on them were popular at the time and Gaz had about a dozen Leeds ones sewn on to his jeans. I had about the same amount sewn on to my Levi's jacket. What on earth were we doing here – right outside the home end?

At first we just received a load of jeers from the Arsenal fans, and then it got a bit more threatening. We decided to leg it, fast! With a bunch of Arsenal fans in hot pursuit, we raced up the road adjacent to the railway line where the away buses used to park, and then suddenly we were among our own supporters and these Arsenal fans were then forced into a hasty retreat. It was crazy, and we lost the game 2-0.

Then it was into Europe and after Leeds United had won the last Inter-Cities Fairs Cup in 1971 the competition came under the jurisdiction of UEFA and was subsequently replaced by the UEFA Cup.

But Leeds's first game in the UEFA Cup in 1971 was a damp squib. On the face of it the result looked quite acceptable; a modest 2-0 victory in the first leg against Lierse SK in Belgium, seemingly setting up a somewhat easy passage through to the next round via the second leg at Elland Road.

Antwerp airport was a tiny airport, so tiny in fact that Mick Collins and I were already outside the airport while Mick's dad was still coming through passport control, about 20 yards away.

The Leeds 'mascot' had travelled with us to Belgium. He wore his distinctive Leeds top hat and tails and his handlebar moustache looked as though it had been freshly waxed for the occasion. He used to smoke small cigarette-type cigars and offered one of the security guards one from his tin, but the guard politely declined.

Chris Galvin and Peter Lorimer got United's two goals to set up that 'easy passage' at Elland Road, but what happened next could quite easily have featured in an episode of *Tales of the Unexpected*.

Even though it was still early in the season, Leeds already had ten games lined up just for September, with the possibility of even more. Sandwiched in between the two legs against Lierse was a match to decide who would keep the Inter-Cities Fairs Cup permanently. Barcelona were the first winners back in 1958 and Leeds were the last winners in 1971 so both teams met at the Nou Camp Stadium on 22 September to decide who would keep the trophy for good. On a personal note this was my first of four visits, to date, to the Nou Camp with Leeds and Revie's side lost 2-1.

Leeds, unbelievably, also lost the second leg of the tie with Lierse SK at Elland Road. It is convenient to blame the fixture pile-up because without doubt that was a major problem in those days as after that defeat at Arsenal came six more matches in the final 20 days of the month.

Having said all that, the second leg against Lierse was embarrassing for Leeds. Prior to this, Lierse had only ever played three times in Europe in their 65-year history, including an 8-0 aggregate defeat by Manchester City in the European Cup Winners' Cup in 1969.

Don Revie had already used a lot of his squad members in the games intertwined with these two Lierse games and the side he put out against Lierse at Elland Road consisted of just four first-teamers.

I consulted my scrapbook for more information on this particular match and a quote from the Lierse manager, Frank de Munck, before the game, said, 'Leeds are such a talented side. Even with so many players injured I do not expect to beat them. As a coach it is my job to be realistic as well as optimistic. We will do our very best, but I think we will be very satisfied if we can avoid a very heavy defeat. This match will be very valuable for our players. It will be a great experience, we will try to win of course, but we must be honest and say that we will be happy if we do not lose by more than, say 2-1.'

By half-time however Lierse had levelled the tie. Revie quickly tried to retrieve the situation and brought off the goalkeeper, John Shaw, who was making his debut for the club, and replaced him with the regular number one Gary Sprake, who mystifyingly had been put on the bench along with another first-teamer, Norman Hunter.

A short while later, defender Hunter was sent on to replace reserve winger Jimmy Mann. Initially Leeds, now with six of the regular first team on the field, looked to be getting back into the game but it was the visitors who struck again just after half-time and finished Leeds off with a fourth goal with ten minutes remaining, winning 4-2 on aggregate.

The next day at school, I was at a loss to explain just what had happened to anyone who asked. Revie meanwhile was adamant that he had not underestimated his Belgian opponents and that Lierse had been worthy victors. But I can clearly remember being disappointed with Revie for the first time. The only consolation for me is that I still have the pennant that was given to Leeds by Lierse before the kick-off.

The matches came thick and fast for the rest of 1971 and it didn't seem long before the New Year dawned on us.

On 5 January 1972, American President Richard Nixon announced the order for the exciting space shuttle programme. A very famous date in this calendar year also came on 30 January – for all the wrong reasons. The British Army killed 14 unarmed nationalist civil rights marchers in Derry, Northern Ireland on a day that was to become infamously known as Bloody Sunday.

For ten days in February the 1972 Winter Olympics took place in Sapporo, Japan. Seven people were killed in Aldershot by an IRA bomb. Later in the year more IRA bombings took place, including Bloody Friday on 21 July when 22 bombs exploded, killing nine people and injuring 130.

Between 26 August and 11 September the 1972 Olympics took place in Munich, West Germany. The Games were overshadowed by the massacre in Munich, in which 11 Israeli athletes, five rebels and one West German police officer were killed. They were murdered by eight members of the terrorist group Black September, who invaded the Olympic Village. In December Apollo 17 successfully landed on the Moon.

Famous names that were born in 1972 include former Spice Girl and singer Geri Halliwell, actor Ben Affleck, comedians Jimmy Carr and Frankie Boyle, singer/songwriter Liam Gallagher and actress Gwyneth Paltrow.

Footballers who were born in 1972 include former Spurs and England midfielder Darren Anderton, Brazilian genius Rivaldo, French superstar Zinedine Zidane and former Leeds United and Holland striker Jimmy Floyd Hasselbaink. Two other Whites, Alf-Inge Haaland and Paul Butler, were also born that year.

For me, a memorable trip to South Wales was one of the early great stories of what was a year never to forget.

It was about 12.30am. I was sat on a Wallace Arnold coach in The Calls, Leeds, and we should have set off for South Wales half an hour earlier. Having disposed of Liverpool in the fourth round of the FA Cup, Leeds now faced Cardiff City at Ninian Park.

However, two days of torrential rain had put the tie in serious doubt and the owner of Wallace Arnold Tours was awaiting a telephone call from Cardiff City giving the many dozens of coaches packed with Leeds fans the green light to start the long journey south.

In those days a journey of this distance would take several hours (twice as long as today), and hourly pitch inspections through the night were taking place in order to inform fans whether or not to travel. The Leeds team bus, incidentally, had been in a Cardiff hotel since 7pm the previous day. Don Revie always insisted on taking his team the night before to an away game no matter what the distance was.

I think it was around 4am when I was informed by the man next to me that the game would go ahead and the coaches began to roll out of Leeds city centre bound for Cardiff at last. Leeds beat Cardiff 2-0 that day with both goals coming from Johnny Giles and there was sporadic fighting between both sets of fans throughout the day. Just before kick-off a Leeds fan ran on to the pitch and laid a Leeds flag on the centre spot.

Several police officers chased after him as the fan raced back into the crowd and over the wall, disappearing among the hordes of Leeds fans massed down one side of the ground.

Just prior to this victory over Cardiff, Leeds had systematically destroyed manchester united 5-1 at Elland Road. There are plenty of cliches in football, one of which is that a team has been 'given a footballing lesson'. Never a truer cliche has been said when you talk about this totally dominating performance from a Leeds side that never gave their arch-enemy a single sniff throughout the whole 90 minutes.

Oh, and just after the Cardiff game on 4 March 1972 the BBC's Barry Davies mentioned in his commentary for *Match of the Day*,

'Poor Southampton don't know what day it is,' as Leeds turned on the style again to embarrass the Saints 7-0 at Elland Road.

Soon we were going to West Ham and it definitely helped having an adult with you there, even if he was in his late 70s.

I travelled down to Upton Park one Good Friday with my grandma's chap, George Dean. George was a remarkable man, and was an accomplished drummer. His biggest attribute though, was that he was a Leeds fan and I went to many games with him.

He also had a remarkable talent for blending in with the crowd. Walking back to the coaches after a 2-2 draw, there was fighting all around us. George quietly ushered me through all the flying bodies and after stepping over a few groaning Leeds and West Ham fans sprawled out on the road we reached our coach unscathed.

The season before I embarked on my role as a Leeds United 'twitcher' the club had travelled to Birmingham's St Andrew's with the slim hope of clinching the First Division title for the first time in their 44-year history. It was April 1965.

Leeds sat at the top of the division while Birmingham sat at the bottom. A certain team from Old Trafford were breathing down Leeds's neck in second place, just one point behind. Despite the positions Leeds only had the Birmingham game left while manchester united had two to play, meaning that Leeds had to win and manchester lose their two remaining fixtures for the Yorkshiremen to be crowned champions.

However, there were catastrophic goings-on at St Andrew's and with around 20 minutes left Leeds were 3-0 down. Though they did finally mount a comeback with three goals from Johnny Giles, Paul Reaney and Jack Charlton, a draw was never going to be enough and Leeds had to concede the title – on goal average. Birmingham were relegated.

The following week, Leeds faced Liverpool at Wembley in the FA Cup Final (after beating manchester united in the semi-final) but lost 2-1 after extra time. They had come so close to winning the coveted double but fate had conspired so cruelly against them. Still, it wasn't bad for a young Leeds team who had only just been promoted to the First Division the season before.

Seven years on and although Birmingham were still in the Second Division, they came up against Leeds again, this time in the 1972 FA Cup semi-final at Hillsborough.

Freddie Goodwin, a former Leeds player under Don Revie in the early 1960s, was now manager at Birmingham and had introduced some of the game's most promising young players, including Trevor

Francis. Leeds, though, were too strong on the day for Birmingham, winning 3-0 to reach the final.

Interestingly, Revie had opted to play David Harvey in goal at Hillsborough in place of Gary Sprake. Revie had remained loyal to Sprake for over ten years, but his costly mistakes had finally led to Harvey being preferred.

The following season, Goodwin paid a record fee for a goalkeeper at the time, £100,000, to take Sprake to Birmingham. There was another factor behind Revie's decision to play Harvey. Sprake had revealed allegations to the press over match-fixing by Don Revie and the Leeds captain Billy Bremner in 1972.

Once extensive court proceedings had ended, and found the allegations to be totally untrue, Sprake was banished from Leeds without a testimonial or a goodbye. To this day Sprake remains the only Leeds player from the Revie era not to be invited to any club reunions or get-togethers, and most of Revie's boys refuse to even speak to Sprake.

※ ※ ※ ※ ※

Just over two weeks after Leeds beat Birmingham City in the 1972 FA Cup semi-final I caught the number 163 bus into Leeds and then walked the two miles up to Elland Road. I was armed with a full token sheet and the right amount of away programmes to qualify for a ticket for the final against Arsenal at Wembley.

These were the requirements back then to prove that you were a supporter who had been to enough games to warrant a ticket. I can't remember how many tokens were actually needed, but my sheet was full anyway. I'd cut out every token from the covers of my home programmes and carefully glued them side by side until there were no empty squares left. I had also brought along enough away programmes; all with different coloured felt pen markings on their front covers from when they had been used for tickets for the previous cup rounds.

It was about 5pm. Only 15 hours to go until the ticket office opened and I would have a ticket marked 'Final Tie' in my hands. Actually, dad and I had already got our tickets through our West Stand season tickets, but ever since I had queued out all night for my 1968 FA Cup semi-final ticket against Everton I had become rather fond of queuing out all night at Elland Road.

It was a great atmosphere and something I had never witnessed before. The sleeping bags, blankets, pillows, cushions, deck chairs, flasks, sandwiches, bars of chocolate, packets of Castle crisps with the small blue bag of salt inside, crates of beer, bottles of wines and spirits, radios, newspapers, magazines, torches but, above all, the camaraderie.

The ticket office used to be at the rear of the West Stand. It was a small booth, hexagon-shaped, with about six serving windows. Two years previously, irate fans had tried to storm the ticket office and hundreds climbed on to the roof when tickets sold out for the 1970 final against Chelsea. Leeds had received less than 19,000 for that match, and could easily have sold well over five times that amount.

There were slightly more tickets available for the 1972 FA Cup Final but not many more. The queue stretched from the ticket office down along the back of the West Stand round the back of the Kop, up along the Lowfields Road Stand and right across the full length of the Scratching Shed on Elland Road. The very end of the queue went back through the gates of the West Stand, only a matter of about 50 yards from the front of the queue.

As people began to settle down for the night the odd guitar could be heard strumming along, often accompanied by a mouth organ. There was even a lad with a flute and he can still be seen around Elland Road today. The lovely smell of fish and chips bought from the shop across the road would linger for hours. There would always be a football being kicked around and when the Peacock pub emptied at around 11.30pm, a massive 100-a-side game on the adjoining Fullerton Park training pitches would go on well into the small hours. I zipped myself into my sleeping bag at about 1am.

The giant sleeping snake that was wrapped around Elland Road all night would begin to stir as it began to get light, and you could feel the excitement begin to buzz around the place. I always felt sorry for people who would arrive at about seven in the morning. They would look at the size of the queue and grudgingly tag on to the back in the forlorn hope of grabbing the last few tickets.

I was about 30 yards from the front of the queue and about an hour and a half later I was sat on the 163 bus home with my ticket zipped safely in my jacket. Well it was Rob Anderson's ticket. I had queued for him as he was unable to go himself but I had loved every minute.

After tea on Friday 5 May, dad and I set off down to London in his Ford Transit. In the back, dad had set it up real cosy. We had an old mattress-type bed each, wrapped in blankets with pillows, a small stove and plenty of supplies. It was raining slightly as we wormed our way through the countryside that surrounds Kippax and joined the A1 southbound.

It was after midnight when we pulled into an empty car park somewhere along Edgware Road. It was still raining as we walked to a nearby chip shop for our supper.

Back at the van, my dad connected the stove to a calor gas bottle, and we had a nice cup of tea with our fish and chips before turning off the inside back light and snuggling up in our beds and drifting off to sleep. It was sheer bliss.

The next thing I remember was the unmistakable smell of bacon wafting up through my nostrils. Dad was stood with the back doors open cooking our breakfast. I walked across the road and bought a couple of newspapers, which were all talking about the 1972 FA Cup Final between Arsenal and Leeds. After breakfast we read the papers with a second cup of tea.

Walking up Wembley Way was just getting better and better for me. This was my third time already and I had only just left school a couple of weeks ago. I called into a toilet, and as I went in, unknown to me at the time, four Arsenal fans walked in after me. I had wondered why dad had come in and was now stood near the sinks watching me pee. There was no evidence that these Arsenal fans were up to no good but my dad was there, just in case.

I had my white butcher's coat on with Leeds patches sewn on and a canvas bush hat with plastic figures stuck to it that I had painted in the brilliant all-white of Leeds. Once inside Wembley Stadium the atmosphere was electric, as it always was, and Leeds fans outsang Arsenal fans, as they always did. Tommy Steele, dressed in an all-white suit, led the traditional community singing. This was the centenary FA Cup Final and the Queen and Prince Philip were present. It was special.

History tells us that Leeds won the FA Cup that day for the first, and to date, only time in the club's history thanks to the only goal of the game from Allan Clarke. What history doesn't tell us is that it was one of the most memorable and joyous occasions that one could possibly spend with his trusty old dad.

※ ※ ※ ※ ※

Molineux was the setting for one of the most disappointing nights of my life, just 48 hours after the FA Cup Final at Wembley. Leeds United had beaten Arsenal to lift the FA Cup and were now just one point away from winning the league and achieving the coveted double, but, alas, the referee and the full cast of the Wolverhampton Wanderers players clearly hadn't read the script.

People still talk today about alleged bribery attempts by Leeds to certain Wolves players to 'throw' the game. This subject has been discussed, chewed over and dissected over the years in countless pubs and publications, but over 40 years on, no one has ever produced any evidence to support this or any other accusations of bribery levelled at Leeds United.

Indeed, Billy Bremner sued the *Sunday People* newspaper over these Wolves allegations and received a sum of £100,000 in damages, a record amount at the time. Even centre-forward Derek Dougan, who played for Wolves that night, appeared in court to speak in defence of Bremner and against other bribery allegations.

Leeds had been forced to play this game on the Monday night after the cup final. Celebrations after Wembley had to be put on hold as Leeds headed straight to the Mount Hotel in Wolverhampton to prepare for what was without doubt the biggest match in the club's history so far.

The Football League had arranged a league fixture against Chelsea four days before the FA Cup Final and the Wolves trip two days after the final. It was left to Leeds to ask the clubs if they would rearrange the dates. Chelsea refused, saying they were going on a tour of the Caribbean a week after the final. Wolves, who were in the middle of a two-legged UEFA Cup Final with Spurs, agreed to play Leeds on the Tuesday, but the Football League secretary Alan Hardaker, who openly admitted to 'loathing' Don Revie, said that if Leeds played Wolves on the Tuesday they would have to do so without their five current England internationals because of an upcoming England v West Germany European Championship game.

The following statement written shortly before the FA Cup Final by *Guardian* reporter Eric Todd, although a tad long-winded, sums the situation up perfectly:

'For the second time in two weeks Fates, with whom may well be associated to the Football League, are making it very hard for Leeds United to win anything. Only in Yorkshire, perhaps, would this be classified as victimisation. Outside it, even those people who hate Leeds as they used to hate Arsenal, Tottenham Hotspur and manchester united, envy is too modest a word, must feel that little effort has been made either to sympathise with Leeds or to try to accommodate them on their final run in for the Double.

'Sympathy can find little room in football these days but sooner or later the League and the Football Association must realise that the football season is far too long and far too congested with a multitude of competitions. There is no space to manoeuvre and none to provide international demands.

'It is as monstrous as it is unfair that Leeds or any club placed similarly should have to play a game a few days before the FA Challenge Cup Final and another one two days after it.

'If Leeds fail to win either the Cup or the League title they need not blame loss of form. They must blame the system. And if Leeds cannot field a full strength side against Arsenal at Wembley, the crowd and the FA can blame the Football League and Chelsea, who have decided that their jaunt to the West Indies, or wherever it is, is more important than trying to help Leeds prepare for their crucial matches. Fair enough. Why should they anyway?

'Not that I am concerned over much with Chelsea or with the European Championship. I am more concerned only that any side, Leeds, Chelsea, Hartlepool or Watford, who have a chance of winning one or both of major competitions this country has to offer is given a reasonable chance of winning them. In this instance Leeds have not been given that chance.

'But Leeds in recent years have been nobody's friends. The authorities closed Elland Road last year after a few yobbos had run onto the pitch regardless of the fact that this sort of thing happens every week on most grounds. Two years ago in between the first of their three semi-finals against Manchester United and the final, Leeds had to play ten games in three weeks and were beaten by Chelsea in a final replay and they finished runners up in the League.

'I believe that Leeds have been treated scandalously and are having to pay the penalty for lack of foresight by the League and the FA.'

So dad and I arrived at Molineux on that dark windy evening and joined the masses of Leeds fans crammed into the South Bank. Half the crowd of 50,000 had arrived from Leeds and the gates were closed almost an hour before kick-off. Some barriers gave way under the pressure and 70 people were injured, and nine were taken to hospital. Thankfully the most serious case was a broken leg.

We were perched high in the corner and we could see outside the ground as dozens of Leeds coaches arrived too late to get in. The Leeds team was decimated from the start. Mick Jones had dislocated his shoulder at Wembley so therefore was unable to play. Allan Clarke and Johnny Giles both played after receiving painkilling injections, and both Clarke and Eddie Gray played with heavy strapping wrapped around their bodies. Terry Cooper was missing with a broken leg and little Billy Bremner had to play up front in the absence of Jones.

Wolves played well above their expectations and early in the second half found themselves two goals to the good. Bremner led the fightback and scored in front of the South Bank to make it 2-1 and from then on Leeds bombarded the Wolves goal in search of the solitary point that would give them the double.

Wolves' goalkeeper Phil Parkes caught, punched and tipped the ball away all night long. Peter Lorimer said, 'The only players who handled the ball better than Parkes were the Wolves defenders, Bernard Shaw and Frank Munro.

Leeds had three stonewall penalty claims turned down by the Welsh referee Alan Gow. Shaw twice handled the ball on the line and Munro held the ball in his hand for what seemed liked five seconds. Norman Hunter said, 'When Munro caught the ball everything went quiet. He could have taken the lace out during the time he held the ball.'

When the final whistle blew at 2-1, the brave Leeds players fell to their knees in disappointment and exhaustion. The coveted double had slipped from their grasp for the third time since their arrival in the First Division only seven years before. The double had only been achieved four times between 1889 and 1971.

My first trip to Molineux had been four years earlier and although it was a very dull affair, Leeds got a goalless draw. That was all we needed on this fateful Monday night but it just wasn't to be.

6

More European Adventures

WHEN I first ventured into Turkey as a 16-year-old, Leeds fans Kevin Speight and Christopher Loftus were 12 and nine years old respectively. Twenty-eight years later they would both be brutally murdered on the streets of the country's capital, Istanbul.

I can honestly say that when I arrived in Ankara for Leeds's first game in the now-defunct European Cup Winners' Cup in 1973, and Ankara's debut in Europe, I was nervous. By now I had been to quite a few games in Europe but the minute Mick Collins, his dad and I set foot in Ankara airport I didn't like the atmosphere. Armed police greeted a couple of hundred Leeds fans as we were shunted on to waiting buses and almost immediately escorted to the ground.

The pitch was surrounded by high fences. I had seen pitches surrounded by fences before on the continent, especially in Italy, but this all seemed much more threatening and I have to say, evil. I also have to report that there was no trouble as such, either on or off the field, but there was a constant uneasy atmosphere throughout.

I have always looked on Leeds's games that season in the Cup Winners' Cup as a tale of centre-halves. Big Jack Charlton was coming to the end of his playing career and had been lined up to take over as manager of Middlesbrough. But for the meantime he was still a Leeds player. However, Don Revie was looking at options to eventually replace Charlton and occupying the number five jersey that evening in Ankara was a new recruit from Huddersfield Town, Roy Ellam.

We had been talking to Ellam and Leeds's Chris Galvin in the airport beforehand, and he had a sound game in the defence, a Joe

Jordan goal earning Leeds a 1-1 draw. Unfortunately Ellam didn't look to be the right replacement for big Jack.

A slender 1-0 win in the second leg, thanks to a Mick Jones effort, was enough to ease Leeds into the second round and in doing so, lined up another trip behind the Iron Curtain.

Carl Zeiss Jena sounds more like the name of a British-born boy with German parents than an East German football club, but the latter is precisely what Carl Zeiss Jena is. We had to go through the usual tiresome paperwork to enter East Germany but, unusually, this time we were offered snacks in the airport on our arrival, free to Leeds fans. Mick's dad sneaked Mick and I a very small sample of German beer in paper cups that we drank secretly, but proudly.

I remember more about our arrival at the airport than the game itself, if I'm honest, but Leeds managed a 0-0 draw which Revie seemed quite pleased with. And big Jack was back at centre-half, or 'Zak Charlton' as the German announcer proclaimed.

I remember the home leg much more because of Leeds's second and decisive goal. Trevor Cherry had scored the cutest of goals to put Leeds ahead at the Kop end, stroking a ball through a crowd of German defenders to deceive the keeper.

The second goal was most memorable. Peter Lorimer prepared to take a free kick which was easily 30 yards out, possibly more. After a massive run-up he delivered a fearsome rocket of a shot which literally knocked the black-clad keeper over as he attempted to punch the ball away and Mick Jones stooped to head in the rebound as the keeper lay helplessly on his back.

Back at home there was another memorable incident in a game against West Ham, which Leeds won 1-0 at Elland Road.

When I started going with my mates on the coach to away matches I realised how dangerous it could be, West Ham being a particularly notable venue. The coaches used to park at the end of a road beyond a small roundabout with a small statue in the centre of it.

If you were walking down this road and you weren't wearing claret and blue then you were a Leeds fan, and you would more than likely receive a slap. I got many slaps over the years, but up to now, none too serious. In fact the worst slap I have received after a West Ham game was in Leeds!

I had been on my own, and I got off the coach at the Calls, and made my way to the train station to catch a taxi back to Kippax. I was just walking under the dark arches near to the station when a few lads came towards me. I had my old silk Leeds scarf on and I noticed that two of them had white trousers on, and one wore a black bowler hat. It was when the film *Clockwork Orange* was showing at some cinemas and you would regularly see lads wearing that type of fashion to football games, so I didn't think too much of it when they came towards me.

Then one of them said something that I didn't hear, and the next thing I was on the floor getting a kicking. It was over in seconds and as they walked away, one of them even shouted back, 'Sorry mate.' I'll never forget that.

As we moved into 1973, on 4 January the longest-running TV comedy series in the world, *Last of the Summer Wine*, aired its pilot programme. Later that month George Foreman defeated Joe Frazier to become boxing's heavyweight champion of the world.

In March London Bridge was officially opened by HRH Queen Elizabeth II. On 4 April the World Trade Center in New York was officially opened. On 2 September J.R.R. Tolkien, author of *The Lord of the Rings*, passed away in Bournemouth at the age of 81. At the back end of 1973, on 14 November to be precise, Princess Anne married Captain Mark Phillips in Westminster Abbey.

In the football world prolific marksman Kevin Phillips entered this world, as did Leeds United players such as Martin Hiden (11 March), Geoff Horsfield (1 November) and Alan Thompson (22 December).

My tale of 1973 begins with an emphatic FA Cup victory but sadly for all Leeds followers this particular year was remembered for all the wrong reasons in the great competition.

I actually stood in the Holte End, which is the Aston Villa home end, in January 1973 along with thousands upon thousands of fellow Leeds fans. Villa weren't playing Leeds though. It was the second replay of a third round FA Cup tie against Norwich City. Having drawn 1-1 at both Carrow Road and Elland Road, the clubs lined up against each other at Villa Park. On this occasion Leeds destroyed the Canaries with a 5-0 win.

Personally, I've always preferred long away trips. The day lasts longer and to be fair, Plymouth fans are a hardy bunch as well. They came to Elland Road in the next round and although they were beaten 2-1, they remained in good spirits and tossed a life-sized blow-up doll above their heads for the entire 90 minutes.

We were progressing in our defence of the FA Cup but we were also into the quarter-finals of the European Cup Winners' Cup and against Romanians Rapid Bucharest the number five jersey had yet another occupier.

This time it was a young Scot, Gordon McQueen, whom Don Revie had paid St Mirren £30,000 for as he sought what he hoped would be the ultimate replacement for Jack Charlton. Leeds travelled to Bucharest with a comfortable five-goal cushion from the first leg at Elland Road and they finished the job with a creditable 3-1 away victory.

The trip to Romania was marred somewhat by Mr Collins falling ill. I don't remember too much about what the problem was but I do remember him being in a bit of pain on the flight and again during the match. A man and his wife, who were on our trip, asked him if he needed help but he said he was OK.

One of the air stewardesses had a bit of a chat with him. I think she was American or Canadian, but she gave him some tablets and a glass of water. Typical of Mr Collins, he just said, 'There's no way I'm missing the semi-final!' But I watched Mick as he looked at his dad and he was clearly worried.

Over the years I used to love going to Yugoslavia, both with Leeds United and on holiday. In April 1973 I travelled there to watch Leeds contest the semi-final with Hajduk Split. They were a brilliant side too, and Leeds had to fight hard to get a goalless draw.

It had only been a couple of weeks since Mick's dad had fallen ill, and he was too ill to travel to Yugoslavia, so I went with a bloke from Seacroft in Leeds who everybody called 'Alki Mick'. I had seen him when we travelled on Wallace Arnold coaches from the Calls in Leeds, and with Mick Collins staying at home with his mam and dad, I latched on to Alki Mick. He was called that because he quite obviously liked a beer or two. He was the first person I ever saw go to the bar and get two pints – both for himself.

He used to wear the same brown corduroy jacket which always looked like it was in need of a good wash, although there was a danger that a good wash could finish it off altogether. His hair was long and straight and his unwashed ears protruded through the greasy strands. He had a scruffy little beard, but he truly was an engaging character, and I travelled many miles with Mick over the years.

Rapid Bucharest had been very physical in the quarter-final and Split were no different. Leeds took a delicate 1-0 advantage to Yugoslavia having been pushed, kicked and hacked almost every time they were on the ball at Elland Road.

Allan Clarke was attacked and abused so much in the away leg that it forced him to react and retaliate against a particularly over-exuberant challenge, so much so that he was sent off. This later prompted Revie to ask UEFA why Clarke had received a two-match ban as opposed to the usual one game, causing him to miss the final against AC Milan with a 0-0 draw in Split having been enough to take Revie's team through. Leeds never received an acknowledgement in any shape or form from UEFA.

%% %% %% %% %%

I've never really liked Sunderland. I don't particularly know why. The 1973 FA Cup Final certainly didn't help. There has never in the history of the FA Cup been a more one-sided game where the best team lost than that game at Wembley in May 1973. Even Sunderland manager Bob Stokoe, a sworn enemy of Don Revie, had to admit, 'I have no idea how the hell we beat Leeds today, but I'm glad we did.'

That aside I still don't like those Wearsiders. We have a decent enough record against them over the years, both at home and away, but there is always something that niggles me about them. Maybe that final in 1973 scarred me more than I think, I really don't know.

Over the years I became friends with a Sunderland fan, Gary Sunderland Lamb (he changed his name by deed poll). He has seen most Sunderland games over the past four decades but he was unable to get a ticket for the 1973 final, which has always made our conversations a lot easier.

It is reported that when the Sunderland team returned home with the cup that year they were greeted by a crowd of around half a million. Yet on the club's final home game of the season, a few days later against QPR, a crowd of only 18,000 turned out. Before that encounter two Sunderland fans were allowed to walk round the pitch carrying a white coffin bearing the words, 'LEEDS DIED – 1973'.

The cup final was a dark day in the history of Leeds United Football Club. Leeds had reached their second successive final and they were overwhelming favourites to overcome Second Division Sunderland.

After being taken ill during the trip to Bucharest in March, Mick Collins's dad never regained his former good health and eventually stopped going to matches altogether. Mick's mam died suddenly in April and Mick had to reluctantly walk away from Leeds United and spend most of his time looking after his dad. I felt so sorry for them both. We had spent some great times travelling together, and I will always be grateful to Mr Collins for letting me tag along with him and Mick.

During the week before the Wembley final with Sunderland I went for tea at Mick's and was told that him and his dad were moving to Scarborough. Less than a week after the final they had moved to the coast and apart from a few letters over the following months, we lost touch and I never saw them again.

I travelled down to Wembley on the Friday night on a Wallace Arnold coach with a bunch of friends, many of them new friends. Amazingly, one of them was called Mick Collins, but the two Micks were not alike in any way. The 'new' Mick was twice as old as me but we got along fine, although our friendship didn't last half as long as with me, Mick and Mr Collins.

He wasn't too bright either it has to be said, but I myself was a bit slow on the uptake on one particular occasion. Mick used to live in a terraced house in the Holbeck area of Leeds, close to Elland Road itself. At first I thought it was a back-to-back terraced house but I later discovered that it was in fact a through terrace. Colenso Mount was the name of his street.

One day I went to see him and noticed a street near him called Bk Colenso Mount. It took me some weeks to discover that Bk Colenso Mount was in fact 'Back of Colenso Mount' and I had been walking past his back door and right round to his front door, thinking they were two separate streets. So maybe its me who's not so bright.

When we arrived in London we strolled along the banks of the River Thames. There seemed to be quite a few more Sunderland fans about than Leeds, but we always knew that there would be no neutrals watching the game today, either in the flesh or on television. Everyone in the world it seemed, except Leeds fans of course, wanted the minnows from Wearside to win the FA Cup. Sadly, they got their wish.

The game itself is still too painful for me to even contemplate thinking about, and although people still talk about how it was so one-sided, with Sunderland scoring from their only chance of the game, that is scant consolation to me.

I received a VHS copy of the match that, for obvious reasons, I have never even opened. I'm not entirely sure how I came to have a copy in the first place but I seem to recall it came from my grandma. Bless her cotton bed socks.

The only thing that kept my spirits alive on that long coach ride home was the fact that in just 11 days I would be back on a plane and heading for the sunny climes of Salonika in northern Greece for Leeds's European Cup Winners' Cup Final against AC Milan. I just wished that Mick and his dad would be going.

%. %. %. %. %.

When we gathered in the airport to fly to Greece for the European Cup Winners' Cup Final I was sat in the bar with the 'new' Mick Collins, and he told me that the taxi was late arriving to bring him to the airport. I couldn't resist asking him if the driver had gone to the right door. He looked at me puzzled. 'You know,' I said, 'did he go to the front door or the back door?' I could see the tumbleweed rolling across inside his head. 'Colenso Mount or Bk Colenso Mount?' I persisted, but there was no change whatsoever in his expression. 'Another pint?' I said and got up to go to the bar, thinking that it may be a long three days ahead.

From the very first time I travelled on an aeroplane I have loved flying and our flight to Greece was right up there with the best. Even these days, I'm still like a big kid when it comes to flying. I love it when the engine roars and the thrust and acceleration send the plane down the runway and up into the clouds.

I was looking through some old postcards recently that I sent home to my ma from games in the 1960s and 70s and on some of them I wrote, 'Great flight here, can't wait to take off again.'

Talking of anoraks, I wish I'd brought mine when we landed at Salonika. We were in the middle of a fierce thunderstorm as we left the airport and headed for our hotel. Three hours later, dramatic forks of lightning punctuated the sky as we took our seats in the totally uncovered Kaftatzoglio Stadium but, as drenched as we were, once the rain stopped about ten minutes before the game, it was so warm that we were snuff dry by half-time.

I had heard beforehand about how much the Greeks admired Leeds but I never imagined the scale of adulation that they held for Don Revie's side. The Greeks in the crowd, to a man, were supporting Leeds and they had been brushing up on their songs too. 'Supa Leeds!' they chanted as they clapped excitedly.

A few thousand Leeds fans were also in attendance, some of whom had donated the odd Leeds scarf or two to our grateful hosts. There were about 200 Italian supporters present, at most. There was a carnival atmosphere around the ground but nothing could prepare the Leeds team for what lay ahead.

Rumours had been circulated among sections of the media that money had changed hands and that AC Milan would be certain winners. Johnny Giles, who was injured and could not play that night, was on the BBC team as a pundit and he has said many times since that the media heard that the referee, Christos Michas, a Greek national, had been 'got at' by the Italian club and that a win for Milan was a formality. It's a fact that the referee even flew into Salonika on the plane carrying the Milan team. The Leeds players who were at the airport at the time have testified to this.

Only four minutes into the game, Leeds were a goal down after Paul Madeley was bizarrely penalised for a foul after barely, if any, contact with another player. The free kick, conveniently from the edge of Leeds's penalty area, was instantly despatched via a deflection and keeper David Harvey's left-hand post.

The score remained at 1-0. This was despite several very strong penalty claims for Leeds including blatant handballs and vicious tackles in the area, all of which Michas nonchalantly waved away. Television footage can still be seen today of this farce of a match and some of the diabolical, some would say despicable decisions have to be seen to be believed.

When the Italians received the trophy they began a lap of honour but a barrage of missiles from the Greek supporters forced the Italians to quickly retreat down the tunnel. So it was Leeds who went on the lap of honour and the crowd went wild and greeted the team with further chants of 'Supa Leeds! Supa Leeds!'

Within days of the final, Christos Michas had been banned from refereeing for life amid sustained bribery allegations and was subsequently given a prison sentence for an accumulation of match-fixing scandals.

On a lighter note, later that evening I was at a banquet that had been provided for Leeds fans, and the main dish that evening was horse burger...and chips.

After Michas had been banned for life, Leeds sought a replay, but UEFA denied their request. MEP Richard Corbett, a lifelong Liverpool fan, started a campaign in 2009 to get the result overturned and the trophy awarded to Leeds, but after delivering thousands of signed petitions to UEFA he was told that although they 'greatly sympathised, too much time had elapsed for there to be an alteration to the winner'.

Corbett said afterwards, 'It is quite obvious that Michas cheated Leeds out of the Cup Winners' Cup and UEFA had a great opportunity to set the record straight, but sadly they failed.'

Thirty-one years after that fateful night in Salonika, Leeds were invited to open the newly refurbished Kaftatzoglio Stadium. We stayed over a few nights and many of the old bars still had framed pictures and newspapers from that final with AC Milan hanging on the walls. Many of the Greeks who were there that night still remembered it clearly. 'He [Michas] brought shame on our country,' one local told us. 'He is a cheat. Shame!' he kept saying over and over.

The ground was unrecognisable from that evening back in May 1973, but the overwhelming enthusiasm from the Greeks towards Leeds hasn't faded one bit. Worldwide there are over 300 Leeds supporters' clubs but there is one, the Hellenic Leeds United Supporters' Club in Greece, that has a special link to the club which was forged that night over 30 years ago and is still as strong as ever today.

7

Battles In Scotland

EVEN these days, White Hart Lane can be a dangerous place for travelling fans. Police offer little if any protection whatsoever. It wasn't a particularly good hunting ground for the team either during the 1960s.

We did however earn a priceless point with a goalless draw there in November 1968. This was the season Leeds won their first league championship.

And fortune favoured us slightly better as we turned into the 1970s and the most memorable game came on 1 September 1973. Leeds demonstrated their awesome prowess as two goals from Billy Bremner and one by Allan Clarke demolished Spurs.

After Bremner's second goal my mate Stan got a smack to the back of his head by an irate Tottenham fan, but Stan just laughed at him.

Leeds found themselves in the UEFA Cup for 1973/74 having finished third in the First Division the previous season and first up was a tie against Norwegian side Stromsgodset where, once again, the Whites had unbelievable support from the Scandinavians.

Stromsgodset are situated in Drammen, a little over 20 miles from Oslo. Drammen is a brilliant, atmospheric town on a river surrounded by steep, wooded hills and hundreds of beautiful wooden houses for as far as the eye can see. In the evening it really is a sight to behold.

In one of these wooden houses at the time lived a young man called Geir Jensen. Before the game in September 1973, we were stood having a beer in a small bar situated just outside the ground when Geir came up to us wearing a Leeds shirt and introduced himself. His knowledge of Leeds was unbelievable. When the game kicked off he was giving us our own running commentary and then, when Allan Clarke scored, he almost pulled John Walker's head off, he grabbed him so tight.

The game finished 1-1 and the Stromsgodset players were visibly happy with their evening's work. Unfortunately for them however, Leeds were in a rampant mood for the second leg at Elland Road and swept the Scandinavians aside by a whopping 6-1 margin. I had acquired a Norwegian friend for life.

Fast forward a few decades and in January 2013 I was in the Leeds end at a freezing cold St Andrew's for an FA Cup replay with Birmingham City. The game was delicately poised at 1-1 when Leeds were awarded a penalty with a little under 15 minutes left. El-Hadji Diouf stepped up to take it in front of the Leeds fans and after bluffing the keeper to dive to his right, simply chipped the ball down the middle for a very cheeky penalty conversion, ensuring a 2-1 victory.

Later on the coach home to Leeds I got to thinking about another cheeky penalty I had seen almost 40 years earlier. It was at Easter Road for the second leg of the second round of the UEFA Cup against Hibernian.

After a goalless draw at Elland Road, the score remained exactly the same after 90 minutes and extra time in Edinburgh so the tie went to penalties.

Hibs legend Pat Stanton took the first penalty, and missed. It would be his last spot-kick before retiring four years later and becoming assistant manager to somebody called Alex Ferguson at Aberdeen. Eight penalties later the score stood at 4-4 with one more to go.

I had been to Easter Road before for the game in the Fairs Cup in 1968 when a Jack Charlton goal earned Leeds a 1-1 draw and progress to the next round following a solitary Eddie Gray goal in the first leg at Elland Road. In fact I had been to Scotland many times before this game. I had seen the so-called angry mobs at Rangers and Celtic and the over-enthusiastic Dundee fans. But nothing, including St James' Park, Maine Road or even Goodison Park, could compare with the fierce hostility that Leeds fans witnessed that night at Easter Road.

When Billy Bremner stepped up to take Leeds's fifth and final penalty, the crowd were screaming at him and the venom coming from over 30,000 mad Scotsmen had to be seen to be believed. Not that it bothered Bremner one jot. In fact he revelled in it, strolling around the penalty area with the ball under his arm and without a care in the world. I remember thinking, as I saw huge veins popping out of thousands of boiling red hot Scottish foreheads, 'Billy, please just take the fucking kick and let's get out of here alive!'

Bremner placed the ball calmly on the penalty spot and amidst the loudest hissing and booing I think I have ever heard, he took a small step back. Then he stood for a few seconds with his hands on his hips and then he walked slowly to the ball, bent down and picked it up. He then scrunched his white shirt sleeve in his right hand and slowly wiped the ball and put it back on the spot. By now, half the crowd had almost turned inside out. They were so incensed. 'Please Billy, take the kick. We're all gonna die here,' I pleaded with him in my mind.

The referee went up to him and had a word in his ear. Bremner then nonchalantly strolled just a couple of feet up to the ball, went to kick it to his left but then with the goalkeeper flying across to his right, he changed direction and cruelly rolled the ball agonisingly for Hibs into the right-hand corner of the goal. Cue instant violence.

The main mob of Hibs fans used to gather on the large uncovered side stand in those days, right opposite to where we were stood that night. They were incensed, outraged and very hostile. As the triumphant Leeds team disappeared down the tunnel the Hibs fans turned their anger on the Leeds fans. We weren't stood together. We were dotted about all over the place and the process of seeking us out began in earnest.

There were several English squaddies in the crowd and they had all been supporting Leeds on the night even though clearly not all the accents hailed from Yorkshire. I got the distinct impression that the squaddies were enjoying this intimidating atmosphere and relished the several sporadic clashes that followed. It was quite surreal to see a smart, close-cropped squaddie fighting side by side with a large, unshaven, scruffy Leeds fan with a tatty Leeds scarf wrapped around his wrist in mortal combat with a bunch of angry Scotsmen. We didn't have time to stop and think that another Scot, Billy Bremner, who had long since departed, was the cause of this escalating riot.

Outside was even worse and chaos ensued as large groups of Hibs supporters ran past us in the opposite directions shouting, 'Get the English bastards!' They were heading for the Leeds fans who were on their way to the train station. But as we arrived at our coaches we were far from safe. Clashes between fans occurred all around and the police seemed powerless as they began signalling for the Leeds coaches to begin their exit from the coach park as quickly as possible. Mounted officers meanwhile looked to be winning the battle in keeping back the hordes of Scotsmen that had now gathered around the coach park.

A small way down the road we seemed out of danger until a large brick was hurled at our coach and came crashing through the window, shattering glass everywhere. Then the driver, insanely, leapt off the bus and began chasing a small group responsible for the ambush down a side street, much against our advice. He returned moments later with his clothes all torn, a bloody nose and minus his watch.

Our long trip back to Leeds was interesting. As our driver struggled with his blocked and swelled nose and periodically asked us what the time was, we wrapped up and consumed a few units of alcohol to combat the ventilation recently installed by our friends back in Edinburgh, and looked forward to the next round of the UEFA Cup.

In the First Division, at the very end of December 1973 Leeds travelled to Birmingham in the middle of what would become a 29-game unbeaten record. But they so very nearly came unravelled as Birmingham led until the very last minute when Joe Jordan converted a low cross from Peter Lorimer to stab home the equaliser past Gary Sprake, who was on his knees.

The game was watched by Birmingham's record attendance of 50,451.

Leeds fans were spread all over St Andrew's that cold afternoon. The majority were behind the goal where we scored, but I was stood with a bunch of maybe a dozen or so towards the corner of a large side stand and we were completely surrounded by City fans. Elated at conserving our ongoing record we instantly went berserk celebrating our goal, sparking a right old fisticuff.

I put in my small contribution but I received a right whack to the back of the head for my trouble. To this day I don't know what made contact with my nut, but it most certainly was an extension to the human body. I had a massive gash to my head, which only started to hurt when our coach arrived back in Leeds a few hours later. It wasn't only Leeds that was throbbing beneath the Christmas lights that night but it had been worth it. Six weeks later Leeds achieved the record of 29 games unbeaten.

As we moved forward into 1974, the year got off to an uplifting start with New Year's Day being celebrated by way of a public holiday for the first time. In February Bob Latchford became the most expensive footballer in Britain following his £350,000 move from Birmingham City to Everton. March saw a change of government with Labour's Harold Wilson replacing the Conservatives' Edward Heath as Prime Minister.

In June the unmistakable voice of Tom Baker was introduced to our TV screens, replacing Jon Pertwee as the new Dr Who. The first McDonald's restaurant in Britain was opened in Woolwich, Ceefax began on the BBC and the IRA continued their bombing campaign with many attacks including Guildford, Birmingham, the Tower of London and the home of former PM Heath. Heath was out at the time and returned just ten minutes after the bomb went off.

Singer Robbie Williams was born in 1974, as were radio DJ and Leeds fan Chris Moyles, former tennis player Tim Henman and England cricket captain Michael Vaughan. The football world was as hectic as ever. Don Revie parted with his beloved Leeds United to become the manager of England, Brian Clough replaced him at Elland Road for an infamous 44 days, Alf Ramsey had been sacked by England, and Bill Shankly left Liverpool after 15 glorious years to be replaced by Bob Paisley.

Leeds won the league, Liverpool won the FA Cup and manchester united were relegated with their former striker Denis Law scoring the only goal of the game for Manchester City at Old Trafford to help send the reds down.

The 1973/74 season was probably my most memorable of all. I have always loved that season. Partly because we won the league of course, but ever so slightly less importantly, manchester united were relegated. In my world, it doesn't get any better than that.

That campaign's FA Cup, however, was a different story. It started well enough. We beat Wolves in the third round and after the disappointment of the previous season's Wembley final against Sunderland, Leeds seemed determined to make amends.

A trip down to Peterborough was next on the agenda, which was a first for me and many of the Leeds fans with me. I went down on the train with my dad and a few of the lads from our estate.

London Road wasn't the best ground I've ever been to but I can still visualise Terry Cooper playing in his white boots. It was all the rage with certain footballers at the time. Alan Ball springs to mind. A couple of over-excited Leeds fans fell through the wooden roof of a hot dog stall as a few others perched precariously in the rafters above the Leeds masses below them.

When Peter Lorimer put Leeds in front it caused mayhem, and two of those fans in the rafters lost their footing and fell, disappearing into the huge swaying body of Whites followers beneath them. By the time Joe Jordan got two more goals and Terry Yorath added a fourth it was all over for Peterborough and the scoreline ultimately read 4-1.

Leeds later took time out from their quest for the league title in 1974 to travel down to Second Division Bristol City in the fifth round of the FA Cup. Billy Bremner scored in a 1-1 draw to bring the tie to Elland Road for the replay. Because of the miners' strike and the power cuts as well as the three-day week, the replay was a midweek afternoon game. However, even that did not prevent over 47,000 cramming into Elland Road. Unfortunately someone by the name of Keith Fear had not read the script and scored the only goal of the game to notch up one of the major shocks of that era's FA Cup as City went through.

Later on in February, as we closed in on our second championship, the score was slightly different to when we thrashed Stoke City 5-1 in 1969. Leeds travelled to the Victoria Ground on 23 February 1974 with 29 games behind them and not one single defeat.

It appeared to be business as usual as Leeds stormed into a 2-0 lead with goals from Billy Bremner and Allan Clarke. Then Revie's side hit the self-destruct button, which was an absolute rarity in those days, and unbelievably Stoke won 3-2.

That defeat threatened to derail the title hopes and three successive defeats from mid-to-late March saw Leeds begin to wobble. Revie however had promised his team back in August that they would win the league and he wasn't going to allow them to throw in the towel.

Leeds did not lose again after that defeat at Stoke and we travelled to Loftus Road for the final game of the season already assured of the league championship.

Three days before we travelled down to London, Arsenal had beaten Liverpool at Anfield which meant that Leeds couldn't be caught at the top of the table. That April afternoon at Loftus Road, Leeds entered the pitch through a sporting 'clap of honour' by the QPR players, and an estimated 20,000 visiting fans including me and dad and a few mates. We were crammed into the open end and were sprawled all along the side to our right.

With nothing to really play for, it was a carnival atmosphere but 'Super Leeds', as they were known, turned on the style with some brilliant exhibitionist play.

Although the result was academic, it was to be Don Revie's last game at Leeds before leaving Elland Road to take up his position as the new manager of England. It was inevitable that his players wanted to send him away with a final victory.

This 1-0 win came courtesy of a solo effort from Allan Clarke to spark jubilant scenes at the full-time whistle. The teams had to retreat down the tunnel as a group of 'home' fans went on to the pitch and started to come towards the Leeds supporters. We found out afterwards that a group of Chelsea followers had infiltrated the understaffed QPR section in a bid to goad the visitors from Yorkshire.

It was then that I witnessed a beautiful sight. Leeds fans, almost as one, swarmed on to the pitch and engulfed the whole field. I don't know if the 'home' fans were attacked or just disappeared under a huge sea of blue, white and yellow. Attention then focused on the tunnel as Leeds fans chanted, 'We want Revie! We want Revie!' The Don and his players then arrived behind the police cordon that had been thrown around the entrance to the tunnel and waved to their fans. Grown men were crying all around me and it all got pretty emotional as the players and Don disappeared down the tunnel. I shed a quiet tear or two myself as my body pounded with pride.

Revie had been destined to leave Leeds to join Everton the season before but, after controversially losing the European Cup Winners' Cup Final to AC Milan in Greece, he vowed to continue and win the league once again with Leeds United, 'Without losing a single game.' Revie's promise to win the league had been fulfilled, and we also came so close to being undefeated. It had been late February before Leeds were finally beaten and they won the title by five points from Liverpool.

Leeds United and Loftus Road appeared together in a popular television programme just a year after. In an episode of *Porridge* screened in November 1975, Fletch (Ronnie Barker) and Blanco (David Jason) plotted against their despicable fellow inmate Norris (Ronald Lacey) who was called 'scum' by other inmates, culminating in Norris, after his release from prison, digging up a field late one night, to find some supposed valuables. Instead huge floodlights came on (it's a pity they weren't there that night in January 1969) to reveal that Norris was in fact digging up the pitch at Elland Road and he was immediately arrested.

The scene, however, was filmed at QPR's Loftus Road, just around the corner from the BBC's studios in Shepherds Bush. A large board with the name 'Leeds United AFC' had been placed on the front of one of the stands for effect.

There was still time for one more game that season as Leeds were invited to play at Middlesbrough in a testimonial for their veteran player Bill Gates. It was champion v champion as Boro had just won the Second Division with Jack Charlton their manager.

My hatred for Middlesbrough had manifested during my first trip to Ayresome Park for this Tuesday night match.

Although Leeds were well supported that night, it wasn't the biggest support I had seen Leeds take away, and Boro fans were cock-a-hoop at gaining promotion and mixing it with the big boys, both on and off the pitch. There were one or two serious incidents that evening and the animosity from the home fans proved enough to merit a response when the teams met for real the following November.

8

Working On Site

JUST three months after descending on London to witness the glorious end to Leeds's 1973/74 title-winning season at QPR we were heading back to the capital, this time to Wembley, to play Liverpool in the FA Charity Shield.

It was my fifth trip to Wembley and there had been big changes at Leeds United Football Club since my last visit there in 1973. Don Revie had left Elland Road to take up the job as England manager and the man who replaced him was none other than Brian Clough. The football world was shocked, and so were the people and supporters of Leeds.

Here was a man who had systematically criticised and viciously attacked Leeds, and in particular Revie, relentlessly for the past seven years and now here he was in the manager's chair at Elland Road.

The man who claimed that the Leeds players should throw all their medals in the dustbin because they had got them by 'cheating', that if Eddie Gray was a racehorse he would have been shot and among many other snipes refused to acknowledge Peter Lorimer at a sportsman's dinner by announcing he was 'going for a piss' was now leading those same players out at Wembley to face FA Cup holders Liverpool.

It was one of the strangest feelings that I've ever known in all my years of watching Leeds United. In later years it seemed alien to have Dennis Wise or even Neil Warnock as our manager, but this whole Cloughie thing was too weird. I cannot recall there ever been a chant or a song from the Leeds fans in favour or in relation to Clough, apart from of course when he was sacked after just 44 days and 'Hey rock n roll, Cloughie's on the dole!' rang out loud from the Gelderd End.

For now however, the Leeds faithful roared their team on but it was Liverpool who took the lead when Phil Boersma scored after 20 minutes, but Trevor Cherry equalised with 20 minutes left. The score was still 1-1 after extra time so it went to penalties after a game that was dominated by the dismissals of Billy Bremner and Kevin Keegan who both threw off their shirts in disgust as they left the Wembley turf. They were both fined £500 by the FA and each banned for 11 games.

The penalties were taken at our end and we were to witness a fine exhibition of spot-kicks, with the first five being coolly dispatched by both teams – Peter Lorimer, Johnny Giles, Eddie Gray, Norman Hunter and Trevor Cherry netting for Leeds. For the first penalty of the sudden-death process Leeds chose goalkeeper David Harvey because apparently he could kick the ball 'really hard'. Harvey kicked it hard, sure enough, but it went about three yards over the bar, then Ian Callaghan stepped up and scored his penalty to give Liverpool the Charity Shield.

As we left Wembley I can still remember Leeds fans raising hell at having to fork out 50p for fish and chips. I had travelled down with a few mates on the train and after a few beers we went for the midnight train back to Leeds. There were large groups of supporters waiting for the train and we were just sat about in the main building while an equally large entourage of Liverpool fans sat some distance away on the opposite side waiting for theirs.

Suddenly, a mob of Cockneys, I think they were Arsenal fans, ran in looking for trouble. Immediately both Leeds and Liverpool fans ran at their would-be assailants and after punching and knocking down the first few they chased the rest out of the building before the police knew what was happening. Then with maybe just the occasional nod to each other both sets of supporters went back from whence they came.

※ ※ ※ ※ ※

Leeds's first game on the continent in the new season's European Cup was away to Swiss champions FC Zurich and it produced a rare defeat. However, losing 2-1 didn't prevent Leeds from progressing to the second round, as victory in the first leg back in Yorkshire was enough to see Clough's team through with a 5-3 aggregate score.

The first thing you notice about Zurich is that it is expensive. I believe that even back then in 1974 we were paying easily the equivalent of around £2 for a pint of beer. Zurich is nice though, and we were made very welcome during our short stay, although we were just into October and the temperature was much cooler than what we had left behind at Yeadon airport.

To compensate for this, John Walker, a few others and I decided to insulate our bodies by way of alcohol. Damn the expense was the general consensus. I had just had a nice raise at my job as a decorator and everything was looking rosy. However, sometimes I cringe when I think back to my job. Not because I didn't enjoy my job – I did – it was just that my employers J.F. Meehan Ltd didn't even know I was here.

Basically I had opted for a job that no one else wanted and this was painting (or priming) new skirting boards, architraves and doors prior to being fitted in new houses on the building site where I was at the time. This meant that I was on my own in a field with my little wireless knocking out tunes and apart from joiners coming from time to time to pick up freshly primed woodwork, no one knew I existed. I had chosen this job especially as when the time came for my quick jaunt into Europe, I would leave mid-morning one day, see the match and be back on site at 8am the following day with nobody any the wiser regarding my absence.

I used to pay labourers on the site to cover for me if by any chance a boss from Meehan arrived unannounced, which didn't happen very often. I had very little if any contact with the other decorators on site and would pay my labourers with a gallon of white paint in return for them saying that I had just nipped off to deliver some skirting boards or something similar, should someone ask.

One of my biggest regrets in football was not having any of my hearses whenever Leeds played Bury. For obvious reasons it would have been a hoot to roll up at Bury in my hearse as there is a pub called The Cemetery not far from the ground. How spectacular would that have been? Me and Paul Bearer getting out with top hat and tails and a dozen lads clambering out of the back of the hearse and straight into The Cemetery for a pint. Unfortunately it wasn't in the dead centre of town.

My memory refuses point-blank to provide me with any data from my first trip to Bury's Gigg Lane in October 1974. I vaguely recollect Peter Lorimer scoring for Leeds in a 2-1 victory in round three of the League Cup, back in the days when it was simply called the League Cup and not the Rumbelowsmilkworthingtonsponsoredbycarling Cup, but unfortunately I can remember little else about that night. When my memory was recently jolted by an acquaintance, I did remember Trevor Cherry scoring what proved to be the winner.

That 2-1 League Cup victory at Bury took Leeds to the delights of Chester in the following round.

Leeds arrived at Sealand Road as reigning league champions while Chester, in stark contrast, were in the Fourth Division. The outcome of this fourth-round tie seemed to be a foregone conclusion. As the 5,000-strong Leeds support began to file into the large open end that evening, none of us were prepared for what followed.

In a nutshell, Chester just blew the champions out of the water and cantered home to the tune of 3-0. It is hard to recall the Leeds faithful ever being so quiet.

To their immense credit, Chester reached the semi-final of that League Cup before losing cruelly 5-4 on aggregate to Aston Villa.

Back in the league, ahead of a home game against Middlesbrough which ultimately finished 2-2, Leeds city centre was absolutely buzzing when the visiting fans arrived in large numbers. 'We're going Boro bashin'! We're going Boro bashin'!' was the war cry from the Leeds fans gathered outside the train station awaiting the mob from Teesside.

Football violence was rife during the 1970s and despite Leeds and Middlesbrough never having played each other for more than ten years, the rivalry between the sets of fans was at fever pitch. The pubs located in the vicinity of Leeds train station, The Black Lion, The Prince of Wales and The Scarborough Taps, were bursting at the seams as police struggled to keep the situation calm.

The Black Lion was a good old pub, full of tradition and home to one of the earliest branches of the official supporters' club, but this time it was absolute bedlam. As I watched a sea of bodies work themselves into a frenzy it took me back to just a few months earlier when Newcastle fans came in to this pub and as they retreated from an onslaught of darts there were so many trying to get out at the same time that they actually got stuck in the doorway as they scrambled to safety.

There is no doubt in my mind that the 1970s was probably the worst decade for football as far as violence was concerned. However the 80s in more ways than one would not be far behind. It seemed to fester at almost every ground in the country, though some obviously more than others.

In August 1974 Carlisle United had started life in the First Division for the first and so far only time in their history. Amusingly, they had swapped places with manchester united who had been relegated.

This season also coincided with my first trip to Carlisle's Brunton Park and in fact it was only Leeds's second game against the Cumbrians, following a 5-2 FA Cup win against them in 1950.

Goals by Joe Jordan and Duncan McKenzie gave Leeds a narrow 2-1 victory and at the end of the season Carlisle were relegated. It would be eight years before we met again when we joined them in the Second Division.

Brian Clough was in charge of Leeds when Carlisle began their one top-flight season but by the time they visited Elland Road he had long since departed after just 44 days in the hotseat but he was back in football early in 1975 when he took over at struggling Second Division outfit Nottingham Forest.

Also in 1975, Margaret Thatcher defeated Edward Heath to become the first female leader of the Conservatives, while a massive Tube crash at Moorgate claimed 43 lives.

In entertainment, Charlie Chaplin was knighted by the Queen at the age of 85. The classic comedy *Monty Python and the Holy Grail* was released. Queen's 'Bohemian Rhapsody', the third-best-selling single of all time, spent nine weeks at number one. The first episode of *Fawlty Towers* was aired on the BBC.

Former Liverpool, Leeds and England striker Robbie Fowler was born in 1975, as were TV chef Jamie Oliver, snooker players Mark Williams and Ronnie O'Sullivan, presenters Ant and Dec and actress Kate Winslet.

Trips to the continent would play a big part in the first half of 1975 but, to begin with, Leeds had to negotiate what turned out to be a far tougher FA Cup fourth round tie against Wimbledon than anticipated.

The Wombles had played at Elland Road as a Southern League outfit, holding the defending league champions to a 0-0 draw. Wimbledon keeper Dickie Guy even saved a Peter Lorimer penalty in front of the Kop. The replay was held at Selhurst Park where Leeds scraped past a resilient Wimbledon by a solitary goal after Johnny Giles had hit a 25-yard effort which was deflected in by defender Dave Bassett.

Meanwhile, the tension between Middlesbrough and Leeds fans heightened even further on a visit to Ayresome Park in February 1975 when a perfect strike from Allan Clarke gave Leeds the win.

On the way to the ground and again afterwards on the way back to the train station the police, for whatever reason, split the Leeds fans up into separate small groups resulting in several supporters being attacked as we walked through a busy precinct area of the town centre. Basically we were a sitting target for the Boro fans walking alongside us or in pubs, and they would just come charging out and take a swing with the boot at any Leeds follower walking past.

This trend continued at Middlesbrough for many years and even travelling by coach had its problems. I was attacked along with my mate Stan after one night game there by a mob coming at us from a graveyard as we walked to the coaches. It became a regular tactic for Boro fans and one that was replicated at Stoke's Victoria Ground at around the same time. Fans would hide behind large headstones before pouncing on an unsuspecting victim walking past.

Meanwhile the trouble on Teesside continued on a regular basis during the 1970s and despite Jack Charlton, who never played for any other club but Leeds, becoming Middlesbrough's manager, and Leeds's popular international full-back Terry Cooper replacing his white shirt with a red one, the animosity never went away.

I have a strong affection for Belgium. Maybe it's because they hate the French, just like us. When me and my mates Gaz, John and Dave rolled into Brussels train station at 6am the day before the second leg of the 1975 European Cup third round, away to Anderlecht, it was cold and snowing and, we had no digs. But a couple of hours later we were in a bar with a hotel sorted. I say 'hotel' but it was more of a hostel; three single beds, a camp bed and a small sink, but it was OK for us for two nights.

Leeds had won the first leg 3-0 at Elland Road but I had to wait until I watched the highlights on the television in my local pub afterwards before I saw two of our goals. Because of dense fog it was impossible to see the other end of the pitch from the Kop, and those two goals were scored at that end. 'Who scored?' chanted the Kop to the South Stand. 'Super McQueen!' replied the South Stand. Then a third goal went in. 'Hotshot Lorimer!' the South Stand responded to further questioning from the Kop.

The referee had said that as long as he could see either goal from the halfway line then the game was playable, and that was OK by us. Having said that, we might have felt differently if we had lost 3-0.

We had arrived in Belgium via a very choppy ferry crossing. The waves were so high that at one point they engulfed the top deck and pasty-faced Leeds fans staggered around the ship as it was lashed from side to side. The following day, the snow had turned to sleet and then to heavy rain turning the pitch into a mudbath.

We had mingled freely with Anderlecht fans all day as we trawled from bar to bar and considering the Belgians were three down on aggregate, they were in good spirits. They had brought about 500 supporters to Leeds a fortnight previously, with many of them sporting large white cowboy hats with their distinctive purple shirts, but one of them who had a large bell wasn't too popular as he rang it constantly throughout the evening. I can still remember the older supporters in the West Stand with blankets draped over their knees throwing stuff at him to make him shut up as he sat with a couple of friends close to the tunnel, but he was undeterred and the chimes continued, despite a few words in his ear from the police and stewards. One of the old guard even threw the cup from his flask at him. I could imagine the old lad saying to himself, 'That showed him.'

There were around 2,500 Leeds fans in Belgium, with hundreds of flags, a lot of which were destined to remain in Brussels. Billy Bremner scored a cheeky goal to make it 1-0 on the night and 4-0 on aggregate but as the game entered the final minutes, the rain came down even harder and there were piles of Leeds flags scattered around the terrace with many just too wet and heavy to retrieve.

I went over to one of these piles and as I examined one of the flags, it became apparent that it was quite possibly the largest Union Jack I have ever seen. Dave and I struggled with it, but we finally got the flag back to our hostel and I attempted to wash it in our small sink. There was mud and sand everywhere from the flag and it was all over the sink and the floor. However, our efforts were worthwhile and we ended up with a brilliant flag with large white letters spelling 'Leeds United AFC' still fully intact emblazoned across the three-foot deep middle band.

Our last couple of hours in the Belgian capital were spent just browsing the shops and I bought my ma a souvenir, the famous peeing boy of Brussels. Known officially as 'Mannekin Pis', meaning 'little pee man' in Flemish, this world-famous landmark stands proudly pissing all over Grand Place, the iconic square in Brussels.

Over the years I have collected countless souvenirs from all over the world for my dear old ma, but as I sat in her house the evening before I was about to embark on yet another foreign journey, she said to me, 'Don't worry about bringing me anything back son, I've got enough now.'

Quietly I was a bit disappointed. Ever since I first went to Scarborough on my own in the late 1960s and brought ma a brass ornament back, I have been collecting mementos for her. Now she was telling me that she didn't need anything else. So, I think in 1998, I gave her my last souvenir – a pair of coasters from Moscow.

During the 1970s there was no such thing as a penalty shoot-out to settle an FA Cup tie – you just kept playing replays until someone eventually won. This happened between Leeds and Ipswich in 1975. A 0-0 draw at Portman Road in the quarter-final saw a replay at Elland Road. It was in this game that I experienced the sheer power of a packed-out Kop. I had been in big crowds before and had a couple of what we called 'terrace tumblers', when as the crowd surged forward you often ended up either face down on the terrace steps or flat on your arse with everyone scrambling to get back on their feet and then helping each other up. This was usually when we had just scored but it sometimes happened even if we got a corner.

We were losing this replay 1-0 until Duncan McKenzie popped up at the very last second to earn Leeds a draw. As McKenzie scored, the crowd of just over 50,000 celebrated like never before. I was stood in the centre of the Kop and as the momentum took hold the crowd quickly surged forward. My feet were literally lifted off the ground as I and hundreds of others were carried along with the crowd. Then I saw a barrier coming towards me at top speed. I lifted my legs as high as I could and unbelievably I was carried over the barrier where I finished my journey with a terrace tumble.

There was never any bother or fighting over these events and everyone helped everyone else. Youngsters who had strayed too near to the back of the Kop and were caught up in the pandemonium were lifted up and passed to the front over everyone's head.

The second replay was held at Leicester's Filbert Street ground where after extra time the teams were still locked at 0-0. The third replay was held two days later back at Leicester. As in the second replay, Leeds fans once again vastly outnumbered Ipswich's but despite being the better side by far, the Whites just couldn't overcome a stubborn Town team. Clarke and Giles scored for Jimmy Armfield's men but Eric Gates hit a late winner to send Ipswich through to the semi-final.

%% %% %% %% %%

In April 1975 Leeds United lined up against Barcelona in the European Cup. It was the first leg of the semi-final and over 50,000 fans were there to see Billy Bremner and Allan Clarke give Leeds a 2-1 advantage to take to Spain two weeks later. Most people thought that this wouldn't be enough to guarantee Leeds their place in the final in Paris and many experts agreed with them.

Early on the morning of the second leg in Spain, I arrived at work on the building site and set out my workload for the day. I placed six pieces of new skirting board across my two old oil drums, and after turning on my wireless I primed them then repeated the procedure. At 9.30am I went into the cabin for my breakfast. The cabin was a wooden hut, like the ones seen on *Auf Wiedersehen, Pet*. I sat down among all the site workers, labourers, joiners, plasterers and electricians, but no painters. They would have their snap in the house where they happened to be working at the time. My small band of 'hired' labourers had been 'primed' and after breakfast I went 'over the wall'. I was on my way to Yeadon airport, which by now had been renamed Leeds Bradford airport.

Those so-called experts may have thought Leeds had no chance of reaching the final but there was never any doubt in the minds of the fans who began to descend on the airport that day. In no time at all I was basking in the Spanish sunshine and loving every minute of it, and the more San Miguel I downed with my mate John Walker the more confident I became that Leeds would piss it to the final.

We were met with one of the most unbelievable sights I certainly have ever seen when we finally arrived at the Nou Camp. Everything seemed to be painted in the blue and red stripes of Barcelona – buses, cars, vans and even motor scooters. Horns, trumpets and drums were being played all over the place and it was difficult to pick out the rather less animated blue, white and yellow-clad United fans who were just content to sit outside the bars and drink until the time came to enter the stadium and hopefully watch Leeds finish the job.

Once inside what I still consider to be the best stadium I have ever been to, apart from Elland Road of course, the noise was deafening. Massive banners were paraded around the pitch depicting Barcelona fans' own interpretation of what was going to happen in the next 90 minutes. One had a huge cartoon of Johan Cruyff driving a tank over some Leeds players while proclaiming 'Advanca Barca!' Another had a Leeds player on his knees and crying with the Eiffel Tower and the European Cup in the background.

Leeds fans tried desperately to make themselves heard but it was to no avail because on top of only being allowed a small allocation, just over 2,000, they then separated the visitors into different parts of the ground so they were just engulfed amid a sea of blue and red. Hundreds of Barcelona banners swayed from side to side and I just wanted the game to kick off.

Just seven minutes after the start Peter Lorimer fired a rocket past their keeper to put Leeds in front. The Barca fans couldn't believe it. I jumped up and I don't know whether you would call it a shout or a scream, I was just making an insane noise (I was told this afterwards by John). It was so loud that it hurt like hell and it hurt for days after, but ask me if I was bothered? Barcelona had been overwhelming favourites to progress to the final.

In the second half centre-back Gordon McQueen was sent off for retaliation and Manuel Clares equalised for Barcelona with 20 minutes left. I hardly saw a ball kicked in the second half. I was so nervous. I turned away and had my head buried in my Union Jack, the one we had brought back from Anderlecht. Every second seemed like an hour, as the home crowd started to vent their anger. This seemed to work in our favour and as the cushions from the main stand began to rain down on to the pitch, the Barcelona players became frustrated and erratic.

When the whistle went, declaring Leeds as the winners 3-2 on aggregate, it was time for the Whites to rise to prominence. The only flags that could be seen now were Leeds tricolours and Union Jacks. Bremner took his players and raced to all four corners of the ground where the Leeds fans were and we danced and celebrated like never before.

Despite me not seeing many minutes of the second half, this game remains today as my most memorable in all my time watching Leeds. Barcelona had been overwhelming favourites to progress to the final. They had the man regarded as the world's best player, Johan Cruyff, as well as a star-studded side including Johan Neeskens, Clares and Juan Manuel Asensi, who had scored in the first leg at Elland Road. This was 1975 and it was also Barcelona's 75th anniversary but Leeds clearly hadn't read the script.

※ ※ ※ ※ ※

The 1974/75 visit to Tottenham Hotspur was not quite as successful as the previous campaign's 3-0 win at White Hart Lane as this time we were beaten 4-2 in the last game of the season.

However, that only tells a fraction of the story. It was a Monday night at the end of April and exactly one month before Leeds would face Bayern Munich in the European Cup Final in Paris. Leeds had already surrendered the championship crown to Derby County. Tottenham, though, were doing battle at the bottom of the table and were in serious danger of being relegated.

Leeds looked to be cantering to an easy victory when they took the lead very early on through Joe Jordan. However, Tottenham pulled one back almost immediately. Peter Lorimer then put Leeds back in front and once again Spurs levelled the score straight away. Then in the second half Leeds seemed to offer little resistance as the

Londoners took the lead and then scored a fourth to earn a victory that saw them leapfrog Luton Town into 19th place and relegate the Hatters instead of them.

Sandwiched in between the European Cup semi-final with Barcelona and the final against Bayern, Leeds found time to take a team to Walsall for Nick Athey's testimonial game. They fielded a full-strength side too with Allan Clarke, Joe Jordan and Duncan McKenzie finding the net in an entertaining 3-3 draw.

A few days later, Leeds used another friendly in their preparations for the final, playing the Scotland U23 national side at Hampden Park, a perfect opportunity for Gaz, John and me to enjoy a few nights in Glasgow. They lost that one 3-2 and it was soon time for the final.

%% %% %% %% %%

The early 1970s saw the introduction of the silk football scarf. I remember where I bought my first one. It was at Leeds Road, Huddersfield, before Leeds's 'home' game against Wolves after the Football Association had ordered the Whites to play their first four home fixtures away following minor crowd trouble at the West Brom match the previous season.

I saw the silk scarves, which were wrapped in plastic covers at a vendor behind the main stand, and immediately bought one. It was white and had the Revie-era blue owl in a circle badge all over it.

In the mid-70s I acquired my first white butcher's coat that any self-respecting fan on the Gelderd End was wearing at the time. I wore my coat for the very first time on my trip to Paris for the 1975 European Cup Final. As my Goblin Teasmaid shook me awake early on the morning of 27 May I noticed that my ma had carefully ironed and laid out my white coat which was totally covered with drawings and slogans I had been adding ever since we beat Barcelona, 'The White Tornados'; 'The Untouchables'; 'Hotshot Lorimer'; 'King Billy' and one for the manager Jimmy Armfield, 'Lord Jim'.

Atop my head would be a white bowler hat, which my ma had lovingly given four coats of white paint and neatly written the words 'Leeds United AFC' on the front. Blue, white and yellow ribbons hung down either side and the small replica European Cup glued to the top was the crowning glory, or so we hoped. I took my bright orange match ticket from the dresser drawer and carefully placed it in my wallet before putting it in my back pocket.

Dad and my sister Julie were also going to Paris but they were on a separate trip as I was taking my girlfriend at the time, Karen. I felt as proud as punch as the local newspapers took my photograph as I boarded the Wallace Arnold coach bound for Leeds Bradford airport.

Paris was swarming with thousands of Leeds fans as we travelled through the streets on our assigned coach to our hotel. I hung my white coat up in the wardrobe and hung my bowler on the coat rack. It was now time for us to sample the Parisian walkways.

For some Leeds fans it was probably the first time they had drunk wine, and they consumed it in copious amounts. Everywhere you looked, Leeds fans were sat outside bars and cafes or just laid in a park with a few cans of beer or bottles of vino as company. There were quite a few Scots hanging around too. They had been to Wembley four days before to watch Don Revie's England beat Scotland 5-1, and after the game they had continued to head south, hop on a ferry and lend their support to Leeds United for a few days.

Scotland is a beautiful place, but for some reason some Scots never seem to rush to get back home. Thousands travelled to Lisbon for Celtic's European Cup Final victory over Inter Milan and a few of them liked it so much that famously they never returned home. That was in 1967.

Karen and I finished the night in a small bar close to the Champs-Elysees, with half a dozen Scotsmen who recounted, more than once, their huge admiration for Billy Bremner.

The next morning at breakfast it suddenly dawned on me – that night Leeds United were playing in the European Cup Final. This was Don Revie's dream. I wondered where he was and if he was thinking about the game. Although he was by now England's manager, he must have harboured some feelings about tonight surely? Would he be in Paris?

Although Jimmy Armfield was now in charge, this was by and large Don Revie's side. I think Jimmy recognised this and even left Duncan McKenzie, one of his own signings and a brilliant addition, out of the side and, some would say blatantly, played 'Revie's team'. This would certainly be the present team's last chance of winning the European Cup, the one trophy that had eluded Revie during his glorious 13-year reign at Elland Road.

The Parc des Princes Stadium was a relatively small ground for a European Cup Final with a capacity of just 48,712, but that didn't seem to bother the thousands of Leeds fans congregating around the stadium.

There had been quite a lot of drinking the night before and many Leeds fans awoke exactly where they fell the night before. For some this meant on the roofs of the shops nestled beneath the Eiffel Tower. The lethal concoction of 'topping up' the previous night's alcohol intake led to a few skirmishes with some Bayern Munich fans and French residents, but nothing on too grand a scale, especially in view for the huge amount of Leeds fans present, who heavily outnumbered the Germans and even the French, who quickly became conspicuous by their absence.

There was a chronic lack of tickets available and it is still estimated that around 15,000 Leeds fans travelled without them. Inevitably scuffles broke out between fans and touts, but this was nothing compared with what would follow later inside the stadium.

It is universally accepted that an injustice of monumental proportions occurred that evening in Paris as the referee, Frenchman Michel Kitabdjian, performed with such obvious bias towards Bayern Munich that he was later banned for life by UEFA following several bribery allegations relating to the game. Several curious decisions littered the match, including one stonewall appeal for a penalty following a foul on Allan Clarke by Franz Beckenbauer inside the six-yard box. A more certain penalty you will never see, as Beckenbauer himself admitted ten years later.

The boiling point was reached by Leeds in the 66th minute when a thunderous volley rocketed through the German defence and flew into the net. Everyone connected with Leeds went mental then, tragedy struck. Kitabdjian, who had clearly signalled a goal, consulted with a linesman on the advice of Beckenbauer, and unbelievably disallowed the goal. The reason given was that Bremner had been adjudged offside. There are two crucial points here: TV footage clearly shows that Bremner receives an 'accidental' push from Beckenbauer, which makes him offside, but even so he is definitely not interfering with play.

Infamous scenes of crowd disorder followed as irate Leeds fans clashed with riot police and tracksuited bodyguards. As the trouble continued, at the other end Franz Roth clipped the ball past keeper David Stewart, who had been magnificent in the semi-final against Barcelona, to put Bayern in front. It was heavily against the run of play but signalled further violence from the Leeds hordes.

A second goal, this time by Gerd Muller, was by now insignificant as the clashes with police continued and hundreds of seats were hurled on to the pitch. My dad was sat in the side stand with our Julie and he shot the violent scenes on his Super 8 cine camera and

I can clearly be seen in the end amid the thick of the violence in my white coat and bowler hat. I am stood motionless throughout, with my large Union Jack folded up around a huge pole and stood by my side. Don't misunderstand me, I'm not trying to paint myself as some goody two shoes, I was literally numb with sadness and disbelief and I was almost oblivious to the scenes going on around me.

I did witness one Leeds fan, however, who was easily in his late 50s, dragged over the wall by the bodyguards and beaten up right there in front of the fans, and there were others who suffered the same fate.

The final whistle came and went totally unnoticed by Leeds fans. The Germans, sensibly and with a little advice from police, decided against bringing the cup anywhere near the Leeds end. The white-shirted Leeds team, some of whom had pleaded earlier in vain for calm from the rampaging fans, were just sat at various points of the pitch totally dejected and demoralised.

Afterwards we met up with dad and Julie and we disappeared into a small bar for a consoling drink and a small bite to eat, but we weren't that hungry. Sporadic trouble continued to flare up with some Leeds fans still angry and by now quite drunk. As Karen and I walked back to our hotel we saw some Leeds fans pick up a man on a moped and throw him and the bike straight through a nearby shop window. Poor chap probably only nipped out to get a bag of snails.

Due to the actions of some of the club's supporters inside the Parc des Princes, Leeds were given a four-year ban from European competition, although this was reduced to two years on appeal. It turned out that Don Revie had been there in Paris, working as a pundit for the BBC. He said, 'Leeds United have received many adverse decisions for many, many years, but this had to be seen to be believed.'

9

Trouble At Home And Abroad

WAITING for my first glimpse of Notts County was not dissimilar to waiting for a bus before it finally arrived in the 1975/76 season.

Leeds hadn't played them for 20 years since I was born, then along they came – twice. Our first encounter was a shock 1-0 defeat in the third round of the League Cup in October 1975, followed three months later by a trip to Meadow Lane for the third round of the FA Cup when Allan Clarke restored the balance with a 1-0 win.

However it proved to be a season of shock upsets for Leeds as we were beaten by Crystal Palace, who were struggling in the Second Division, 1-0 at Elland Road in the very next round.

In between those two matches we were away to Manchester City and on my first two visits to Maine Road I saw two defeats, 1-0 in 1967 and 3-1 in 1968, but that was nothing compared to the good hiding I got there in 1975.

It was Boxing Day – literally – and Paul Madeley had just given Leeds a priceless 1-0 victory. Now, with the game over, the hard work started for the Leeds fans. The away buses used to park in a park-type area next to a pub. It was almost a two-mile walk (or run) from the ground and it was like an obstacle course for away fans. The police were always conspicuous by their absence along the way and consequently visitors would be easy prey if you strayed away from the main pack of your own supporters. It was a bit like a lone wildebeest finding itself wandering into a mob of lions or crocodiles.

On this dark festive afternoon I was with two mates walking back to the coaches in the safety of hundreds of Leeds fans. We had our silk Leeds scarves on but in the dark they could have been any light colour, white or sky blue. We were doing well and we were nearing the final corner into which we turned to get on to our buses. Then, as we chatted away, we strayed over to the wrong side of the road, straight into a pack of lions with City shirts on.

All of a sudden, with a cruel trick of the street lights, our Leeds scarves became white – bright white. They surrounded us and I just blurted out, 'Run towards the coaches, they're just up there.' But it got worse for me when I became that lone wildebeest. One of my mates managed to run back across the road to the safety of two coppers who were just stood there chatting, and the other lad just started crying.

Now I must explain that this lad was a year older than me, but he was a midget. He was less than four feet high and just looked like a young kid. The City fans left him alone and turned their attention, i.e. boots and fists, to me. I tried to carry out my original plan of running towards the Leeds coaches, which I could actually see the tops of in the distance over a fence. But as I made my move I was punched, tripped and then kicked. I curled up in a ball as big hobnail boots came at me from all directions. I thought I was going to die.

Then suddenly the thugs disappeared. I'm not sure to this day why they stopped. It was either the police or Leeds supporters who came to my rescue, but I was off like a greyhound and I certainly didn't look back. When I got back to the coaches a group of fellow Whites were stood by the corner, chanting, 'City where are you?' If I had been a bit bigger and perhaps braver I would have gone over and punched every one of them, but this little wildebeest learned a valuable lesson that day. Never again did I stray from the main pack. No sir.

Even in later years when they decided to park the coaches a little closer to Maine Road there were still plenty of scuffles between City and Leeds fans. We were once attacked by a group of City fans when they came racing out of a side street. It then turned into a bit of a slapstick comedy routine as our lot started running at them and throwing nearby traffic cones at them and it actually worked.

We played one more match, a 4-0 win at home to Leicester City, before we moved into 1976, a year that saw the first commercial flight on Concorde take off. John Curry won gold at the Winter Olympics in Innsbruck, Austria, to become Britain's first gold medallist in skating. It was the only medal Great Britain achieved.

Prime Minister Harold Wilson retired with Jim Callaghan winning the race to replace him in 10 Downing Street. Sid James of *Carry On* fame died of a heart attack on stage at the Sunderland

Empire Theatre. The summer Olympics took place in Montreal, Canada. The Damned released the first single, 'New Rose', that was labelled as punk rock.

The summer of 1976 produced record temperatures and a famous drought which seemed to last a lifetime. Britain's James Hunt became Formula One world champion. Sweden's Bjorn Borg won the first of his five successive Wimbledon men's singles titles. The Sex Pistols unleashed several swear words on *Today* with Bill Grundy, following the release of their debut single 'Anarchy in the UK'.

Television presenter and model Abi Titmus was born in 1976, as were Spice Girl Emma Bunton, six-times Olympic cycling gold medallist Sir Chris Hoy, comedian Ross Noble, yachtswoman Ellen MacArthur, actress Martine McCutcheon and actress and presenter Lisa Riley.

Liverpool won their ninth Football League title and their second UEFA Cup. manchester united were stunned as Second Division Southampton overhauled the reds 1-0 to win the FA Cup at Wembley with a terrific goal from Bobby Stokes seven minutes from time.

My tales of a scorching hot year begin with a scary trip to West Ham but a visit to the capital wasn't the only journey in 1976 where trouble reared its ugly head.

George Dean wasn't with me for the February 1976 game at West Ham but I was beginning to wish he was. I was with my mate Gaz and a few others and once again we stood down that same side. A lot of known Leeds hooligans hadn't travelled to West Ham because an FA Cup tie was taking place that same night at Elland Road between Newcastle and Bolton, and a lot of fans had gone there instead.

Consequently, away supporters were a bit thin on the ground, and I remember looking behind me and seeing moving shadows silhouetted on the underside roof behind us, as fighting erupted at various points during the game. It was pretty scary going back to the coaches too and we all breathed a heavy sigh of relief when we reached our bus, even though it was a windowless and draughty journey home for many after a 1-1 draw.

Already out of the FA Cup and the League Cup, we went on to finish the season fifth in the First Division table before heading to Amsterdam in the summer of 1976 for a pre-season tournament that was the scene of some of the most violent clashes I have ever seen.

Four teams – Leeds, Anderlecht, Borussia Moenchengladbach and the hosts Ajax – competed in the competition and fans from them all were in the stadium at the same time. There was only a handful of supporters from Germany but there was a large following for both Anderlecht and ourselves, who had been drinking together without the merest hint of trouble.

The games were on a Friday night and Sunday afternoon and after trouble broke out during the first match it escalated further on the Sunday. Ajax fans attacked the Belgians and then turned their attention to us. Mayhem followed and there were dozens of casualties on both sides, including broken bones but thankfully nothing more serious than that.

Back home, we won 5-2 at Bradford City in the October. Despite several Leeds players switching to Bradford City towards the end of their careers, there is an intense rivalry between the supporters.

It may be because of the close geographical proximity of the two, or some believe it to be as a result of Leeds fans setting fire to a chip van while playing Bradford at Odsal Stadium in 1986, not long after the tragic fire at Valley Parade. Many say that it is because there are a large number of Leeds fans living in Bradford but this reason is rubbished by the Leeds United Bradfordians.

Most of them were supporters of Bradford Park Avenue and hated their neighbours City. When Park Avenue went into liquidation in 1974 and disappeared from football, rather than support Bradford City, Park Avenue fans took up supporting Leeds United. They still do today, in their thousands. Bradford Park Avenue now play in Conference North with some degree of success but the Leeds United support in Bradford is as strong as ever.

My earlier trips to Valley Parade will have been in the mid-to-late 1970s for West Riding Cup fixtures. I can't recall the games in great detail, but there was a jolly pub (The Belle Vue) over the road from the ground putting on strippers for pre-match entertainment for just a 10p admission charge.

Another pub just down the road was called the Royal Standard. It was from here that the Yorkshire Ripper used to stalk some of his victims.

As the season continued, 1976 became 1977 and in the calendar year that followed the Sex Pistols were sacked by EMI after their less-than-gentlemanly guest appearance on *Today*. Presenter Bill Grundy was sacked by ITV for egging them on.

Fleetwood Mac released the album *Rumours*, featuring 'The Chain', later to become a regular sound for any BBC Formula One viewer. Red Rum won the Grand National for the third time. Street parties were aplenty throughout Britain as the Queen celebrated her Silver Jubilee.

Britain's Virginia Wade won the women's singles title at Wimbledon. The first *Star Wars* film, which had already been released in America, was screened for the first time in Britain. The Yorkshire Ripper was believed to have claimed his sixth victim, Jean Jordan in Manchester, the first outside of Yorkshire. Marc Bolan, lead singer of T. Rex, was killed in a car crash two weeks before his 30th birthday.

Wings released 'Mull of Kintyre', which was to become the biggest-selling single of the year, spending nine weeks at number one (four of them in 1978). Among others there were also number one singles for Brotherhood of Man, Abba, Leo Sayer, Rod Stewart, Elvis Presley and two from David Soul.

The greatest Olympic sailor in history, Ben Ainslie, was born in 1977, as was Peter Phillips, son of Princess Anne and the Queen's first grandson. *Lord of the Rings* star Orlando Bloom also came into the world and heading the other way comic genius Charlie Chaplin passed away.

In the football world Wimbledon, champions of the Isthmian League, were elected to the Football League, replacing Workington. Don Revie resigned from the England manager's position and took over as boss of the United Arab Emirates. Ron Greenwood, later in the year, was confirmed as the new England gaffer.

Liverpool won their tenth league title and their first European Cup with a 3-1 victory over German side Borussia Moenchengladbach but missed out on the treble following a 2-1 defeat to manchester united in the FA Cup Final. Kenny Dalglish became Britain's most expensive footballer following a £440,000 move from Celtic to Liverpool. England failed to qualify for the following year's World Cup.

Leeds United reached the semi-finals of the FA Cup, going down 2-1 to manchester united at Hillsborough, and in the First Division they finished tenth – a cause not helped by a defeat to a club who now featured an Elland Road icon.

Bristol City had been promoted to the First Division and had also secured the services of Leeds favourite Norman Hunter in October 1976 for a fee of just £40,000. Leeds manager Jimmy Armfield surprisingly thought that we no longer required the services of the brilliant defender who had played 723 times for the club. Hunter announced his disappointment but went on to record three brilliant seasons with City and won their Player of the Year award each time.

We travelled down to Ashton Gate just two months after Hunter had left and as we piled into the away end at Bristol it was one of the strangest experiences that I have ever had, to see Norman Hunter in a red shirt and, even worse, playing against us! The loudest chant of the day was for Hunter from the Leeds fans.

Having said that we didn't see much of him that day or anyone else in the other half of the field for that matter. The game had kicked off enveloped in thick fog and the referee had real trouble following the action, as did we. At half-time he abandoned the match with the score standing at 0-0.

As with the FA Cup fixture back in 1974 we had travelled down by train and the fog was so thick that many Leeds fans lost their footing and slid down a large grass banking as we all filed along a thin track back to the train station. Of course their mates did everything to help them back up, once they had stopped laughing that is. The game was eventually replayed in glorious May sunshine but we lost 1-0.

10

The Wild Hearses

I PAID £200 for my first hearse. It was an Austin and I called her Doombuggy. Twelve people could easily fit in the back, which came in handy when it came to driving it to Elland Road for the games. I would drive down Lowfields Road and into the car park behind where the Pavilion now stands. The police would take off their helmets as a dozen of the lads piled out of the back and filed across into the Gelderd End.

This was during the late 1970s and at that time there was a band on the scene from Leeds called The Sneakers and they were absolutely brilliant. They almost made it big-time and it was disappointing for all when they disbanded around 1980. The band got to know the hearse and at the gigs the lead singer, Russ Elias, would announce, 'Are the "Hearse Mob" in?' We would all start cheering and pogoing up and down like lunatics as the band played a song called 'Dead on Arrival'. Ah, those were the days.

Doombuggy even played her part when she led a protest march by me and a load of mates as we marched through Leeds city centre to Tetley's Brewery when they dared to put one penny on the price of a pint of bitter in 1981. Once our voice had been heard we all headed off to Elland Road and a 0-0 draw with West Brom.

Back then, when a hearse was in its working life, it didn't require an MOT so eventually the wear and tear would show underneath and eventually the chassis collapsed on my dear old Austin and I had to search for a replacement.

That search ended in the barn of a remote farm close to Ripon in North Yorkshire. A dilapidated old 1962 Ford Zodiac hearse was home to around a dozen chickens. Sadly I evicted those poor chickens when I thrust £80 into the palm of the rather surprised farmer. And after some makeshift repairs by a mate of mine I chugged out of the farmyard with a large bang and a stream of black cloud following me all the way back to Leeds.

About four weeks later my Zodiac hearse was a gleaming, shining black monster glistening in the bright sun. I sighed with deep satisfaction. The straight-six engine had been completely overhauled and was spotless, thanks to my good old father-in-law Harry Hemsley, top bloke and top mechanic.

The interior was decked out in black fur. Black velvet curtains hung from brass rails. Phantom side pipes were fitted to the new sills and even a new horn that played the death march was fitted. The old hubcaps were replaced with state-of-the-art smoothies, which were finished in gleaming chrome. A mechanical skull's head came out of the glove compartment at the flick of a switch on the dashboard. Macabre and sombre instrumental music from the b-side of David Bowie's new album *Low* came out of the brand new cassette player trimmed with black fur.

In the back of course was a coffin, a very nice pine affair, complete with brass handles, white silk lining and of course a full life-sized skeleton. The jewel in the hearse's crown was a fully stocked bar lined in lush green velvet with half a dozen optics containing several spirits (what else would there be in a hearse?). There was also a full complement of beers and lagers. I called her Rehearsel, misspelt to contain the word 'hearse'.

The bar was a definite winner with judges up and down the country as it toured custom car shows nationwide, winning several trophies. In one show, at Birmingham's NEC, Rehearsel was pitched at the side of Alice Cooper's black 1954 Chevrolet convertible. It was gorgeous. Unfortunately, the man himself wasn't there but I felt sure he would have approved of Rehearsel.

Attending the shows with me and the missus, Wub, was my mate Paul Booth, although he was called Paul Bearer on show days. We had some right laughs, and Rehearsel's first outing was the first Custom Car Show put on by the *Yorkshire Evening Post*. It was held in 1979 at the now demolished greyhound stadium which was just opposite Elland Road.

Paul and I were dressed in top hat and tails, black gloves and dark glasses. We also had hundreds of black balloons with a lovely skull and crossbones on them to give away to the kids and anyone else who wanted one. Rehearsel was of great interest to thousands of people as they peered hesitantly into the dark fur-clad rear that surrounded the coffin. We won the Visitors' Choice prize that day. First show, first trophy.

As well as being great to look at, Rehearsel could shift a bit too. I was once invited to take her on the drag strip at Melbourne near York but, speeding got the better of me one afternoon in May 1981. I had been on a cruise through the centre of Leeds with other custom cars and I was rushing back home to watch the FA Cup Final on TV when all of a sudden I saw a blue flashing light in my rear view mirror. Two officers approached my car and began looking around it, but they were visibly taken aback when I stepped out of my hearse dressed in my top hat and tails, gloves, glasses and a white painted face.

'What's the problem?' I asked, trying to act normal. Neither of them spoke for a second or two, and then one walked towards the front of the car and held in his hand the Jolly Roger flag that was attached to my aerial. 'This must be held on pretty firmly,' he said. I was puzzled. He then leant into the car through the open window and had a good look around, including a long glance at the coffin in the back.

'Do you know what speed you were doing back there?' he asked. '30?' I replied. He turned around and looked me straight in my white face. '96.4 miles an hour sir. That's precisely what speed you were going when you whizzed past us back at the Gaping Goose. We had trouble catching up with you didn't we Ron?' he said to his colleague, who just nodded. I momentarily thought about telling him that she could actually do 120mph quite comfortably, but quickly thought better of it and graciously accepted my ticket and subsequent endorsement.

The hearse featured in the popular car magazine of that time, *Custom Car*. They came up from Croydon and did a photo shoot at Killinbeck Cemetery just outside Leeds. That day had to be seen to be believed. The magazine owners fended off protests from the superintendent in charge of the cemetery by thrusting three £10 notes (which was quite a lot of money in 1979) into his top pocket. This made the superintendent very compliant and he even offered the best potential shots behind certain prominent grave stones. Afterwards, Paul and I were taken to the nearby pub, The Melbourne. A perfect end to a perfect day.

I had some great times with my hearses, like the occasion I had my coffin nicked out of the back of Doombuggy while I had a pint in the Nags Head before the UEFA Cup match at home to Valletta. Some of the lads had taken it and left it in another pub and ran off. I had to go to Leeds police station lost property department to retrieve it. The faces on the officers when in walked Paul and I fully kitted out in our top hat and tails – priceless.

I was once waiting at some traffic lights in the early hours of the morning in Doombuggy when one of the lads, who was asleep in the coffin, woke up and as he lifted the lid, a nurse in the car at the side of me shrieked and shot straight through the red lights. Luckily, because of the time, there was very little traffic around. It could have been much worse.

Then there was the time when I wished that a hole would appear and I could go down it. Paul and I were travelling back from a show in Rehearsel when we suddenly realised that we had inadvertently joined a funeral procession. I couldn't believe it. Here we were dressed head to foot in undertakers' outfits, with a Jolly Roger flying from the aerial, driving slowly caught in between the two black family Daimlers with the real hearse just yards away. I quickly did a u-turn over the central reservation and just hoped and prayed that the mourners behind didn't follow me.

11

Romanian Border Run

TWO items of real note made up the first few weeks of the 1977/78 season. The first came in August as Leeds were drawn to face Rochdale in our first competitive game against them and what would prove to be our only one until 2014.

Leeds won fairly easily with goals from Joe Jordan, Trevor Cherry and a belter from Carl Harris without reply as we progressed as far as the semi-final, where we lost 7-3 on aggregate to Nottingham Forest.

But for any Leeds follower, what happened just a few weeks later – on 8 October to be precise – was unthinkable.

We were back at Ashton Gate nearing the end of the game with the score locked at 2-2. Then, Norman Hunter picked up the ball midway in his own half and surged forward.

Leeds fans watched in silence as he carried on into our half, past one man, then another, then another, then he hit the ball from about 25 yards out and the whole world spun into slow motion as the shot curled over David Harvey's outstretched, despairing hands and into the top corner of the net. Bristol had won 3-2 and our former hero had scored – against us!

Progress in the League Cup continued in the latter part of the year before the arrival of 1978, which saw John Travolta and Olivia Newton-John dominate the music charts, spending 16 weeks at number one with two hits from the film *Grease*, 'You're the One That I Want' (nine weeks) and 'Summer Nights' (seven). Boney M, however, had the biggest-selling single with 'Rivers of Babylon'. There were also number ones for Kate Bush, Abba, the Bee Gees and the Boomtown Rats.

Gordon McQueen became the most expensive transfer between two English clubs following his move from Leeds to manchester united. Brian Clough's Nottingham Forest were crowned champions of England, Ipswich Town beat Arsenal 1-0 to win the FA Cup and Liverpool retained the European Cup with a 1-0 victory over FC Brugge at Wembley. Argentina won the 1978 World Cup on home soil, beating Holland 3-1 after extra time in the final.

I was 22 and my single life was over after I had tied the knot with Bev, but for how long?

During 1976 I was taking time out from my decorating work and had gone to work for a clothing firm where my dad was the transport manager and my sister Julie also worked there. I was a driver and thoroughly enjoyed my time, which also saw me meet a lovely girl called Bev, who used to work on reception. We very quickly became an item and two years later we were married.

We had a brilliant courtship and she seemed to fully understand and accept my passion for Leeds, but when we got married everything went rapidly downhill. We were wed in April 1978 – a midweek, to avoid clashing with a Leeds fixture. But the very next morning, our first as a married couple, her first words to me were, 'You won't be going to QPR on Saturday will you Gaz?' I couldn't believe it and we were separated and divorced within a matter of weeks, in fact it was over before the World Cup had finished in Argentina. I have not seen her since.

Leeds finished 1977/78 in ninth spot in the First Division then kicked off the following campaign at Arsenal on a day that saw plenty of trouble inside the ground.

The police, in their wisdom, had allowed Arsenal fans to enter the Clock End that was predominantly occupied by Leeds supporters. Fighting broke out everywhere, on the terraces and downstairs in the bar areas. Tony Brown, from Kippax, was making his first visit to a football match and was clearly shaken by events going on all around us. 'I thought you said there was no trouble at games anymore,' he shouted to me over the melee.

Just then an Arsenal fan went flying past us and rolled down the steps before ending in a crumpled heap at the wall. Tony looked at me. What could I say? I just shrugged my shoulders. This 2-2 draw was Tony's first game – and his last. To be fair, these incidents of trouble were rare occurrences over the years, and by and large it was always a good day out at Highbury.

In November there was more trouble during a 1-1 draw away to Wolverhampton Wanderers. The South Bank at Molineux was a massive covered terraced end and, more often than not, both Wolves and Leeds fans would be in there together, inevitably causing no end of problems. On this occasion a group of us were walking under a subway towards the back of the South Bank when we were attacked by a mob of Wolves fans. One of our lot, Billy, suffered from difficulties as a result of thalidomide but he protected himself as well as the rest of us, in fact more so.

As the Wolves fans ran off, Billy was still piling into one of them, who by now didn't know what day it was. Then with the police arriving I shouted to Billy, 'Come on mate, leave him, let's go!' But it was too late, as this poor Wolves lad slowly slid down the wall of the subway leaving a trail of blood above his head and close to unconsciousness.

The copper grabbed hold of Billy. I watched as Billy pushed his jacket sleeves up slightly to reveal his short hands and then he began to cry. The copper was completely taken aback, immediately letting go of Billy and slapping the cuffs on this Wolves fan, who by now had slumped to the ground and was totally out of it.

I put my arm around Billy and said to the copper, 'It's OK mate, I'll see to him, he'll be OK,' and led Billy away while he was chuckling under his coat. The officer took the Wolves fan and bundled him into the back of a police van, calling him 'lowlife' for attacking an invalid.

The dawn of 1979 would eventually see Conservative leader Margaret Thatcher begin her 11-year reign as the first and only female British Prime Minister, succeeding the outgoing Labour leader Jim Callaghan.

Sid Vicious, the former Sex Pistols guitarist, was found dead in New York following an overdose. He was on bail for the murder of his girlfriend Nancy Spungen. The very first issue of *Viz* was published in Newcastle. Trevor Francis became Britain's first million-pound footballer following his move from Birmingham City to Nottingham Forest. Francis later justified the fee with the winning goal in the European Cup Final against Malmo.

Forest also won the League Cup but were runners-up to Liverpool (their 11th title) in the league. Arsenal won a dramatic FA Cup Final 3-2 against manchester united with three of the goals coming in the last five minutes.

On 5 September Manchester City broke the British transfer record when they paid Wolves £1.45m for Steve Daley. Just five days later that was topped following Andy Gray's £1.5m move from Aston Villa to Wolves.

Singer/songwriter Will Young was born in this year, as was Rugby World Cup winner Jonny Wilkinson and former Liverpool and England striker Michael Owen.

Among the chart-toppers of 1979 were artists such as Village People, Blondie, The Police, Ian Dury and the Blockheads and Pink Floyd with the classic 'Another Brick in the Wall'.

My stories from 1979 start with a chilly trip north to Hartlepool United and I remember my first trip to their Victoria Ground as though it was yesterday. It was freezing cold and stank of fish. It was the third round of the 1979 FA Cup and after the game fell foul of the freezing temperatures it was rescheduled for a midweek slot a couple of weeks later. It was still bloody cold though as Leeds fans filed into the small ground.

'Could the Leeds fans please move to their right and down to the far side of the stand to allow your fellow fans who are still queuing outside to get in,' said the club's crackling tannoy system. Some people were predicting an upset due to the adverse conditions, and Leeds manager Jimmy Adamson, who wasn't particularly popular with the majority of us, certainly didn't fill us with much confidence when he told the press, 'This will be a very difficult game and we will have to be at our very best if we are to avert this potential banana skin, and end up in the fourth round draw.'

United fans needn't have worried though, as an early goal from Paul Hart settled the jitters, and following further goals from Arthur Graham, Carl Harris, Frank Gray and two from his brother Eddie, Leeds ran out convincing 6-2 winners.

One high point of 1978/79 was the run to the semi-finals of the League Cup but that ultimately ended in defeat against Southampton.

This was a heart-breaking League Cup semi-final. Leeds were seemingly coasting to a first leg victory at Elland Road with two goals from Tony Currie and Ray Hankin. But then the crowd of 33,500 watched in disbelief as Leeds imploded and let the Saints back into the game and the final score stood disappointingly at 2-2.

That said, the Leeds fans were fairly optimistic for the second leg as thousands headed to the south coast for the showdown. In those days we used to frequent a smashing little pub in Winchester called the Heart and Hand, run by a lovely old lady called Doris Tilly if my memory serves me correct. These were the early days of the Kippax Branch and this was one of our first pre-booked pubs.

Things soon livened up in the Heart and Hand and there was a tense beer-drinking competition going on. Eddie Lowther and Ian 'Trapper' Robinson were our two fastest drinkers with neither possessing a clacker. This meant they could sink a pint of lager in seconds. The lads each placed a bet on their favourite to win and the money was piled high in the ashtray between them as they went head to head. It has to be said that the audience were also drinking heavily as well and for the life of me I can't remember who won! I do know it didn't last long.

Unfortunately the game didn't go our way and a solitary goal from Terry Curran won the tie for Southampton. Terry is often knocking around the betting shops in Kippax and seems to do all right too, but every time we meet he has this unhealthy obsession of talking me through his goal back on a cold January night at The Dell.

As we raced towards the end of the 1970s Leeds were still notching up away wins at Old Trafford, apart from in 1979. Leeds had always been well supported there but the fans had never really been allowed to congregate together. In those days it was like that. There were no tickets, it was cash only and you could literally end up anywhere in the ground.

That afternoon in 1979, Leeds fans for the first time at Old Trafford managed to keep everyone together. Thousands of leaflets had been posted and handed around Elland Road for weeks leading up to the game. They had precise details of how to stick together and where to go. This was not a hooligan operation but a concerted effort to support the team as we knew they should be supported.

Leeds fans filled the entire Scoreboard End and carried on almost to the halfway line on the cantilever side. Unfortunately our team couldn't live up to our enthusiasm and we ended up losing 4-1 with a certain Andy Ritchie grabbing a hat-trick. But never again would Leeds fans be separated at Old Trafford.

Leeds did finish fifth in the First Division in 1978/79 and along with West Bromwich Albion they set a domestic record that due to cup rule changes will never be broken as the two teams played each other seven times.

The two league games resulted in wins for the away sides while Leeds lost out in the FA Cup 2-0 at The Hawthorns after a 3-3 draw at Elland Road. The clubs had already met three times in the League Cup second round with Leeds winning the second replay at Maine Road thanks to a goal from Paul Hart.

After two relatively good attendances, the Maine Road match was poorly attended with just over 8,000 turning out on a bitterly cold and wet October night. It was later estimated that just 500 of the crowd were from the West Midlands.

In the late 1970s our famous Kippax Branch had been born and we kicked off the 1979/80 season by travelling to Ashton Gate by coach, stopping off at several watering holes on the way there and back.

Coming home from the 2-2 draw we broke down on the motorway and the coach was stood on the hard shoulder as the police arrived in the distance. It wasn't quite dark and as they approached we all had the same thought.

We looked across a field and naturally assumed that there would be a pub behind that hedge and on the main road. With that, 50 of us hopped over the fence and dashed across the field with the police car travelling at speed towards the next exit from the motorway. Amazingly there was a pub just yards up to the right. By the time the police arrived, the last few of our lads were just getting into the pub. The police saw the funny side and let us remain there until our coach was fixed.

A somewhat less memorable trip came on 4 September with Leeds going down 7-0 away to Arsenal in a League Cup replay.

It was bad. We got slaughtered. The atmosphere on our coach back to Leeds was a tad bizarre to say the least. About five or six pounds of raw sausage ended up being thrown all over the coach, sticking to the seats, the windows, just about everything.

I, as chairman of the branch, was hauled into the offices of Wallace Arnold in Leeds the following day and warned that if this sort of thing ever occurred again, we would have to look elsewhere for a coach company. We paid for the cleaning of the coach and there was never any more trouble on the coach. Not for many years anyway.

After the riots in Paris in 1975 and the club's subsequent ban from Europe, it was to be four years before we were competing on the continent again. The four-year ban had been cut to two but we failed to qualify until 1979. It was worth the wait though.

What better place to reboot your European adventures than the sun-kissed island of Malta? Hiding in the Mediterranean Sea between Sicily and North Africa, this beautiful island was the idyllic setting for Leeds's long-awaited return to European competition and our fans were there in their droves to witness it.

We were also pleasantly surprised to be welcomed by hundreds of Maltese Leeds fans. This figure has significantly increased over the years and they make regular trips to watch Leeds over the season. One of those fans is their ambassador, a splendid chap by the name of Hilary Attard.

One thing that struck me immediately about Malta was the 'Britishness' and almost all of the taxis were clapped-out Morris

Oxfords or Morris Travellers. Once an important part of the British Empire, Malta was heavily bombed during the Second World War by the Italians and Germans for two years until the British Army, Royal Navy and the RAF gained the upper hand and sent Hitler and Mussolini packing. Even our hotel was an ex-army barracks.

But evidence of those bombings was to be seen everywhere as we strolled around the magical city of Valletta, though at times it was difficult to differentiate between a bombed building and an ancient ruin.

Even the venue for the match had British connections and was called the Empire Stadium. It was even more like Britain once you entered. The pitch was made entirely of hard sand, just like Blackpool. There was also a bizarre method of score-keeping in place – by way of a structure with white discs attached to it. The number of discs on either side depicted the number of goals scored by either side. At one point it looked as though they might run out as Leeds came tearing out of the traps and Arthur Graham thumped in a hat-trick, but the Whites took their foot off the gas and only added one other goal to their tally, courtesy of Paul Hart. It was a comfortable 4-0 lead to take into the second leg at Elland Road two weeks later.

After the game we still had a few days to enjoy Malta and my favourite place was a small harbour town called St Paul's Bay, very picturesque with plenty of bars. We spent more time here than anywhere else.

Another thing that created an impression with me as the buses that shunted people around the island. They were small with possibly 40 seats at the most, but they carried easily three times that amount of passengers and never passed a stop or left anyone. The driver's cockpit was adorned with pictures and statues of either Jesus Christ – or Elvis!

Incidentally, the Empire Stadium was closed two years later after numerous complaints from foreign clubs.

Before the second leg in Leeds I was in the Nags Head on Vicar Lane in the centre, and you may recall some of my mates nicked the coffin out of the back of my hearse that was parked just outside, and left it in another pub before walking out. Something else funny happened that evening in the form of Valletta's goalkeeper Frank Grima. He was by far the most agile and acrobatic keeper that I had ever seen and he won the home crowd over from the start.

Despite Leeds scoring their fastest goal in Europe, with just 20 seconds on the clock when Alan Curtis slotted home, they were constantly thwarted by Grima as he soared through the air like some superhero, tipping, punching and catching almost everything that was thrown at him.

Even a well-taken penalty from Kevin Hird was brilliantly tipped over the bar and although two more goals came from Paul Hart and Ray Hankin, Grima left the pitch to a hero's welcome from the home crowd. The very next night Grima was back at his job as an airline courier.

Later that same month we were in Romania to play Universitatea Craiova in the first leg of the UEFA Cup second-round tie.

As Romania was still very much a communist country, upon advice from our travel agent we had opted to stay in Yugoslavia and commute to the match when the time came. It was a good call.

Our hotel and surroundings were very good and we quickly made ourselves at home in a couple of nearby bars. We weren't far from the border with Romania, in a small town which is now in Serbia, and when it came to matchday, our coach duly arrived and we filed aboard.

We were introduced to our driver, who called himself 'Stavros', and he was absolutely mental. Our journey to the border took us through the Transylvanian mountains and at times there was a sheer drop on either side of us but that didn't mean that Stavros slowed down, on the contrary. We shot through those mountains at close on 70 to 80mph all the way and I swear that the coach was just inches from the roadside and a certain tumble down the mountainside. We had stocked up with beer before we set off and by the time we got to the border there wasn't a drop left anywhere on board, with most of us opting to stare down a bottle than out of the window.

Yugoslavia was, in a sense, a communist country too, but nothing compared to its counterparts. The thing that struck me about Romania was that no one seemed to smile and everywhere appeared grey and dismal but, the beer was cheap.

Universitatea Craiova were United's opponents and we were soon on the back foot. The Leeds fans were a constant source of interest to the Romanians and their attention was certainly focused more on us than the game itself, despite their team running out 2-0 winners.

When the match finished we braced ourselves for the return coach trip back across the border and through those mountains once again. More for medicinal purposes we asked Stavros where we could stock up with beer. He told us that there was a small shop that sold everything, including beer, just before the border. What he failed to tell us however, was that the small amount of Romanian currency we had changed for the day couldn't be taken back into Yugoslavia. It had to be spent in Romania or surrendered by law.

This turned out to be easier said than done and we simply couldn't get rid of our money. We had all slightly overdone it with our alcohol supplies but because it was so cheap, we each still had loads of currency left.

Outside the shop were lots of small children and they were there for a purpose – food. Although they weren't exactly starving to death they had learned that tourists couldn't take their money with them so they would line up and ask for cakes and biscuits and as it was a simple choice between giving them lots of buns and sweets and stuff or giving your money to the guards on the border control, it was a no-brainer.

We enjoyed our last day in the relative comfort of a bar close to the hotel and even Stavros called in to say goodbye. It turned out that the border run was a trip he did regularly and as we looked across and saw a coachload of tourists waiting to go across to Romania, we waved to them as Brod said to me, 'God help 'em!'

Unfortunately Leeds were unable to turn the tie around in the return leg at Elland Road, going down 2-0 and 4-0 on aggregate, making the trip to Romania our last competitive game in Europe for another 13 years.

As the new decade arrived, 1980 would be a year of big events. The SAS stormed the Iranian Embassy in London, killing five out of the six terrorists and freeing all the hostages. Queen Elizabeth II became the first British monarch to make a state visit to the Vatican and John Lennon was shot dead in New York.

Also departing this world in 1980 were horror film director Alfred Hitchcock, Joy Division lead singer Ian Curtis and *Pink Panther* genius Peter Sellers.

Liverpool and England captain Steven Gerrard was born in this year, as was Leeds United's Alan Smith, whose career went rapidly downhill after his departure from Elland Road.

The early part of 1980 began for me with a trip to Sheffield United for a meaningless friendly match one cold Friday evening.

A hardy bunch of us had returned to the Shoreham End. I have absolutely no idea why, and there were only 12 of us, but we did. It wasn't long before we were spotted in a corner of the stand and, heavily outnumbered, we were attacked by hundreds of rampant Sheffield United fans, no doubt intent on revenge for their beloved 'end' being taken with relative ease by Leeds supporters on an embarrassing number of occasions.

After about 20 minutes of abuse and taunts but no actual violence the police moved in and removed us. We thought they were going to eject us but they marched us straight into a detention cell in the corner of the ground. We were then questioned as to what we were doing there and what our intent was. We assured them we had no 'intent' other than to simply watch the match, which we were now missing. The officers then disappeared and left us huddled over two desks playing simultaneous football games with three coins and two combs as we listened to the chants of 'We all hate Leeds and Leeds and Leeds' in the stands above us.

With about 20 minutes remaining the police returned and we were put down the side to watch what was left. Leeds were losing 2-0 but then when Gary Hamson pulled one back our celebrations aroused more attention so we were rounded up again and escorted from the ground. Happy days!

Talking of ejections, I was actually removed from Villa Park by police after I persistently stood on a barrier with my mate Butter holding a massive 'Adamson Out' banner during a 0-0 draw in April that year. Jimmy Adamson resigned from his post as Leeds manager a few months later, shortly after a home defeat by Aston Villa.

We drew 1-1 at Old Trafford earlier on in 1979/80 but it was the game at Elland Road, the final one of the season, that stood out for most Leeds fans of that era.

Gordon McQueen had controversially been transferred to manchester united and returned to his former home to line up in the unfamiliar red and black of the enemy. Leeds were rampant that afternoon and ran out 2-0 winners but the icing on the cake came when McQueen conceded a penalty to set up the second goal, right in front of the Gelderd End, as we finished 11th in the First Division.

During the summer of 1980 and ahead of the new campaign we took part in the Edi Naegli Tournament in Zurich along with the Swiss city's two main teams, FC Zurich (FCZ) and Grasshoppers, plus German side Eintracht Frankfurt.

We played both of the Swiss clubs and lost to them both – 1-0 in the semi-final to Grasshoppers and on penalties to FCZ in the third/fourth place play-off.

The two teams despise each other and while both sets of their fans fought, Leeds supporters were more interested in venting their anger towards manager Jimmy Adamson. I'll never forget his face as he walked out on to the pitch with the team before kick-off and was immediately met with a tirade of 'Adamson out!' chants from behind the goal.

He had been receiving quite a bit of stick from the fans for a few months but he must have thought he was safe from them as they travelled to Switzerland. He wasn't.

Massive demonstrations against Adamson at Elland Road and at away games by Leeds fans had to be broken up almost every week by mounted police. Two months into the new season Adamson quit and walked away from football for good. He was replaced by Leeds hero Allan Clarke.

The hatred, unfortunately, had become so bitter and personal that while the Yorkshire Ripper was still at large, police would come into the pubs around the city centre and play a tape recording of a Geordie voice which they believed to be that of the Ripper. Almost to a man Leeds fans would shout, 'That's Jimmy Adamson. Go and arrest him now, he's down at Elland Road.'

In December 1980 I first went to Swansea City for an away game on what was a bitterly cold evening. It was billed as a 'Special Match' and was being played as part of a deal that had taken Swansea's Alan Curtis to Leeds.

I travelled down to South Wales with three mates in a car and I can't recall much about the game itself but I do remember, like most of the crowd, waving to the inmates in the nearby prison that overlooked the ground. They were all looking out through the barred windows and could see most of the pitch.

Cardiff City are fierce rivals of Swansea and I wondered to myself what it would be like for a Cardiff fan who was banged up in there. He would have the opportunity to watch every Swansea home game for free. Or on the other hand would he simply ignore them and read a nice book instead or watch *Porridge* on TV perhaps?

Yorkshire Ripper Peter Sutcliffe was finally, after a six-year investigation, caught in 1981 and charged with the murder of 13 women. Following the trial, which lasted just 14 days, he was found to be guilty of all 13 counts plus seven further charges of attempted murder and sentenced to life imprisonment. Mark Chapman was also given life for the murder of John Lennon.

Buckingham Palace announced the engagement of Prince Charles and 19-year old Diana Spencer, while Bucks Fizz won the Eurovision Song Contest with 'Making Your Mind Up'.

Also in the music world John Lennon had two number one singles, 'Imagine' (four weeks) and 'Woman' (two weeks), but Adam and the Ants topped that with nine weeks at the summit with 'Stand and Deliver' (five weeks) and 'Prince Charming' (four weeks). Queen and David Bowie also hit top spot with 'Under Pressure'.

Notable footballers born in 1981 include Peter Crouch, Zlatan Ibrahimovic, Gareth Barry, David Villa, Joe Cole and El-Hadji Diouf. The classic football film *Escape to Victory*, featuring the likes of Pele, Bobby Moore, Osvaldo Ardiles and Mike Summerbee, was released (in America it was simply called *Victory*). Don't be fooled by thinking Sylvester Stallone made some quality saves in one of the final scenes. Stand-in actor and Ipswich Town goalkeeper Paul Cooper can claim the credit for that.

Tottenham Hotspur won the 100th FA Cup Final by defeating Manchester City 3-2 in a replay following a 1-1 draw. Liverpool won the European Cup for a third time, 1-0 against Real Madrid in Paris, Aston Villa were crowned English champions and England qualified for the 1982 World Cup following a 1-0 win over Hungary at Wembley, their first qualification for 20 years since 1962. In 1966 England were hosts and in 1970 they were holders so did not have to qualify for either. And it's best not to go there in relation to 1974 and 78.

There was a special victory at Old Trafford in February 1981 as Brian Flynn scored the only goal of the game to seal a win notable for the fact that, due to a kit mix-up, Leeds actually played in manchester united's shorts! Leeds haven't tasted a league success at Old Trafford since that great day.

The 1980/81 season ended with Leeds finishing ninth in the First Division and the penultimate game took place at Brighton & Hove Albion.

We arrived on the coast to be greeted by wall-to-wall sunshine. When we came out of the ground after a 2-0 defeat you would have thought we had won the cup. Leeds fans were all stripped to the waist and were dancing around and chanting, 'We are Leeds! We are Leeds! We are Leeds!'

I'm not sure but this may have been where the shirts-off craze began for Leeds fans because the following season they were once again bare-chested as they sang themselves hoarse inside the Goldstone Ground – despite it being a freezing cold, early-March night match teeming down with rain.

12

What Trouble At West Brom?

O UT of the 17 meetings in Wales between what was Swansea Town – later known as Swansea City – and Leeds United, only two of those meetings have come outside of the second tier of English football. One was an utterly disastrous match at the start of the 1981/82 season in the top flight and one came in League 1 in 2007.

Swansea started out as Town in 1912 and became City in 1969. Over the years they've had some fairly high-profile managers including former Liverpool star John Toshack, Tommy Hutchison, who once scored at both ends in the 1981 FA Cup Final between Spurs and Manchester City, and three former Leeds players – Terry Yorath (1986–89 and 1990–91), Micky Adams (1997) and Brian Flynn (2002–04). Leeds started brightly on their patch, winning two and drawing one of the opening three meetings in South Wales. However, we now have to go back to 1964 to see our last victory there.

The opening day of the 1981/82 campaign saw Leeds in a rebuilding period as they were in the latter stages of losing all the great stars that Don Revie had produced and developed, but it wasn't going well. Former Leeds hero Allan Clarke was now manager and was valiantly trying to get the club back on track.

Alan Curtis had come up through the divisions with Swansea in their rise from the fourth tier but had joined Leeds in 1979. Now though, he was a Swansea player again, leaving Leeds less than a year after he had arrived at Elland Road.

This was the first competitive fixture against Swansea for many years and attracted plenty of interest among the travelling Leeds fans. The Kippax Branch alone took four coaches. I had booked us into a pub just a couple of miles out of Swansea. I had spoken with the landlord, Pete, on the phone and he had given me a route there to avoid a police cordon that he knew was being set up to prevent Leeds fans from arriving too early.

It certainly was a scenic route and I have to say that the views, as we entered the valleys, were breathtaking. It was a boiling hot day and as we arrived at the pub, the landlord welcomed us with open arms. It was a massive place and there was ample staff to cope with over 200 of us.

My biggest problem that day was force-feeding our lot. Unknown to me, Pete had laid on tons of free food. There were some big lads on our coaches with hearty appetites but that day they hardly put a dent in it. There were quite a few barrels in the cellar that needed changing however.

Now, it has to be said that I'm not the biggest fan of Wales, but the welcome we received in the pub that day was second to none. And also there is a surprisingly large number of Leeds supporters living in that part of the world.

Sadly, there was an even warmer welcome awaiting us that afternoon that the 5,000 Leeds fans present will never forget. Swansea were on fire and our solitary goal from Derek Parlane paled into insignificance as the rampant Welsh side fired five past us, including, inevitably, one from Curtis.

The result was the start of a difficult period for the club that lasted through the remainder of 1981 and in to 1982, a year that saw the Falklands War run from 2 April until 14 June and end in victory for Britain.

The Eurovision Song Contest was held in Harrogate with Nicole of Germany claiming top spot. In the Queen's Pearl Jubilee year the future King of England, Prince William, was born. Channel 4 was launched with its flagship first programme, *Countdown*, which still runs today. The film *Gandhi*, which won eight Academy Awards, was released in the UK.

Two famous Arthurs passed away in 1982 – Lowe (Captain Mainwaring in *Dad's Army*) and Askey (comedian), as did actors Harry H. Corbett, Marty Feldman and Kenneth Moore.

In the music world it was a busy year for Black Sabbath. Lead singer Ozzy Osbourne bit the head off a live bat on stage, guitarist Randy Rhoads, at the age of just 25, was killed in a freak plane crash and Osbourne married his manager Sharon Arden.

'Come on Eileen', by Dexy's Midnight Runners, was the best-selling UK single of the year, with 'House of Fun' by Madness, 'Eye of the Tiger' by Survivor and 'Beat Surrender' by The Jam also hitting the top spot in the UK charts. The 500th UK number one went to Nicole with a single entitled 'A Little Peace'.

In the world of football England crashed out of the World Cup in Spain without losing a match as Italy went on to win the tournament following a 3-1 final triumph over West Germany. Aston Villa won the European Cup, making it six English victories in a row. Tottenham won the FA Cup for a second year in a row following a 1-0 replay victory over QPR and Liverpool were crowned champions of England.

But for Leeds United, there were good reasons why 1982 was most definitely not a year to remember.

Fighting between Tottenham and Leeds fans reached epic proportions during the 1981/82 season. Tottenham beat Leeds 2-1 in May and three games later we were relegated to the old Second Division. Hundreds of fans clashed outside the Leeds end afterwards, but this was nothing compared to the ugly scenes when the teams met in the fourth round of the FA Cup in January.

Almost 10,000 Leeds fans descended on White Hart Lane on a cold January afternoon to see their team go down 1-0. Fighting continued outside the ground before, during and after the game as hundreds of fans clashed. A Norwegian Leeds supporter was seriously hurt when he was pushed into the path of a bus. Another White was thrown through a shop window and a Tottenham fan had his head shoved through the window of a funeral director. Scores of followers from both teams were injured or arrested or both as fighting continued long after the final whistle and dozens of Leeds coaches were attacked.

Having been to Rochdale in 1977 for a League Cup match we were next there in March 1982 for a friendly – and sat on the very same grass banking we had done five years previously.

Trevor Cherry was on the scoresheet once again and two goals from Leeds-born Terry Connor saw the Whites score three goals, as they had done in 1977, but this time Rochdale also scored three.

The only contact with Rochdale since is when we have stopped off for a drink there on our way to fixtures on the wrong side of the Pennines – well, until the FA Cup of 2014.

%% %% %% %% %%

The final game of 1981/82 saw us away to West Bromwich Albion and what a night it was – but for all the wrong reasons, other than an unbelievable travelling support where the Leeds contingent did not stop singing for the entire match. Talk about noisy, this was deafening.

This was the first season of the FA's new rule of three points being awarded to the winners of a match though that wasn't Leeds's priority. Not for the first time they needed a point from the last match but this time it was at the wrong end of the table.

As it was, West Brom won 2-0 to pretty much relegate Leeds to the old Second Division. A draw would have ensured United's safety and relegated the Baggies. Sadly it was all too much for Leeds fans and there was a bit of a riot. Well, quite a lot of a riot actually. Fences were pulled down and general mayhem ensued as angry supporters confronted police officers on the pitch.

One lasting memory I have of that night is seeing Allan Clarke later on TV. He had just managed his last game for Leeds as he was sacked a month later, and he was asked for his thoughts on the night. 'It's very sad,' he said. 'But the Leeds fans have been magnificent tonight.' When asked about the trouble, he said, 'What trouble, I never saw any trouble.' While trying to get Leeds fans off the pitch, a police horse was deployed and it came within inches of standing on Clarke's foot as he stood near the dugout. The reporter asked him about the horse. 'What horse?' he replied. 'I never saw a horse.'

I needed that bit of mirth that night as I later shed a quiet tear on to my pillow.

Mathematically, though, Leeds weren't relegated yet, as we were still fourth from bottom. Stoke needed to beat West Brom at home to avoid relegation themselves and send Leeds through the trapdoor.

I went down to Stoke three nights after the game at The Hawthorns, with a few mates in the car. We were in the bizarre position of wanting West Brom to win which would relegate Stoke instead of us. We lived in desperate hope. That hope disappeared in a second when we arrived at the ground to a carnival-like atmosphere with both West Brom and Stoke fans chanting in unison, 'We all hate Leeds and Leeds and Leeds.'

The four of us stood among the crowd near the halfway line while across in the far corner there were about 100 other Leeds fans, who like us were clutching on to the final straw. As the league table stood, Middlesbrough and Wolves were already relegated on 39 and 40 points respectively, Stoke were third from bottom on 41 and Leeds were just above them on 42.

Not surprisingly, Stoke scored early and added a second goal shortly afterwards. We were stood close to one another, though not side by side, when one Stoke fan gleefully said, 'This is great, I wish I was near those Leeds fans over there.' Big Mally tapped him on the shoulder from behind and said, 'I'm Leeds mate.' Then Tony away to his right said, 'Same here pal.' I was to his left and said, 'Me too mate.' Gord was stood directly in front of him and turned round and said, 'Do you want to make something of it?'

This Stoke fan didn't know what to do. Neither did his mates, who must have thought there was a load of us around them. They started to move away and didn't even look back, even when Stoke scored a third. 'I've seen enough,' said Tony. 'Let's get back to Leeds.'

Stoke won 3-0 which meant we were relegated as the Potters leapfrogged us. All four teams above us – Sunderland, Stoke, West Brom and Birmingham – had 44 points.

13

Chester Or Whitby?

AFTER relegation in 1982 Leeds travelled to Blundell Park, Grimsby, for their first game of the season in the Second Division, their first in that tier for just under 20 years. Author Simon Inglis captured Leeds's arrival on the east coast with this thinly veiled compliment, 'The sight of the brand new Findus Stand was just too much for some Leeds fans who were so overcome with emotion that they kicked out the back of the stand and relieved themselves in neighbouring gardens.'

Around 600 supporters stayed overnight in Cleethorpes, which is where the ground actually is, and apart from one or two minor scuffles with the locals the police reported 'little trouble from the Leeds supporters'.

Leeds have quite a following from this area with branches from both Grimsby and Cleethorpes but they, and the masses of fans from all over the country packed into Blundell Park, quickly learned that Leeds weren't going to get it all their own way in this difficult division, coming away with a hard-fought 1-1 draw thanks to Terry Connor. Grimsby's equaliser was met with a rousing, 'You only sing when you're fishing!' from the mocking away fans.

Dropping into the Second Division meant that Leeds once again locked horns with Fulham and we went there in September 1982 hardly having set the division on fire.

Our first two games saw two draws. But then three straight wins at Leicester City and Sheffield Wednesday and at home against Derby County put us in good heart for our jaunt down to west London. This was to be a strange day to say the least.

I don't like to use the word notorious but, that was most often spoken in description of our very own Kippax Branch of the official Leeds United Supporters' Club. Admittedly we did use the Jolly

Roger as our emblem, but this was a tongue-in-cheek response to the conformist branches which would hide behind each other, whispering behind their hands while reporting our latest misdemeanours to the hierarchy.

Basically we were just a bunch of lads who enjoyed a day and night out. There's no denying that we got into some scrapes but I can honestly say that we never started any of them – not one.

Drinking was made illegal on coaches by The Transport Act 1980, but only on those coaches designated to travel to sporting events. This seemed to be, and indeed was, yet another act of victimisation of football supporters because, although The Sporting Events (control of alcohol etc) Act 1985 states 'sporting' it does actually mean football. Not cricket, not rugby, not tiddlywinks, just football. To this day the debate on drinking on coaches for sporting events, or otherwise, remains shrouded in mystery and contradictions.

Be that as it may, the Kippax Branch made a conscious decision to stick rigidly to this law and for the first time we ran a dry bus to an away game, in this instance to Craven Cottage. It was a strange experience, I have to say, and it hadn't gone unnoticed by other Leeds supporters' branches either. All the way to London we came across other coaches in service stations and the conversation soon got around to us having no beer on board. No one could believe it. These were just some of the many comments we received en route:

'Why? Have you been warned off by the LUSC committee?'

'I can't believe it. No drink at all. Who said? The police?'

'What? You haven't even got one can of beer on your coach?'

We arrived at the ground with a spring in our step and simply oozing with sobriety. Relegation to the Second Division had been a hard pill to swallow and many Leeds fans did seek the odd drop or two of the hard stuff to get them through what is still referred to as the 'Dark Years'. During these seasons many a Leeds fan was nicely topped up, me included, and often watched the game with a hand over one eye so as to focus on the players.

That day in September at Fulham we even left our infamous Jolly Roger on the coach as we took up our position in the open end for visiting fans. It was there that I managed to knock out an Irishman. It wasn't deliberate of course. 'Belfast Bill', as we called him, was stood with us near a crush barrier. Bill followed Leeds all over the country, leaving his home near Belfast in the early hours of the morning to hitch a lift on the many lorries making their way across the Irish Sea to England. I had met Bill six months previously while watching Leeds in a friendly match against Glentoran in Northern Ireland.

He was still at school, yet he was hitching a lift to Leeds's games week in week out.

We lost 3-2 at Fulham but when Arthur Graham scored our second goal I jumped up and accidentally caught Bill with my fist, sending him crashing into the barrier where he hit his head, rendering him unconscious. St John's Ambulance staff soon brought Bill round but Leeds couldn't find a third goal.

Leeds continued to come to terms with life in the Second Division as the season progressed and they closed out 1982 with four unbeaten games to usher in a new year that saw the BBC's *Breakfast Time* become Britain's first national breakfast television programme. It was followed a month later by TV-am's *Good Morning Britain* output on ITV.

Only 42 per cent of the population voted in the General Election as Margaret Thatcher was re-elected as the British Prime Minister. The Compact Disc (CD) was marketed in Britain for the first time and one of England's finest actors, David Niven, who was author Ian Fleming's first choice to play James Bond, died of motor neurone disease at the age of 73.

Ultravox, Simple Minds, The Cure, Duran Duran and Def Leppard were among some of the major players in the music industry.

In football, England failed to qualify for the 1984 European Championship in France. Liverpool dominated the English game again with triumphs in the League Cup (beating manchester united 2-1), and the First Division, the latter for a record 14th time. England's six-year dominance of the European Cup ended as former Liverpool striker Kevin Keegan won the trophy with Hamburg after they beat Juventus 1-0.

The Second Division fixtures continued for Leeds and in February 1983 the club visited the Abbey Stadium for the first time as they took on Cambridge United.

It had been snowing before we arrived in Cambridge and we had to walk across two park football fields to get to the ground from the coaches. As we walked and chatted, a lad appeared in the middle of us and started carrying on for no apparent reason. We tried to ignore him but he persisted in being a nuisance and shouted in my face, 'I'm Cambridge, come on Leeds, do you want some?'

We started laughing at him, but he had been drinking and wasn't going to go away. He then took a swing at me and missed by a mile. The trouble was, I had been drinking as well and I swung back at him so hard that I spun round, lost my footing and slid down a grass banking. I was covered in slush and mud as I scrambled to get back to my feet as the lads were laughing at me. 'Where is the twat?' I said, trying desperately to regain some street cred. 'He's miles away,' said Paul. 'Legged it over there somewhere when you slid down that banking.'

I had dried out by the time we played them again the following season and our long walk to the ground went unhampered this time as I took my seat in the rickety old stand with the rest of the lads. That second game was in 1984 and we've not been back since.

Although we all wanted to go back to the First Division straight away, it didn't happen and by the time of our penultimate game of the season – away to Shrewsbury Town – we knew we would be remaining in the second tier for at least another year.

The Shrews were another side I saw for the first time that campaign and the only thing worth reporting about a dour trip to Gay Meadow was this bloke in a boat. Fred Davies used to sail up and down the River Severn, which ran alongside the ground, retrieving the match ball after it had been booted over the Riverside Stand.

Apparently, on one foggy day Fred chased a ball down the river only to discover that when he got there he had been chasing a swan. Fred died many years ago but the tradition was kept alive right up until Shrewsbury Town moved grounds and Gay Meadow was demolished in 2007.

The actual boat that was made and used by Fred stands today in the National Football Museum as a reminder of a great piece of English football history.

Leeds finished eighth in the Second Division that season before the new campaign at least presented the opportunity for a return to Chester City in October.

Sealand Road was precariously straddled across the England/Wales border. The pitch and the stands were in Wales but the offices, although joined on, were in England. Nonetheless Chester is a fantastic place with endless black and white Tudor buildings and when we returned in 1983 to exact revenge for that League Cup defeat ten years earlier by winning 4-1 in the same competition, some of us managed to catch a few glimpses of a wonderful city.

So much so in fact that when Leeds returned for a hastily-arranged Friday night friendly the following year, my mate Pete and I invited our other halves to join us for a few nights to sample those sights we had recently discovered.

As we sat in a pleasant little pub hours before the kick-off, news filtered through to us that the game had been cancelled. No reason was given but Leeds would definitely not be playing in Chester that evening. Pete ordered another round of drinks and as more followed we assessed our situation. We knew that Leeds United reserves were playing Whitby Town the following day, because we had toyed with the idea of going there for the weekend instead, but loyalty to the first team was paramount so here we were, stranded in the heart of Chester.

As the evening progressed, Pete and I deduced that because of this evening's postponement, Leeds might field the first team at Whitby. 'We should go to Whitby,' was the general consensus between Pete and myself.

This however would conjure up one or two tricky obstacles. First, we were currently situated on the west side of England and Whitby, the last time we looked, was on the east. Secondly and potentially slightly more prickly, was the fact that we had promised the girls a weekend in Chester. Pete and I decided that we would 'work' on the girls individually once we had retired to our respective rooms and consequently submit our request to return to Yorkshire immediately after breakfast the following day. With the added sweetener of a weekend in Whitby, who could refuse such a tempting offer?

The next morning, bright and early and still gobbling toast down our throats, we threw our bags in the boot of our car – a fantastic blue American Oldsmobile with a smooth draylon interior that was simply divine. It truly was like driving a luxurious, fully furnished lounge on wheels with a fully stocked drinks cabinet to boot.

So as the girls in the back and my co-pilot Pete sipped chilled white wine, I thrust the car into gear and set about getting us from one coast to the other. The eastbound M62 quickly disappeared beneath us, so too did the glorious *Heartbeat* countryside, and less than three hours later the four of us were checking in to a hotel overlooking the glorious Whitby harbour.

We had lunch in a nearby pub and then Pete and I made our way to the ground, leaving Lesley and Joanne to meander through the delights of this beautiful town and with the massive ocean now to the east of us. Meanwhile in the Whitby Town clubhouse, Pete and I were like two schoolkids as we discovered that our assumption had been correct and that Leeds were indeed fielding a full-strength team. For the record we won 9-0 and captain John Sheridan missed a penalty.

Back to the 1983/84 campaign and as the end of the year approached Leeds were still trying to string together the results to get them in the promotion race.

The year 1984 was made particularly famous by George Orwell's 1949 novel *Nineteen Eighty-Four*, in which he predicted a concept named 'Big Brother' that saw every citizen in society constantly under surveillance by the authorities. By 2014 that seems about right.

In the music world, Bob Geldof and Midge Ure co-wrote the Band Aid single entitled 'Do They Know It's Christmas?', raising awareness of famine in Ethiopia. It became the biggest-selling single in history in the UK at the time, moving a million copies in the first week.

Frankie Goes To Hollywood, however, dominated the 1984 UK charts with three singles making it to number one including 'Two Tribes', which remained at the summit for nine weeks. Unbelievably a track called 'Agadoo' by Black Lace, a party piece that would be annoyingly played at many a wedding, also made the top spot.

In football, Liverpool were dominant again, this time claiming three trophies – the League Cup for a fourth consecutive year, the First Division for the 15th time and the European Cup for a fourth time. To complete the domestic Merseyside domination of 1984, Everton beat Watford 2-0 at Wembley, witnessed by a teary Elton John, to claim the FA Cup.

Liverpool's European Cup success meant English clubs had now been crowned champions of Europe for seven out of the previous eight seasons.

In the FA Cup, Leeds and Manchester City, via Kippax, had a certain connection. During the 1980s our Kippax Branch used to play a group of City fans at football every FA Cup Final day. We used to then all go for a drink together.

This was fine, but we decided in January 1984 to all meet up in their supporters' club after the game at Maine Road, which ended in a 1-1 draw. This turned out to be a big mistake. Leeds fans in their club – it was unheard of.

The atmosphere was tense to begin with but became much worse when one of our lads, Tony, won the raffle and the prize was a City football. This was the same Tony who used to play practical jokes all the time and got hit in the face with a slab of tarmac at Burnley.

We all cringed when Tony held the ball up in the air and said, 'What do I want this shit for?' I saw about half a dozen of our lads look up to the heavens and then bury their heads in their hands.

Then it started. Glasses and chairs were thrown about every-where, mostly at us, as we headed for the door. About a dozen bouncers and several police officers became involved and we were ushered to our coach that had been hidden around the corner in a cul-de-sac, pursued by a rather large and rather angry mob of City fans. We continued our association for many years with the Denton and Gorton branch of the City Supporters' Club but we never met up again on matchdays.

The 1983/84 FA Cup third round saw Leeds paired with Scunthorpe United, who were then of the Fourth Division.

Scunthorpe were still playing at the Old Show Ground – they were four years away from moving to Glanford Park, the first purpose-built football stadium of the modern era – and I had two trips to their former home in the space of a month.

The initial tie at Scunthorpe was drawn 1-1, as was the replay at Elland Road, so a second replay was required and we returned to the Old Show Ground once again.

We made our way back there hoping that we could put an end to this valiant effort by a Scunthorpe side, who at the time were managed by former Leeds favourite Allan Clarke. Tommy Wright scored in all three of the games against the Lincolnshire side but we lost the third of those 4-2. Leeds were already deep into one of the darkest periods in the club's history.

Twenty days before my first birthday back in 1957, Leeds United went down to Fratton Park and beat Portsmouth 5-2. The legendary John Charles scored two goals, so too did Chris Crowe, and the great Georgie Meek got the other one. Twenty-seven years later I made my first trip to Fratton Park. Leeds had last played at Portsmouth in 1964 and we were all looking forward to notching up another 'new' ground for the Kippax Branch.

One of our more senior members, who sadly is no longer with us, was big Pat Connor. On that February 1984 day Pat sat on the coach and ate a large jar of gherkins. By the time we had reached the pub on the outskirts of Portsmouth he had thrown the lot back up into the empty glass container.

They were all still fully intact and were all back in the jar, complete with their original 'juice'. Pat then screwed the lid back on and put them under his seat. When we got back on the coach after the pub stop, the jar had gone. The driver claimed he hadn't seen it and to this day I wonder if he and his family had feasted on gherkins all of the following week.

I'll leave you with that thought as I inform you that we won 3-2 that day courtesy of Tommy Wright, Andy Watson and Peter Lorimer.

Two months later we travelled to Huddersfield Town and there were always thousands of Leeds fans present for away games at Leeds Road. There was a huge stand down the side and an open end, both of which would be full of visiting supporters.

Things got a little out of hand, however, in this Second Division game there. Peter Barnes and Tommy Wright scored in a 2-2 draw but the match was marred by Leeds fans behind the goal trying to bring down the huge fence that separated them from the pitch.

With the fence badly damaged, order was finally restored as hundreds of police officers were deployed to curb the threat of a pitch invasion. Bizarrely, the only arrests made were two unlucky souls who were caught on a closed-circuit camera rolling a joint in a completely different stand from where the trouble was occurring.

The draw was followed by four wins from the last five games to see Leeds, under Eddie Gray, end up tenth in the Second Division.

14

Policing Our Own

NOTTS County joined us in the Second Division for the 1984/85 season and we met on the opening day at Meadow Lane. Before the game, we were drinking in a pub called the Bull and Butcher on the outskirts of Nottingham. We had been there before and got to know the landlord pretty well but after about an hour or so some unwelcome visitors came calling. Forest fans were on their way up to a game at Hillsborough and must have heard we were in this pub and thought that it would be a hoot to come and stir up some trouble.

There were two coachloads of us and to be honest the Forest fans didn't stop too long and the last thing I can remember of them is running up the road with Stevie chasing them with a large umbrella from the beer garden. As we settled back down to our beer, the police were the next to call on what was turning out to be a busier day than expected and despite the landlord, Pete, saying that we hadn't instigated the trouble, they asked us to leave and to get back on our coaches immediately.

Once we were on them we were escorted away by a couple of police bikes and a van. I had a hunch that they were not taking us to the Notts County ground and I was right. About a quarter of an hour later, we were escorted into a large police compound, and as I looked back I saw a couple of officers starting to close the large gates behind us. I jumped off the coach via the rear emergency door and went over to one of the officers. To this day, I can't remember what I said to him but I remember pointing in the other direction and as he looked, I made a dash through the closing gap between the gates and I set off running like I'd never run before.

I was 28 years old. I had absolutely no idea where I was or where I was going. I could hear footsteps running behind me so I just kept running for dear life. Then after what seemed an eternity this voice shouted, 'Christ, slow down will yer?' I looked round and it was Sharpy. He had followed me out of the gate and they were his footsteps I could hear behind me, and he didn't have a clue where we were either.

I went in a phone box and phoned a taxi from one of the adverts on the board by the phone. 'Certainly sir, where do you want picking up from?' Was he having a laugh? 'I have no idea where we are, but we want to go to Meadow Lane.' 'Yes sir, but I need to know where you are, so we know where to come.' This went on for some time, suffice to say that we got to the ground with ten minutes of the game gone. However, the rest of our lot got there with ten minutes left of what was a 2-1 win. Isn't our police force just wonderful?

Through what would turn out to be an eight-year spell in the Second Division, Leeds's only victory at Grimsby Town came on 8 September 1984 when goals from George McCluskey and Peter Lorimer earned a 2-0 victory.

By and large the people and the police were very hospitable to Leeds fans and one pub near the ground used to reserve half of its space for visitors from Elland Road. Cleethorpes is a pretty good night out and the Pleasure Island theme park on the front is OK too.

I am privileged to have been the president of both Cleethorpes Whites and Grimsby Whites over the years and my wife Lesley and I have had some very pleasant stays in The Wellow on the seafront. Prominent members include Andy Hartley, Roger Dixon, Brett Taylor and dear old Mo, but one member has very strong links with Leeds United; Ray Hardy now resides in Cleethorpes but was the head groundsman at Elland Road alongside John Reynolds for the great Don Revie team.

Later that month one of Revie's greats, Eddie Gray, took a young Leeds side to Gillingham for a League Cup tie.

He had been player-manager for a couple of seasons but by this time had hung up his boots and recruited the veteran Peter Lorimer to continue as his 'old head' on the pitch.

Leeds won 2-1 at Gillingham and 3-1 at Elland Road for a 5-2 aggregate success and it looked as if there might finally be light at the end of the ever-darkening tunnel that fans were currently peering through.

A couple of months later we paid what was only our second visit to Oxford United. Earlier in 1984 we got hammered 4-1 in the League Cup and in November that same year, for a Second Division game, I got hammered.

I'm afraid I was a bit drunk as we entered the Manor Ground. We'd had a good stop-off somewhere for a drink on the way down and I had managed to get past the coppers and stewards and into a stupid little corner stand that only held about 200 people, if that. I slumped into my seat and tried to focus on the match. We had missed the kick-off.

I wasn't the only one of our lot who was watching the game with one hand over an eye to focus. Then Stan leant heavily into his seat and slurred to the man behind, 'What's the score mate, are we winning?'

We were sat among the more, let's say, mature section of Leeds fans, complete with flasks, sandwiches and blankets and they clearly weren't best pleased that firstly, we had arrived late and secondly we appeared a bit wobbly. 'Leeds are two up,' said a stern voice behind us. 'Oh, nice one!' said Stan. 'C'mon Leeds!' he shouted.

After about 15 minutes we became a real pain in the arse when we decided that we wanted to stand behind the goal with the rest of the Leeds fans. About 60 of us got up and moved towards the gate into the open end, standing on a few toes as we did so. The little steward didn't want to let us through, but thought better of it, so we hurriedly disappeared in among the crowd as the police began to arrive.

Meanwhile the game was taking a turn for the worse and after pulling a goal back, John Aldridge added another to equalise for Oxford. Things then went from bad to awful and in no time at all it was 4-2 to Oxford.

Minutes later there was an incident over on the left of the pitch. Aldridge and Peter Lorimer were involved in a fracas, and Lorimer ended up on the floor. Aldridge had elbowed Lorimer in the face. Aldridge got booked and Lorimer unbelievably was sent off. Aldridge went on to score his hat-trick as Oxford romped home 5-2. This sparked off a bit of unrest in the Leeds end and a wooden television gantry that was situated right in the middle of the fans began to shake as it was pushed from side to side.

Now a lot of people have claimed that a TV crew were injured as the gantry was taken down. This isn't true. The crew had scarpered before it was dismantled! There was some TV equipment and other stuff still in the gantry and as things looked to be getting uglier by the second, we, the Kippax, stepped in. We surrounded the collapsed gantry to prevent further damage and looting. We were close to getting arrested when the police arrived but thankfully they believed our story.

Slow down everyone, Doombuggy's coming

A Yorkshire Post clip of Leeds fans at Yeadon Airport bound for the 1975 European Cup Final in Paris

Gary's looking forward to Paris for the European Cup Final

Gary's sister Julie, in Paris '75

He's still kept it – his European Cup Final ticket

You can't find a better coat than this in fashionable Paris

Bizarre case of a coffin in John's pub..

Landlord John Richmond had grave doubts when one of his regulars told him someone had dumped a coffin in the lounge bar of his pub.

He couldn't believe his ears. He thought the drinker had downed one too many. But he decided to check up . . just in case.

And then he couldn't believe his eyes . . . for lying on a table in the middle of the room was a coffin, draped with a dark red cover, shroud and cross. So John got on the phone to the police and told them of his unwanted gift.

The police arrived . . and promptly asked John if the casket was occupied. "No," said John. So they all took a closer look and found it empty. Then the police picked it up and carted it away as lost property to Millgarth police station, Leeds.

WERE THEY JOKING?

John, landlord at The Grange, Dibb Lane, Oakwood, Leeds, said: "I was in the cellar when someone shouted down that six lads had left a coffin in the lounge. At first I just thought they were joking.

"But by the time I had checked and phoned the police, these lads had disappeared, leaving the coffin behind. Now it is in the police lost-property office waiting to be claimed. I have a receipt for it.

"It details one coffin, one chalice and one shroud. It says if they aren't claimed in one month they are mine.

"But I won't be using them just yet," said John.

Anyone wanting to claim the funeral outfit should contact the lost-property department at Millgarth police station.

Gary's coffin gets stolen

Leverkusen 1978

Dusseldorf 1978

Craiova in the UEFA Cup '79

Chief barman Gary at the Crawshaw Show 1980 with his proud Rehearsel

Having a drink at the bar

Rehearsel at the Crawshaw Show in 1980

Gary, on the left, helps out with the Adamson Out banner in 1980

A local paper in Ikaast, Denmark, captures the Leeds fans on camera in 1981

Gary's flag and coffin as the Adamson debate dragged on in 1980

Ikaast, Denmark in 1980

It's time for pre-season action in West Germany in 1981

On the way to Hillsborough for the FA Cup semi-final with Coventry City – a policeman won this particular FA Cup

Moscow Airport on the way to Tokyo in 1991

At an eerie Nou Camp in 1992 for the replayed European Cup tie against Stuttgart

Istanbul 2000 – RIP Christopher Loftus and Kevin Speight

Istanbul on the night two Leeds fans were murdered – tanks were aplenty

Fenerbahce fans with a Leeds fan a year after Galatasaray – Fenerbahce fans were Leeds fans on this particular night

Andy Starmore and his sons Harry (left), Russell and mum Malena at Gary and Lesley's (Wub) wedding at Elland Road – where else would it be?

Andy Starmore, Frank Van Grunsven and Gary Edwards

Fun and frolics on the ferry heading for Dublin

Gary shows off Doombuggy at the 1979 Knutsford Show

Tokyo in 1991

Authors Gary and Andy with the legendary Don Revie sandwiched in between

This incident was in fact used in the Popplewell Report on football violence the year after following the Heysel disaster. It mentions the Kippax Branch 'policing' their own supporters to prevent further trouble. We were also mentioned in the report elsewhere regarding an incident at the end of that same season at Birmingham City. Don't misunderstand me, we weren't exactly angels, but there is a certain limit as to what should go on.

We stopped off at a pub on the way home and watching the game again on *Match of the Day*, it was clear that Aldridge had whacked Lorimer in the face with his right elbow. Even Jimmy Hill admitted that Lorimer was hard done by but mentioned the 'unruly element' of Leeds fans raising their ugly heads yet again. Incidentally, the Lorimer/Aldridge altercation can be viewed on YouTube. Make up your own mind.

Live Aid is surely the biggest memory to come out of 1985. Two concerts on the same day – one at Wembley Stadium and one at the John F. Kennedy Stadium in Philadelphia. Phil Collins actually played in both arenas with an Atlantic flight on Concorde sandwiched in between. Other performers included the likes of Status Quo, Duran Duran, a young U2, Bob Dylan, The Who, David Bowie, Dire Straits, Sting and the act that stole the show, Queen. There were many other fantastic artists who took to the stages in what was simply an amazing spectacle, raising money for the famine in Ethiopia. It was the brainchild of both Midge Ure and Bob Geldof who managed to pull off an astonishing event.

Also in 1985 BT announced the beginning of the removal of the red telephone boxes, a massive earthquake hit Chile, killing 177 and leaving over a million people homeless, Mohamed Al-Fayed bought Harrods, *Back to the Future* was released in cinemas and depressing soap opera *EastEnders* began life on BBC One.

In the football world there were three major tragedies – Heysel Stadium saw 39 fans killed as a result of violent clashes before the Liverpool v Juventus European Cup Final. Valley Parade, Bradford, saw 56 lose their lives after a massive fire and at Birmingham City, on the same day as the Bradford disaster, a young Leeds United fan also died.

In March 1985 I celebrated my 29th birthday away at Fulham, when I was part of a contingent of 4,000 travelling Leeds fans who easily made up half of the attendance. Tommy Wright scored two smashing goals to earn United a comfortable 2-0 win.

That was the day I saw and chatted with Don Revie. He was stood downstairs under the open end at half-time with Leeds chairman

Leslie Silver, and he talked and shook hands with dozens of fans for what seemed an eternity.

As more supporters became aware of his presence, I remember Leslie saying something like, 'You OK Don? Shall we go?' But Revie, who had left Leeds 11 years earlier, had no intention of going anywhere as he was worshipped by adoring fans for what would be the last time I personally met him.

The season ended on 11 May 1985 and there can be no more memorable day at St Andrew's for Leeds fans than that particular Saturday afternoon – but tragically for all the wrong reasons.

Birmingham had already been promoted to the First Division and Leeds still had an outside chance of going up themselves but they had to beat Birmingham and then rely on three other teams all losing. Neither of those things happened.

United lost 1-0, but a battle of major proportions occurred on and off the pitch as Leeds fans fought with police on the terraces and on the field of play. Before the game, 7,000 visiting supporters had been herded through just two turnstiles by a heavy-handed West Midlands Police force. Tempers frayed during the game and when Birmingham scored, the whole place erupted with away followers smashing through the fences and on to the pitch to avoid being crushed by police charging them with riot shields and batons.

Eddie Gray came on to the pitch to appeal for calm as the game was stopped and the players taken from the field until order could be restored. The match eventually concluded at around 6pm.

Around 200 fans were involved in the fracas and 125 of them were arrested. A further 80 supporters and 96 policemen were injured.

When Birmingham had scored and complete mayhem and carnage ensued in the Leeds end, four young boys from Northampton got separated. One of them, 15-year-old Ian Hambridge, was attending his first football match. When police charged at the Leeds fans, a wall collapsed, crushing Ian and many other spectators as well as many cars outside the stadium. Ian died in the early hours of the following morning in Midland Neurological Hospital in nearby Smethwick with head and chest wounds.

On the same day as the Birmingham v Leeds game a fire broke out just before half-time at Valley Parade where Bradford City were playing Lincoln City. The blaze quickly raged out of control and sadly 56 people perished. Saturday 11 May 1985 was indeed a black day.

15

We're From Longtown

THE original sight on which St James Park in Exeter now stands was once used to breed and fatten pigs until it became a football ground in 1904. Far be it from me to draw comparisons, but to say that Exeter City have hardly set the world on fire is only 'scratching' the surface.

My first visit as a Leeds fan to Exeter City came courtesy of Liverpool Football Club. After their fans' involvement in the Heysel Stadium disaster in 1985 all English clubs were banned from Europe, including pre-season friendlies. However this wasn't strictly true. The ban should have read, 'Only Leeds United and their fans are banned from Europe.'

UEFA ignored the fact that many English clubs played pre-season games in Europe during the following summer, including Liverpool themselves (who played in Italy). Leeds were scheduled to play in a tournament in Germany but UEFA prevented them from taking part because they were 'English'. Leeds had to pull out and Luton Town took their place!

Leeds were even banned from venturing into Wales. When Newport County asked United to play them in a friendly to raise much needed funds for their survival, Leeds agreed but UEFA didn't. So while English clubs were playing all across Europe, Leeds's only two friendlies that summer were at Swindon Town and Exeter City.

A couple of months into the season, Maine Road was the venue for Leeds's first game in that most prestigious of competitions, the Full Members Cup. In October 1985 we traipsed across the Pennines to witness Peter Lorimer put away the perfect penalty for Leeds in the second half. On any other evening this would have been just the ticket, but for City sneaking six goals past Mervyn Day at the other end.

We were sat in the Platt Lane Stand that evening, behind the goal with the mighty Kippax Stand, which was where the majority of City's hardcore fans congregated, away to our right. As I looked at the Kippax Stand that evening I thought of all the scrapes we'd had in there over the years.

Leeds fans had been in there on several occasions. The police would split this very large stand (it ran from one corner flag to the other) in half for our visits and unfortunately some violence occurred.

There was one occasion when Leeds fans filled this entire stand themselves. It was for the 1973 FA Cup semi-final against Wolves, but most of the fighting that day inside and outside the ground was between Leeds and City fans.

As I looked at the Kippax Stand during the cup tie it was deserted. The crowd was just over 4,000 that evening and half were Leeds fans. The Full Members Cup, or Zenith Data Systems Cup or Simod Cup or whatever it was called, was an utter waste of time.

A month later I first set foot inside The Den in 1985 and witnessed a 3-1 defeat of Leeds by Millwall. But it was the crowd that remains in my memory to this day.

Millwall fans have a number of 'firms' among their ranks such as The Treatment, The Half Way Liners and Bushwhackers, and after the final whistle no one in the ground moved. Despite tannoy announcements asking the home fans to start leaving the ground, they chose to stay and simply stare at the 3,000 Leeds supporters crammed into a crumbling old corner terrace beneath a rusty old floodlight pylon.

There was a noticeable lack of children or families in the ground. It just seemed to be full of angry thugs. When we finally did leave, sporadic fighting took place all the way along the short walk back to the coaches. Several coach windows were smashed and fighting between Millwall and Leeds fans continued en route back to the train station.

'No one likes us!' sing the Millwall fans, and seemingly they don't particularly like each other either. Clashes erupted during their FA Cup semi-final against Wigan at Wembley in 2013 when they fought battles in their own supporters' section.

But the first recorded violence involving Millwall fans, mainly dockers, can be traced back to 1906 when they clashed with West Ham at Upton Park. They had their ground closed three times before 1947 and in 1950 a referee and both his linesmen were ambushed outside The Den.

Their history is littered with other incidents including knocking the Newport County goalkeeper unconscious in 1920 after he jumped into the crowd having been pelted with missiles, attacking referees and away team buses, and even in 1965 throwing a hand grenade on to the pitch at Brentford.

Following the riot at Birmingham on the final day of 1984/85, Leeds had been fined £5,000 but just two months into the following season trouble flared at The Den, resulting in the FA making all Millwall's games all-ticket but banning Leeds fans from away games altogether.

The first of this ban was at Brunton Park against Carlisle United. Dozens of Leeds coaches travelled north under the guise of fishing buses, shopping excursions and the like, and our branch posted as a stag party heading for Edinburgh.

We stopped off at nearby Longtown and as we had a pint or two we agreed to get taxis into Carlisle and travel separately thus attempting to enter the ground incognito. Three of us, all trying not to make eye contact with the rest of the Leeds fans, finally arrived at the turnstile. We must have stuck out like a sore thumb as one of the stewards said to us, 'Where you from lads?' 'Longtown,' I muttered, sounding like a cross between a Scotsman and a Cornishman.

'There are turnstiles open at the other end for Leeds fans,' said the doubting steward. Thinking that it may be a trap, I continued with the charade saying, 'No mate, we are from Longtown, we're working up there.' Unbelievably he let us in with a warning, 'OK,' he said, 'but watch yourselves in here, it's the home end.'

Frankly we didn't give a toss. We were in the ground, that's all that mattered to us. It soon became apparent that Leeds fans were situated all over the ground and the police set about escorting large bunches of them across to the away end. We leapt over the wall and joined one of those bunches walking around the pitch, much to the loud boos of the Carlisle fans. Our day was made complete when Andy Linighan and Andy Ritchie gave us another 2-1 victory.

Another of the games we were banned for was on 7 December at Plough Lane, the home of Wimbledon.

The trip to Wimbledon was no different to how we approached getting to Carlisle. The crowd at Plough Lane was only 12 less than had been at Brunton Park, but around 2,500 Leeds fans were in that figure of just 3,492. This is the lowest league crowd that Leeds have played in front of.

That same defender Dave Bassett, who played for Southern League Wimbledon against Leeds in the FA Cup back in 1975, was manager at the now-Second Division club when Leeds rolled into town. Bassett defended Leeds fans by saying, 'The Leeds fans are brilliant and they are welcome here any time.'

Wimbledon had been elected to the Football League in 1977 in place of Workington and after an indifferent start they were storming up through the divisions. Before the game Leeds manager Billy Bremner had told his team they were likely to need 'tin hats and helmets' to deal with Wimbledon's 'high rise approach'. 'It will be like the Alamo!' warned Bremner.

In the event, goals from Ian Snodin, Ian Baird and Martin Dickinson eased Leeds to a 3-0 victory. I remember there were no TV cameras at Plough Lane that day but a Leeds fan in front of us in the main stand (the only stand as I recall) videoed the whole game. This rare, often wobbly recording, was shown several times during the next few weeks in the old Supporters' Club at Elland Road.

When our 'shopping trip' left Plough Lane after the game we headed off into London for a few light ales. We regrouped at midnight at the Embankment and as we hung around our coaches we chatted with some of the residents of 'Cardboard City'. This is where many of London's homeless sleep in cardboard boxes. Despite their misfortune, there were some great characters and as we shared a beer with some of them, a cardboard box next to us began to move.

Then, all of a sudden, a head popped up through the lid and a voice exclaimed, 'By, it's great to hear Yorkshire voices. I'm from Sheffield. I'm a chef.' One of the lads left our 'head chef' a couple of beers and I apologised to him for not having any wine to leave him for his next recipe and we were on our way up north.

Plans to ban Leeds fans from the next away game at Hull City were scrapped by the FA. Meanwhile, Wimbledon continued their upward surge and in 1986 they were promoted to the First Division. Plough Lane became a very inhospitable place to go to. Wimbledon contained the notorious 'Crazy Gang' of Vinnie Jones, Dennis Wise and John Fashanu, and many a top team fell foul at their home.

The tiny dressing rooms were a key part of Wimbledon's success. The chairman, Sam Hammam, would have the heating turned on full. The toilets wouldn't flush and Hammam would put salt in the sugar bowls before giving the visitors their half-time cuppa.

The rule of all-seater stadia and the restriction for improvement to Plough Lane saw the club move to Selhurst Park to share with Crystal Palace in 1991. There are few memories of Wimbledon v Leeds games at Selhurst Park, but a couple stand out.

Tony Yeboah's second goal in a 4-2 win in 1996 was the best of Yeboah's Leeds goals by far, and when Vinnie Jones returned to play for Wimbledon in 1992, whenever they played Leeds he would give the United fans the 'Leeds Salute' every time he came over to our side to take a corner or a throw-in. God bless Vinnie.

We were allowed in for the game at Hull City on 22 December but Billy Bremner's side – he had taken over from Eddie Gray in October – came back empty-handed after a 2-1 defeat. Just for good measure, we received a brick through the coach window as we left the outskirts of Hull.

The Hull game sent us towards 1986, a year that saw Prime Minister Margaret Thatcher open the M25, Mike Tyson win his first world boxing title by defeating Trevor Berbick in Las Vegas to become the youngest man to win a world championship at 20 years and four months, Alain Prost become Formula One world champion and Boris Becker win Wimbledon for a second year running, still at the tender age of 18.

Notable films released in 1986 were *Top Gun*, *Platoon*, *Crocodile Dundee* and *Aliens*. Floyd Gottfredson, long-time artist of Mickey Mouse comics, passed away at the age of 81 and the space shuttle *Challenger* exploded 73 seconds after launch, killing the crew of seven astronauts, including schoolteacher Christa McAuliffe.

Argentina won the World Cup after defeating Germany in the final 3-2 in Mexico. In my 1986 football world we start with what could easily have been a football tragedy.

Comedian Roy 'Chubby' Brown is a Boro season ticket holder, but even he admits that 'sunny' Middlesbrough is not exactly the most glamorous place on earth. In a nutshell it is a depressing place. Away fans at Ayresome Park used to be shoved and crammed into a decrepit old corner section and it was in here that there was very nearly a terrible tragedy in March 1986, a game that was drawn 2-2.

It was less than a year on from the Heysel Stadium disaster and lessons were supposed to have been learnt. But there were too many Leeds fans packed into one area and several parts of the old walls surrounding us collapsed, causing panic as dozens of us had to scramble to safety on to the pitch. It was an absolute miracle that nobody lost their life that day and that is in no way an exaggeration.

However, I have one or two happy memories of going to Ayresome Park, like the time we were in a pub on the outskirts of Middlesbrough as guests of our Teesside branch of Leeds fans when in walked Boro's Craig Johnston. It was just after 8am and when Johnston sat down with a few mates with a pint, we assumed that he wasn't down to play for Boro in seven hours' time, but he was, and he hit the bar beforehand.

A month later we went down to Portsmouth and won 3-2. The Leeds end was open back then, as were many grounds in those days, and with 5,000 visiting fans crammed in, Noel Blake immediately scored for Portsmouth.

Leeds fought back and two goals from Andy Ritchie and one from Ian Baird put us 3-1 in front and despite another goal from Blake in the final minutes, we returned to Yorkshire with all three points.

It is interesting to analyse the three goalscorers that day. Ritchie was playing on a week-to-week contract at Elland Road after a knee injury had prevented Portsmouth from signing him only a week previously. At the time Leeds were 17th in the Second Division and Portsmouth were second. Ritchie of course was born on the wrong side of the Pennines, which is never good, in a small town near Salford, and had scored a hat-trick against us at Old Trafford in 1979. So understandably it took me some time to warm to him when he signed for us and made his debut two days before my 27th birthday in 1983.

Much of Ritchie's four-year spell at Leeds was spent in contract dispute. One entire year of his time was spent on that weekly deal and he was clearly disappointed when the move to Portsmouth fell through. He said at the time, 'If Portsmouth win promotion and come back in for me then the offer of First Division football has got to interest me.'

After Ritchie's first goal, a stunning 20-yard flyer, he clenched his fist and thumped his right knee and said, 'There's nothing wrong with this knee.' However, after the game, and possibly with the prospect of signing for Pompey, he said, 'I tried to cross it and was as surprised as anyone when it went in.' Portsmouth never came back in for Ritchie and in August 1987 he signed for Oldham Athletic for £50,000.

As a testimony to his unhappy spell at Leeds he said, many years later, 'My lowest point at Oldham was better than my highest point at Leeds.' A couple of years ago during an interview on BBC Radio Leeds, I questioned Andy, or 'Stitch' as he is known, about this off-hand comment and he laughed and just shrugged his shoulders. That said, to be honest, he didn't seem a bad chap really.

Baird, the scorer of Leeds's second goal that day, was born in Rotherham, but despite this he still considers himself to be a southerner. He used to attend many supporters' functions and would always deny being a Yorkshireman – very strange indeed. He left Leeds the following season and joined, you've guessed it, Portsmouth. However, Baird was a big hero of the Leeds fans and always gave 100 per cent whenever he pulled the white shirt over his head. He still remains a cult figure among the Leeds faithful of that day.

Blake scored both Portsmouth's goals that day. He moved north and joined Leeds in 1988 along with fellow Portsmouth player Vince Hilaire.

In April 1986 we won 1-0 away to Bradford City, less than a year on from that terrible fire at Valley Parade which resulted in the deaths of 56 people. My first thoughts after the tragedy were that I'd been in that stand on those previous visits with Leeds and running along the back was a long tunnel. It never struck me at the time of course, but the tunnel only seemed to have two exits, one at either end. This, combined with the wooden structure of the stand, surely contributed to the horrific loss of those treasured lives.

The first time I saw Leeds play Bradford in league action was that victory. While Valley Parade was being rebuilt, City were playing their home games at Elland Road, Huddersfield and Odsal Stadium, home of Bradford Northern Rugby League Club. When Leeds played at Odsal in 1986, a regrettable incident where a chip van caught fire among the Leeds fans caused a pitch invasion and multiple brawls between both sets of supporters.

After two seasons at Odsal, City returned to their newly refurbished and impressive Valley Parade. Although the away end was proportionally smaller than the rest of the ground it was good to see City back home.

16

Members Only

OUR game at Millwall on 8 November 1986 was an 11am kick-off and Leeds fans had been travelling down all through the night. A couple of hours later after a 1-0 defeat we were all sat on a stationary coach. Stationary because it had broken down only yards from the ground.

We were still sat on this coach at 3pm surrounded by a few very nervous policemen. The pubs began to close and Millwall fans spilling out instantly spotted us – a sitting target and about 100 of them swarmed around the coach, totally ignoring police instructions to move on. It was an uneasy stand-off. They wouldn't come on board (luckily) and we certainly weren't getting off.

Eventually a mechanic arrived to fix our coach. He was drip white and shaking like a leaf, as were some of the police I have to say, at the prospect of an almighty punch-up. He managed to do a quick bodge-job to get us moved out of harm's way but not before we had a pool ball thrown through the window.

I can still see my mate Stevie hanging out of the bus where the window had been and with the aid of a sweeping brush as a paddle he began singing the tune of *Hawaii Five-O* as we made our way back up the M1. We even had our branch flag, which was a Jolly Roger, confiscated from our coach because, according to police, it could be seen as provocative. Provocative at Millwall? I ask you.

Football is a funny old game and even Leeds fans had cause to chuckle when we travelled to Stoke City in December 1986. The previous season Leeds had been hammered 6-2 by Stoke and when we returned in 1986/87, manager Billy Bremner announced, 'We were trounced here last season 6-2, I can assure you, that won't happen again.' Billy, God rest his soul, was right – we were beaten 7-2!

The Leeds goals by Ian Baird and John Sheridan, however, were easily the best of the game. Sheridan's penalty kick was amazing.

Undeterred, after the game Bremner said, 'Forget the result, did you see and hear our fans today, they were truly magnificent. They sang throughout the game to lift our team, they are without doubt the greatest supporters in the country. I just wish my lot could have done them justice.'

The opening days of 1987 soon came around, a year in which Terry Waite, the special envoy of the Archbishop of Canterbury in Lebanon, was kidnapped in Beirut, U2 released their album *The Joshua Tree*, *The Simpsons* first appeared on TV screens in America and the first Rugby Union World Cup took place in New Zealand with the hosts becoming triumphant.

Maggie Thatcher was re-elected for a third term in office as Prime Minister while the Great Storm occurred on the south coast of Britain, with hurricane winds killing 23 people.

Uruguayan football genius Luis Suarez was born in 1987, as was another great, Lionel Messi, England's goalkeeper Joe Hart and tennis Grand Slam winners Novak Djokovic, Andy Murray and Maria Sharapova.

A bitterly cold day was encountered when Leeds met non-league Telford at The Hawthorns in January 1987, in the third round of the FA Cup. The tie had been switched from Telford's Bucks Head ground amid fears of crowd trouble.

The game itself was a complete farce as the surface was rock hard with sheets of ice covering an already snow white pitch. The FA were reluctant to postpone the match because of the previous rearrangement, plus they would no doubt have been conscious of a potential cup upset. Leeds narrowly scraped past Telford 2-1 with both goals scored by fan favourite Baird.

In the next round we were drawn away to Swindon Town, a club I had first visited for a sixth-round game at the County Ground in 1970 when Allan Clarke scored twice to see off the Second Division outfit. The two teams met again the following season with Leeds winning 4-0 at Elland Road.

The 1986/87 FA Cup run for Leeds was dogged by FA decisions all the way through. Because of a relatively minor incident the previous season at a league game at The Hawthorns against West Bromwich Albion, in which a small wooden shed was set alight, the FA obstructed Leeds in almost every round.

Leeds were drawn away against non-league Telford in the third round, but, as previously mentioned, the FA moved the game to – unbelievably – The Hawthorns! What was also unbelievable was the headline in the *Yorkshire Evening Post* when the news broke of the tie being switched from Bucks Head. Probably the only newspaper that Leeds fans could relate to had turned its back on the club.

On Tuesday 16 December the headline on the front page of the *Post* announced, 'Come on Telford!' I couldn't believe what I was reading. Our very own local and respected newspaper had joined the ranks of the national media and other clubs and had turned against us.

The article beneath the hurtful headline read, 'For the first time in its history, the *Yorkshire Evening Post* today hopes that Leeds United will LOSE a match. It is monstrously unfair that, due to police intervention, Telford United will be obliged to give up home ground advantage on January 11. That is why we are hoping for a different result on January 11. We do so sadly. We have always carried a rattle for Leeds United. We will continue to do so. But we will be taking 90 minutes out on January 11.'

Leeds fans were dumbfounded at this attack on them, and many refused to buy the paper again. I didn't buy a copy for over ten years and I only did so again when the whole regime and writing team had been replaced.

We went on to beat Telford, then Swindon, then QPR at home and then won away at Wigan in the quarter-final. The semi-final against Coventry City at Hillsborough was fixed for a 12.15pm kick-off, the first time that a semi-final had been switched to an earlier start time. All Leeds flags (not Coventry) were banned from the ground. Days before the game at Hillsborough, the *Post* put out a 'Wembley Special Edition'. 'We're with you all the way United!' they proclaimed. Cheeky bastards.

All the cup games during that run, with the exception of the home tie against QPR, were switched to early kick-offs to deter Leeds fans or at the very least make it difficult for them to attend.

Interestingly, Swindon's manager Lou Macari said on the evening of the Leeds game, 'Leeds fans are not a problem to us, and they are welcome here any time.'

Swindon Town were not really well known for their hooligans, but they had got quite a few, although, to be fair, as a travelling Leeds fan I never witnessed them. During the 1970s, Swindon had a mob called Swindon Town Aggro Boys (STAB). During a game against Wrexham, STAB were responsible for pelting the opposing goalkeeper with carrots.

During the 1980s a hooligan gang known as Swindon's Southside Firm (SSF) emerged and in one incident, Macari walked straight into a group of around 100 SSF members chasing Northampton

Town fans up the road. Macari said the incident was 'worse than a Celtic–Rangers game'.

My wife Lesley always chuckles when she reads through the dog-eared pages of my diaries from when I was a kid in the late 1960s and early 70s. One repeated line throughout my recordings is, 'It was windy'. I've always hated the wind. It plays havoc with my hair.

And it was sure blowing a gale when we converged on Wigan for our FA Cup quarter-final there in April 1987. Leeds had been given a meagre 2,500 tickets and venues had been set up all over Leeds city centre that were showing the game live on big screens for those not lucky enough to have got a ticket. There were police roadblocks surrounding Wigan early on the morning of the game, turning back any Leeds fans who didn't have tickets.

Wigan were then in the Third Division and Leeds sat in the top third of the Second but it was always going to be a difficult game, particularly with the high winds circling around Springfield Park.

Things were tense among the travelling Whites herded into what looked like a temporary open end, and by half-time there was no score. Then in the second period, Leeds's John Stiles, son of Nobby and nephew of John Giles, raced deep into the Wigan half and let fly with a thunderous shot that, partly aided by the strong wind, opened the scoring. Micky Adams eased away all the tension by adding a second to send Leeds into the semi-final.

Incidentally, another indication of the FA's intention of hampering United's road to Wembley at every opportunity came when striker Ian Baird was suspended for the game at Wigan. He had received a two-match ban following an accumulation of yellow cards and was due to miss the two league fixtures prior to the quarter-final, but manager Billy Bremner said, 'At least we'll have Bairdy back for the Wigan match.' Then the FA altered the situation and instead awarded Baird two one-match bans and arranged it so that he missed the cup tie and a league game, instead of the usual two successive games – it was unbelievable.

This was unprecedented and I wrote to the FA asking them to clarify why they had chosen to implement this kind of arrangement, especially as it had never been done before. In due course I received a curt reply from the FA simply showing me an extract from the rules stating that they *could* do it. They never addressed my initial question, which was *why* they had done it?

The facts were that prior to the Wigan cup match Leeds had a league game against Grimsby on the Saturday before and another one, a rearranged fixture away at Portsmouth, the following

Tuesday. The FA believed that Leeds had deliberately rearranged the Portsmouth game so that Baird could play against Wigan. Leeds strenuously denied this, pointing out that they were still fighting for promotion too and that every league game was just as vital to the club as a cup game.

Incidentally, during the Portsmouth match Baird was almost arrested. A policeman alleged that Baird had made a 'V' sign to the Pompey fans and told referee David Elleray. Subsequently, Baird was charged with bringing the game into disrepute, which further threatened his chances of playing at Wigan.

As if proof were needed that Leeds receive unfair treatment from the authorities, when Baird left Leeds to join Middlesbrough the following season his new club got to the Zenith Data Systems Cup Final at Wembley against Chelsea. But because Baird had played for Leeds in the same competition he was cup-tied. Baird said, 'I was due to serve a one-match suspension but the FA confirmed that the ban would be served by missing the Zenith final despite the fact that I was cup-tied and ineligible to play in the game anyway. After the way I had been dealt with while playing for Leeds I couldn't believe it. The suits in the ivory towers had done me a huge favour rather than hammer me like they had in the past.' The 'ban' enabled Baird to play in a vital league game instead.

%% %% %% %% %%

One of the funniest sights I have ever seen was a policeman standing at the top of Penistone Road as we walked down to Hillsborough for the 1987 FA Cup semi-final between Coventry City and Leeds. He was holding a homemade, hardboard FA Cup which was over ten feet tall and he was having all sorts of trouble holding on to it in high winds.

It all started at 6am on 12 April in the Anchor pub in Allerton Bywater village, just a couple of miles from Kippax. The FA were still placing obstacles in Leeds fans' route to the final (hopefully) and had rescheduled the kick-off to 12.15pm for this, the biggest Leeds game for a decade. I believe it was also the first time that an FA Cup semi-final had not kicked off at the traditional 3pm.

So, as a result of these newly imposed FA rules, we rescheduled our own arrangements and the pub opened five hours earlier than normal. Me and my mate Gordon had made that ten-foot high FA Cup which was sprayed silver and it had blue, white and yellow ribbons draped from the handles as it stood proudly outside the pub awaiting the 30-mile trip down the M1.

We were travelling to Sheffield on a double decker bus, and immediately had difficulty getting our 'FA Cup' on board. The bus was already overloaded and also, because of the low headroom inside, the cup had to be strapped to the outside of the bus and held from the inside by 'designated' passengers upstairs and downstairs. The driver, who was not our usual driver, was slightly reluctant to have this thing flapping from the outside of his bus, but after a lengthy discussion and our assurance that it would be safe, although I cannot remember putting anything in writing to that effect, we were allowed to take it with us.

On our arrival we walked proudly down the hill towards the ground with our giant cup and this is where we encountered the 'fussiness' (for the want of a better word) of this over-zealous policeman, who said, 'You can't take that in with you!' We offered no resistance whatsoever and Gordon responded immediately. 'OK mate, here you are – it's all yours,' he said as we handed him our personal work of art, including the bright ribbons.

Other police officers were clearly sniggering and fans were laughing out loud as this hapless copper stood alone with our cup as it swayed violently back and forth in the wind, knocking his helmet askew as it did so. 'You can pick it up after the match!' he shouted to us as we disappeared down the hill to the match. 'No problem mate,' I shouted back. 'You keep it.'

Once again, Leeds fans had been short-changed with the designated end of the ground for an FA Cup semi-final and I must say that the Coventry supporters looked nice and cosy in the newly covered end at Hillsborough. 'It was more convenient to put Coventry fans in that end because of the route they travelled to the ground,' said an unconvincing police statement. Two-thirds of the 51,000 crowd were Leeds fans and thousands packed into the Leppings Lane Stand, including myself.

First Division Coventry were overwhelming favourites to beat Second Division Leeds but by half-time we were a goal up thanks to one of the best goals I've ever seen scored by a Leeds player. David Rennie met a cross from Micky Adams perfectly to head home after less than 20 minutes. Leeds held the lead until the 70th minute when combined defensive errors allowed Coventry to equalise and then almost cruelly City went in front 2-1.

However, Leeds, under manager Billy Bremner's fighting spirit, forced extra time when Keith Edwards scored the equaliser in front of the delirious Leeds fans at the Leppings Lane end. In the ninth minute of extra time David Bennett forced the ball over the line in front of those same Leeds fans to send Coventry to Wembley and their first FA Cup triumph.

Despite the fact that Keith Houchen was in an offside position (undisputable on TV evidence – he was in fact stood *behind* Leeds keeper Mervyn Day) when Bennett scored and the fact that Leeds had been robbed so many times over the years for the self same but reverse situation, I was genuinely pleased for Coventry City, especially when they beat Tottenham in the final.

However, one good thing to come out of that afternoon at Hillsborough was the fact that Leeds fans finally received some praise from the police and the footballing authorities (and the *Yorkshire Evening Post*) for their 'impeccable behaviour'.

In the writing about matches at Hillsborough I have realised something rather important, particularly with all the FA Cup semi-finals I've attended both at Hillsborough and elsewhere. For the games in 1967, 1968, 1970 (three), 1972, 1973 and 1987, on three occasions I have watched the game from the side and Leeds have won every one, 1970, 1972 and 1973. I have watched the rest from behind the goal and we have either lost or drawn them. I now know from where I'll be watching my next semi-final.

% % % % %

In 1986, after an altercation at West Bromwich Albion I was arrested and banned from all football grounds for six months. I immediately appealed in court through my solicitor. The ban was lifted but upon my arrest my LUFC membership had been confiscated by West Midlands Police and returned to Leeds United. The card was essential to gain entry at any away game.

The problem was getting it back. I requested a meeting with the general manager at Elland Road, Alan Roberts, and soon found myself in his office deep beneath the West Stand nervously holding a cup of tea. It was Leeds's policy, I was told by Alan, not to return a card following an arrest watching United, and after all, although my ban was lifted immediately, I was still guilty as charged of the offence at The Hawthorns.

'But,' said Alan, 'in view of your great support for this club, and bearing in mind we are playing at Wembley in a few weeks [Leeds were taking part in the Mercantile Credit Tournament] I'm going to return your card.' I could have kissed him. 'But officially you are still banned by the club until the end of the season,' he added. 'So I must ask you to keep a low profile. My neck is on the line here mate.'

I decided not to travel on the supporters' coaches until the end of the season, so for the next away game in April 1987, which was at Shrewsbury Town, a match we would win 2-0, I went in the car with Sharpy and a couple of the other lads.

As we trundled through the sunny countryside I passed two cans of beer back and opened another myself. 'Lovely scenery Gaz,' I said to our driver sitting next to me. 'It's gonna be a good day, I can feel it. Just get past that car in front, we've been following him for miles now.'

At the first opportunity we pulled alongside the other car to overtake and as we drew alongside I couldn't believe my eyes. We were the only two vehicles for miles around and in the other car was none other than Alan Roberts. He had just seen me take a large swig of my beer and as we just looked at each other, he smiled at me and cocked one hand towards me in the shape of an imaginary pistol and pulled the 'trigger'. I hoped he realised that I couldn't take much more of a lower profile than snaking through small country roads miles from anywhere. The next time we met, a few years later in Germany, we never mentioned the incident.

A couple of weeks after the visit to Shrewsbury, and with the impending end of a season that would ultimately lead to a play-off final against Charlton Athletic, I took my first trip to Reading Football Club, or 'Reeding Soccer Club', as a Canadian tourist once said to me while on a ferry in Scandinavia.

Elm Park is not the best ground I've ever been to, I have to say, and coupled with a 2-1 defeat it meant I had a right miserable day. John Pearson, or 'Near Post' Pearson as he was called because of his flick-ons (although he was also called 'Lead Boots' by some fans), scored our goal and that was about the only thing worthy of note. We had though beaten Reading at Elland Road earlier in the season 3-2 after being two goals behind at half-time.

We qualified for the play-offs by finishing fourth in the Second Division and in the semi-finals we came up against Oldham Athletic.

Oldham have remarkably similar traits to that of Barnsley. They both have a meagre (except when they play Leeds) attendance at a ground that is not exactly Wembley Stadium and, they are both a thorn in the side of Leeds. As you approached Boundary Park you could be forgiven for assuming that the stadium was derelict and that you have been the victim of a prank that had sent you to the wrong ground. Even for night games, the half-dozen or so light bulbs perched on a couple of towers didn't exactly convince you that there is a football pitch on the other side of the crumbling brick walls.

Knee-deep in mud, you finally got to squeeze through one of the foot-wide turnstiles and then you were confronted by a lush green playing surface, a lush green *plastic* playing surface. Oldham were one of only a handful of clubs in the Football League to install an artificial playing surface. It was a massive advantage to them however, as visiting teams struggled to literally get to grips with it. Plastic pitch or not, even when Oldham reverted back to grass, Leeds still found it difficult to win at Boundary Park. You could count on Mickey Mouse's hand the times that Leeds have ever won at Oldham but, incredibly, one time when we were defeated at Oldham we actually 'won'.

The 1986/87 season saw the first play-off system for promotion and relegation, leading to the two-legged semi-final against Oldham.

United took a slender 1-0 advantage to Boundary Park for the second leg and considering our record there, fans were far from optimistic of progressing further. Predictably Leeds found themselves 2-1 down on aggregate, but then with only seconds left on the clock Keith Edwards stabbed the ball home to clinch victory on the away goals rule.

It had been a long time since Leeds fans celebrated a goal with such ecstasy while Tommy Wright, who had only recently left the club to go to Oldham, had to be consoled as he walked down the tunnel in tears. The result gave us a final against Charlton Athletic, again over two legs.

% % % % %

I've always liked The Valley. It has a friendly, homely feel about it, and I've not witnessed one speck of trouble on any of my travels there so far. Charlton have moved about like cuckoos over the years and have had several different grounds, including sharing Selhurst Park with Crystal Palace towards the late 1980s. This wasn't a particularly happy hunting ground for Leeds and we played there in the play-offs against Charlton in 1987 and although we lost 1-0, we had won 1-0 in the first leg at Elland Road so the tie went to a replay at Birmingham's St Andrew's.

Charlton aren't the best-supported team in the land by any stretch of the imagination but, as thousands of Leeds fans descended on St Andrew's for the replay, I really felt sorry for the small handful of Charlton's followers, maybe 100 in all, engulfed by the mass volume of Whites in the pubs and the area surrounding the ground. That pang of sympathy had disappeared within two hours.

This was the first season of league play-offs in England and the format was different to the one currently in use today. Back in 1987, the bottom three clubs of the First Division (Aston Villa, Manchester City and Leicester City) were relegated automatically and the top two from the Second Division (Derby County and Portsmouth) were promoted automatically.

Then the team who finished fourth from bottom of the First Division (Charlton) had to compete with the three sides who finished behind the top two in the Second Division (Oldham, Ipswich Town and Leeds).

After 90 minutes at St Andrew's the score was still 0-0 and the game went to extra time, but then with five minutes left of the first period, John Sheridan curled in a superb free kick to put Leeds ahead and within touching distance of a division they had not graced for five long years.

Those dreams were shattered in the closing minutes when Charlton inexplicably scored two goals to retain their First Division status. Leeds fans all around us were in floods of tears. It was devastating. I will never forget the look of anguish on the faces of people around me.

As Charlton celebrated in the far corner in front of their small bunch of happy fans, Leeds boss Billy Bremner went to all of his players, who were slumped to the ground and filled with agonising despair, and embraced each and every one of them as though they were his own kin.

Brave Leeds, against all the odds, had come so close to achieving their own unique 'double' of the FA Cup and promotion to the First Division. Then, motivated by Bremner, the Leeds players who were visibly drained and saturated made their way towards the main bulk of fans down the large side of the ground. Shirts, socks, even shorts were launched into the appreciating crowd. Some players, including Neil Aspin, were left wearing only their jock straps and little else.

Then for fully 20 minutes, with Charlton and their fans long since gone, 16,000 fans on the terracing and maybe 20 staff and players on the pitch bonded like I had never seen before. These kinds of scenes will be treasured by everyone who was there and were only repeated years later one evening in Rome but that's another story for later.

It was Peter Shirtliff who scored both of Charlton's goals. He had not scored once throughout the entire season but, with just seven minutes left of extra time in this play-off final replay he popped up with two.

17

Paying Tribute To The Don

IT was sunny when we travelled to Barnsley on the opening day of the 1987/88 season. It was baking hot in the sunshine and as we crammed together on the open mound watching Leeds play out a 1-1 draw thanks to Bob Taylor we were at the mercy of the burning sun, which never changed position for the whole 90 minutes. As a result of this, Leeds fans had a precise line down the centre of their faces. One half was untouched by the rays but the side nearer the sun was a deep, throbbing pink. As supporters mingled that evening back home with jester-like faces, the conversation started something like, 'Been to Barnsley this afternoon then?'

I remember thinking that if someone's wife had been 'done in' at home during the afternoon, the husband would have a concrete alibi if he had been at Oakwell. The police would have simply looked at his face and ruled him out of their investigation.

In early October we travelled to York City for a League Cup tie. I have watched Leeds play at Bootham Crescent on numerous occasions down the years but this match was the only time we have played a competitive fixture there.

The amazing John Sheridan grabbed a goal in each half, followed by a header from Taylor and a tap-in from Peter Mumby, who only played for Leeds eight times. This was his only goal for the club.

Penned in to three small pens behind the goal, Leeds fans chanted to their colleagues congregated in the side stand, 'Leeds fans, Leeds fans give us a song! Leeds fans, give us a song!' To which the 'side-standers' responded with, 'Leeds fans where are you?' It was all quite funny. It even forced a smile on some of the York fans, despite their team getting hammered 4-0.

Later that month, around 7.30am on a cold but sunny Sunday, our coach had just pulled into Leeds city centre after a long journey back from Plymouth. We have often arrived back from Plymouth at this time from an evening fixture at Home Park, but this had been a Saturday afternoon game – and what a match it had been too. Taylor had scored for Leeds and Ian Snodin had grabbed another two. Unfortunately Plymouth had scored six.

The reason we had been late in getting back to Leeds was probably in protest at having to chew up 516 miles. Our coach had broken down. Luckily it was right outside a country pub about 150 miles north of Devon. Our trusty coach had been coughing and spluttering since we left Home Park but had bravely soldiered on, until now.

It was near to closing time and I went into the pub with the driver to use the telephone to ring for help. There were only three people in the pub and I asked the landlord if we were OK for a quick drink. 'How many are there of you?' asked the landlord. 'Well, it's a minibus-ful,' I answered. 'If you behave well enough, you'll be OK for a drink,' he said. So while the driver was on the phone I went back out to our 74-seater double-decker coach and beckoned them all in. Initially, I steered clear of the landlord for the first 20 minutes, but once he realised we weren't such a bad bunch, and more importantly, saw his till ringing away merrily, he was more than delighted.

Four hours later with our coach fully repaired and us fully replenished, we all climbed back on board. As we left the pub with the landlord grinning like a Cheshire cat, the three locals who had been in there when we arrived, were still at the bar, albeit asleep, still holding their pint glasses.

Our final appearance at Elm Park, Reading, just before Christmas in 1987 yielded a treasured 1-0 victory thanks to a conversion from the spot by the ever-reliable John Sheridan. Reading then left us for pastures beneath as they crashed into the old Third Division, and by the time we travelled back to Berkshire in 2004 they had moved to their new Madejski Stadium and we had been relegated from the Premier League so we met them in what was by then the Championship – oh happy days. After yo-yoing up and down the divisions, we managed to pin Reading down to a few league fixtures over recent years but as yet Leeds have still to notch up their first win at the Madejski.

Calgary in Canada was the host of the 1988 Winter Olympics with the summer tournament taking place in Seoul, South Korea. Elsewhere in the sporting world of 1988, Ayrton Senna became

Formula One world champion and Sweden dominated tennis with Stefan Edberg winning Wimbledon and his compatriot Mats Wilander stealing the show by claiming the Australian, French and US titles. Australia defeated New Zealand to win the Rugby League World Cup while Holland won football's European Championship by beating Russia in the final.

The Liberal Democrats were formed in 1988, as were Al-Qaeda by Osama Bin Laden. The Iran/Iraq war finally ended with around one million people losing their lives and in music, Celine Dion won the Eurovision Song Contest for Switzerland while a huge concert at Wembley Stadium took place to celebrate the 70th birthday of imprisoned ANC leader Nelson Mandela.

Back in the world of Leeds United, as police forces go, the West Midlands Police Force (WMPF) is pretty well down the table as far as our fans are concerned – as far as football fans in general are concerned actually.

On a 1986 visit to West Bromwich Albion's home, The Hawthorns, just under half of the supporters on our coach were arrested by heavy-handed police as we walked to the ground from the coach park.

'Heavy-handed' was the phrase used by several witnesses, called to give evidence in subsequent court hearings. Our 'crime' had been to sing Leeds songs while walking up the road – nothing more, nothing less.

My own brush with the WMPF came two years later on a cold January 1988 afternoon at The Hawthorns. Leeds were winning quite easily with goals coming from John Sheridan and Gary Williams before the referee blew for half-time. The second half continued in a similar fashion and it wasn't long before John Pearson made it 3-0.

As we celebrated the goal, I became aware that I was being watched by two policemen, and then suddenly I was being marched down the steps of the stand and around the pitch. As I arrived at the far corner flag in the grip of my two officers, Sheridan paused from taking a corner and winked at me.

I had got to know 'Shez' quite well. He liked the odd drink and he had attended many supporters' functions – but my escort didn't appreciate that and I was put in handcuffs and hauled the final few yards and out of sight of the crowd. I missed a late fourth goal by Leeds as well as a consolation from West Brom's Andy Gray.

My day in court duly arrived and I walked into Smethwick Magistrates' Court with my two witnesses, Ray and Dave. Both were wearing ill-fitting brown suits from the early 1970s and wearing ties that resembled upside-down kites with knots the size of Frank Bruno's fist. My solicitor didn't exactly fill me with hope either, admitting to me that this was his first football case.

Half an hour later we emerged from the courtroom after the judge had fined me £195 and given me a six-month exclusion order preventing me from attending football matches during that period. Neither of my witnesses were given the opportunity to say anything on my behalf, but I had told my solicitor beforehand that it was likely I would be given a ban and he was to immediately appeal against this, which he did, successfully.

The police had said that I had been gesturing to West Brom fans after their team equalised in the first half and generally being a nuisance. My comments that it was 2-0 to Leeds at half-time and that I wasn't even there when West Brom scored were totally ignored.

Billy Bremner is officially the Greatest Ever Leeds United Player but unfortunately when he became manager of his beloved club, fate conspired against him with agonising defeats in the FA Cup semi-final and the play-off final and early in the following season, 1988/89, he was relieved of his duties by Leeds chairman Leslie Silver following a 1-0 defeat at home to Watford in October.

But there was no bitterness or resentment from Bremner, who simply said, 'Having played for the greatest club in the world, all that's left is to manage the greatest club in the world, and I've done that.'

Howard Wilkinson, a dour yet surprisingly humorous Yorkshire-man, was the next man in the Elland Road hotseat. 'You can take route one back to the top flight if you are prepared to back me with transfer funds,' he told his new directors and Silver.

To their credit, Leeds put up the requested funds and although a serious attempt at promotion was out of the question at that time, the summer of 1989 saw some incredible signings including Gordon Strachan, an absolute steal from manchester united for just £300,000, and so-called bad boy Vinnie Jones from Wimbledon. The newly proclaimed 'Sergeant Wilko' had signalled Leeds United's intent to the rest of the league.

Those transfers all came in a year of events that included George H.W. Bush succeeding Ronald Reagan as the 41st President of the USA, German tennis ace Boris Becker winning his third and final Wimbledon championship and claiming the US Open as well, and the Hillsborough disaster resulting in the deaths of 96 Liverpool fans at their FA Cup semi-final against Nottingham Forest.

Indiana Jones and the Last Crusade was the highest-grossing film at the box office. Del Boy fell through a bar in a classic episode of *Only Fools and Horses* – shown for the first time and repeated countless times for years to come. Arsenal won the First Division title in dramatic circumstances at Anfield. With the score at 1-0 to Liverpool the Merseyside outfit would have been champions but with seconds remaining Michael Thomas scored for the Gunners, handing the crown to the Londoners.

Leeds's 1988/89 season ended at Gay Meadow on 13 May and while we were leaving sleepy Shropshire following a 3-3 draw with Shrewsbury Town, no one could have predicted the mayhem that was to follow as our coach headed north to Stafford and a few welcome pints.

The Staffordshire police immediately rounded us up and told us that Wolves fans were on their way home from their game at Preston North End and the force didn't want any trouble, so we had to move on.

It was getting dark as we pulled into a small town called Alsager in Cheshire, and at around 10pm as a few of us sat playing dominoes in a pub, all hell broke loose outside. Macclesfield Town fans, who had been to Wembley to see their side lose to Telford in the FA Trophy Final, clashed with some of our lads in another pub further down the road and the next thing we knew we were embroiled in the biggest brawl I've ever seen. It lasted easily for over half an hour (some reports say longer) with residents fleeing for cover. The first police car on the scene unbelievably locked its doors and the four officers wouldn't get out until reinforcements arrived.

The result of the ensuing carnage was a fan from each side in a coma, eight in hospital, including two policemen, and our entire coach, including the driver, being arrested and locked up. We were released the following day at 10.30pm, over 24 hours after the incident had begun. In hindsight we probably would have been better staying in Shrewsbury for the evening.

%. %. %. %. %.

A tribute to Don Revie
10 July 1927–26 May 1989

Howard Wilkinson had breathed new life into Leeds since the moment he took over in 1988 but one man actually brought Leeds United Football Club *to* life – Don Revie.

In 1961 Revie stepped up to be player-manager of Leeds United and it wasn't long after that he hung up his boots for good. He had been good in those boots too. As a player he won the FA Cup, he was Footballer of the Year in 1955, he played a starring role in the 1950s 'Revie Plan' and he played six times for England.

But it was when he donned his manager's tracksuit that we began to see the real greatness of Don Revie. He surrounded himself with his own hand-picked backroom staff and using unknown youngsters at the club, he nurtured and moulded a tough fighting unit and brought in Scottish veteran midfielder Bobby Collins from Everton to add much-needed experience and guidance for these younger players. To this day many older Everton fans still see letting Collins go as one their club's biggest mistakes, while many older Leeds fans see it as one of Revie's greatest decisions.

A young Jack Charlton was by his own admission 'a one-man awkward squad' and had great difficulty in conforming to any sort of rules. He had been at the club since the early 1950s, but Revie gradually turned Charlton into one of the finest centre-halves in the world. Charlton played 773 games for Leeds and never kicked a ball for any other club, while he also won 35 caps and the World Cup with England.

Charlton said of Revie, 'I don't care about public acclaim or perception of Revie. His achievements on the pitch spoke for themselves. He was terrific. I owe everything to the man.'

Meanwhile those unknown youngsters such as Gary Sprake, Paul Reaney, Norman Hunter, Paul Madeley, Billy Bremner and Peter Lorimer to name but a few were fast becoming household names and Leeds were also becoming a much more attractive footballing side to watch.

An extremely gifted footballer in the form of Johnny Giles was added in 1963 and, by 1964, Leeds were promoted to the old First Division. It is well documented how agonisingly close Revie's young side came to honours in those early years, but between 1968 and 1974 the team, now with the added wizardry of winger Eddie Gray and the firepower of Allan Clarke and Mick Jones, won six major trophies.

During that time, Revie was voted Manager of the Year for 1969, 1970 and 1972. As well as appearing on TV's *This Is Your Life* he was also awarded the OBE. Revie left Elland Road for the England job in 1974 and it was to be another 16 years before Leeds lifted their next piece of silverware, the Second Division championship with Howard Wilkinson.

Revie had his detractors (he still has) but, over the years, these people have had far too much coverage, and most of it jealous drivel for me and millions of like-minded people. If anybody at any club other than Leeds had achieved anywhere near what Revie did in those years they would have been given a knighthood almost immediately.

He was a great family man and he channelled this commitment to Leeds United. Again it is well documented how he looked upon everyone at Elland Road as part of his family. From the laundry staff, the groundstaff, the coach driver Jim Lister, the players' wives and girlfriends and of course his players and backroom staff, everyone was equal in the eyes of Revie.

His daughter Kim said of her dad, 'He was someone who inspired love, loyalty and devotion in all those that really knew him. He had a gift for making you feel you could achieve anything, overcome any odds. A few of his favourite sayings seemed to reflect his attitude to daily life. Common sense and the courage to apply it and from the "Keep Fighting" sign he had above the Leeds dressing room.

'The media perception of him bore no resemblance to the dad I knew and loved so much – honest, compassionate, charismatic, funny, generous to a fault and always, always caring, with an extraordinary ability to make even casual acquaintances feel part of his extended family and in some definable way, protected by his warmth and strength.

'He believed in manners and discipline and could be strict for sure, but always fair. Dad was a great leveller of people and situations. No matter what role a person played, who they were, or where they came from, they were no more or less important to him. Everyone counted and everyone mattered. He cut through pretension without even being aware he was doing it. He was always himself in any and every situation.'

Lord Harewood was the president of the Football Association from 1963 to 1972. He was the first cousin to Her Majesty Queen Elizabeth II, the first grandchild of King George V and Queen Mary and the eldest nephew of King George VI. The Queen made him a Knight Commander of the Order of the British Empire (KBE) in 1986 and he was appointed an honorary Member of the Order of Australia in 2010. He was also the president of Leeds United for 50 years.

He told Leeds author David Saffer in an interview shortly before his sad death in July 2011, 'On our travels it was clear that Don Revie had put the club on the world stage. In Sydney once, I recall arriving at our hotel when the porter took our luggage and saw the address label. He dropped everything. "Leeds – Leeds United, the best club in the world," he exclaimed.

'Don's legacy was one of winning. He also treated the team and backroom staff as members of a family. Don looked after them all in a way few managers anywhere could live up to. There is no doubt that Don made Leeds United. They had been a minor affair until he arrived and put his imprint on the club. Under Don, Leeds became a major club and other clubs were frightened of us. Don is undoubtedly the most important person in the history of Leeds United.'

Revie's ever-present sidekick on the Leeds bench was trainer/coach Les Cocker. Les, as well as a host of other duties, was primarily responsible for the superb fitness of Revie's squad and was a key staff member of the England World Cup-winning group of 1966. Les died while taking a training session at Doncaster Rovers, who were managed by Billy Bremner, in 1979. His son Dave remains a big Leeds fan to this day.

We touched earlier on the 'Revie Plan' and author Robert Endeacott once asked Dave Cocker for any little-known Revie facts. 'Don always carried around his payslip from the famous Man City "Revie Final" of 1956 in his wallet,' said Dave, 'forever willing to show it to anyone who asked. I think it was about £20, which included his FA Cup-winning bonus.'

Revie had great affection for the Leeds fans too, although it is true he did at times show frustration at some comments from fans, which he took personally. Leeds were famous for being able to score a goal and then shut up shop to ensure those two points (as it was then) were safe in the Elland Road coffers. You could almost guarantee that the opposition would not equalise once Leeds had scored and then adopted these tactics.

However, some fans didn't like this approach and that disappointed Revie. He told *Yorkshire Evening Post* reporter Phil Brown in 1970, 'What these fans need to understand is that we are playing in some cases, with our cup commitments, twice as many games as other teams and it is vital that we conserve our energy whenever possible while maintaining our league form.'

Above all Revie loved and appreciated the Leeds fans, and much the same as today's group, his players were always out and about in the community on non-matchdays. I remember them coming to my school sometime in the late 1960s.

Almost all of the Leeds players lived in the Leeds area in those days and many within walking distance of my school, Garforth Comprehensive. This particular day, Revie arrived with Gary Sprake and Paul Reaney and they set up some tables for them in the music room. Mr Alwood, the music teacher, sat quietly and proudly at the back of the room as three Leeds legends replaced the recorders, guitars, cymbals and triangles for an hour.

I was sat next to Tony McKenna who wasn't remotely interested in Leeds or football, he had only seen this as an opportunity to miss a lesson but, he became more and more interested as the hour progressed. 'I like this fella,' he said to me, as Revie addressed the small audience. 'What a man.'

Revie talked in great detail of his time at Leeds United both past and present. There are two other thoughts that spring into my mind about that day. One was talking to Revie afterwards and him signing the back of a music song sheet that I had secretly removed from one of the walls minutes earlier and the other thing was that Gary Sprake was wearing a bright red pullover. It's funny how things stick in your mind isn't it?

On 29 May 1989 I attended Revie's funeral at Warriston Crematorium in Edinburgh. It was here that I met his son Duncan for the first time and we have stayed in touch ever since. Revie had developed motor neurone disease in 1987 and his last public appearance at Elland Road had been in April 1988 when he attended a match in his honour. I'll never forget that day. It was heartbreaking to see Revie in his wheelchair, flanked by his beloved Leeds players and led by his right-hand man Billy Bremner. The disease had intensified so much that Revie could hardly speak.

I stood on the Kop with thousands of others and tears streamed down my face as Revie, struggling to hold the microphone, thanked all the players (who had arrived from all over the world) and supporters for coming and said that he would 'see us all again soon'.

They say that 'behind every great man there's a great woman' and that's certainly true of the lovely Elsie Revie. After her husband's death, Elsie retained strong ties with the club, until her own untimely passing in 2005.

In 2010 Jim Cadman, an entrepreneur from Stourbridge, got together with renowned sculptor Graham Ibbeson with an idea to create a long-overdue statue of Revie. Ibbeson, like Revie a Yorkshireman, had created many prominent statues in the past including Les Dawson, Freddie Trueman, Eric Morecambe, Laurel and Hardy, Dickie Bird, William Webb Ellis and Cary Grant. This one of Revie in my opinion is one of his best.

On 6 May 2012, 40 years to the day since Revie's team had won the FA Cup at Wembley against Arsenal, Jim Cadman, a Birmingham

City fan (Leeds had beaten Birmingham in that year's semi-final), addressed thousands of sun-drenched onlookers and special guests as the statue was unveiled on the Lowfields Road, fittingly on the other side of the road from the statue of his 'sergeant' Billy Bremner.

It had taken two years of solid effort from Leeds supporters all over the world to raise the required £90,000 for the statue. The Don Revie Tribute Committee, headed by Cadman, had deliberately avoided funding from huge corporate magnates such as McDonald's and Coca-Cola as well as the club itself. Instead the statue was, as the plaque beneath it declares, bought and paid for entirely by Leeds United supporters.

God bless, Don.

18

An Eventful End
At Bournemouth

VINNIE Jones was an instant hit with the Leeds faithful. But, even though he sat on the bench at Newcastle United for the opening game of the season on 19 August 1989, he was fully clothed and the only kicks he got were returning the ball to his team-mates in a 5-2 defeat.

His little jaunts up and down the touchline kicking the ball back didn't go unnoticed by the travelling Leeds fans and the cries of 'Vinnie, Vinnie, Vinnie, Vinnie' would soon top the Elland Road terrace charts. Vinnie also became a firm favourite with the disabled supporters at Elland Road and when the team came out of the tunnel, he would always devote time to them for chats and photos before rejoining his team-mates for the pre-match warm-up.

He then quickly started a trend in and around Leeds by sporting a skinhead-type crew cut with a distinctive 'V' at the back. Hairdressers were soon inundated by hundreds of Leeds fans of all ages wanting to emulate their new hero, resulting in several youngsters being sent home from school. Vinnie was an undoubted revelation for Leeds United and despite his bad-boy tag, he was a vital part of the team and was booked just a couple of times all season.

Gordon Strachan played in every single game that season and with further additions to the squad in Mel Sterland, Gary Speed, Chris Fairclough and Lee Chapman, Leeds stormed up into the First Division as champions, leaving the rest in their wake.

As Leeds raced to promotion from the Second Division in 1989/90, goalless draws with Port Vale at home (March 1990) and away (September 1989) passed virtually unnoticed. Leeds favourite Neil Aspin had recently left Elland Road in July 1989 to join Port Vale and became an instant success before being awarded a testimonial in 1994 – a match that was graced on the pitch with the presence of Vale fanatic and nifty footballer Robbie Williams.

There is a teeny bit of history between Leeds and Port Vale, which goes back to 1920. United's first game in the Football League was against Port Vale but there's also another little story attached to it. Eight games into the 1919/20 season Leeds City were expelled from the Football League and Port Vale were appointed to take over City's fixtures. Within hours of City's demise, a supporters' group founded Leeds United Football Club.

United lost that first encounter against Port Vale at the Old Recreation Ground in Hanley on 28 August 1920, but fittingly their first victory in the league came just seven days later with a 3-1 victory at Elland Road against the Valiants.

In 1989 we travelled to Stoke in what I think was that awful Full Members Cup. This cup was also called the Simod Cup and the Zenith Data Systems Cup and it was an utter waste of time. It was created by the FA after the Heysel Stadium disaster in 1985 and the subsequent ban on English clubs from European competition. It was meant to be a substitute competition for the top two divisions.

It created little interest from anyone, except for a December night in Stoke. One player who I used to hate with a passion was Stoke's Chris Kamara and he played in the Victoria Ground fixture. With the teams level at 2-2 at full time, the game went to a penalty shoot-out. Kamara had kicked lumps out of the Leeds players throughout the game and the fans were screaming for his blood, and that group included new signing Chris Fairclough, who was sat with the supporters.

We won 5-4 on penalties and months later Kamara turned from villain to hero and signed for Leeds – and we loved him!

Barnsley Football Club are like an annoying little gnat when it comes to Leeds United. No matter how hard you want to knock its head off, it just keeps buzzing around and blowing raspberries at you.

Barnsley habitually live near the bottom of their division but despite not beating anyone else, they nearly always beat us. Even when Leeds were crowned Second Division champions in 1990, the only team to beat us at Elland Road that season was Barnsley in March. This was despite us leading with a Chris Fairclough goal for much of the game.

They did the double over us that season as well, thanks to a 1-0 win in front of their own fans in December 1989, but at least we defeated them at Oakwell in the Full Members Cup. Take that you Tykes!

In 1990, Margaret Thatcher resigned as Conservative leader with John Major taking over, therefore becoming Prime Minister without being elected by the public. England and Arsenal defender Tony Adams was jailed for four months following a drink-drive charge. England bowed out of the World Cup at the semi-final stage, going down to Germany on penalties, and the Germans went on to get revenge on Argentina, who beat them four years previously.

This time it was 1-0 to the Germans in what was quite possibly the most boring final in history. A penalty in the last five minutes settled the issue.

A victory for Leeds at Oxford in March 1990 became part of Howard Wilkinson's crusade towards promotion back to the First Division. Once again Leeds fans were crammed into the open end and down the side as United cruised to a 4-2 win, after being two goals behind.

The TV footage of the game became famous for showing football's first 'Flying Fan'. After Chris Fairclough scores the goal that puts United in front, a Leeds fan dressed in all-white can clearly be seen 'gliding' above the heads of his fellow jubilant Whites before nose-diving and disappearing never to be seen again.

%, %, %, %, %

My first two visits to Bournemouth's Dean Court, both in 1988 (March and September), were pretty uneventful really and both were goalless. But by golly the next trip, on the final day of the 1989/90 season, was red hot in more ways than one!

Leeds sat at the top of the Second Division with Sheffield United and Newcastle United both breathing down our necks. Any of the three could win the league but ultimately it was in our hands. If we won we were up, simple as that. I didn't want to contemplate a draw and all the different scenarios it would throw up.

The game at Bournemouth was on a scorching hot Bank Holiday Monday. We travelled down on Sunday morning and booked into our hotel, The Treetops, situated just off the seafront at Bournemouth.

Leeds had voiced concern to the FA over the fixture being held over the Bank Holiday weekend but the FA didn't share United's concern. We frequented a number of pubs and bars around the town during our first night and soon discovered that there were already quite a number of Leeds fans present. We were told by a lot of the publicans and doormen that all the pubs would be closed on the day of the match due to police orders.

The next morning, after breakfast, we hired a fleet of taxis at the hotel and asked them to take us to a pub that would be open. Within five minutes we were in a pub that had the front doors closed but the back doors were open. When we walked in, there were hundreds of Leeds fans already there. It was the same in the few other pubs we went in.

We arrived at the ground a lot earlier than usual to soak up the atmosphere and it soon became apparent that there were thousands of Leeds fans without tickets. There was a very heavy presence of armed police with shields, helmets and loud dogs. The odd skirmish broke out between supporters and the police but to begin with it was all pretty low-key.

As the kick-off fast approached, tempers became frayed and the feuding became more frequent and much more intense. Running battles occurred between heavily armed police officers and Leeds fans, many wearing only shorts and trainers and sporting huge beer bellies. Eventually police ordered everyone with tickets to go into the ground and all those without to congregate in a large car park close to the ground.

It was estimated that there were easily over 10,000 Leeds fans either inside or outside the ground as the game kicked off. We were in the main stand and most of our supporters were behind the goal to our right. There were, however, large numbers of Whites all around the ground.

When the game kicked off I felt more nervous than I had felt at a match in years. This was it. Shit or bust. We were 90 minutes from the First Division or heartbreak. Leeds settled down quickly and looked confident. This was a good sign. Harry Redknapp was the Bournemouth manager and his son Jamie played for the Cherries, for whom there was a lot at stake too. If they lost and other results were unkind to them, they could have been relegated to the Third Division.

At one stage Sheffield United were leading at Leicester, and Newcastle were losing at Middlesbrough. With our score still at 0-0 that put the Blades in pole position. News then filtered through that they were two up and the nerves were jangling among Leeds fans.

Then Chris Kamara crossed and Lee Chapman met it perfectly to head Leeds in front. Our supporters erupted. I looked out of the back of the stand where I could see the thousands in the car park surrounded by hundreds of police officers and going absolutely mental. I hugged my mate Pete so hard that I almost stopped his circulation. When the final whistle blew and Leeds had won 1-0, United and their hosts exited the Second Division in different directions.

The pubs were definitely closed that night except for a small handful that were only letting in locals. A group of us opted for an Indian restaurant where we ate and drank wine, beer and champagne like never before witnessed. Later, we did blag our way into a small local pub and stayed there for the rest of the evening.

My last recollection of that glorious night was sitting on the edge of a grassy cliff edge with my mate Lunge. We had a large bottle of bubbly each and we chatted for hours about the following season and our visits back to the 'big grounds' after an eight-year absence. All the time our little legs were kicking away as they dangled over the edge. We were like two schoolkids. It was fantastic.

Unfortunately there had been a lot of trouble and I was watching the news bulletins on the TV in our room to see that they were all about Leeds fans running riot and clashing with police. The aftermath was all too evident the next morning as we strolled along the seafront for the last time before heading back up north. Piles of burnt-out deckchairs were still smouldering and dozens of Leeds fans were curled up everywhere, still asleep.

What is not widely known though is that the previous night, vans carrying Bournemouth hooligans armed with baseball bats ambushed unsuspecting Leeds fans making their way back to their hotel drunk and alone.

19

A Question Of Love
Or Fear?

IT was a sunny afternoon in June 1990 and I was stood waiting to be served at the bar at Ripon races when this lad came and stood next to me. He looked at the Leeds United tattoo on my arm and said, 'See you're back with the big boys then pal,' in a broad Scouse accent. I spied his tiny Everton badge, but pretended I hadn't seen it. 'Who are you mate,' I replied, 'Tranmere?'

I couldn't resist it. Leeds had just been promoted back to the First Division and this must have been this cheeky Scouser's way of welcoming us back. We got chatting and the lad was OK to be fair, but little did we know our teams would meet on the first game of the new season in a little over eight weeks.

It was sunny that day too as Leeds returned to the big time with a bang. The 34,000 fans had no sooner settled in to Goodison Park when Chris Fairclough headed Leeds in front, triggering the long-overdue chant of 'United are back!' from the travelling Whites.

Leeds were two up just before half-time when Gary Speed pounced on a loose ball caused by team-mate Imre Varadi to stab it home in front of the home fans in the Gwladys Street End.

Bizarre scenes then followed during the interval when Everton goalkeeper Neville Southall emerged from the tunnel several minutes before his team-mates and sat at the foot of the post in front of the Leeds fans in the Stanley Park End. Southall was unhappy at Everton and had put in a transfer request just two weeks before this game. The ever-reliable Leeds fans taunted the portly keeper as he indulged in what the media dubbed as his 'sulking session'.

Things got worse for him too during the second half when Speed returned the compliment to Varadi who then put Leeds in a seemingly unassailable 3-0 lead. However a spirited comeback made the score 3-2, but Leeds weathered the storm and actually should have made it 4-2 when Gordon Strachan squandered a late chance but, more importantly, United had signalled their return in style.

*%, *%, *%, *%, *%*

Although not widely recognised, Luton Town have had their fair share of hooligans. The MIGs (Men In Gear) were formed when their predecessors, the BOLTs (Boys Of Luton Town), found themselves otherwise detained as guests of Elizabeth Regina and unable to embark on further aggro. The MIGs had a pretty fearsome reputation, at least locally, taking on Millwall, Cardiff and even the local Hells Angels.

But the reason I'm talking about hooligans is that because of hooliganism Leeds fans were banned once again, this time from Luton Town, despite not even ever hearing of or indeed seeing the MIGs.

Having said that, it wasn't just Leeds fans who were banned from Kenilworth Road, it was all away fans, and this was because of an incident in March 1985. It was then that Millwall supporters wreaked havoc on Kenilworth Road, smashing 700 seats, invading the pitch and launching missiles at the opposition. Margaret Thatcher, along with the Sports Minister Colin Moynihan, who was widely regarded as a puppet to Thatcher, sought to put an end to the violence and in an unprecedented move tried to get all clubs to ban away fans.

This, not surprisingly, fell on deaf ears everywhere apart from Luton, who were the only club to support Thatcher but, interestingly, in doing so they were denied inclusion in the League Cup.

As things turned out, we never played Luton during their ban on away fans and at the start of 1990/91 they lifted that sanction. Personally however, I still had to attend the 1-0 defeat at Kenilworth Road that season behind enemy lines.

You see, after a misunderstanding at a game at Chelsea and a subsequent court appearance in west London, I had my membership temporarily suspended by Leeds United and was asked not to watch Leeds until things could be cleared up. So that's how I ended up in the Oak Stand down the side with my mate Billy Burton who had got me tickets via a London address.

I'm glad to say that shortly afterwards and following another court appearance, this time at Knightsbridge Crown Court, I was acquitted of all charges, which meant that I could now grow my hair back, grow my beard again and stop wearing a hat and glasses.

For all the trouble Leeds fans did find themselves involved in, however, they showcased their positive side following the tragic death of York City player David Longhurst due to a heart attack suffered during a match in September 1990 against Lincoln City.

The following year a stand at Bootham Crescent was rebuilt and renamed in honour of Longhurst and Leeds were invited as the opponents for the official opening in October 1991. Our supporters turned out in great numbers to mark the occasion.

In the summer of 1990, Leeds played a friendly at Tranmere Rovers, and being the considerate man I am I whisked my beloved missus Lesley away for a few nights in Liverpool before travelling on through the Birkenhead Tunnel into The Wirral to sample the delights of Tranmere.

I think we won that night, but after the game we travelled back through the tunnel and enjoyed our final night in Liverpool by drinking in one of the many 'Caverns'. The next morning at breakfast, Lesley remarked how much she had enjoyed herself despite it being primarily a football trip. She hadn't been to the game the night before, instead opting to stay in a restaurant we had been in, but she added that she really had enjoyed the few days away.

While she was talking I had the morning paper in my hand and as usual I was removing the crossword page to hand to her when suddenly my eyes were drawn to the fixtures section for that evening. Under the headline 'Central League', which was the reserve league back then, it read, 'Liverpool Res v Leeds United Res – KO 7pm'. I was just about to say, 'You've never been to Anfield have you?' when I decided against it.

Was the reason for me not asking the question down to my love for Lesley, or the fact that if I had have asked, I would have had to sleep with one eye open for some considerable time afterwards? I think the latter was closer to the mark.

Sunderland's chairman Bob Murray announced in 1990 that only 500 away tickets would be made available for Leeds United's game at Roker Park that December. This was a ludicrous decision and resulted in pockets of Leeds fans appearing all over the ground, resulting in the inevitable scuffles that broke out.

Meanwhile the bulk of away supporters were penned in to a corner of the side stand like sardines while the rest of the ground was nowhere near full. It was an insult. The satisfying thing was that

Leeds, thanks to Mel Sterland, came away with all three points and it made for a most enjoyable journey home.

In 1991, the Gulf War took place following Iraq's invasion of Kuwait. An inquest into the Hillsborough disaster recorded a verdict of accidental death in relation to the 96 Liverpool fans who lost their lives in 1989, leaving relatives of the fallen angered and still trying to get justice to this day. Bryan Adams remained at the top of the English charts for 16 weeks with '(Everything I Do) I Do It For You', eventually displaced by U2's 'The Fly'.

Arsenal lost just one match throughout the 1990/91 season to be crowned champions of England while for Leeds, the year would begin with an FA Cup match at Barnsley.

Even when we 'beat' Barnsley at Oakwell in the FA Cup in 1991, it didn't count. Leeds were in the lead going into the closing stages when Barnsley threw everything at the visiting defence in one last desperate attempt to force a draw. The resulting shot was so far off target from the Barnsley forward that his winger jumped up and stopped the ball with both hands from almost hitting the corner flag. He had stopped the ball to save some time, but instead it dropped back into the path of the surprised frontman who immediately latched on to it and fired an unstoppable volley past Leeds keeper John Lukic.

Barnsley mockingly celebrated the goal knowing full well that the referee, George Courtney, would disallow it for an obvious handball but, staggeringly, Courtney gave the goal, sparking unbelievable scenes from both sets of players and fans alike. I can still picture Courtney's face as he was jostled by justifiably irate Leeds players in the tunnel after the game. He was mortified. He clearly hadn't seen the handball (the only person in Oakwell not to) and simply couldn't understand what all the fuss was about. I would have loved to have seen his reaction when he finally saw the replay of the incident on TV.

I don't need to tell you the sort of reception Courtney got in the replay at Elland Road, suffice to say United were in rampant mood and cruised to a 4-0 win. We would then be eliminated in the fourth round by Arsenal after a tie that needed three replays.

In the autumn of 1990, Howard Wilkinson had sadly decided that he saw no further use for Vinnie Jones and the midfielder played just once in 1990/91 before being shipped 30 miles down the M1 to Sheffield United. Even so, and despite playing just over 50 games for the Whites, Vinnie still remains a hero to Leeds fans to this day. These days Vinnie proudly strolls around Beverly Hills wearing his

Leeds United tattoo after his remarkable career took him to the dizzy heights of becoming a Hollywood actor.

Gary McAllister had joined the bandwagon in the summer of 1990 and after missing just one game all through his debut season at Elland Road he helped Leeds to a very creditable fourth place in the final table in what was their first year back in the top division.

Nobody knew it at the time but McAllister would go on to become a great servant of the club, playing nearly 300 games before leaving for Coventry City in 1996.

20

Champions Again

IN the summer of 1991 a few of us had met David Wetherall, who was a great bloke, on the streets of Tokyo. We were there for Leeds's exhibition match with Brazilian club Botafogo. We saw Wetherall at around 4am as he was trying to get in a nightclub with David Batty and Gary Speed. They were refused entry but we saw them later in the Hard Rock Cafe.

Back at home, I have witnessed two memorable Leeds 4-1 victories at Villa Park over the years, both with unbelievably stark consequences.

During the 1981/82 season, goals from Arthur Graham and Terry Connor plus two from Frank Worthington crushed Villa 4-1. Six games later we were relegated from the old First Division.

Ten years on, goals from Rod Wallace and Mel Sterland, plus two from Lee Chapman, once again crushed Villa 4-1. At the end of the season the heartbreak of 1982 would be completely banished.

After a 2-0 win for Leeds at Luton towards the end of 1991, followed by a home victory by the same margin in early 1992, the only contact we had with Luton for the next 13 years was when we stopped at the same off-licence on the outskirts as we headed home after a game in London.

These stops were something that our lot began to look forward to. Our coach would pull up and while the off-licence was doing a brisk trade, others would be in the surrounding chicken shops or the Chinese takeaway before we all took part in a cricket match against the ethnic locals in the nearby church car park.

This did indeed become a regular feature during our stops on the outskirts of Luton, and our hosts got to know our routine and from which Leeds game we would be arriving from. Early on any given Saturday evening they would be waiting with bats, balls and beer-crate wickets.

Unfortunately, probably due to the large alcoholic intake that most of our members had indulged in throughout the day, I can't remember us ever winning a single innings.

The arrival of 1992 gave us a year that would see boxing's world heavyweight champion Mike Tyson receive a six-year prison sentence for the rape of 18-year-old Desiree Washington while over 500 people perished following a massive earthquake in Turkey.

Pakistan beat England to win the Cricket World Cup for the first time, Sweden won the ice hockey world championships in Prague and Denmark shocked the football world by winning the European Championship in Sweden, beating hot favourites Germany 2-0 in the final.

The beginning of 1992 in my world began with a fantastic trip to Yorkshire rivals Sheffield Wednesday.

Our best performance at Hillsborough came in 1992. Leeds were battling it out for the league title throughout a long season and were neck and neck when we travelled to Sheffield to play a vastly improving Wednesday side, who would finish third in the table at the end of the season.

The game, which was televised live, had been eagerly awaited by both sets of fans and TV pundit and self-proclaimed 'Leeds hater' Emlyn Hughes had written in one of that morning's Sunday newspapers, 'I hope Leeds get slaughtered.'

Hughes had been a footballer, of sorts, and he played for the great Liverpool. But he was hated by almost everyone. Not just by opposing teams and fans but by his own team-mates. Just ask renowned Liverpool hardman Tommy Smith.

It was one of the most satisfying matches I have ever been to as Leeds tormented and dazzled their opponents and thrashed them 6-1. Even Wednesday's goal came from a hotly disputed penalty. Gordon Watson dived in the Leeds penalty area and TV footage clearly showed him tripping himself up to earn a penalty, which former Leeds hero John Sheridan, embarrassingly, converted.

The referee had been fooled by Watson's theatrics but Wednesday's manager Trevor Francis hadn't and much to his credit he substituted Watson, whose appearances for the club were limited from that day onwards.

The season continued and so did the title hunt so there was a capacity crowd for our visit to Maine Road in early April 1992.

We were breathing down the necks of manchester united in a race for the championship but they were overwhelming favourites. Our 4-0 defeat that afternoon didn't help our cause but I still believe that that defeat gave Leeds and Howard Wilkinson a massive kick up the arse that they sorely needed for the final push.

※ ※ ※ ※ ※

I think one of the last times we occupied the precarious away end at Sheffield United – the Shoreham End – was quite possibly one of the greatest days of my life.

It was a Sunday lunchtime and Sheffield United fans have never been particularly fond of Leeds, but they had good cause to positively hate us on this fine sunny day in April. As the large, police-escorted entourage of coaches carrying Leeds supporters weaved through the narrow streets leading to Bramall Lane, hundreds of home followers gathered outside their pubs with pints in hand and not even a hint of happiness on their distorted faces. They knew, just as well as us, of the vast importance of this game. If we won and our dear friends manchester united lost at Anfield later that afternoon then we, Leeds United, would be the First Division champions.

The tension was unbearable as Leeds and the Blades fought toe to toe for superiority. The home side were in no mood to gift their neighbours any advantage and drew first blood but Rod Wallace equalised shortly before half-time to send the sides in level. Leeds went in front in the second half through Jon Newsome but our joy was short-lived when Lee Chapman put through his own goal to level the scores once again.

It was that sort of afternoon and with the game heading for a draw, a mix-up in the Blades' defence saw Brian Gayle head over his own goalkeeper to give Leeds a victory and send our fans into unbelievable scenes of rapture. We passed those same pubs on the way out and the sight of those thoroughly dejected home supporters will live with me forever. It was glorious.

Once back in Leeds we settled down in a pub to watch part two of this already crazy day, at Anfield, knowing anything but a victory to the visitors would give Leeds the title. To coincide with Ian Rush putting Liverpool ahead I knocked over a full table of drinks and by the time I had replenished everyone with a huge grin on my face, Mark Walters scored a second goal for Liverpool and Rich jumped up and knocked the fresh round of drinks over.

Any other time this would have resulted in a mass brawl but the circumstances on that glorious April afternoon in 1992 were completely different as Leeds were crowned league champions.

As a result of this glorious outcome:

Our hoodoo at Old Trafford would continue throughout the 1990s and although we gained plenty of draws, we never managed a win. That said, in 1992 both teams were involved in a two-horse race for the league title but throughout that campaign, arrogant manchester united never once acknowledged that there was another 'horse' involved.

History shows us that eventually Leeds became champions with relative ease, winning the title by four points. To this day though, Ferguson and the reds still feel that Leeds didn't win the title – manchester united lost it.

manchester united had not won the league since 1967 and quite frankly that looked set to continue for some years to come. That was until our manager Howard Wilkinson inexplicably turned into a Martian. Wilkinson had transformed Leeds from a struggling Second Division team into league champions in four short years. Now, though, he appeared to lose all will to continue as a member of the human race and pressed the self-destruct button. Everyone was baffled and rumours were rife that he had been abducted and something else placed into his body. Even Mulder and Scully would have been hard-pressed to solve this.

They say that one man doesn't make a team, but that is precisely what happened when just months after guiding Leeds to their first title since 1974, Wilkinson gave manchester united a lifeline in the form of Frenchman Eric Cantona, and never sought to replace him.

Frank Strandli doesn't count. I remember Wilko saying, 'We don't need Cantona, we've got Frank Strandli,' but you never knew when Wilko was joking and when he wasn't because his face never altered. 'Gave' is the operative word here as Leeds received around £1m for Cantona and never filled the subsequent gap.

The following season, defending champions Leeds avoided relegation by a cat's whisker. And, unfortunately, manchester united never looked back.

Two interesting facts come from this amazing season for Leeds United. Leeds were the last club to be crowned First Division champions before the top flight in England was rebranded as the Premier League, and Howard Wilkinson remains – at the time of writing – the last English manager to win the country's top division.

21

Unsuspecting Lions And Giraffes

W HEN Leeds began their pre-season schedule for the 1992/93 campaign as league champions, Stromsgodset were first on that agenda so it was off on another little jaunt into Drammen.

Geir Jensen had invited Lesley and I to stay with him at his house high up in those hills. What he had neglected to say was that he lived with his elderly parents and his brother who was out of town for a week. This of course wasn't a problem, but during our stay I saw another side of Geir that I hadn't witnessed before.

Like the rest of us, Geir likes the odd drop of alcohol and he tends to get rather loud and boisterous. Never violent but over-exuberant, shall we say. While we are happily quaffing large amounts of beer he likes nothing better than chinking your glass with his and shouting, 'Yorkshire and justice!' He has gone through this routine for many years and we still have no idea what he is on about.

He has an impressive collection of Joshua Tetley's memorabilia, most of which was provided by Lesley during her near 40 years of working at the world-famous Leeds brewery – sadly no longer with us thanks to the Danish company Carlsberg.

I was once out with Geir and a few of my mates in Oslo when we passed a bar called Churchill's. Winston is a hero of mine so, naturally, I wanted to go in and have a pint, but Geir was reluctant. 'It's crap in there,' were his exact words. But I had to insist, and in we walked.

As I approached the bar, the landlord, a larger-than-life Cockney, said, 'Sorry lads, I can't serve you.' I explained that we were with him, 'That Norwegian over there,' and as I turned round to point to Geir, who had turned his back so as not to be seen, the landlord said, 'It's him I aint facking serving!'

It transpired that Geir had been a bit 'boisterous' a few nights previously in this very bar and he had been asked to leave. That was the reason Geir didn't want to go in. The landlord agreed to give us a pint, except for Geir, who sat there like a naughty schoolboy.

It's a perfect set-up for Geir in his wooden home. His parents live downstairs and he and his brother live upstairs. His lovely parents can't speak a word of English but they made us breakfast every morning, which we sat and ate in their kitchen. But Geir was always very quiet at home and one day as I walked down the hall with no shirt on after getting washed and brushing my teeth, he quickly stressed to me that I must put a shirt on while we were in a communal part of the home. Geir has stayed many times at our house and Lesley remarked, as we sat in their living room, that she didn't know he could be that quiet and rather civilised. 'Neither did I,' I replied.

Geir was so drunk on one occasion when he stayed with me that I convinced him that he had eaten one of my dog's legs! Cybil only had three legs and when we arrived home one evening after pushing the Viking longboat out a tad too far, I cooked us both a giant turkey leg each. A couple of hours after our midnight feast and a few more beers I had him believing that he had just gorged himself on one of Cybil's legs.

The walls in the living room in Geir's part of the house were covered in English nostalgia. Almost every Scandinavian I have ever met loves the English and British way of life. Silk scarves from the 1970s were all over the walls; 'Mud' and 'Slade' and even a light blue one with 'Showaddywaddy' emblazoned across it. There was also an original framed newspaper announcing, 'John Lennon Shot Dead'. Geir is certainly a top Leeds fan and a great character.

Another Geir I have known for many years is Geir Magne Fjellseth, who is another devoted Leeds fan and avid Status Quo fanatic. He has been to see Quo many times. Making a trio of Geirs is Geir Wang.

Don't get me started on the Runes as there are Rune Roaslvig, Rune Radfal, Rune Kristian Monsen, Rune Reitan – the list is endless.

Svend Anders Karlsen-Moum and Erik Sveen are regular Norwegian visitors to these shores but some Norwegians go a step further and move lock, stock and barrel to these shores. Kjell Skyerven has been residing here for many years while last year, frustrated at not being able to attend as many Leeds games as he would like to, Cato Visdal Mikalsen left Norway and now lives deep in the heart of Leeds.

And many Norwegian footballers are Leeds fans too. Eirik Bakke, Alfie Haaland and Gunnar Halle all played for Leeds. Tore Pedersen played for Wimbledon and Blackburn Rovers in the Premier League before moving to Eintracht Frankfurt in Germany and although he didn't join the Whites, he sports an excellent Leeds United tattoo on his arm. He was even once told off by his fellow Blackburn defenders when he was caught secretly celebrating a Leeds goal from Gary McAllister – against Blackburn!

May the Viking invasion of Leeds continue but, I still don't like them killing those poor whales for 'scientific research'.

※ ※ ※ ※ ※

As league champions, Leeds United travelled to Wembley to play FA Cup winners Liverpool in the 1992 Charity Shield as a curtain-raiser to the new season. We used to frequent Wormwood Scrubs prison quite a lot in those days. We still do. Purely from a visitors' prospective of course.

Among the prison warders there is a large contingent of Leeds fans and we would readily accept their invitation to join them at their club whenever we were in the area. This trip to Wembley was such an occasion. It was always a laugh passing through the guarded gates and past the famous Wormwood Twin Towers and we would be hurried along by the guards as we stopped to have photos taken of us and our flags draped over the gates with the towers in the background.

We would then make our way to their club, tucked away down the side of the main building, where a pint of John Smith's would be around £1 and a pint of lager not much more. Once we were suitably refreshed, around a dozen prison officers joined us as we boarded our Wembley-bound coach, many of them sporting Leeds tattoos on their forearms.

It was a gloriously sunny day inside Wembley as thousands of bare-chested fans gave their tonsils a right good airing. In the line-up was a certain Frenchman by the name of Eric Cantona, who enjoyed the day more than most by scoring a hat-trick.

I was told by someone afterwards that it was a great game for neutrals to watch but I wouldn't know about that. I class myself as a Leeds fan, not necessarily a football fan. I want to see Leeds win and I'm not there to be entertained but, on this particular day, I experienced both.

It all started with the first of Cantona's goals after about half an hour but that was quickly cancelled out by Ian Rush. Classy left-back Tony Dorigo restored United's lead just before half-time and we then retired to the bars downstairs. As it was a nice day and we were winning, no one batted an eye lid that the beer was almost three times dearer than what we had been paying back at the club.

Dean Saunders drew Liverpool level once again, before Cantona added another two to set Leeds up for victory with three minutes left. However, Gordon Strachan then entered the fray as a late substitute and with his first touch dragged the ball over his own line to give the scoreline a much more balanced look than the game itself had actually been.

That was no matter to the Leeds fans as a huge snake of them doing the conga made its way down the back steps and out into the streets. We found ourselves upstairs in a private club not far from Wembley itself. I've absolutely no idea how we got in, but we were still in there at 10pm. We then had a nightcap in our club at Wormwood before retiring to our hotel bar a few miles away.

Leeds finally returned to continental football with a European Cup match at Stuttgart. It had been 13 long years since United last competed in Europe and it was here that I renewed my acquaintance with general manager Alan Roberts.

Leeds had annoyed their fans by bringing in a scheme which meant that tickets could only be purchased through the club. Normally that would have created no problem but Leeds were charging more than face value for the tickets. Fans unsurprisingly objected.

Even the organiser of the group I regularly travel with, who usually stuck rigidly to club rules and regulations imposed whenever we ventured abroad, chose to organise his tickets independently. The Leeds fans had been warned that anyone who arrived with tickets not purchased from the club would not be allowed in the ground. Alan warned of 'stringent checks at the turnstiles'.

We travelled regularly to Germany for pre-season friendlies and I was always impressed with how clean, friendly and efficient things were; Stuttgart, Dusseldorf, Leverkusen, Marburg, Koln, Bremen, Hannover, Hamburg, Frankfurt, Freiburg and many more, were all spotless, and of course German beer is second to none.

Our hotel in Stuttgart in 1992 was no different from the high standards we were used to and we quickly ditched our bags and found the hotel bar. Word was spreading that thousands of Leeds fans were expected to arrive without 'official' tickets. In fact every supporter we saw had purchased their tickets from a source other than the Elland Road ticket office. It was also rife on the streets and in the bars that people without tickets direct from Leeds wouldn't get in.

Big Mick had suggested that we arrive at the ground early in case there were any problems getting in, so we set up camp at a bar within walking distance from the stadium and enjoyed a few more beers in the glorious sunshine. Leeds fans were everywhere and apart from a few minor scuffles with Germans, overall things were pretty calm.

It did however get a little more heated as fans met Alan Roberts outside the ground. He was addressing Whites from within the stadium through a wire fence and repeating the threats that those without officially-sourced tickets wouldn't get in. There were loud and angry protests with many of the visitors waving 'German' tickets at Alan.

The noise alerted the police who apparently until now were not aware of the self-imposed ticket policy. As Alan retreated back to the confines of the stadium, a man with a large dark green jacket on, who we rightly assumed to be a ground steward, told the gathering crowd that there would be no trouble gaining admission and he and his colleagues set about directing us to the relevant turnstiles.

'Welcome Leeds!' this man kept saying as he ushered people around. Once inside the ground there was the ridiculous situation of some supporters being separated by a large fence from others, and notably the smaller set of fans were those who had bought tickets from the club.

Eric Cantona had played only a very minor role when Leeds won the league but it was hoped that he would be much more involved this season and become a major part of the Leeds set-up. Unfortunately it was here in Stuttgart that the Leeds fans began to see Cantona for what he was really worth to the club. He was a passenger for most of the game against the German champions and tended to disappear for lengthy spells throughout the 90 minutes. That contributed, it has to be said, to the 3-0 defeat.

The second leg at Elland Road a fortnight later seemed a formality for the Germans, especially when they equalised an early Gary Speed goal to make it 1-1 on the night and 4-1 on aggregate. Then minutes later, Leeds scored with a Gary McAllister penalty following a series of onslaughts on the German defence, and goals from Cantona and Lee Chapman levelled the tie at 4-4 with ten minutes remaining.

The noise at Elland Road was incredible as Leeds surged forward. Desperately Stuttgart replaced an attacker and midfielder with two defenders as they sought to keep a rampant United at bay. A small knot of Stuttgart fans cheered along with their mightily relieved team when the final whistle went with the tie still at 4-4, meaning that Stuttgart went through on the away goals rule.

But the Leeds team received an ovation from an appreciative Elland Road crowd who, although not achieving the deserved passage into the next round, knew that their heroes had given their all on a memorable night.

It was the following evening when I received a telephone call from John Martin, who asked if I was watching the TV. I switched it on immediately and news was breaking on BBC's *Look North* programme that Leeds may be awarded the tie against Stuttgart. I knelt down in front of the TV and turned up the volume. 'Leeds United may, and we stress the word may, still be in the European Cup after dramatic news emerged from Germany this afternoon,' said announcer Harry Gration.

It transpired that German fans who supported a rival German team to Stuttgart had brought it to the attention of UEFA that Stuttgart had fielded four foreign players at Elland Road. In 1992 only three foreigners were allowed in a team and these fans who watched the game live on German TV pointed out that when Stuttgart brought on those two defenders at Leeds, one of them was Swiss international Adrian Knup which meant they then had four foreigners on the field, contrary to UEFA rules.

News continued to filter through as *Look North* went out live and by the following morning UEFA had declared the game at Elland Road null and void and after awarding Leeds a 3-0 victory, ordered the teams to play off in Barcelona.

The following week, after hasty travel arrangements by Big Mick, we jetted off towards the Spanish sun and were soon quenching our dry throats with gallons of San Miguel and sangria on Las Ramblas.

I've seen Leeds play four times at the Nou Camp, but this was by far the weirdest occasion. The Nou Camp, or Camp Nou as it is officially called in Spanish, is, after Elland Road, by far and away the best stadium I've ever been to. Seemingly unaltered since I first went there in 1971, it has a capacity of 100,000 and its record attendance is 120,000, but on a balmy evening in early October 1992 the attendance for this Leeds v Stuttgart showdown was just a few hundred over 7,000.

It was mostly Leeds fans in attendance, with very few neutrals, and the few coaches carrying the Stuttgart fans were actually driven into the ground and parked behind the goal. It was eerie seeing thousands and thousands of empty seats but the match itself was incredibly tense and the score at the interval was 1-1. Then Carl Shutt made us very happy indeed when he fired Leeds in front and subsequently into the next round to face Glasgow Rangers. There were one or two sore heads next morning at breakfast but no one who was there will ever forget that game.

I had first been to Ibrox back in 1968 for an Inter-Cities Fairs Cup tie and by the time of my return in October 1992, new stands now dominated the ground, although noticeably they were not joined together but instead had large corner gaps separating each one.

This particular journey was the small matter of a tie with Rangers in the European Cup for which away fans had been banned from both games to apparently avoid crowd trouble.

The day before the first leg at Ibrox, I arrived in Edinburgh with a mate of mine, Billy Burton. We had arranged to get tickets for the game via a newspaper reporter friend and they came from a Rangers director on the proviso that we remained quiet at all times, so on arrival at the ground we instantly became incognito.

Our transaction was sorted that evening in a bar on Rose Street and it became obvious that Leeds fans were everywhere keeping a low profile – sort of. Apparently, that morning, Edinburgh Zoo had been like a scene in a Russian spy film with large brown envelopes containing match tickets being swapped right under the noses of unsuspecting lions and giraffes and suchlike.

Supporters of both clubs had secretly agreed, in large numbers, to exchange tickets for each of the games. With our priceless tickets in our hands we had a cracking night around Edinburgh including a bar that had a female stripper plying her trade in an iron cage as the punters drank, chatted and stared.

The next morning we drove to Glasgow and booked in to the Copland Hotel which is situated directly behind the Copland Road Stand, the home end at Ibrox, then went into the city centre to sample the local fayre.

Within the first two minutes of the game Gary McAllister scored for Leeds. Everyone in the ground rose to their feet – but for different reasons. Me and Billy were clutching the air and saying 'yes!' through gritted teeth. All around us they were calling for blood.

Once everyone settled down, Leeds fans were getting ejected all over the ground. Over in the stand to our right about 50 were escorted out by police and dozens more were being led away right in front of us. It was like something out of a Masonic convention with everyone winking at each other and 'secret hugs' going on all over the place.

Meanwhile, Billy and I remained 'incognito'. But, then we, or should I say, 'I', gave the game away. Actually it wasn't me who gave the game away – it was our goalkeeper John Lukic.

Leeds were looking comfortable and Gordon Strachan had already had a goal disallowed for offside that would have made it 2-0. To make things interesting, at the other end of the pitch, Lukic decided to make a game of it and minutes before half-time he promptly punched the ball into his own goal. This was where I came in.

'Lukic! You useless bastard!' I shouted as I rose to my feet. It's hard to explain, but this was a split second before the Rangers fans in our end had realised that they had scored. Billy, bless him, quickly pulled me down into my seat.

The home supporters then began to celebrate and we became lost in the ensuing euphoria. Once order was restored, some Rangers fans made it clear to Billy and I that they knew we were from Leeds but they treated us OK.

As the night wore on Ally McCoist made it 2-1 to Rangers and after the game we made our way to the hotel bar where we watched the match again. I can't remember the reason why, but the game wasn't allowed to be shown live on Scottish television. Instead it was shown in full an hour after the final whistle. TV footage clearly showed that Strachan's 'offside' goal was onside by a country mile and that would certainly have made a difference as far as Leeds were concerned, but it wasn't to be our night.

The next morning at breakfast we noticed a couple wearing Rangers colours on the next table. 'Morning,' said Billy. 'Morning,' came the reply, in a Yorkshire accent. I couldn't resist. 'Where you from?' I asked. I nearly choked on my square Scottish sausage when the lad replied, 'Leeds, Meanwood.' Billy beat me to it, 'What the fuck are you doing supporting these?' 'Oh, I used to have a season ticket at Elland Road, but I came up here to see a game and fell in love with 'em. Great atmosphere innit?' he said, as if to condone what he had done. 'By the way, this is my mam.' This bloke was about 40 years old and he had brought his mother to a hotel in Glasgow. What goes on at Ibrox stays at Ibrox I suppose.

As we headed back home, the general consensus was that 2-1 would not be enough for Rangers and Leeds were expected to win the tie. Unfortunately another inept display from Lukic and an even worse performance from Eric Cantona contributed to Rangers winning the return by the same scoreline – 2-1 – and going through 4-2 on aggregate.

That meant Leeds's European Cup campaign would not continue into 1993, a year that saw Czechoslovakia split into two to become the Czech Republic and Slovakia, ITV's GMTV replace TV-am and tennis star Monica Seles get stabbed in the back in a tournament in Hamburg by an obsessive Steffi Graff fan.

In Japan, 385 people were killed following a huge earthquake. Less than a month later an earthquake off the coast of Japan triggered a tsunami, killing a further 202.

England footballers Ross Barkley and Alex Oxlade-Chamberlain were both born in 1993 and sadly, heading in the other direction, World Cup-winning captain Bobby Moore passed away.

The rest of Leeds's season was not much to write home about as the champions failed to mount a serious defence of their crown and ultimately finished 17th, just two points outside the relegation zone, but for the club's youngsters the campaign ended with a simply glorious outcome.

The youth team reached the final of the FA Youth Cup and picked up an oh-so-sweet victory over two legs against a manchester united squad that contained the likes of David Beckham, Gary Neville, Nicky Butt and Paul Scholes.

The first leg was played at Old Trafford and to emphasise the importance placed on this competition by Ferguson, the crowd was 30,562 – 6,000 of those had travelled from Leeds. The Whites won the first leg 2-0 against the favourites for the tournament – thanks to goals from Jamie Forrester and Noel Whelan – and set up a tasty return at Elland Road the following week.

Much had been said about the attendance which was a record, but for the second leg over 31,000 turned up and I realise this sounds biased, but this was never mentioned in the national press. It hardly received coverage either when Leeds won the final 4-1 on aggregate. Forrester had scored again at Elland Road and Matthew Smithard added the second goal with Scholes scoring from a penalty for the visitors.

As yet another example of the arrogance and expectancy of manchester united, Leeds, as winners of the FA Youth Cup, took part in an exhibition match in Holland against Feyenoord in Eindhoven but when we arrived by ferry to support our youngsters, we were amused to see posters everywhere in town advertising the match.

The posters announced that it was manchester united who would be playing, and not us. These posters had clearly been printed before the final in England. The name Leeds United had been written over manchester's in pen.

The following year saw Lillehammer in Norway hosting the Winter Olympics, in which Great Britain and Northern Ireland competed together and won two bronze medals. Meanwhile, the Channel Tunnel was officially opened. Labour leader John Smith died of a heart attack in London, with Tony Blair taking over as leader. The first UK National Lottery draw also took place.

British tennis star Laura Robson was born in 1994, in Melbourne, Australia. Also entering this world was One Direction's Harry Styles, Olympic diving medallist Tom Daley and Paralympic gold winner Ellie Simmons.

Ayrton Senna was killed after an accident in the San Marino Grand Prix. Nelson Mandela became the first black president of South Africa and Colombian footballer Andres Escobar was shot dead outside his house in retaliation for him scoring an own goal during the 1994 FIFA World Cup. Brazil went on to win the tournament, beating Italy 3-2 on penalties following a goalless draw.

Cups also provided some of the main on-field talking points over the next couple of seasons for Leeds and in the third round of the 1993/94 FA Cup we came up against Crewe Alexandra for the first time in any competition.

The Whites won 3-1 at Elland Road and the game had additional interest to me as my mate and a fellow resident of my village of Kippax, Shaun Smith, was the captain of Crewe.

Shaun spent ten years with Crewe and scored the winning goal in their Second Division Play-Off Final victory against Brentford. In total he played more than 450 times for the club, scoring 39 goals from his left-back position, and was their supporters' Player of the Year in 2001.

Later that same month Leeds went to Blackburn Rovers and David Batty did something that helped me overcome my sadness at his 'passing over to the other side'.

Batty had left his home-town club in October 1993 and crossed the Pennines to join Blackburn under their multimillionaire owner Jack Walker. It was pure sacrilege of course and Leeds fans didn't take it lightly.

Admittedly there was a lot of bad 'politics' going on at Elland Road at the time and Howard Wilkinson, who had already allowed Eric Cantona to go to Old Trafford for relatively little, now allowed

Batty to cross the forbidden border and opted to replace him with quite possibly the worst footballer ever to make it as a professional – Carlton Palmer.

Billy Bremner is easily the most recognised number four in Leeds's entire history but Batty had worn this number with pride and with total acceptance and pure adulation from the Elland Road faithful. Now not only was a man with a head no bigger than a tennis ball wearing number four but even worse, Batty was now wearing a red rose over his heart in a Blackburn Rovers shirt.

I personally found it hard to cope with. I felt like Batty was having an affair. I cannot ever remember a player leaving my club that has had such a profound effect on me as when Batty went to Blackburn.

Sir Matt Busby had died a week or so prior to this fixture and the media in all its forms was bursting at every seam to announce what was undoubtedly a sad loss to football. Busby was a great manager, there is absolutely no denying that but, so too was Don Revie. And these were the foundations of what was to prove an explosive afternoon at Ewood Park in front of millions watching on television and it is still talked about today.

In the wake of Busby's death, the Football Association had asked for a minute's silence to be held at all league matches that weekend. The overwhelming majority adhered to this request. Leeds fans were angry. Why hadn't the FA asked for the same respect when Revie had died five years earlier?

Word was rife among Leeds fans arriving at Ewood Park on that winter afternoon that the name of Don Revie would be sung during the minute's silence and that is precisely what happened.

I had taken a flag with the words 'Don Revie OBE' sprayed on it and this appeared on the front of every single tabloid the following morning with predictable headlines like 'Scum' and 'Animals'. Pictures of Leeds supporters appeared with circles around their head saying, 'Do you know this fan?' I remember going for a Chinese takeaway on the High Street back in Kippax with my flag late on that Sunday night and people saying, 'We've seen that flag on telly this afternoon, you were bang right to do what you did.'

The next day, *The Independent* wrote, 'Supporters of Leeds United sent ripples of shock and distaste through the nation yesterday when they chanted in defiance of the minute's silence being observed for Matt Busby before their match at Blackburn Rovers. Their invasion of this show of respect for a great football manager included, among other things, shouting the name of their own hero Don Revie.

'Similar breaches of etiquette disrupted the solemn occasions at other grounds including Chelsea and Liverpool, but none provoked such a strong reaction. Those responsible for the disturbance at Blackburn have been banned from watching Leeds for the rest of their lives.'

There are three interesting points raised here by the writer of this article, Peter Corrigan. Firstly, he refers to Busby as 'great' but somehow denies the same accolade to Revie (even as I write this, the Microsoft Word spellchecker is telling me to put Revie in lower case). Secondly, Leeds fans didn't shout the name of Don Revie 'among other things', they chanted the name of Don Revie only; and thirdly, not one single supporter was banned over this incident because, quite simply, no one was doing anything against the law.

An evocative website called Life, Leeds United, The Universe and Everything is run by Rob Atkinson and he said of that day, 'The chanting of Don Revie's name at Blackburn was a very necessary stand against the establishment view that Busby was a saint and Don was a sinner. It was a statement of our reverence for Don Revie, against a background of organised and compulsory mourning for someone who was a hero only to those at Old Trafford.

'It was an assertion of the fact that nobody tells us when to show respect, especially when no bugger showed any respect for The Don in life or in death. The FA couldn't even be bothered to send a representative to Don's funeral, the hypocrites. Why the hell is there such disparity, and more to the point, why the hell are we expected to just put up with it and go along with such blatant hypocrisy and double standards? Are we supposed to have no pride?

'The players from any era who were wheeled onto camera to criticise the actions of the Leeds fans at Blackburn have one thing in common. They haven't got a bloody clue what it's like to be a fan. They're players, club employees, and they come and they go, even the best and most loyal of them.

'Not one of them knows what it is to be a fan and continually have the media's favourite bloody football club shoved down your throat, to the exclusion of everything and everyone you care about as Leeds supporters.'

I contacted the club very early the following day to voice my concern at the media hype and hysteria aimed at Leeds fans that was prevalent in all the newspapers, on the front and back pages. I also asked why the club seemed so reluctant to defend the name of Don Revie. To be fair they were under immense pressure from the media to 'act'.

I received assurances from the club and also in writing later from general manager Alan Roberts that the club knew the feelings of many of our supporters. Mr Roberts also wrote, 'I fully endorse your sentiments, but unfortunately at times, this club does seem to show a lack of sincerity with many long-term employees as well as Don Revie.'

Once the dust was allowed to settle after the Ewood incident, the Kop at Elland Road was renamed The Don Revie Stand which brings me back to David Batty. He openly gesticulated at Leeds fans in disgust that day, and others showed their disapproval including Gary Speed and Gordon Strachan, but no one except Whites understood this protest.

I got over my personal loss of Batty that day but I am delighted to say that the Prodigal Son returned to Elland Road in 1998, via Newcastle United, a much better player than the one who had defected in 1994 and I'm also glad to report that I gradually resumed my personal friendship with my former hero.

Finally on this rather tetchy subject, Brian Clough was despised by Leeds fans much more than Busby, but when Clough died, Whites supporters' silent tribute at the following game was impeccable.

I can count on one hand the times I've left a game before the end, but something always happens when I do. This happened against Oxford in the fourth round of the FA Cup in February 1994.

We had drawn 2-2 at the Manor Ground and were expected to beat them in the replay at Elland Road. As usual however, Leeds didn't read the script properly. After going a goal up they found themselves 2-1 down with the game heading rapidly towards the final whistle. To be fair Oxford looked the more likely to score again.

'I'm off for a pint,' I said to my mate. I walked out of the Gelderd End and as I walked past the back of the West Stand there was a huge cheer. Leeds had scored. Hundreds of Leeds fans, me included, raced into the West Stand to watch it again on the big screen. It was 2-2 and now there would be extra time. I knew it would be too late to get a pint now, but that didn't matter – let's beat these twats now.

Seconds before the end of extra time and with the game heading for penalties Oxford scored again and the final whistle blew. I was gutted. No chance of a pint back in Kippax and we had been knocked out of the FA Cup.

The theme of cup ties against lower-division opposition continued the following season when, in September and October of 1994, we faced Mansfield Town over two legs in the second round of the League Cup.

Mansfield did exact some form of revenge 24 years after our FA Cup fifth round victory back in 1970 when they came to Elland Road, still as a Third Division outfit, and went away with a 1-0 win in the first leg.

Leeds couldn't break them down in the return at Field Mill and a 0-0 draw was enough to see Mansfield through. I don't know if my old school pal with the enormous ears was at either of those games but I bet his many teeth were forming the hugest of grins.

The following January an FA Cup tie away to Third Division Walsall would get 1995 under way and later in the year British boxer Frank Bruno became the new WBC heavyweight champion of the world, Pierce Brosnan played James Bond in the 16th 007 film *Goldeneye*, just under 23 million people tuned in to watch Princess Diana give a revealing interview to *Panorama*'s Martin Bashir and the Queen wrote to the Prince and Princess of Wales, urging them to divorce.

Serial killer Fred West hanged himself in custody while awaiting trial. His wife Rosemary West was sentenced to life imprisonment for the murder of ten women, with the judge saying she would never be released. Comedians Larry Grayson and Peter Cook both passed away, as did American actor and singer Dean Martin.

The Walsall tie was taking place around ten years after our previous visit there, but by this time they had moved to a new ground – the Bescot Stadium.

David Wetherall scored late in the game to level the score at 1-1 and take it back to Elland Road. Wetherall was on the scoresheet again in the replay and, along with a hat-trick from Philomen Masinga and one from David White they beat the Saddlers 5-2.

We would go on to beat Oldham Athletic in the fourth round before losing at manchester united in the fifth. We also finished fifth in the Premier League, as we had done in 1993/94, and with changes in the qualifying criteria we entered the UEFA Cup for the following season.

22

The Best Christmas Ever

IT was because of our game at West Ham in August 1995 that our supporters' branch, the Kippax, was banned from the official supporters' club, although on this occasion, it had nothing to do with the Hammers.

It was our first away game of the season and the sun was shining. We had started the new season with a new coach company and a new driver, although the girl in the front seat who had been sent by the company to sell pop and crisps didn't last too long. 'You're not gonna sell much of that on here love,' said Webby, as he made his way to the back of the coach. 'Come back here and have a can of lager.' Poor lass, she just sat quietly reading her book all the way to London and back.

It was the driver, however, who turned out to be the problem. He had absolutely no idea where he was going. Initially, he had difficulty in finding London, and then we arrived at Gillingham's ground and then when we drove past White Hart Lane, the lads grew a little concerned. We eventually got to Upton Park with 20 minutes of the game gone.

As you can imagine, tempers were frayed, but one lad, 'Blockhead' (self-explanatory), took things just a tad too far. I was forced to intervene when I saw that he was sat right behind the driver and had wrapped a bootlace around his neck and was pulling it quite tight.

Other incidents occurred throughout the journey home and just as I had expected, a report from the coach company was sent to the supporters' club. Suffice to say, this, and a culmination of other events, not all entirely our fault it has to be said, resulted in the expulsion of the Kippax Branch. At least we won at West Ham, 2-1, thanks to Tony Yeboah.

In recent years I became friends with many West Ham fans, one of them having moved to Kippax. Alan, known as 'Geezer', and his mates would come and have a pint with us when West Ham visited Elland Road and we would do the same down in London, although the first time we met down there it almost ended up in disaster.

Four of us had arranged to meet Alan and his mates in the Wakefield Arms, which is where the hardcore of Hammers fans have their pre-match drinks. When we got there, Geezer hadn't arrived and as we stood outside discussing our next move we were joined by a dozen or so West Ham fans, all six-foot-plus and all with shaven heads.

We were just seconds from being smashed to a pulp when Geezer arrived. I have never been so thankful to hear a Cockney accent in my life. 'Hallo mate,' he said. 'Been here long, sorry I'm late, come on I'm parched.' With that we went inside and had a few pints, but I can't say it was the most relaxing hour's drinking I've ever had.

Naturally, I've never been keen on France or the French, but I must admit to liking the south of France and when Leeds were paired with Monaco in the first round of the UEFA Cup in September 1995 I couldn't have been happier, even though they are regarded as being French despite being their own principality.

We were based in Nice for our trip, just a very short distance from Monaco and the famous Monte Carlo race circuit, regarded by many experts as the most dangerous in the world. Unfortunately there was no racing while we were there, but just walking along the roads and streets where they do race was enough to at least get a feel of what it must be like. The luxurious homes nestled in the steep hills, and the picturesque skyscrapers overlooking the circuit, are breathtaking.

Of course there are many casinos too and a few of us mixed with the bigwigs for a minute or two! It is slightly expensive in this part of the world but you make the best of it while you're there. Many James Bond films have been made in Monaco and you could instantly see why.

Nice is nice as well, but we had to laugh as we were drinking outside a bar on the seafront and watched as one of the waiters came out every hour and altered the beer prices on the blackboard on the pavement. The cost was going up by the hour and by the time we moved on elsewhere, the price had more than doubled from the first pint we had there in the afternoon.

The Stade Louis II is pretty iconic too and very striking with huge arcs that dominate its appearance. Though it is a very small stadium with a capacity of just 18,500, this is mainly due to four massive columns occupying each corner. There were no turnstiles either, just glass doors to enter through.

Howard Wilkinson had unearthed an absolute gem of a player the previous season and he certainly tore into Monaco on this warm evening. The hosts had absolutely no answer to our goal machine that was Tony Yeboah. He fired home a bullet in the first half and got another two after the break. Poor old Monaco didn't know what had hit them as they trooped off the pitch shell-shocked after a 3-0 defeat.

Afterwards we sought out a couple of back street bars where the price of beer was still quite reasonable for where we were, around £3.50, although it wasn't quite a pint. I ordered a bottle of the house wine, which if I'm honest would have been better poured over my chips. Sorry, pommes frites.

Leeds lost the second leg 1-0 at Elland Road but went through 3-1 on aggregate to set up a second-round tie against Dutch side PSV Eindhoven, which took place in October.

The well-established airline Ryanair has a brilliant distinctive blue and gold livery. Unfortunately its other features leave a lot to be desired. But the company does fly to Holland.

It claims to be an inexpensive airline which is true for the first half-dozen passengers to book, but not so for the rest. It sells sandwiches and snacks coming in at around a million quid each and sells warm beer and wine for much the same.

These days it sells whisky in a bag. For a very reasonable £10 you can purchase your very own teabag-sized polythene sachet of whisky for immediate consumption. For your purchase price you actually receive *two* small bags of whisky. Once purchased, and having lowered your very own free table and acquired your very own free thin plastic cup, it is time to open the first bag of your whisky consignment. But be warned, you will find no perforated line with which to assist you in your quest to consume your newly acquired 'liquid gold'. No problem, just bite off the corner and serve.

But that's easier said than done I'm afraid. The minute you squeeze and pierce the bag between your teeth, your eyes are attacked by a small but powerful squirt of whisky as it is jettisoned from your three-inch square sachet, leaving you to suck the tiny droplets of whisky remaining in your tiny crumpled bit of polythene. Trying to remain undeterred you immediately turn your attention to your second sachet lying there on your free table. But unfortunately because airlines won't let you carry knives, scissors or even a small butane gas blowtorch anymore, the procedure is pretty much the same. The whisky incidentally is called Bullseye, which could explain why it always ends up straight between your eyes instead of down your throat.

I have flown with Ryanair possibly around 50 times, maybe more, and I have yet to encounter a smooth landing. Many of my flights have been in to or out of Ireland and invariably there is a contingent of priests or nuns on board and as we bounce on to the runway it's not unusual to see the men and women of the cloth praying, crossing themselves and looking up to the heavens.

It's amusing too how the airline plays a trumpet tune over their tannoy system each time one of its planes hops, skips and jumps into its destination. As the catchy toe-tapping tune dances around the cabin, passengers can be seen holding each other's hands, often drawing blood, as the plane hurtles down the runway swaying violently from side to side, throwing almost cheekily your crumpled whisky bags to the floor, still with unexplored droplets of whisky smiling at you from within.

Our Ryanair flight to Holland from Leeds had lasted just over an hour, but for all intents and purposes this was a hopeless trip. It was the second round of the UEFA Cup against PSV and we had already lost the first leg 5-3 at Elland Road. And it was Halloween as we landed unceremoniously at Eindhoven airport. At least back then they still had good old-fashioned whisky miniatures with an easy-to-use screw-top.

Like the ticket situation a few years earlier in Stuttgart there were ticket restrictions placed upon Leeds fans but this time it was instigated by the Dutch police. We were left under no illusion that only fans travelling with an official match ticket from Leeds United and arriving on official transport would be allowed into the stadium.

It was a very strict operation and around 500 supporters travelling from Amsterdam were stopped on a train and detained until the game had finished because they had purchased tickets from an unofficial travel operator. Although their tickets were quite valid for the game, they would not be allowed entry because they had not been bought from Leeds United.

I know some Leeds fans, including married couples, who had got tickets via legitimate contacts in Holland but once they arrived at the turnstiles they were turned away as soon as they were identified as being English.

Leeds used to go to Holland quite a lot on pre-season tours, especially in the 1970s. Holland had a fearsome reputation for hooligans and we had experienced this first-hand when we played in Amsterdam in August 1976. Consequently, we were warned to expect much of the same when we played PSV in a pre-season friendly in 1979. Although it was only a friendly there were plenty of fisticuffs over the three days we were there.

The violence seems to me to be purely a club thing as far as Dutch fans are concerned. I used to follow England everywhere in the late 1970s and into the 80s but whenever we played Holland, thousands of bright orange shirts would be everywhere and there was very little trouble. Even now whenever Holland are on the TV, you find yourself having to turn the colour down a bit because of the mass orange blur on the screen.

I remember being in a pub close to Trafalgar Square one evening after we had drawn with Holland 2-2 at Wembley. Ruud Gullit had played an absolute blinder and scored both of Holland's goals, and we drank with dozens of 'tulips' long into the night without so much as a cross word.

On this night in 1995 I sat with about a dozen mates on the top floor of a Chinese restaurant in Eindhoven. It was about three hours before kick-off and as we noshed on large salt and pepper spare ribs, Peking duck and three tons of fried rice, we looked down at the street entertainment as hundreds of Leeds and PSV fans fought a pitched battle while armed police watched on. Inside the ground 'official' Leeds fans certainly gave a good account of themselves vociferously, but it was to no avail as the Whites crumbled to a miserable 3-0 defeat. Once back on the plane we put the 8-3 aggregate loss behind us and ordered a few whiskies, screw-top, 1995 style.

Although Leeds couldn't notch up a league win at Old Trafford during the 1990s, it was a different story at Elland Road as we used to beat manchester united on almost every occasion. One of those victories stands out for me.

It was Christmas 1995. manchester united arrived cock-a-hoop and expecting an easy win, but this was Christmas Eve and my beloved team had a last-minute present for us Leeds fans. We beat them comfortably 3-1 and with the game being recorded at home I could watch it again.

But I went one better than that, I took the video out of the player and wrapped it up in Christmas paper. I then put a tag on it saying, 'To Gary, Merry Christmas, Love, Gary' and placed it under the tree. It was the best Christmas ever.

I need another present from Leeds. That 3-1 video slotted nicely into my collection. I have us winning against them 1-0, 2-1, 3-1 and 5-1. I need us to win 4-1 to make the collection nice and neat, then we can move on to 6-1 and so on.

In 1996, Princess Diana agreed to give Prince Charles a divorce, Take That announced that they were splitting up, and former scout leader Thomas Hamilton gunned down 16 children, their teacher and himself at a primary school in Dunblane, Stirling – the same school that future Wimbledon champion Andy Murray attended and indeed he was in class that day.

The Duke and Duchess of York were divorced after ten years of marriage. The 1996 Olympic Games took place in Atlanta, Georgia, USA. Britain's Damon Hill became Formula One world champion. Former Liverpool manager Bob Paisley passed away, as did former Dr Who actor Jon Pertwee.

The big story of the second half of the season for Leeds was our progress in the League Cup and having got past First Division Reading in the quarter-finals, we had a two-legged semi-final against Birmingham City – also of the second tier – in February.

We won that tie 4-1 on aggregate after a 2-1 victory at St Andrew's in the first leg and a 3-0 scoreline at Elland Road in the second but, if we had known then that we would witness an abysmal performance in the final, I would hazard a guess that most of the 36,000 Leeds fans who were at Wembley would have been happy for the run to have ended against the Blues.

Two days after the second leg of that semi-final came perhaps my personal (and possibly only) highlight of Vale Park when Thomas Brolin played there for Leeds.

The vastly overweight Swede wasn't exactly a success at Elland Road, but during this FA Cup fifth round replay he showed glimpses of why Howard Wilkinson had parted with £4.6m to bring him to Yorkshire the year before.

Brolin's link-up play and at times quite majestic talents were in evidence in front of thousands of mesmerised United followers. He was inspirational in both of Gary McAllister's goals that saw Leeds edge past Vale 2-1. Brolin's engineering even managed to make Carlton Palmer look good in short spells.

Sadly, Brolin's obvious talent was rarely seen at Leeds and he clashed many times with Wilkinson who once accused him of 'not pulling his weight'. Considering the Swede's excess poundage, this was quite a statement from his manager.

%% %% %% %% %%

It was good to be back at Wembley after a four-year absence as swathes of Leeds fans decked in blue, white and gold swarmed up Wembley Way towards the twin towers for the League Cup Final against Aston Villa.

Leeds weren't having a particularly good season while Villa were plugging away for a European slot, but honours had been even in the Premier League with both clubs winning their home fixture.

Leeds were widely tipped to lift the League Cup for only the second time in their history. That view was endorsed by the 36,000 Leeds fans inside the stadium as the game got under way.

Howard Wilkinson's team formation was puzzling though. It appeared that he was employing his prolific goalscorer Tony Yeboah in a much deeper role than he was used to, while using Andy Gray, who was primarily a winger, as a lone striker. Leeds struggled throughout and were fortunate to be only a goal down at half-time.

Frustration grew among the fans and that turned to anger as Villa went two up ten minutes into the second half. 'Why is Brolin on the bench?' chanted the Leeds fans. Ten minutes after Villa's second goal, Wilkinson brought Brolin on, but it was all too late and Villa added to United's woe with a third two minutes from time.

The protest chants against Wilkinson were actually louder than the Villa fans' celebrations. Wilkinson had got his tactics disastrously wrong and there was serious doubt among the Leeds faithful regarding his position as manager. He had gone from winning the Second Division and First Division in three seasons to within a point of relegation the following campaign, and he no longer seemed to have the commanding grasp and superb man-management skills that had been prevalent in previous years.

I'll never forget the look of disappointment on thousands of young Leeds fans' faces, many painted in club colours, as we trudged away from Wembley. And I was even more disappointed when I saw Wilkinson on TV the next day, saying, 'I can't understand why the Leeds fans were so angry.' Wilko's days were surely numbered.

Five games into the following season, Leeds suffered a humiliating 4-0 defeat at the hands of manchester united at Elland Road. One of the goals came from a certain Eric Cantona who Wilkinson had sold, unbelievably, for around £1m. Even more annoying to Leeds fans was the fact that Cantona alone turned out to be the catalyst that Alex Ferguson's team had been lacking and in turn transformed their whole future.

It is well known that Ferguson was on the brink of being sacked after failing to win the title in 1992, making it 26 years since they had last won the league. Instead it was Howard Wilkinson who got the sack, just two days after that 4-0 defeat.

%% %% %% %% %%

A friend of mine, Richard, runs a great pub in the delightfully named village of Wetwang, 12 miles out of Bridlington. He and his lovely missus, Linda, are mine hosts of the Black Swan.

Richard, of course, is a Leeds fan. Linda, unfortunately, is a Pompey fan, bless her.

But there's a lad who frequents the pub who supports Darlington Football Club. His name is Darlo, obviously. Darlo, in true Quakers tradition, hates those 'monkey hangers' from Hartlepool, but when it comes to Leeds we've only played them a handful of times and none of the encounters were anything to write home about.

The very first meeting between the two clubs was in September 1996 when Darlington held Leeds to a 2-2 draw at Elland Road in the first leg of the second round of the League Cup. Up in Darlington, Rod Wallace and Ian Harte scored to set up a home tie against Aston Villa in the next round.

You will recall that Villa had beaten Leeds at Wembley the previous season and they went and did it again, 2-1. But this time we couldn't blame Howard Wilkinson. This one was the fault of George Graham, who replaced Wilkinson in September 1996.

We settled into life under Graham as we continued through the season and into 1997, which would see Diana, Princess of Wales, die in a car crash in Paris. Tony Blair became the new Prime Minister following a landslide victory for Labour and the largest remaining British colony, Hong Kong, was transferred to China. No fewer than 160 vehicles were involved in an M42 motorway pile-up in Worcestershire.

Teletubbies was aired on BBC for the first time and elsewhere in TV, Tim Vine and Julia Bradbury presented the launch of the new station Channel 5. J.K.Rowling's first Harry Potter novel, *Harry Potter and the Philosopher's Stone*, hit the book stores. The Duke of York opened Sunderland's new stadium, The Stadium of Light. Derby County moved to their new Pride Park Stadium, opened by the Queen. With new grounds going up seemingly every other week, Sir Stanley Matthews officially opened the Britannia Stadium, new home of Stoke City.

By February 1997 we were preparing for our final visit to Roker Park, where the Leeds players and fans have had many battles over the years.

This occasion saw a fine 1-0 win for Leeds and was memorable but for an incident still talked about today that wasn't even connected to the goal.

Ever since Graham had taken over as manager he steadfastly refused to play fans' favourite Tony Yeboah. He had been leaving Yeboah on the bench and basically ignoring him. It can't be put any plainer than that.

However, this particular afternoon, some fierce tackling by both sides meant that substitute activity was frequent which, consequently, meant that Graham reluctantly had to send Yeboah on. Almost immediately, Yeboah received the ball on the halfway line and seeing the Sunderland goalkeeper off his line, he shot for goal. With the keeper frantically scrambling back, the ball flew over his head and crashed on to the top of the bar before bouncing over for a goal kick.

The Leeds fans were behind that goal and chanted Yeboah's name continuously for around 20 minutes. After the game, when asked what he thought of Yeboah's spectacular effort, Graham shrugged his shoulders and said, 'I never saw it, I was fastening my shoelace.' For the following game, Yeboah once again appeared on the list of substitutes.

I have had a few drinks with Gaz Sunderland and we usually meet at his local pub in Seaham. On this particular day we arrived with our coach and nearly 60 lads piled inside, to be met and served by none other than 'Five Bellies' himself. His best mate Gazza had bought his mother a house on the seafront just around the corner from the pub.

In 1997 Sunderland moved to their new ground, The Stadium of Light. Before one Leeds game there, Gaz managed to get around 20 of us into a club just over the road from the stadium. It was packed, as you would expect, with Sunderland fans. I thought to myself, 'We'll be OK, Gaz will know most of this lot.' Then, after about ten minutes, one of our lads asked Gaz, 'Where's the bog mate?' to which Gaz replied, 'I've no idea bonnie lad, I've never been in here before.' 'Oh, fuck!' I thought.

We were getting some icy stares as we mingled near the bar. We were the only ones in the club without colours on and we stood out like hell. I don't know if they thought we would have been too much to handle, or they simply couldn't be bothered, but we were the last 20 to leave the club.

Leeds went on to finish 11th in the Premier League under Graham while the following season saw the division joined by another Yorkshire club, who were playing in the top flight for the first time in their history.

These days the away end at Oakwell is a fairly impressive large covered stand, but not so long ago it was just a huge open terraced mound exposed to all the elements. For the 1997/98 season, a monumental effort had seen Barnsley propelled into the dizzy heights of the Premier League and we turned up in our droves, after a long trek down the M1, to be met by a typically cold November torrent of rain, wind and hail.

The coach park at Oakwell is a steep grassy slope which has its predictable winter problems as dozens of coaches take on the form of Torvill and Dean, constantly slipping and sliding in the mud and jostling for a place where the drivers can be sure that the coach is still where they left it when they return.

As Leeds fans stood drenched behind the goal protected only by thin black bin liners, kindly provided by the friendly Barnsley stewards for just one South Yorkshire pound each, we soon found ourselves in the usual routine of being two goals down. But as we peered through the horizontal downpour, Leeds staged an amazing comeback and goals from Alfie Haaland, Rod Wallace and Derek Lilley had us dancing about like thousands of full bin bags in a fountain as we celebrated a 3-2 win.

*% *% *% *% *%

A tribute to Billy Bremner
9 December 1942–7 December 1997

It was December 1959 when there was a knock on the door of 35a Weir Street, Stirling. James Bremner opened it to two men asking to see his son, Billy. The two men were from Leeds United, the chairman Harry Reynolds and his manager Bill Lambton, and they had come to sign Billy. Celtic, Arsenal and Chelsea had given Bremner trials, but it was Leeds who had eventually won the signature of this 17-year-old flame-haired, pasty-faced ruffian from one of the roughest and toughest areas in Scotland – Raploch.

Leeds were virtually unheard of in Scotland and indeed by the end of that season they had been relegated to the Second Division. Billy had scored his first goal for the club in a 3-3 draw at Birmingham in March 1960, just a month after his debut. He was playing at right-wing while at inside-right that day was the senior pro at the club, Don Revie, who got the other two goals.

Revie had taken Billy under his wing, and he became inspirational in keeping him at the club when he became manager the following season. Billy was extremely homesick in those early days and often made his way back to Stirling. On more than one occasion, Revie arrived, sometimes in the dead of night after driving alone from Leeds, knocking on the door in Weir Street, to persuade Billy to come back to Leeds. Billy had a fiancée, Vicky, who was the main reason for him returning north at every opportunity. It was Revie who managed to talk Vicky into eventually moving to Leeds, and that solved the problem, with the happy couple finally settling in Leeds, thankfully for everyone concerned with Leeds United.

Billy became the linchpin in the Leeds side as they sought promotion from the Second Division. The rest as they say is history as Revie moulded a side together that became the best in Europe.

Although a dynamic midfielder, Billy scored some vital goals for Leeds, including winners in three FA Cup semi-finals. I was surrounded by hundreds of beer-stained Celtic fans when he scored an absolute corker at Hampden Park against Celtic in the 1970 European Cup semi-final. Billy had almost signed for Celtic back in 1959. Rangers were also interested but lost interest on account of him being a Catholic. Celtic still wanted to sign Billy but his dad, James, thought it best to avoid the religious situation in Glasgow and advised his son to ply his trade in England, where there were 'less religious boundaries'.

Returning home from a holiday on the west coast of Scotland in 2000, I called at Weir Street, to see for myself the street that holds massive historical significance to Leeds United. To my horror I discovered that number 35a was the only house in the street to have been demolished. All that remained was a huge grass square.

During a pre-season tour of Scotland in 2011, Leeds held a 'Leeds on the Road' event. These are designed to give supporters from the host area a chance to see and speak to the United team and management. This particular one was in Stirling so a few mates and I jumped in a taxi at the train station and went the short distance to Weir Street. The driver was a Celtic fan as well as being a big fan of Billy but he told us Weir Street was no longer there. He would take us to the site anyway as it was only a few minutes away. Now all that stands on the site of Weir Street are some offices. It's all very sad.

Often labelled 'ten stone of barbed wire' Billy was one the nicest blokes I ever met. The last time I spoke to him was a fortnight before his sad death from a heart attack in 1997, just two days before his 55th birthday. I don't mind admitting that I shed a tear that day.

In his youth Billy was a programme seller at Stirling Albion and that club has always had a great affection for the 'wee man'. When Stirling held a benefit evening on behalf of Billy, I was honoured to be asked to write about my memories of him in the special brochure published for the event, which I treasure.

I was slightly bemused as well as privileged when a stage play about my life watching Leeds United toured the country in 2010. One particularly moving part of the play, *Paint it White*, received great acclaim. It was when the actor who played me (Gary Dunnington) sat and talked to the Billy Bremner statue at Elland Road asking him for guidance in helping the club out of their predicament of playing in League 1.

On the pitch Billy was incredible and he won the vote to be named as the Greatest Ever Leeds United Player. He covered every blade of grass and was Footballer of the Year in 1970. Even when he became manager of the club he loved in 1985, he instilled that same passion into his players.

In 1987 he took Leeds to the FA Cup semi-final (regular territory for Bremner as a player) but they agonisingly lost to Coventry 3-2 after extra time.

I can still see Billy politely wiping his muddy hand prior to shaking hands with Her Majesty the Queen before receiving the FA Cup at Wembley in 1972.

When I'm working in the area of Leeds where Billy lived, I often park outside his old house while I have my lunch and reminisce over the countless memories he gave me as a Leeds fan. The overhead kick he scored when we thrashed Chelsea 7-0. The quick free kick he scored against Leicester while the defence were still turned around organising the keeper. His last-minute goal against Standard Liege in the Fairs Cup. Him dancing, jigging and somersaulting all over the pitch, after he had won the toss of a disc in Naples. His very cheeky penalty at Hibs in the UEFA Cup. His winning header in front of the Kop at Anfield in the UEFA Cup semi-final. Him leading the players across to the Leeds fans when we had beaten Barcelona in the European Cup semi-final at the Nou Camp.

The people now living in the house at Temple Newsam in Leeds must think they are under observation for something!

One morning in 1972 I was in between exams at my school and had four hours to kill, so a classmate, Gareth Wilson, and I caught a train from Garforth and went to watch Leeds in a training session. Sometimes hundreds of people lined the fence that ran along the edge of Fullerton Park training pitches, which were next to the West Stand car park, to watch Revie's boys put through their paces by Les Cocker, Revie and often Syd Owen too. People would scramble to return a ball that had been hoofed over the tall wire fence into the car park, and it was on one of these occasions when I was getting a ball that I saw Billy walking over the road towards Sheila's Cafe.

I went and told Gareth and the two of us followed him in. Everyone had autograph books with them then but we didn't even have a pen, let alone a piece of paper. I have no idea how I remember this, but at school the boys either had a briefcase or a satchel. I had a briefcase and Gareth had a satchel and both of them were full of pens and writing paper, but both were back at the school.

There was nobody else in the cafe except us three and a girl behind the counter. We stood there awkwardly and, without saying a word, she handed us a white paper sandwich bag and a pen and nodded across at Billy, who had his back to us looking out of the window.

Nervously we walked over to Billy and asked for his autograph. He had a dark jersey on and just said in a strong Scottish accent, 'Sure boys, here, sit down,' and pulled out a couple of chairs. We chatted for a few minutes although I can't recall one word that was said, and then we shook his hand and left, completely starstruck. We then ran outside, over the road and down past the back of the Scratching Shed waving our signed sandwich bags in the air and giggling like the two schoolkids we were.

% % % % %

One of the funniest things I have ever seen on a football pitch occurred at Selhurst Park. It was January 1998 and Leeds were playing Crystal Palace.

Tomas Brolin is widely recognised as being the worst Leeds player ever. However, I beg to differ on that point. In my humble opinion that unfortunate title belongs to only one man. This player's surname is the same as that of a world famous golfer from the 1960s whose first name was Arnold, and his christian name begins with a 'C' and comprises of seven letters.

Anyway, I digress. Brolin was now playing for Crystal Palace and had taken the field against his old club hoping to prove everyone wrong. In the first few minutes Brolin was involved in a collision with

Leeds's Bruno Ribeiro (possibly the smallest player on the pitch) and had to receive medical attention.

While he was off the field, Leeds scored and then Brolin re-entered the game nursing six new stitches and the biggest head bandage anyone had ever seen. Honestly, it looked like he was concealing a police helmet under his new bandage. Poor Brolin had only been back on the field for two minutes when Leeds added a second goal to eventually win the game 2-0.

Leeds fans were massed down one side of the ground as usual and whenever Brolin came anywhere near them, he was the victim of much hilarity. While trying his best to get on with the game and ignore his recently acquired white headgear, the hapless Swede went in for a challenge against Gary Kelly. Suddenly the ball left Kelly's boot and in a split-second had knocked the bandage clean off of Brolin's head. This left thousands of Leeds fans rolling about with laughter. They were crying and holding their stomachs to stop them hurting with the huge guffaws that echoed all around that stand.

I remember being doubled up and begging for people around me to stop laughing. Even the Leeds players, and Palace players for that matter, had to turn away to hide their glee. It really was one of the funniest things I have ever seen.

The incident was a light start to a year that saw Great Britain and Northern Ireland win one bronze medal at the Japanese Winter Olympics, the Union Jack dress worn by Geri Halliwell be sold at Sotheby's for £41,320 and the Likoshane massacre in Yugoslavia trigger the beginning of the Kosovo War.

The film *Titanic* won 11 Oscars including Best Picture. Bear Grylls, at just 23 years old, became the youngest British climber to reach the summit of Mount Everest. Hurricane Mitch hit Central America and killed an estimated 18,000 people.

The 1998 FIFA World Cup was won by hosts France following a 3-0 victory over Brazil in the final. Arsenal become only the second team in English football history to win the league and cup double twice.

In the summer of 1997, Bolton Wanderers had left their old Burnden Park home and taken up residence in a new venue, the Reebok Stadium, and Leeds's first visit there in April 1998 yielded a thrilling 3-2 victory as the Trotters were blitzed by our foreign 'H' bombs, Alfie Haaland, Gunnar Halle and Jimmy Hasselbaink.

I like the Reebok. I definitely think it's the best of the 'new' grounds, which in the 1990s seemed to spring up everywhere from Stoke to Sunderland, Derby to Huddersfield and elsewhere.

George Graham guided Leeds to fifth in the Premier League that season but he wasn't to remain at Elland Road for too much longer with the situation coming to a head a short while after a September 1998 clash at White Hart Lane against Tottenham Hotspur.

There was an unhealthy atmosphere surrounding the meeting but for different reasons to previous visits.

Out-of-work and disgraced manager Graham had been offered a return to football management by Leeds United. Graham had been banished from football following a much publicised ban for taking bungs for players, having been paid in the region of £285,000 by Norwegian football agent, Rune Hauge, as a bung in the transfer of Danish international John Jensen to Arsenal in 1994. A Premier League inquiry found Graham guilty and he was banned from football for a year.

In 1996 Leeds employed Graham, but controversy surrounded the visit to Spurs as it was widely believed that Tottenham chairman Alan Sugar wanted Graham at White Hart Lane, the fierce rivals of the Scot's former club Arsenal. Sugar had said at the time of the bung scandal that 'Graham should not be touched with a barge pole', but seemingly changed his mind on the subject.

I was chatting to Leeds chairman Peter Ridsdale at Leeds station as we prepared to travel to Tottenham. The question on every Leeds fan's lips was, 'Is Graham going to Spurs?' Ridsdale all but told a few of us that morning that he was and he also added that Graham had tried to sell David Batty to Tottenham only days before.

The game that afternoon was a pantomime, an absolute farce. Leeds fans chanted, 'Who's our manager?' throughout with their side comfortably winning 3-1. The fans indirectly received the answer when Graham, still on the Leeds bench, switched the tactics. He substituted almost all of the attackers, including Tony Yeboah. As Yeboah left the field and walked in front of the Leeds dugout he removed his shirt and threw it on the floor in front of Graham.

The game finished 3-3. Shortly afterwards, Graham had reneged on his long-term contract at Elland Road and became manager at Tottenham.

Having finished fifth the previous season, Leeds qualified for the UEFA Cup and were paired with CS Maritimo in the first round with the two legs to be played later in September.

Maritimo ply their trade on the holiday isle of Madeira, which is very popular with the senior end of British tourists. I have no idea why though, as everywhere you go you are confronted by some of the steepest hills that you will ever have to encounter.

We were quite drunk as we landed at Madeira's Funchal airport and it was well after midnight. We had been told beforehand that aviation experts consider this airport as the second-most dangerous in Europe, behind Gibraltar. I for one am glad I was drunk when we landed after I had seen the airport and its runway in the cold light of day. It had an extremely short runway as you descended between the surrounding mountains. The runway, which had a car park underneath it, jutted out into the sea supported by large concrete columns.

Madeira itself is very green and mountainous. We had a great time in the bars but the thousands of flowers everywhere played havoc with my hay fever, forcing me to counter this by rapidly topping up on my previous day's alcohol intake. Having said that, none of us were half as drunk as the hundreds of aged British tourists who had bought tickets for the game and some of them, well into their 70s, were so intoxicated that they were turned away by the police.

Because of the obscene power of television the game was switched to a later kick-off so it could be shown on Portuguese TV and this in turn gave the already wobbly spectators more drinking time.

Leeds had a slender 1-0 lead from the first leg at Elland Road, which was cancelled out by half-time, and the game went to penalties. By the time Lee Sharpe tucked away Leeds's final and winning penalty it was almost midnight.

As fans celebrated with the players, manager George Graham could be seen disappearing down the tunnel never to be seen again prior to his move to Spurs, with his former assistant David O'Leary eventually taking over.

In the next round we were handed a tie against AS Roma, with the first leg to be played away from home.

Italy is a fantastic country for a holiday but not for a football match. Even if you arrive a couple of days before the game, the polizia know what time you'll be at the airport and they greet you in their hundreds and whisk you away, under armed escort with sirens and flashing lights, through the streets full of tourists and bewildered shoppers, to your hotel. They close down the bars in the centre, despite protests from the owners, and they generally make life difficult for you during your stay.

We always try to befriend the owner of the bar, if we can get near enough, and have a quick word before the polizia arrive to force a shut-down. Usually we end up sneaking back to the same bar in small numbers and drinking behind closed doors without the slightest hint of trouble and without the police provocation and more importantly with the owner's till playing a merry tune to his ears.

If you are in large groups you are followed by the polizia, even if you are genuinely sightseeing at the Coliseum or the Vatican, or some other Roman attraction. On matchday it gets even worse. With the promise that there is food and beer in the ground, the polizia attempt to herd you on to coaches to the stadium with as much as three hours to go before kick-off.

I fell for this trick once. I was in the ground over two hours before the game with thousands of other Leeds fans and the polizia had shut down the bars. We were sat around in one of Italy's most famous football stadiums eating ice cream. How humiliating is that? I have never fallen into that trap since.

After losing the leg 1-0 we were kept in the ground for a further hour. Leeds were unable to overturn this deficit in the second leg at Elland Road and a 0-0 draw was enough to put us out of the competition. To make things worse, I'd taken my young nephew Scott to his first Leeds game that night.

In 1999, England's football manager Glenn Hoddle, in an interview with *The Times*, claimed that people born with disabilities are paying for sins in a previous life. Two days later Hoddle was relieved of his duties by the FA.

The euro currency was launched but Britain remained with sterling. The Millennium Stadium was opened in Cardiff, later in the year hosting the Rugby World Cup with Australia beating France in the final.

manchester united won the FA Cup but opted not to defend it in the 1999/2000 season because they wanted to concentrate on the FIFA Club World Championships in Brazil. Former England manager Bobby Robson was appointed as the new Newcastle United boss.

The draw for the third round of the FA Cup saw Leeds United – of the Premier League – paired with Conference side Rushden & Diamonds and tickets were as scarce as the proverbial rocking horse shit as Whites fans scrambled for their share of a record crowd of 6,431 at Nene Park.

We were actually driven into the stadium complex still on our coaches and within yards of our seats behind the goal. Although in charge for long periods of the game, Leeds couldn't penetrate Rushden's defence and then in the dying minutes the Conference side came so very close to pulling off a major cup shock. I wasn't the only Leeds fan who was praying for the final whistle. When it finally came, Leeds fans were the more relieved despite their side having had possibly 75 to 80 per cent of the play.

The Leeds public was intrigued by this tussle and a crowd of over 39,000 for the replay at Elland Road supported this. Some 4,000 Rushden fans were packed into the South Stand with huge expectations and these turned into a real possibility when their side took an early lead to stun the home crowd. Luckily, this Leeds team was a well-drilled outfit and eventually overcame the feisty Northamptonshire side with a solid display and three goals.

In the closing minutes, Rushden brought on former Leeds favourite and 1992 league championship winner Chris Whyte. The applause was as loud as for any of the goals, and afterwards Whyte and his team-mates indulged in a lap of honour and received a standing ovation from the Leeds crowd.

Hundreds of Rushden fans flooded the radio phone-ins and online forums afterwards to heap praise on the behaviour of the home supporters. One said, 'We were apprehensive about the welcome we would get but we needn't have worried. They were incredible.' Another on a forum said, 'There are many Leeds fans here in the Northampton area and they'd been telling us that the Leeds fans would welcome us with open arms and they were right. They are certainly the best fans that I've ever seen.'

Rushden went on to gain promotion to the Football League the following season and even had a brief affair with League 1 before financial difficulties hit the club hard and they slid out of the league. Worse was to come in 2011 when they were expelled from the Conference and liquidated. A new club rose from the ashes. AFC Rushden & Diamonds now play in the United Counties League and share their ground, The Dog and Duck Stadium, with Wellingborough United.

Leeds reached the fifth round of the FA Cup, losing to Spurs after a replay at White Hart Lane, and O'Leary guided the team to fourth in the Premier League to set up another UEFA Cup campaign the following season.

23

Galatasaray

THERE are two treasured possessions in my house that are not connected to football (not counting the missus of course). One is a beautifully framed picture of Winston Churchill and hanging proudly alongside him, there is a magnificent framed painting of Her Majesty, Queen Elizabeth II.

A problem of massive proportions occurred however. The Queen knighted Alex Ferguson. People say that they know exactly where they were when President Kennedy was assassinated, when Elvis died or 9/11 happened. It was 12 June 1999 and just after 11.30am when I heard the devastating news of this knighthood. I was totally stunned. I left work early, and wandered the streets for a while to gather my thoughts. I played it over in my mind. She had given Ferguson the OBE in 1984 but I had shrugged it off, thinking 'She doesn't really know what she's doing,' and I gave her the benefit of the doubt. Besides, I reasoned that they would take it back from him once the hierarchy realised their dreadful error. However, time elapsed and he got away with it.

Being the compassionate and forgiving type that I am, the Queen remained on my wall. But this latest outrage was just too much to bear. The Queen was placed in the cupboard under the stairs and 'She' was told in no uncertain terms that this was unacceptable. I then wrote to Buckingham Palace and told Her, at length, of my concerns. I did receive a reply from the Queen, but sadly, no apology.

After two long weeks I hung the Queen back on my wall but she knew I was still disappointed. Then just over four years later, showing a complete lack of remorse, the Queen unbelievably awarded David Beckham the OBE. Once again a letter was sent to Buckingham Palace and once again, I received no apology. In fact this time, She completely passed the buck, claiming that the Prime

Minister, who was then Tony Blair, made all these decisions, and my letter had been forwarded to No 10 Downing Street. I received a nice letter from Mr Blair, but once more, no apology was forthcoming. As you can imagine, I was inconsolable.

I have to say that the situation as it stands at this moment is one of unease. Should the Queen go off the rails one more time, it would surely signal the end of my long affection for Her Majesty. Just suppose for instance that She decides one day to award Wayne Rooney an MBE or even a 'Slimmer of the Year' award. Of course, the latter is highly unlikely, but you can rest assured that the Queen is indeed on very thin ice.

Later that summer, Birmingham City were the hosts for Jimmy Hasselbaink's final appearance in a Leeds shirt. It was a friendly at the end of July 1999 and just the week before, Hasselbaink had asked for a massive increase on his already massive contract. Leeds offered him a new and improved contract but he turned it down and promptly handed in a transfer request.

'One greedy bastard! There's only one greedy bastard,' was the welcoming chant from the travelling fans as he ran out for the last time. Several flags were draped across the front fence and the wall at the back of the stand, all with a similar message, 'Greedy Jimmy' and 'Judas'. For the record we won 1-0, courtesy of a goal by Alan Smith, a player who himself would endure the wrath of Leeds fans when he defected to Old Trafford five years later.

When the draw was made for the UEFA Cup and our ball came out with Partizan Belgrade, I was really looking forward to the visit. The next day, because of the ongoing conflict in the Balkans, the tie was switched to Heerenveen in Holland and for the September trip we would be based in Amsterdam. 'Well,' I said to the lads, 'I suppose that'll have to do.'

We had a good few days among the canals and pushbikes, as well as the naughty shops and smoky cafes, and a 3-1 victory at Abe Lentra Stadion sent us back across the English Channel to Blighty with a huge smile. Lucas Radebe scored one of those three goals while he was sat on his arse and a winner by Darren Huckerby, who I have to say was miles offside, finished the job at Elland Road a fortnight later.

If we thought Switzerland was cold back in 1974, we got one hell of a shock when we landed and slid along the runway before coming to a halt just yards from the terminal at an iced-over Moscow airport in November 1999. Airport workers didn't bat an eyelid, suggesting to us that this was a normal kind of thing. We were there for the second leg of the second round of the UEFA Cup and it was absolutely freezing.

The authorities and police at the airport were very strict. They were almost like robots. Two regular Leeds travellers known as the 'Leicester Twins', intriguingly called so because they are twins from Leicester, were quite drunk as they entered the main passenger terminal and due to the reason that they could hardly stand, let alone get their tickets and passports ready, they were fortunate not to be the first casualties in the Russian capital. There would be quite a number of those during the next few days.

Moscow is undoubtedly the most corrupt place by far that I have ever been to. Persecution is there for all to see and the police, or KGB as they are sometimes known, harass their own people and while we were in town they harassed Leeds fans too. They would ask if you had your passport with you and no matter which answer you gave, it was the wrong one.

Say 'yes' and you were bundled into a car or van because 'you shouldn't carry it with you'; alternatively say 'no' and you were bundled into a car or van because 'you should keep it with you at all times'. In both instances you were handed an on-the-spot fine which I doubt very much reached the police station's treasury department.

One evening a few of us were walking around the city when I genuinely thought I was suffering from a stroke. I lost all feeling in my face and started to panic a bit as I felt all around my face with ice-cold hands. Then I realised that I wasn't having a stroke, my beard had frozen up. At that moment an unmarked car pulled alongside us containing at least five police officers. Aware of what they had been doing regarding the passport, and other scams, we didn't hang around and walked briskly in the opposite direction ignoring their calls of 'Halt!'

Our hotel was called the Intourist and was easily the tallest building in the area, towering above even the Kremlin. I think just about every bedroom was taken by Leeds fans and there were numerous bars and a nightclub all in the confines of the hotel. There was also an abundance of ladies of the night, who we discovered were supplied and governed by the KGB, hanging around the lobby and in the ground floor bar.

American dollars was the currency in the hotel, although they did readily accept sterling. It was a reasonable price for the beer too and in some bars within easy walking distance of the hotel we were paying around 20p for a large slug of proper vodka.

On our way to one bar we ventured into an underground subway and were met by the sight of hundreds of locals seeking refuge from the icy conditions. People were stood around chatting, others were sat about smoking, drinking, eating and sleeping. They were totally oblivious to us as we walked past. Many were under blankets despite it being very warm down there, due to warm airducts.

Leeds had arrived in Russia with a 4-1 lead over Lokomotiv Moscow from the first leg, and to be honest the away match proved just as easy as we cantered to a 3-0 victory. Throughout the 90 minutes thousands of bare-chested Leeds fans wearing traditional Russian fur hats embraced the icy conditions full on as the now familiar chants of 'We are the Champions! Champions of Europe!' emanated from their mouths accompanied by frosty breath.

The trip to Lokomotiv Moscow was my first trip to Russia and on our return flight home Big Mick took off his headphones and announced, 'I don't believe it. We've drawn Spartak Moscow in the next round. We'll be back here in a month.'

Unbelievably, it was even colder than the previous time as our plane's landing gear met with the thick runway ice and I drained the last drop of my 'medicinal' whisky. The awaiting police cordon was just as pleasant as before as we shuffled through customs and on to the awaiting buses. Teeth chattered loudly as we made our way to the Intourist and before long we were having warm docks of wine in TGI Friday's just around the corner.

We had already had a fair dollop of the stuff when we heard that tomorrow's game against Spartak had been postponed and would now take place in Bulgaria the following week. We were then faced with the arduous task of three days in Moscow drinking more warm wine, copious amounts of beer, chased down by numerous tots of whisky, vodka and Jagermeister – and no football.

The beer in Sofia was even cheaper than we had become used to but unfortunately the riot police at the game were the worst we had encountered anywhere on our travels. We found out later that one Leeds fan had been stripped to his Y-fronts and locked in the back of a police van for the duration of the match. When he finally got his clothes back, his wallet was completely empty, and he was released without charge. One armed police officer in a bar close to the ground became so obsessed with crushing a few skulls with his baton that he had to be restrained by his own officers and ushered away.

The ground was totally dilapidated and obviously unfit to put on a game and certainly unfit to house any spectators. The few seats that were in the Leeds end were bent over and unfit to sit on and others had mangled and twisted rusty iron legs. Leeds lost the game, the first leg, 2-1, but afterwards most of the talk in the bars was stories of police brutality on Leeds fans. Countless fans were detained without a charge during the game and several others reported having money and even passports taken from them. One lad, John, who was on our trip, had been beaten, robbed and even threatened at gunpoint by the riot police.

In the return leg at Elland Road, Lucas Radebe scored the only goal of the night to put Leeds into the next round on the away goals rule.

It meant we would still be in Europe as the new millennium dawned and in 2000, Charlie Kray, one of the infamous Kray brothers, died of a heart attack while in Parkhurst Prison on the Isle of Wight. Brother Reggie was released from Broadmoor Hospital on compassionate grounds due to bladder cancer and died a few weeks later. The Tate Modern art museum was also opened.

Chelsea beat Aston Villa 1-0 in the last FA Cup Final at the old Wembley Stadium. The European Championship, hosted by the Netherlands and Belgium, saw England bow out at the group stages with two defeats but a memorable 1-0 win over Germany. Prior to England's exit UEFA threatened to expel them due to violence from the fans.

The Queen Mother celebrated her 100th birthday and reality TV show *Big Brother* was aired for the first time on Channel 4.

Leeds were drawn in the fourth round against AS Roma and our second trip to Rome in as many years was much the same as the last one, except for the score. The heavy police presence was once again prevalent everywhere but we had sussed things out a little from last time, and did our drinking a short walk from the centre and away from the law.

The game itself at the Olympic Stadium finished with a promising goalless draw, setting up a mouthwatering clash for the home leg. Back at headquarters, Leeds won a tight match with a terrific goal from Harry Kewell, earning a place in the quarter-finals.

Kewell was an extremely gifted footballer but he didn't endear himself to a lot of Leeds fans, including myself. With Leeds in serious financial difficulty in 2003, Kewell left to join Liverpool, the club he said he had always been 'a total fan of'. The fee was a mere £5m. Nothing near his real value but his agents threatened Leeds that Kewell would leave on a Bosman free transfer the following season if they didn't comply. In effect they bullied Leeds's inexperienced chairman, Professor John McKenzie, into accepting this meagre sum. Then both Kewell and the agent took a huge cut from the fee, leaving Leeds with less than £2m from the deal.

Kewell further angered Leeds fans when asked how he would feel wearing the red shirt of Liverpool. He replied, 'It'll feel bloody good to put on another shirt.' And with an insult to his former team-mates at Elland Road, he added, 'I'll finally get to play with some great players.' He played just 90 times in five seasons for his 'boyhood heroes'. His final insult to Leeds, and in particular the fans, would come in 2008 when he signed for Galatasaray.

Back in England, the Premier League campaign took us to Bradford City the following March and saw us come up against an unexpected figure. Goalkeeper Neville Southall remained at Everton for some time after that half-time bust-up against Leeds back in August 1990 but he put in a further two transfer requests. There was also an enquiry for him from Old Trafford but Ferguson was far from impressed with Southall's 'hostile phone manner' so he opted for a large Dane with a big red nose instead.

In February 2000 Southall was installed as player/coach at Bradford City, in their first season in the Premier League, and due to goalkeeping injuries he was forced to put on the gloves to face Leeds once again.

Leeds won 2-1 with two goals from Michael Bridges and this was Southall's one and only appearance for Bradford. He went on to sign for a further five clubs – York, Rhyl, Shrewsbury (twice), Dover and Dagenham – but he didn't play a single game at any of them.

In Europe we returned to the Czech Republic, as it was by the spring of 2000, 30 years after our visit to Sparta Prague. Leeds coasted through their UEFA Cup quarter-final first leg against Slavia Prague at Elland Road with a sterling performance that earned a massive advantage to take to Prague the following week.

Prague is a great city and cheap too, as long as you stay away from the tourist trail, and I must admit to seeing much more of the city's attractions than I had as a 12-year-old on my last visit. We lapped it up in the many exotic bars but the beer was much dearer than in the sidestreet bars hidden away from the paying tourists. In some of these a large and strong beer, the original Czech Budweiser, cost around £1, up to four times less than just 30 yards away.

Kewell scored for Leeds in the Generali Arena but we lost 2-1. However that 3-0 cushion from Elland Road had been more than enough to put us into our first European semi-final for 25 years. Sadly, it would be a semi-final remembered for completely different, horrific reasons.

Galatasaray Football Club and their supporters aren't exactly known for their hospitality. Their history is littered with violence, both on and off the pitch. Many English clubs have had to run the gauntlet of hate when visiting the infamous Ali Sami Yen Stadium. Galatasaray fans even lie in wait at the airport for their visitors to arrive. Police stand by and do nothing as banners are unfurled in the arrivals lounge, 'Welcome to Hell' being the most popular welcome message.

Chelsea encountered trouble there and our dear friends from across the Pennines at Old Trafford were attacked, players and fans alike. As the team entered their hotel in 1993, a bellboy went up to Gary Pallister and ran his finger across his throat simulating a knife while other staff members watched on smiling. This sort of thing is widely accepted in Istanbul and it is even, it seems, tolerated by UEFA. More on that shortly.

It was in the final hour of 5 April 2000 when we touched down at Istanbul for the first leg of the UEFA Cup semi-final and within minutes people were relaying phone messages around the plane that some Leeds fans had been killed in the city. I felt numb. I was sat next to my mate Webby, a strapping six-and-a-half-foot skinhead. 'Wonder who it is?' he said. 'Looks like we're not off to bed tonight mate.'

Our group of 50 walked through customs and Webby and me unfurled a flag I had made for the trip. 'Hello Hell. We are Leeds!' it said. I had no idea when I was painting it just two days earlier the significance that those words would hold. We held it up to the mob waiting in the airport. They were shouting at us, waving their fists and many running their fingers across their throats. The police were simply smiling. It all seemed like a bad dream. We were in for an unforgettable few days.

News kept filtering through that two Leeds fans had been killed, maybe more, but we had no idea what had happened or more importantly who they were. We arrived at our hotel and literally threw our bags on to our beds and we were out on the streets of Istanbul within minutes. We went into a couple of bars but the atmosphere among our lads was subdued. We still had no idea what had occurred or how many had been killed or who they were.

I had a phone call from my wife Lesley and from other people back home asking if I was OK. It was all over the news back in the UK. The latest reports said that two Leeds fans had died. We were followed to every bar by a handful of police who kept a distance and never approached us. The locals literally acted as if nothing had happened. It was a surreal atmosphere.

We stayed out in the bars all night and returned to the hotel at around 7am, where we were met by around 40 police officers who told us we would be under hotel arrest for the rest of our trip and would be escorted to the ground that evening. There was still talk of the game being postponed but we were left completely in the dark as to what was going on.

We found out the names of the murdered Leeds fans later that morning. They were Christopher Loftus and Kevin Speight. The hotel bar reduced the price of the beer for us, its 'captives', but the atmosphere was as nullified as I can ever recall. Anger was already beginning to simmer among our number and when the bar ran out of beer I really thought it would erupt there and then. I really did think that the slightest thing could light the fuse and set off the tinder box that was there within us all.

The hotel staff seemed to realise the intense pressure building among us and an emergency supply of beer was hurried by a dray wagon through the busy streets to our hotel in less than half an hour.

When the time arrived to go to the game, which – despite reservations from Leeds United – UEFA had ruled must be played, we filed on to our coach under heavy police escort. We found out later that the same routine was being carried out at other hotels across the city where Leeds fans were staying. We also discovered later that many supporters had been prevented from flying from England once news of the tragedy unfolded.

The hatred from the home crowd as we neared the ground had to be seen to be believed. We were travelling slowly in the traffic and although there was a heavy police presence, they did nothing to stop Turkish fans banging on our windows, throwing stones, spitting and dragging their fingers across their throats with pure venom.

Then, as the ground came into view, our tinder box erupted and a few of us jumped out of the emergency door at the back of the coach and went for the nearest Galatasaray fans, who promptly retreated back into the baying crowd. The police, who up to now had been ignoring everything before them, began to attack us and beat us back on to the coach. It was incredible.

Once inside the stadium, the visitors were surrounded by riot police as the rest of the crowd whipped up so much hostility that the stadium instantly became a pure cauldron of hate. Any lingering thoughts that the Turks would show any remorse for the murder of two Leeds fans, attacked and stabbed to death the night before, disappeared completely.

Indeed, once the teams had emerged from the tunnel under numerous police shields, Galatasaray refused to hold a minute's silence as well as refusing to wear black armbands. In response, the

Leeds fans turned their backs for two minutes, to the applause of the Leeds team who of course were wearing armbands.

The game had become irrelevant to everyone connected to Leeds United, players and fans alike, and a 2-0 defeat simply subsided into oblivion.

The road outside the end designated to Leeds fans had finally been cordoned off and there was just a long line of coaches, headed by a police tank, waiting to take supporters back to their hotels. One coach was missing – ours. Because we had jumped off the bus earlier and despite the furore going on all about us, the driver had the audacity to call us hooligans and had refused to come back for us.

We were taken back to our hotel on a police coach which had officers on board, but they were very relaxed and genuinely seemed to enjoy being among Leeds 'hooligans', so much so that, and you couldn't possibly make this up, one of the officers handed one of our lads his machine gun and then his pistol. It was bizarre to watch this young officer clearly admiring his hardware in the hands of a Leeds fan. Luckily, the weapons were soon handed back and we could all put our heads back above the seats.

Upon our arrival at the hotel we were told that we were still under hotel arrest, but by now we had all had enough and in small groups we began 'escaping' through the doors of the adjoining Chinese restaurant and out into the night.

For the second leg at Elland Road two weeks later, UEFA banned Turkish fans from travelling, but it was a futile gesture and left the question of what they would have done if the tragic events in Istanbul had been reversed and two Galatasaray fans had been murdered on the streets of Leeds, but in all sincerity, I think we all know the answer to that.

The moronic fans from Old Trafford who came to a game at Elland Road shortly afterwards displaying a flag that said 'Istanbul Reds' – they truly have short memories.

As a matter of record we drew the second leg 2-2, though in between the two fixtures Villa Park was the scene for Leeds's first game following the murders of Christopher Loftus and Kevin Speight. Players from both teams laid wreaths at the Leeds end of the ground in remembrance of the two fans prior to the kick-off.

Although the UEFA Cup run had ended under a tragic cloud, Leeds went on to finish the season third in the Premier League – enough to earn themselves a crack at the Champions League, the modern-day version of the European Cup.

24

Many Memorable Trips

THIRD place in the Premier League had been enough to see Leeds into the qualifying stages of the Champions League where they were pitted against 1860 Munich. United were armed with a slender 2-1 lead from the first leg at Elland Road but this game had been highly controversial with Leeds manager David O'Leary claiming, 'That was by far the worst display of refereeing I have ever seen in my life, either as a player or a manager.'

Goals from Alan Smith and Ian Harte had given Leeds a 2-0 lead as the clock moved into the final minutes. Then the Cypriot referee, Costas Kapitanis, surpassed his already dismal display and sent off Leeds's Olivier Dacourt and Eirik Bakke within two minutes of each other and then against nine men Hassler pulled a goal back for Munich, incredibly seven minutes into injury time. The players, O'Leary and the crowd went mental.

As Leeds fans descended on the beer capital of the world for the second leg, bright sunshine assisted our quest for lashings of real German lager. A beer marquee right outside the ground was our last port of call before we took up our positions inside, where once again Smith came up trumps and his goal ensured a passage into the first group stage with a 3-1 aggregate victory.

After the great victory in Munich, Leeds fans were understandably upbeat and pretty confident as we entered the mighty Nou Camp for our next game in the Champions League. Unfortunately though, for the thousands of travelling Whites perched high up in one corner of this huge stadium, this wasn't to be the glorious night we were expecting.

Leeds were under the cosh from the start and remained there for much of the game, and in the end I suppose the 4-0 scoreline could have been even worse. They had been severely injury-hit for this first game of the group stage but it was David O' Leary's job to now pick his battered troops up, who were already being written off by the media, and prepare them for the rest of the group games.

A fine home win against AC Milan had improved the situation somewhat as Leeds returned to Istanbul for their next away Champions League match.

It was astounding how FIFA and UEFA allowed a game involving Leeds United in Istanbul to go ahead so soon after the atrocities in the very same city just six months earlier. But on reflection, Sepp Blatter isn't exactly known for his tact, diplomacy or indeed his sense of justice is he?

Even when we touched down at Istanbul airport we were still being haunted by Galatasaray. Their team had arrived from their match at Glasgow Rangers and we had to stay on the plane until they had cleared customs and departed the airport, to avoid any confrontation.

Just 138 Leeds fans were allowed to travel to Istanbul for the game against Besiktas. Heavily outnumbered by Turkish riot police, we passed slowly through customs before being escorted by police officers to our coaches. We were then driven to the Bosporus which is a strait that separates Europe from Asia, and we were then frog-marched once again all of 30 yards to a pleasure boat anchored at the side of the water.

My arguably provocative flag announcing 'Hello Hell We are Leeds' had been replaced by a much more sedate flag with the simple word 'LUFsea' written upon it. We had known about this so-called 'free pleasure cruise for the Leeds fans' beforehand, hence my seafaring themed banner. I had also brought along some pirate hats.

This boat trip was designed to keep the few Leeds fans who had been lucky enough to be included in the strict official travel plans, enforced by the club in conjunction with UEFA, out of the centre of Istanbul. Worse still, it was to be a dry boat, but there would be a firework display just for our benefit.

Or at least it would have been a dry boat if John hadn't spied a stash of bottles of red wine secreted behind the ship's temporary closed bar. We sat quietly at a table close to the bar watching the fireworks while we polished off a bottle or two and then some more before we were rumbled by one of the ship's staff. By then there were only two bottles left. The other 12 were empty and resting at the bottom of the Bosporus.

We disembarked and were given an embarrassingly large police escort to the stadium where we were shown to our allocated pen.

The atmosphere inside was entirely different to that of the Ali Sami Yen Stadium where we had played Galatasaray. The Besiktas players applauded the Leeds players on to the pitch and handed bouquets out to fans.

We were soon joined in our designated part of the ground by Turkish fans. They were supporters of Fenerbahce, also from Istanbul and the arch-rivals of Galatasaray. Some Leeds fans had been drinking with them on that fateful night six months earlier. Fenerbahce supporters hated their rivals with a passion and welcomed Leeds fans with open arms.

One of our lads, Collar, had managed to get into the stadium carrying a box containing dozens of cartons of orange juice, laced with large amounts of vodka and then carefully resealed. We then proceeded to drink them greedily with our Turkish hosts. By the time the police became aware of our tipsiness, the cartons had been emptied and flattened.

In between the Barcelona and Milan matches Leeds had beaten Besiktas 6-0 at Elland Road and this encounter ended 0-0, but the evening had tempered my raging hatred of at least some Turkish citizens.

The cup action continued at home and during a League Cup fixture away to Tranmere Rovers, Leeds were in a comfortable 2-0 lead when it all went a bit pear-shaped.

One of the Rovers players had an amazingly long throw on him and he had been very dangerous with a ball in his hands. I'm not sure if it would be allowed now, or even if it was legal back then, but he would wipe the ball with a towel which the ball boy had handed to him and he would then walk up the nearest aisle in the stand and head up the steps.

He would then run back down and as he got to the touchline he would throw the ball right into the six-yard box. It was entirely down to this tactic that we conceded three goals and were knocked out of the competition.

⁄⁄ ⁄⁄ ⁄⁄ ⁄⁄ ⁄⁄

Leeds went to AC Milan needing a point to progress to the second group stage of the Champions League. Milan had already been assured of qualification.

Fully aware now of Italian police pre-match tactics we made our way to a few tram stops from the centre of Milan but we were still met by bars that had been closed down by the polizia. Undeterred, we headed into some of the sidestreets and eventually came across an Indian restaurant.

Totally oblivious that there was indeed a game on, never mind a ban on Leeds fans drinking alcohol, the staff rushed around putting tables together to accommodate about a dozen of us. It was around mid-afternoon and there was no one else in the restaurant except us. We ate like lords and drank copious amounts of wine and beer, and as we settled our bill, the owner came across with the guest book, which we were all happy to sign.

'Gary Kelly' signed, so too did 'Lee Bowyer', and then when it came to my turn I signed 'Carlton Palmer'. With everybody laughing, the owner and waiters were anxious to get in on the joke. 'He is Carlton Palmer, our head coach,' said John in his Whitby-Italian accent, while pointing at me. They couldn't believe that they had the famous 'Leeds United' team in their restaurant and although they didn't refund our money, they brought over a couple more bottles of wine which we consumed purely as a matter of gratitude. 'Goodbye Senor Palmer,' said one of the waiters as he shook my hand as we walked out. I must admit to having pangs of guilt over our deceit, but apart from our skin colour and body physique – me weighing possibly six stone more than Palmer – we both possess an uncannily similar football ability. Neither of us can head, trap, pass or kick a football to save our life.

Once in the San Siro, Milan missed a first-half penalty and then just before half-time Dominic Matteo met a Lee Bowyer cross to head home the most famous goal of his career. Songs about that goal are still sung today by the Leeds fans. Despite Milan equalising, the subsequent 1-1 draw was sufficient to send both teams into the next stage.

After the game, the polizia once again kept Leeds fans in the stadium for over an hour. But this time we were truly glad that we had stayed behind. Once everyone had left the stadium, except for the Leeds fans and the British press, the Leeds team emerged from the tunnel and came across to 7,000 of us. There then followed a sing-song between fans and players that was incredible and had to be seen to be believed.

Commentator Alan Green, for BBC Radio 5 Live, said afterwards, 'That was the best example of player–fan bonding that I have ever seen.'

Incidentally, Barcelona were knocked out as a consequence.

*** *** *** *** ***

A home defeat by Real Madrid in the first round of the second phase had put a slight dent in the hopes of Leeds as once again they entered the Olympic Stadium in Rome in December 2000.

Backed once again by huge numbers of Leeds fans, the game this time was against Lazio, who share the ground with Roma. Leeds stunned their Italian hosts and a goal from Alan Smith cemented a fine win that once again bounced the Whites back on track in their quest for European glory.

The goal had been right out of the top drawer. A superb one-two between Mark Viduka and Smith sliced through the Lazio defence and Leeds then set their sights on Belgian champions Anderlecht with the fixtures to resume in February 2001.

A lot would happen in 2001. An earthquake in India killed just under 20,000 people, George W. Bush succeeded Bill Clinton as the new President of the USA while the world would watch in shock as the twin towers of New York's World Trade Center were attacked by two hijacked planes. Two other planes were taken, one crashing into the Pentagon and the other going down in open land due to passengers fighting the hijackers. In total 2,996 people perished and Al-Qaeda later claimed responsibility. War broke out between the United States, Britain and other allies in Afghanistan.

Sweden's Sven-Goran Eriksson became the first foreign England manager. Liverpool were 'cup kings' as they won the League Cup, the FA Cup and the UEFA Cup, with midfielder Steven Gerrard also winning the Young Player of the Year award.

For Leeds, two victories over Anderlecht in February then set up a visit to Real Madrid the following month.

*% *% *% *% *%

Leeds changed their kit to all-white in the early 1960s because of Don Revie's admiration for Real Madrid and here they were, 12 years after the great man's sad death, face to face with the 'Immortal Spaniards'.

When Leeds played Real Madrid at the Bernabeu Stadium they were accompanied by 6,000 vociferous supporters. It was about a quarter of an hour into the game when I joined them. While queuing to enter the ground my legs suddenly started to give way, no doubt because of the strenuous afternoon I had just had in the shopping malls of Madrid and sightseeing. Others who were with me beg to differ and blame my unsteadiness on one too many light ales in the Spanish sunshine which, quite frankly, is absurd and to be honest, hurtful.

Whatever the reason for my Bambi-like antics, the police refused to let me in. I offered no resistance and calmly staggered across the street and snuck into the bar that I had been in not 20 minutes ago. I met Collar in there and here's the clever part. I said to him, 'I'm just going to have a small beer to sober me up.'

This, along with the thought in my head that I was in danger of not getting in to see Leeds, quickly got me thinking straight and with the feeling back in my legs, I strolled confidently back across the road to the stadium, but this time just a little further up from where I had been refused entry. It was at this point that I felt for my wallet to get my ticket out and discovered that my wallet was no longer there. My money, my cards, and my match ticket had gone.

Thinking carefully now and with the aid of that small beer I devised a cunning plan to gain entry. I walked a little further up past the Leeds turnstiles and arrived at what looked like some sort of hospitality entrance, and more importantly there were far less stewards and police around. I took a step back and weighed the situation up. I could see through a glass door that there was a long tunnel in which two suited men were stood talking. I could also see part of the pitch beyond them.

Quietly I opened the door and slipped inside. It was dark in the entrance and the two men were completely unaware I was there; they were heavily engrossed in conversation and both were smoking. I walked closer and closer. When I was less than five yards away, one of them turned to me and said something and then with the adrenalin pumping through me I started to walk towards them and then I just ran as fast as I could in the direction of the pitch. Hopefully I could disappear among the crowd and, unbelievably, this is precisely what happened.

I made my way behind the goal in the lower tier and stood with a few lads who I knew and a lass called Marie, and then I just began to mingle here and there. Although there were seats, no one was actually sat in them and there was a really relaxed atmosphere in the Leeds end, aided also by alcohol I suspect, but it worked for me. My ticket had been for the upper tier but that didn't matter one jot to me. I was now sober enough to watch the game. Despite losing 3-2 it was a good encounter from which Leeds can consider themselves very unlucky.

During the second half my wallet was handed to me. My Leeds United member's card with my photograph on was in my wallet and luckily this lad recognised it as mine and after 'doing the rounds' among Leeds fans it was eventually passed on back to me. It still contained some money (I had no idea how much was in it to begin with), my ticket, and my bank cards. At least I'd got the right result, albeit extremely luckily.

I found out months later that my wallet had been picked up from the floor outside the turnstiles where I'd been turned away. Whoever first picked it up – thank you.

※ ※ ※ ※ ※

'Leeds United are the weakest side left in the competition,' declared Deportivo La Coruna midfielder Victor, the day before the teams locked horns in the quarter-final of the Champions League. Leeds though, clearly hadn't read the script and that in turn delighted the Elland Road crowd during the first leg as Leeds swept away their Spanish opponents with goals from Ian Harte, Alan Smith and Rio Ferdinand without reply completely blowing Deportivo out of the water.

When the final whistle went, Elland Road echoed to the tune of, 'Three-nil to the weakest link!' The comment made by their manager Javier Irureta afterwards was truly priceless, 'If you sum up the goals, one was from a free kick and the other two came from corners. If you take these situations out, we kind of matched them.'

I loved it in La Coruna. It's a beautiful city on the north coast of Spain with bars aplenty. We spent most of our time in the Orzan district which was close to their Estadio Riazor which is situated right on the coast.

Thousands of bare-chested Leeds fans mingled with the locals and the atmosphere was great. Almost all the Deportivo fans we spoke to genuinely believed that their team would overturn the three-goal deficit they suffered at Elland Road (they turned around a 3-0 scoreline to win 4-3 against Paris Saint-Germain in a previous match), and once the game kicked off we got the feeling that their confidence wasn't too misplaced.

Leeds were under a lot of pressure from the start and apart from a couple of threatening counter-attacks we were pretty much defending most of the night. Early and late goals from Deportivo had fans from both sides on the edge of their seats, for totally different reasons. I had not been more relieved to hear the full-time whistle since our European Cup semi-final triumph at the Nou Camp in 1975.

Leeds won through 3-2 on aggregate, which incidentally was the same as in Barcelona in 1975, but if you go with the logic of the

Deportivo manager Irureta the score should have been 0-0 in that second leg in La Coruna. Deportivo's goals came from a penalty and a free kick, so we 'kind of matched them'.

We also hadn't been in the last four of the European Cup since 1975.

%. %. %. %. %.

The first leg of the eagerly-awaited semi-final with Valencia was a slight disappointment for the vast majority of Leeds fans. Although the Whites had most of the play, goalkeeper Nigel Martyn was also called into action on a couple of nerve-racking moments. The game finished goalless but one consolation as we headed to Spain for the second leg was the fact that not conceding an away goal at Elland Road could be an advantage in our favour.

As with La Coruna, Valencia is also on the coast. Sitting pretty on the east it looks out on to the deep blue Mediterranean Sea and once again, the shirts were off as Leeds fans of all shapes and sizes baked unashamedly in the red-hot sunshine.

As we drank in the many bars along the promenade, news filtered through that Lee Bowyer had been banned from playing in this second leg. It later transpired that, for whatever reason, UEFA had looked at an incident on video involving Bowyer in the first leg at Leeds, and decided to ban him because he appeared to stamp on a Valencia player.

When you saw the incident, which was right in front of the dugouts and the linesman, it was clear that it was an accident, but more importantly the referee had seen it and decided not to punish either player on the night. The official that night was none other than the Italian Pierluigi Collina, widely acknowledged as the world's best referee, and he was astonished by UEFA's actions. 'I saw the incident clearly,' he told the press, 'and in my opinion, no further action was deemed necessary.' Unfortunately UEFA saw it differently.

Bowyer was the leading scorer in that competition and finished joint top scorer overall, even making UEFA's team of the competition, but the organisation would not let him play that evening in Valencia and he was sorely missed in the engine room as we crumbled under intense pressure from the hosts.

The imposing Mestalla Stadium was bouncing and despite a significant support from Leeds, we couldn't hear ourselves speak, let alone sing. The stadium is made up of three-tiered stands surrounding the pitch that are extremely steep and can create an intimidating atmosphere. Although feeling slightly deflated after a 3-0 defeat we managed a few more beers afterwards on the promenade before returning to our hotel bar, well out of the way of the hundreds of waving red and yellow Valencia flags that by now were appearing everywhere, and quite frankly were getting on our nerves.

25

No Really Mate,
Who Was He?

WE returned to Madeira in 2001 once again in the first
round of the 2001/02 UEFA Cup, having finished fourth
in the Premier League the previous season, but this time
the first leg was away, and the runway had been extended somewhat
– not that we noticed as we rolled off yet another late flight.

The game against Maritimo had been postponed by a couple
of weeks following 9/11 and as with the last time, pre-match
entertainment was traditional folk dancing and fans from both
teams mingled freely without the merest hint of trouble and of
course once again there was a cluster of senior British tourists.

One flag draped over the wall in the Maritimo section amusingly
exclaimed, 'Fuck You Bin Laden!' Leeds lost this encounter 1-0, but
three goals without reply at Elland Road would see them through
to the next round quite comfortably.

After the dizzy heights of the Champions League, Leeds had
missed out to Liverpool on qualification for Europe's top competition
for 2001/02. We didn't know then the devastating effect of not
qualifying for the Champions League, but for now we had a couple
more jaunts across Europe to contend with in the UEFA Cup.

Victory over Maritimo set us up nicely for a journey deep into
the heart of France in the next round. As I've said on more than one
occasion I'm not a big fan of France or the French but our trip to
Troyes was quite pleasant for the second leg.

Troyes is situated on the Seine River about 150 miles south of
Paris and its people were most welcoming. With it being a Bank
Holiday most of the bars were closed, but entertainment and
lashings of beer in the town square more than made up for that.

Eventually, several bar owners, noting the impeccable behaviour of the Leeds fans and more importantly their willingness to purchase large amounts of alcohol, began opening their doors.

We had won the first leg 4-2 at Elland Road and a 3-2 defeat in France saw us secure a thrilling 6-5 aggregate victory and took us once again to Zurich in November when we squeezed through 4-3 on aggregate against Grasshoppers.

Once again supporters from the two Zurich teams fought each other outside the ground, and apart from a slight altercation near the train station, Leeds fans were not involved.

I thought it would be interesting at this point in the story to name my own 'six pack' of the dearest and cheapest alcohol I've sampled while globetrotting with Leeds United. Note the dates.

The most expensive are (all per pint): Djurgarden, Sweden (£2.50, 1984); Tokyo nightclub (£10, 1991); Oslo, Norway (£7, 2004); Stavanger, Norway (£6.50, 2005); Dublin (£6, 2008); Sandefjord, Norway (£11, 2010).

Sounding more like a Happy Hour, the cheapest are: Kuala Lumpur (60p per pint, 1994); Local bar, Moscow (25p large vodka, 1999); Johannesburg, SA (50p per pint, 1999); Sofia, Bulgaria (50p per pint, 1999); Local bar, Prague (20p large vodka, 2000); Bratislava, Slovakia (60p per pint, 2010).

In 2002, Queen Elizabeth II celebrated her Golden Jubilee. The Winter Olympics took place in Salt Lake City, Utah. The Queen's sister Princess Margaret died of a major stroke in her sleep, aged 71, and the Queen Mother made her final public appearance at the funeral. At the age of 101 on 30 March the Queen Mother passed away.

The 2002 FIFA World Cup took place in Japan and South Korea with Brazil claiming their fifth victory following a 2-0 win against Germany in the final. England's Stuart Pearce (40), Lee Dixon (38) and Matthew Le Tissier (33) all retired from the game.

In February 1984 a goal by George McCluskey gave Leeds a fine 1-0 Second Division victory at Cardiff City but sadly that remains our last triumph there to date. The following season Cardiff were relegated and our paths would not cross again until January 2002 and the third round of the FA Cup. Leeds were riding high in the Premier League and Cardiff were struggling in the Second Division.

Things looked to be going OK for Leeds when Mark Viduka scored after 12 minutes. But things changed dramatically in the second half when referee Andy D'Urso (who minutes earlier had been struck by a missile thrown by Welsh fans) sent off Alan Smith for an apparent elbow incident. TV footage afterwards appeared to exonerate Smith, but the decision undoubtedly altered the course of the game.

Cardiff, sensing they could salvage a draw and consequently a replay at Elland Road, began to throw men forward against the ten men of the visitors. They forced an equaliser and then unbelievably grabbed a winner in the closing minutes, sparking pandemonium among the home fans.

Cardiff chairman Sam Hammam has been blamed, quite rightly in my opinion, as one of the main reasons for the ugly scenes that followed. Despite being warned several times by the police to sit down, he persisted in goading the Leeds fans and walking around the pitch patting his head with his hands in what is now commonly known as doing 'The Ayatollah'.

Not surprisingly, Leeds fans were incandescent with rage, but it also sparked off the Cardiff supporters too. When the final whistle went and as Leeds players raced for the tunnel, thousands of home followers invaded the pitch and made for the Leeds end. Some attempted to scale the walls and get among the visitors. Luckily, several hundred Leeds fans raced forward to prevent this from happening and that persuaded the home fans to look elsewhere for their 'bit of fun'.

Eventually police restored order but the trouble continued outside on the way back to the Leeds coaches and trains. Even police officers were attacking Leeds fans with batons and several of them, witnessed by many, were saying things along the lines of 'you English bastards shouldn't be here anyway'. Many were scrunching up their uniforms so that their numbers could not be seen on the shoulder, before launching into innocent Leeds fans, including women and children, who were screaming and crying. One supporter was savaged by police dogs as he stood near his coach. His injuries were horrific and eventually after many TV appearances he was awarded substantial damages.

I wrote, as did countless others, to South Wales Constabulary to complain and I received a letter from Superintendent Twigg who promised to investigate the accusations. Several weeks later I received a further letter which basically said it had been impossible to uncover any guilty officers, but he promised that certain procedures would be re-addressed (now where have I heard that before?). Mr Twigg also thanked me for bringing this to his attention. Cardiff City Football Club were fined a mere £20,000 by the FA.

In Europe, victory over Grasshoppers in the previous round of the UEFA Cup subsequently took us to yet another previously visited destination, Eindhoven. By now visible cracks were beginning to appear in the relationship between chairman Peter Ridsdale and his manager David O'Leary and defeat against PSV – Leeds lost the second leg at Elland Road 1-0 a week after the goalless draw in Holland – would be O'Leary's last European encounter with the club.

O'Leary guided Leeds to fifth in the Premier League in 2001/02 but by the time the Whites went to Ukraine in the following season's UEFA Cup he had been replaced by that cheeky Cockney, Terry Venables.

We were based in the fine city of Kiev, before flying into Donetsk for the match against Metalurg Zapor and a slender 2-1 aggregate win over the Ukrainians threw up a contest between 'El Tel' and Tel Aviv.

Because of the ongoing trouble in Israel, Leeds's tie with Hapoel Tel Aviv was switched to Florence in Italy. Several Hapoel players had been openly criticising Alan Smith, calling him a 'thug' among other things. It was a clear attempt by the Israelis to goad Smith into a confrontation but the player answered his critics in perfect style. Leeds triumphed 4-1 in Florence and Smith scored all four.

The next European trip was to the sunny climate of Malaga and after a credible goalless draw in Spain, Leeds were expected to progress to the fourth round, but a shock 2-1 victory by Malaga ended the exploits in Europe of Venables's men.

It remains United's last game in European competition to date but, much more importantly, it signalled the beginning of Leeds's disastrous downward spiral into the darkest depths of the Football League.

In 2003, over ten million people throughout the world protested against the probability of war in Iraq. Weeks later, American and allied forces began the invasion. On 22 July Iraq President Saddam Hussein's two sons Uday and Qusay were killed by troops. Later in the year Hussein was captured in Tikrit.

Concorde made its final flight and Russian billionaire Roman Abramovich purchased Chelsea for £150m from Ken Bates, who bought the club 21 years earlier for £1. In a dramatic final England won the Rugby World Cup by defeating Australia 20-17 after extra time.

The Premier League campaign continued and was a troubled one for Leeds, and by the time an away game at Charlton Athletic arrived in April there had been a change again in the manager's office with Peter Reid taking over from Venables.

What followed was a performance and result that stands out from the rest at The Valley as Leeds won 6-1 thanks to a hat-trick from Mark Viduka, two from Harry Kewell and a further penalty by Ian Harte.

It gave the Whites a real boost towards their target of Premier League survival, though it still hadn't been confirmed by the penultimate game of the season away to Arsenal – the top flight's defending champions, who were bidding to retain their crown.

Many Leeds fans were in fancy dress, as is customary for the final away game, but there was a deep sense of nervousness hovering above the 5,000 travellers massed in the Clock End.

Leeds, however, got off to the best possible start when Harry Kewell scored a stunning opener after just five minutes. Thierry Henry levelled for Arsenal but five minutes into the second half the visitors regained their lead with a Harte free kick, but Arsenal equalised again through Dennis Bergkamp. Arsenal needed to win to keep their title hopes on track but Mark Viduka sent the away supporters into dreamland with a winner two minutes from time.

I can remember being more relieved than I had ever been in my whole life as Leeds fans smiling and crying at the same time hugged each other. About 20 in fancy dress then started a massive conga.

As always with Leeds, there was a downside to this particular afternoon, well two actually. The first was that by beating Arsenal we had inadvertently handed the Premier League trophy to those pillocks from Old Trafford. I watched on the news later that evening and saw hundreds of their fans dancing around and cheering every time Leeds scored each of the three goals. I really didn't know whether to laugh or cry. One consolation I told myself was that I would never in a million years ever cheer one of their goals, not even if my life depended on it.

To make things even worse, the second downside was that our victory at Highbury turned out to be just a stay of execution as we were relegated the following season anyway.

Early in that 2003/04 campaign we were away to Leicester City, who had been promoted to the Premier League at the end of 2002/03. Over the years, Leeds fans were gradually moved from behind the goal at Leicester's Filbert Street home and put down the side into a grotty old stand with a very poor view of the pitch. Although it held fond memories of my early days supporting the Whites, I certainly wasn't sad to see the back of Filbert Street when the club moved to a new stadium, imaginatively called The Walkers Stadium – after their sponsors Walkers Crisps – in 2003.

Filbert Street was demolished in 2002 but we didn't play Leicester in their first season in their new ground because they had been relegated to the First Division in 2001/02. They came straight back up and we only had to wait until September to get our first glimpse of the Walkers Stadium when they came back up to the Premier League.

We'd had a pretty poor start that season but Leicester hadn't won a game for six weeks. Inevitably our encounter was shown on Sky Sports. I use the word 'encounter' loosely. We unveiled our new signing for this game, our first and only Brazilian, Jose Vitor Roque Junior. The legendary veteran 'Rocky' had played 50 times for Brazil and had won the World Cup, and he had won the Champions League with AC Milan, so he was seen as a real scoop by Leeds. Manager Peter Reid proudly announced, 'He is a big boost for the squad. He can play left-back or left centre-half and he is another quality player at the club.'

Eyebrows were raised higher than Roger Moore's on *Spitting Image*. 'How come Leeds have managed to get him?' the media gasped. 'Especially in their financial position.'

Well, I think I have the answer to that particular poser. I don't for one minute believe it was the real Roque Junior. Not by any stretch. It is my belief that the real man was met at the airport, tied, gagged and bundled into the boot of a waiting car and replaced by an imposter who clearly had never kicked or headed a football in his entire life.

Given the job of securing and inspiring the defence, Rocky spent the entire game at the Walkers Stadium looking behind him as every ball either sailed over his head or whizzed past it. Thankfully Leicester declared at 4-0, but the Leeds fans couldn't believe what they had just seen.

Four months later Leeds offloaded Rocky. He had played just seven times, had been on the losing side six times, had been booked four times, sent off once and his defence had conceded 24 goals. I never found out what happened to this imposter but the real Roque Junior went on to continue playing for Brazil.

I was on holiday a few years back having a drink in my favourite bar in Key West, Florida. I was sat at the bar in the Bottlecap when this lad came over and having seen my Leeds shirt, introduced himself as a Leicester City fan. We got talking and he said, 'I can remember beating you lot 4-0 a bit back. You had a big black lad at centre-back. He was really shit, who was that?'

I laughed and replied, 'Roque Junior from Brazil.' He then laughed as well and after taking a gulp of his beer he said, 'No really mate, who was he?'

Less than two months after that defeat at Leicester we travelled to Portsmouth and suffered a 6-1 defeat that contributed to our eventual relegation and fall from grace that had the whole football world rejoicing like never before.

Portsmouth have since gone on to suffer the same fate as Leeds did, as too have several other clubs. As president of the Kippax Flat Earth Society I can only loosely use the comment, 'What goes around comes around.'

Reid lost his job two days after the defeat at Portsmouth and club legend Eddie Gray took over for a second spell in charge, this time in a caretaker capacity, and he would oversee an excellent result at manchester united the following February.

The memorable win at manchester united came in 2004, a year that saw serial killer Dr Harold Shipman found dead in his cell, while more than 225,000 people were killed in a massive tsunami in the Indian Ocean on Boxing Day.

In sport, Middlesbrough won the first trophy in their 128-year history by beating Bolton Wanderers to claim the League Cup. FC Porto won the European Cup under the guidance of Jose Mourinho and a month later he became the new manager of Chelsea.

England were defeated 6-5 on penalties by Portugal at Euro 2004, and Great Britain won nine gold, nine silver and 12 bronze medals at the Olympics in Athens.

Over the years I've travelled to Old Trafford by car, train, coach, bus and even taxi. We once turned up at Old Trafford for an evening game on a Leeds Transport double decker bus. This was just for a reserve fixture.

On one occasion I travelled with a few mates on the train. To avoid police harassment we had travelled on a service train and not the usual football special. We did this so that we could catch a later train home, once everything had died down. But, after the game, the police forced everyone back to the station en masse. This resulted in a somewhat lengthy altercation with some home fans.

That in itself wasn't much of a problem but the police suddenly became very heavy-handed, wielding batons and generally making it uncomfortable for Leeds fans. It was then that I spied a taxi in a side street. 'Come on, let's get in that taxi,' I said to Rolf. 'Where to?' he said. 'Back to Leeds,' I said. 'It'll be a lot easier than hanging around here for two more hours.' And that's what we did. It was only £60 between five of us. Now that's a bargain.

This was in 2004. Alan Smith had earned Leeds a 1-1 draw but that would be made largely irrelevant in the eyes of fans by the eventual relegation and Smith immediately jumping ship to sign for manchester united. He was banned from the Kingdom of Leeds forever.

A month later we travelled to QPR's Loftus Road for a 2-0 defeat – though to Fulham, who were sharing the ground as work was taking place on their Craven Cottage home.

Leeds haven't played Fulham since, which is a great shame as it has deprived fans the opportunity to see the statue of Michael Jackson that was unveiled outside the stadium in 2011.

Jackson, who was made entirely out of white plastic, had become Fulham's number one supporter when he attended a game in 2009. Despite this being the only game that the alleged singer had ever attended, Fulham's crackpot chairman Mohamed Al-Fayed made the decision, without discussion, to erect a statue in recognition of their international celebrity supporter.

'Bizarre' was just one of the words used to describe the statue. Others were far less complimentary. But Al-Fayed simply said of Fulham's fans, 'If some stupid fans don't appreciate such a gift, they can go to hell. I don't want them to be fans. If they don't believe in things I believe in, they can go to Chelsea, they can go anywhere else.'

The statue was removed in September 2013 after Al-Fayed sold the club to new owners, and Fulham went on to be relegated at the end of the 2013/14 season. Al-Fayed then claimed that relegation was a result of the statue being taken away, saying, 'This statue was a charm and we removed the luck from the club and now we have to pay the price.'

※ ※ ※ ※ ※

We blitzed Bolton Wanderers 3-0 at the Reebok Stadium in 2002 with goals from Danny Mills, Robbie Fowler and Jason Wilcox, but our luck ran out in May 2004 when after going ahead through a Mark Viduka penalty, for no apparent reason he then inexplicably pressed the self-destruct button and was dismissed.

Bolton then easily pushed our ten men aside and ran out comfortable 4-1 winners. This defeat all but condemned Leeds to relegation and it turned out to be Viduka's last goal and last appearance for the club, as he, and others, jumped a sinking ship.

The Reebok is nestled in sloping green hills outside of Bolton. A few weeks after this defeat I disappeared out of the way on holiday and I drove past it on the motorway on my way to Oban on the west coast of Scotland, but I couldn't bring myself to look at it.

26

Father Cadfan

J UST over 30 years after a raucous night in Edinburgh I returned to Easter Road in July 2004 and witnessed Leeds capture what remains the club's last silverware to date. After having just been relegated from the Premier League weeks earlier Leeds beat Hibernian 3-1 to win the coveted Whyte and Mackay Challenge Cup.

Leeds had secured their first trophy for 12 years having qualified for the final by having Whyte and Mackay as their sponsor. Hibernian were also sponsored by the Scottish whisky manufacturers, the only other club to be sponsored by them in fact but, hey, a trophy is a trophy!

Right from the start, the Hibs fans began taunting the 2,500 Leeds followers with chants of 'There's only one Alan Smith,' in reference to Smith's recent departure from Elland Road and across the border to Old Trafford. We responded with a resounding, 'We've got Ricketts!' in proud defiance.

Michael Ricketts went on to score twice for Leeds along with one from Frazer Richardson. And despite winning it, the cup could not be presented to Leeds because of trouble inside the ground between home and away fans. It was decided by both clubs to adjourn any presentation to prevent further agitation. Admittedly, it was nothing compared to the scenes that had occurred back at Easter Road on that November night in 1973, but it was sufficient to mean that the first time any fan saw the trophy was at our own Kippax Branch function in Leeds a month later.

Manager Kevin Blackwell personally brought the trophy along to the Viaduct pub where, I have to say, copious amounts of alcoholic beverage were consumed by our White Rose branch as we celebrated in style.

Prior to the 2004/05 season we hadn't visited Rotherham United since December 1982 but almost 22 years on we were back at Millmoor, still finding our feet after relegation from the Premier League but tipped to dispose of the Championship's bottom club, who were yet to win all season.

It was Monday 29 November and the TV cameras were there, no doubt hoping for an upset. In the TV gantry that evening was a certain Neil Warnock, manager of Sheffield United, Leeds's fierce rivals that season.

Millmoor was full to its creaking rafters with a sell-out crowd of 8,860. Around half of those had travelled down the M1 from Leeds and the majority were housed behind one of the goals. Just to our left was the TV gantry. Warnock was spotted immediately, grinning through the glass at the rather irate Leeds faithful.

Worse was to come when Rotherham went into the lead. This created pandemonium among Leeds fans as Warnock could be seen quite clearly smiling from ear to ear. Things were fast turning ugly as missiles were launched at the gantry. The game finished 1-0 to Rotherham, but Warnock had long since been moved by police and stewards. Rotherham were relegated at the end of that season.

Our Boxing Day 2004 visit to Sunderland was certainly an eventful day. Early that morning we were stood outside the pub waiting to get picked up by our coach for the trip north. It was dark, cold and icy and we were freezing our nuts off. I happened to look down at the ice-covered car park and saw what looked like a £20 note under the ice. 'Oh, look,' I said, 'there's a 20 quid note there.' Tico laughed and said something like, 'Yeah, OK mate.'

I chipped away at the ice and sure enough it was a £20 note. It was soaking wet and with bits of ice on it. It was £20 nonetheless. 'I'll get a round in with that when we get back tonight,' I said, folding it carefully and putting it in my shirt pocket. 'Too right you will,' said a rather irate Tico. 'You jammy bastard.' I told him that he'd had every opportunity to pick it up before me, but he wasn't having any of it.

After our fine 3-2 win that afternoon, our coach stopped at a nice-looking pub in Spennymoor. It was in the middle of a housing estate and appeared the perfect watering hole for an hour. There were around 50 of us in the pub and a couple of Sunderland fans, who were none too pleased. Not only had we just beaten their team, we had taken over their pub.

We were playing darts, cards or dominoes and were totally oblivious to the Sunderland fans. Then, as me and Neil chatted away like two old women supping our pints, I looked around and noticed that our lot had gone. Not only that, the pub was now full of Sunderland fans. No one noticed that we were Leeds supporters and I said, 'We'd better get out of here and find our lot.'

As we got to the double doors leading outside, we heard the Mackems shouting and swearing at our coach as it drove away down the road. 'They've gone without us,' said Neil, quite calmly. We pushed through the Sunderland fans, which really threw them and took them aback somewhat. Then I said, 'Come on lads, coming through.' You could have cut my Yorkshire accent with a blunt knife. 'Fuckin' ell,' one of them said, 'There's a load of 'em still in here.'

Some of them panicked, though there were only two of us, and then it was total pandemonium when our bus (we found out later that they had quickly noticed Neil and I weren't on) turned round and headed back towards the pub and parked about 30 yards away.

All hell broke loose as the Sunderland fans all raced back inside the pub. Neil and I calmly strode on to the bus. Then the locals got their courage back and came back out of the pub and towards the coach. We knew that if we stayed on the bus the windows would certainly get put through, so we got off.

When our lads left the pub the first time they had sensed trouble and had taken some pool cues to use as protection. There then followed an awkward silence and a stand-off ensued. There we were, stood with our backs to the side of the coach and facing about 60 or 70 of them stood across the road. All it would take was for someone to sneeze and it would have kicked off big style, of that there is absolutely no doubt.

Just then one of their lads, a stocky skinhead who looked to be in charge, came across and said, 'Look lads, there's no need for any trouble, give us our cues back and we'll call it a draw.' Slowly the cues were handed back, but no one even blinked as everyone was staring at everyone else. 'OK, lads, let's go,' shouted Ralph. 'Back on the bus, come on.' Slowly we all climbed aboard backwards and never once took our eyes off of the Sunderland fans.

The coach doors closed and Steve, our driver, accelerated as though he was at Brands Hatch. In the distance we could see some of them angrily waving their fists but we had managed to get away unscathed and with no bloodshed. No sooner had we got through the doors back at our pub two hours later, than Tico shouted to me, 'Get that 20 quid out!'

The round of drinks cost me just over £28!

In 2005, a concert featuring many artists at the Millennium Stadium, Cardiff, raised £1.25m for the victims of the previous year's tsunami in the Indian Ocean. Prince Charles married Camilla Parker

Bowles at Windsor Castle and Labour won the General Election to remain in power.

Dr Who returned to our TV screens on the BBC after an absence of 15 years with actor Christopher Eccleston playing the Doctor and Billie Piper as his assistant. Liverpool became champions of Europe for the fifth time after a thrilling victory over AC Milan that saw them come from 3-0 down thanks to an inspirational captain's job by Steven Gerrard to draw 3-3 before beating the Italians on penalties.

After seeing Leeds finish in the 19th hole of the Premier League in May 2004 and subsequently suffer relegation, it's no wonder that many fans took to drink. I know I did. Let's be honest, it wasn't a brilliant period in our history.

Kevin Blackwell had only a couple of players with less than three weeks to the beginning of the Championship season and when the start did come, we had a team consisting mainly of loan players. We even had Ricketts – Michael Ricketts to be exact.

To be fair, we did score the fastest goal of the entire 2004/05 season when Jermaine Wright put Leeds ahead against Burnley after just 12 seconds in November 2004 – but we still lost 2-1.

As previously mentioned we gave Rotherham their first win of the season, and we were all pretty glad that we'd had that drink on New Year's Eve as we started 2005 with a forgettable 2-0 defeat to Crewe Alexandra at Elland Road. I had wrapped myself around quite a few glasses of alcohol and I had to watch most of the match with a hand over one eye to avoid seeing 44 players – it really does work if you ever find yourself in that position.

One morning I stirred in a hotel room, it was early April, and as everyone does, I thought back to what had happened the night before and a huge smile appeared on my face, even though my eyes had not yet fully opened.

A few of us had decided to stay over after the Watford match at Vicarage Road and we had been rewarded with a victory (it would be the only one in Leeds's final five games) so we had pushed the boat out so to speak. Over a messy curry and a lethal concoction of lager along with huge dollops of wine and whisky we discussed our club's current predicament.

We were back in the second tier. We had been knocked out of round three of the League Cup and the FA Cup and yet here we were mopping spilt curry off the tablecloth with our chapattis and discussing the prospect, after our recent win, of building a team around Sean Gregan.

The fact that Gregan (I'm sure he won't mind me saying this) had an arse so big that it can be seen from the Moon had escaped us. So too, apparently, did the fact that our ranks consisted of such household names as Steve Guppy, Leandre Griffit, Martin Woods, John Oster, Nathan Blake and Julian Joachim. Perhaps I'm being a bit unfair on these lads because we were also blessed with the presence of a certain Marlon King for nine games, including five as a substitute.

So, wedged at 14th place, we eventually finished what had been quite a dull season. Just for the record, Nottingham Forest and Gillingham went down with Rotherham.

Gregan was still at the seat of the Leeds team at the start of the 2005/06 season as they saw off Millwall 2-1 in the opener at Elland Road thanks to a brace from David Healy, a firm favourite with the fans. Leeds, of course, would go on to the play-off final, but it was the result at Southampton that was without doubt the highlight of the season.

Four of us had decided to fly down to Southampton for a change as we prepared to take in the November encounter. I must admit it was strange being sat in Leeds airport with the kick-off just two and a half hours away and still 235 miles away from Southampton.

Following our heavy drinking of the previous season we had begun to slow down which was a good job as it turned out. Our plane soared into the sky and down again in Hampshire so fast that I only had time for two whiskies. It took us 25 minutes to arrive and our taxi driver, after trying to tempt us to indulge in a different kind of exercise close to the docks, dropped us off at a pub that was full to the brim with Leeds supporters.

I have talked a lot about new grounds and in 2001 Southampton were another to switch as they moved from The Dell to the St Mary's Stadium. Four years on from that we saw what is easily the most dramatic of games between the Saints and Leeds on the south coast.

A Southampton side containing a very little Dennis Wise and a very young Theo Walcott stormed into the lead and at half-time they were three up. With just over 20 minutes left of the second half, Kevin Blackwell brought substitute David Healy on and Leeds immediately pulled one back through Paul Butler. Five minutes later Robbie Blake gave the travelling fans a glimmer of hope by making it 3-2.

Those supporters were in raptures seven minutes from time when Healy equalised with a penalty and then incredibly two minutes later the on-loan Liam Miller scored the winner to spark off unbelievable scenes in the Leeds end and leave Saints manager Harry Redknapp with his head buried in his hands. We were staying the night in a Premier Inn and the faces on the Southampton fans in the hotel bar were not happy ones!

This game sparked off a sequence of four wins on the trot, something that hadn't happened for five years. This was followed by two successive defeats, but that was countered by another four wins on the bounce – Leeds United, it appeared, were on the up.

The following season, however, after playing just one game, Sean Gregan left the club with an ambitious move to Oldham Athletic. Reports that he was the man behind the phenomenal fashion business Jacamo are as yet unconfirmed.

Later in the month following the Southampton drama came a visit to Millwall, by now also in their new home after relocating from Cold Blow Lane and The Den to a new stadium, imaginatively called The New Den. We picked up the points there thanks to an own goal that secured a 1-0 win.

Although not half as bad as the 'old' Den, Millwall is still a menacing place to travel to and from. Afterwards, thousands of Millwall fans, some waving Turkey flags in reference to two Leeds fans murdered in Galatasaray in April 2000, lined the streets of Bermondsey as the away buses snaked past them, with many of the buses carrying a souvenir that had been deposited through the window.

How does their song go again? 'No one likes us?' Too bloody right they don't.

It was soon time to get going with 2006, a year in which Liberal Democrat leader Charles Kennedy resigned after admitting he had a drink problem and Queen Elizabeth II celebrated her 80th birthday.

Great Britain won one silver medal at the Winter Olympics in Turin, Italy, the BBC announced that *Grandstand* would cease to be broadcast within the next year after nearly 50 years on our screens, England bowed out of the World Cup at the quarter-final stage after a defeat to Portugal on penalties and following the tournament, Steve McClaren replaced Sven-Goran Eriksson to become the 12th England manager.

Former national team boss Ron Greenwood passed away and following 93 years at Highbury, Arsenal moved to their magnificent new stadium, The Emirates.

The 2006 highlight, or should I say lowlight, for me, would come in Cardiff. A few other stories prior to that first though.

In what was our second season in the Championship we were in contention for a return to the Premier League and eventually qualified for the play-offs by finishing fifth, helped by a 1-0 win at Crewe Alexandra in April that was slightly upstaged by the fact that I took a monk to the game.

Father Cadfan from Herefordshire joined me on the Kop as part of a BBC documentary. It was his first football match but after a dour afternoon I would wager that Father Cadfan was more than happy to be back behind his plough at the monastery the following morning.

A 2-0 defeat at Preston North End on the final day meant that we finished fifth and Preston nipped above us to finish fourth, setting up a play-off semi-final between the two teams with the first leg at Elland Road and the return at Deepdale.

During the rise of Don Revie's young Leeds team in the early 1960s, one of the most physical teams around at that time were Preston. Leeds were labelled as physical, even 'dirty' in many newspaper offices, but there were others who escaped the same attention such as Everton, Sunderland and even Bury, all of whom were undoubtedly just as physical, if not more than Leeds ever were. Preston beat Leeds 2-0 in 1964 in what was described as an x-rated encounter.

Four decades after that game I paid my first visit to Deepdale, with Leeds running out 4-2 winners, but the following season produced the most memorable of tussles in the play-offs.

A workmanlike performance from Preston earned them a 1-1 draw in the first leg at Elland Road, prompting their manager Billy Davies to proclaim 'job done' in the newspapers and hint that the second leg was a formality.

Kevin Blackwell wasn't entirely happy with Davies's statement and prior to the second leg at Deepdale he simply pinned the newspaper article to the door of the Leeds dressing room. This certainly had the desired effect on his players who ran out deserved 2-0 victors with goals by Rob Hulse and Frazer Richardson taking them to the Millennium Stadium for the final. Preston, incidentally, hold the current record for play-off appearances, eight. But they have yet to gain promotion via this route.

%. %. %. %. %.

One of my encounters with Watford brought about my only visit to date to the Millennium Stadium in Cardiff and I have to say I was very impressed with it. Much more impressed than I was with the Leeds performance that day against the Hornets in the play-off final of 2006.

We should have known what to expect earlier that morning as we had breakfast in our Welsh hotel. The landlord, who claimed he was a Leeds fan, informed us that it had just been on his radio while he was cooking our bacon and eggs that Kevin Blackwell had revealed his side for the big game and that the formation was to be just one up front. That's just one lone striker. It was as if Leeds were playing for a draw in what was, after all, a 'cup final'.

No one could quite believe it, including it appears, Watford's manager Aidy Boothroyd, who said afterwards, 'Once the Leeds team and their formation was announced, I tweaked ours and added an extra striker.'

It just wasn't fair to the 36,000 Leeds fans who filed into the stadium that afternoon. From the first minute Leeds were on the back foot and the only surprise to everyone was that we were only one goal behind at half-time. As expected, Leeds went further behind during the second period and then with the score standing at 3-0, Blackwell's decision to throw more strikers up front was met with derision by the supporters, who knew it was a vain attempt and much too late to have any impact on the game.

The booing from the travelling Whites was disappointing as the clock ticked down, but totally understandable under the forlorn situation we found ourselves in. Once again in a stadium where Leeds fans had vastly outnumbered their counterparts we were left to wonder what direction the club was heading in.

This was Ken Bates's first season in charge as chairman of the club and word was rife among fans that Leeds, who were just about getting on top of crippling debt inherited from the previous regime headed by Peter Ridsdale and David O'Leary, would still owe a considerable amount of money should they return to the Premier League within a certain period. This in turn fuelled speculation that this was the reason for Leeds seemingly taking their foot off the gas as they neared possible promotion. And it wouldn't be the last time that such rumours were to surface.

%, %, %, %, %

At a very early age, I had been struck with the cleanliness of Scandinavia and this has been prevalent on my many visits since and none more so than when we rolled into Sarpsborg once again for a friendly against SK Sparta Sarpsborg in July 2006.

The Leeds team had obviously long since changed from back in 1970. We drew this game 2-2 and our two goalscorers, Ole Heiren Hansen (own goal) and Eirik Bakke (penalty), were only seven years old at the time of the previous match, but the enthusiasm for Leeds has increased on a scale that is unimaginable.

I too have changed a little since then. I used to collect beer mats and I still have one with the name of Bryggerier emblazoned on it. This is the name of the local brewery and nowadays I am able to witness this fine product first hand although, be warned dear friends, it's far from cheap. I've no idea how much this beer was back in the days of British decimalisation, but today a pint of the local brew can set you back anything up to £8. Ouch!

In the 2006/07 Championship season we resumed our meetings with Luton Town with the Hatters having been promoted from League 1 at the end of the previous campaign.

We headed to Kenilworth Road in October 2006 with John Carver in caretaker charge after the departure of Kevin Blackwell and returned having been beaten 5-1.

Just months later Carver had joined Luton as assistant to Blackwell but at the end of the season everyone would be reunited in League 1.

That came in 2007, when England suffered a 5-0 whitewash to Australia in the Ashes series Down Under, Laura Pearce became the first contestant on Channel 4's *Deal or No Deal* to win the top prize of £250,000 and on 27 January the final edition of the BBC's flagship sports programme, *Grandstand*, was aired.

Al-Qaeda threatened to either kidnap or kill Prince Harry during his forthcoming tour of duty in Iraq and back at home, six years after the old Wembley closed, the new 90,000-capacity stadium was opened, with its arch dominating the London skyline. The first FA Cup Final at the new venue saw Chelsea beat manchester united 1-0.

In 2002 Boothferry Park was demolished and Hull City moved to a brand new ground – the KC Stadium. Leeds to date have never had a great deal of luck at this ground, but bizarrely when we did manage a 2-1 win there in January 2007, we actually dropped a place in the league, thrusting us into the depths of the Championship table along with Hull. We never recovered while Hull did manage to get themselves out of trouble and the following season, unbelievably, they were promoted to the Premier League.

Southend-on-Sea was one of the places that had eluded us over the years. But we did finally get our visit to the seaside in March 2007 and it was OK. We stayed in a motel-type complex that resembled a ranch from *The High Chaparral* or something of that nature. It did however have its own late bar and large concert room, which we made a mental note of for after the game.

Roots Hall is a compact little ground with not the best vantage points for away fans, or I would guess for home fans either, but it was a glorious mid-March afternoon as play got under way.

Leeds looked much the better team and should have scored inside ten minutes but it was Southend who got the first goal. It was about now that anyone listening to the match on their radio could be forgiven for thinking that they had tuned into a game in Moscow by mistake. An error by big Lubo Michalik gifted the hosts an unexpected lead with about half an hour gone and seconds later at the other end, Kishishev was denied the equaliser by the crossbar.

Leeds did manage to get that equaliser through David Healy with just two minutes remaining. Healy had only been on the pitch for five minutes. Then in the final minute of stoppage time Simon Francis handled the ball right in front of the referee, Nigel Miller, who immediately pointed for a penalty. As Healy hurriedly picked up the ball and put it on the spot, Miller pointed his finger somewhere else and instead awarded a free kick to Southend.

This occurred at the opposite end to us and we could not see what was happening. We did see Leeds boss Dennis Wise running up and down the touchline screaming at the referee. Then a split second after Southend took their free kick, the final whistle went. It was a bizarre end to a game from which Leeds should easily have taken all three points.

After a few drinks along the cold seafront, we returned to our ranch and our very own bar. As we headed for the bar through the reception we could hear loud, strange noises coming from the concert room. Andy said, 'It sounds pretty lively in there, let's have a look.' It was as if we had stumbled upon a set from Bollywood. There must have been five or six hundred Indians celebrating a wedding. Most of us are partial to the odd curry or onion bhaji so we snuck in as incognito as possible. Of course we were quickly rumbled, but we were allowed to stay and even danced with the new bride. In fact one of the lads danced with the groom.

After that infamous FA Cup tie we did not visit Colchester United again until the 2006/07 season with Leeds and Colchester now in the Championship. Again we lost, this time a 2-1 defeat in April 2007.

Things went from bad to worse as Leeds were relegated at the end of that season to League 1 to create the unbelievable scenario of Colchester being in a division above us. They say revenge is a dish best served cold and the following season Colchester dropped into our division and battle commenced.

The whole world was focused on the ensuing League 1 battles between Leeds and Colchester. For the next two seasons Leeds travelled to Colchester, who by now were playing at a stadium known as Cuckoo Farm, registering 1-0 and 2-1 victories respectively, before soaring back to the glorious heights of the Championship. Take that Colchester!

27

Hereford?
Cheltenham? Yeovil?

T HE opening game of the 2007/08 season, our first fixture in
League 1, was away at Tranmere Rovers and that particular
visit to Prenton Park is a pleasant memory.

It was a 2-1 win and also the first match of that amazing unbeaten
run by the team that is mentioned more than once elsewhere on
these pages.

A few days later came our first – and so far only – game against
the mighty Macclesfield Town, a 1-0 win earned thanks to the
equally mighty Ian Westlake.

Less than 3,500 fans, the vast majority from Leeds, swelled
Macclesfield's Moss Rose ground for this eagerly-awaited League
Cup first round tie.

On Macclesfield's bench that evening was Asa Hartford, who
was assistant manager to Ian Brightwell. Leeds fans of a certain age
will remember Hartford, who was on the verge of signing for Don
Revie's great side of the 1970s. That was until a hole in his heart was
detected and the deal was called off.

A notable fixture away to Nottingham Forest in August 2007
is certainly worthy of a special mention. As well as beginning their
first season in League 1, Leeds had also been severely handicapped
by a vigorously disputed, and much-publicised 15-point penalty by
the Football League.

Undeterred and under the grossly unlikely leadership of Dennis
Wise and his assistant Gus Poyet, Leeds had begun the season in fine
style, winning their first two games. Backed vociferously by hordes
of fans, goals by Tresor Kandol and Jermaine Beckford gave United a
pleasant 2-1 victory and brought their tally to just minus six points.

As the players and management embraced in what was to become a familiar sight that season, the supporters chanted, 'Six more points to go before we get to zero', and defiantly, 'Fuck off to the Football League!' Leeds went on to wipe out the 15-point deficit in their first five games.

Leeds didn't play Bristol Rovers in a league game between 1962 and 2007 so I personally never got to visit their Eastville Stadium. Financial difficulties forced Rovers to move from Eastville in 1986 and after ten years playing in Bath at Twerton Park they moved to their present ground, the Memorial Stadium in Bristol, in 1996.

Relegation to League 1 meant that at least we got to visit a few new grounds, which included the Memorial Stadium. Because of the St Paul's Festival on the same day our scheduled first visit there was moved to a Friday evening kick-off in September 2007.

Although it was early in the season, Rovers were flying high and a tough game was expected but Wise and Poyet saw their side cruise to a comfortable 3-0 victory.

With all those different homes you would have thought that Rovers' nickname would have been 'The Cuckoos' but they are in fact known as 'The Pirates' due to the famous maritime history of Bristol.

That said, many Rovers fans call themselves 'The Gas'. When they played at Eastville Stadium there was a gasworks close by and the strong smell of gas was always very prominent.

Supporters of their fierce rivals Bristol City began calling Rovers 'The Gasheads' or 'The Gas' but far from having a derogatory effect, Rovers fans actually liked the name and it has stuck with the club ever since. Each season, the number 12 squad shirt is allocated by the club to 'The Gasheads' as a mark of respect to their fans as 'the 12th man'.

Just over a fortnight later Leeds went to Gillingham for a game that is still remembered today by the majority of Whites.

Dennis Wise, long despised and hated by Leeds fans, was now in charge. His assistant was Gus Poyet, who supporters took to immediately, but it took a long time for them to adjust to Wise – in fact most never did.

Despite the slightly alien relationship of Wise and Leeds, the beginning of 2007/08 was so successful that it equalled the club's best start to a season. Not since the days of Don Revie had Leeds won their first seven matches.

There will be more on that amazing start later but it was the siege mentality that Leeds adopted in the face of fierce provocation from the Football League that was undoubtedly the catalyst for the success.

Over a period of just two months United were docked 25 points; ten at the end of 2006/07 for entering administration and a further 15 points weeks before the start of the new season for the unprecedented charge of Ken Bates buying back the club without a Company Voluntary Arrangement. This meant that Leeds would begin their first ever season in League 1 on -15 points. It was ludicrous.

By the time Leeds rolled into Gillingham they had won their first seven games, wiping out the penalty and starting to climb the table. They were fully expected to continue their winning ways against a struggling Gillingham side.

It was business as usual as Sebastian Carole fired Leeds in front after half an hour but referee Danny McDermid had ideas of his own. Within five minutes either side of the interval McDermid had sent off Leeds strikers Tresor Kandol and Jermaine Beckford, who were the division's two leading scorers, and the nine men had to defend ferociously for the rest of the game.

With Kandol now standing among the Leeds fans on the terraces the match entered stoppage time and although Beckford's dismissal was the only interruption of the second half, Gillingham equalised in the seventh additional minute followed by the immediate full-time whistle blown by McDermid.

Furious Leeds fans vented their anger at the officials and Wise and McDermid clashed as they both approached the tunnel. In the aftermath, both accused each other of swearing at them.

Wise was fined £5,000 and given a three-match touchline ban. McDermid came up in front of the League Committee but escaped any punishment.

Not surprisingly, years after the 1990 riots, Bournemouth fans still hate and resent us Leeds supporters. The police are no different. When we visited there in 2007 they insisted on an evening kick-off to deter travelling fans and even when thousands of Leeds fans still arrived, they restricted our every move and tried to make sure we didn't enjoy this particular visit to the seaside.

The pitch had even been turned around at a 90-degree angle since our last visit, to disorientate us, but a 3-1 victory soon pissed on their parade.

The *Bournemouth Echo* had splashed reminders of the riots back in 1990 all over its pages prior to the match, a quite irresponsible thing to do given that those riots were 17 years before and a lot of the

Bournemouth fans would still have been in nappies back then. They may not have even been aware of what happened on that scorching hot Bank Holiday but now they had been fully informed.

It was interesting to note that following the match the *Bournemouth Echo* failed to mention that there were 14 arrests made in this 2007 clash and all 14 were Bournemouth fans.

Hereford United. Hereford United! I never imagined for one minute that we'd be playing a game of football against Hereford United. Absolutely no disrespect to Hereford whatsoever but as I would later think about Yeovil, the same thing could be said of Hereford. Where the f*** is Hereford?

Well, it is in England, just. Sixteen miles from the Welsh border in fact. They are English though, no doubting that, and it's a lovely part of the world. I'm saying there's no doubting that but, strangely, they do have another name – Henffordd – which is Hereford in Welsh. Way back in 1189 King Richard the First described the city as 'Hereford in Wales'. Are they really English? I'm beginning to wonder. They even won the Welsh Cup in 1990.

After 88 years of Leeds United's existence the club headed off to Hereford for the very first time in November 2007 for the first round of the FA Cup.

Every fan of a certain age remembers non-league Hereford United knocking the mighty Newcastle United out of the FA Cup in 1972. Ronnie Radford and Ricky George scored one each to sink the Magpies on a very muddy Edgar Street pitch.

As if that wasn't funny enough, my favourite story from that memorable occasion was the one about a policeman who was on duty. Constable 578, Grenville Smith, takes up the tale, 'When Radford scored the crowd ran on to the pitch, but I was ahead of them, cheering. I threw my helmet into the air and caught it. It was then that I remembered myself and began running around shouting, "Get off the pitch." What a day though.'

Smith is now a director at Hereford and will always remember that day back in January 1972.

Due in no small part to the influence of their player-manager, Leeds legend John Charles, Hereford were elected that same year into the Football League. The club are known for their floating support. Their fans turn out in their thousands when the team are doing well.

This was evident when Hereford climbed the league and reached the old Second Division in 1976. However the crowds disappeared as the team then plummeted to the depths of the league and back into non-league football in 1997. They returned to the Football League in 2007/08 and that's where we, Leeds United, came in.

Leeds were also spiralling towards the bottom of the Football League and were plying their trade, for the first time in their history, in the third tier of the English game. It was also the first time that Leeds had been in the first round of the FA Cup and the TV cameras were present at Edgar Street to capture a dour 0-0 Friday night draw.

The highlight of that evening was getting a phone call from one of the lads back home in Leeds telling me that my mate Stuart had just been on the TV. He was sat down at the front of the stand in his wheelchair decked in his Leeds hat and scarf. The cameras had caught him perfectly, fast asleep, mouth wide open and snoring his bloody head off!

The replay at Elland Road was even worse as far as Leeds fans were concerned. Somebody by the name of Lionel Ainsworth scored the only goal of the night to send Leeds out of the cup at the very first hurdle.

Flippin' heck, we're off to Cheltenham next. I thought Hereford was bad enough. Cheltenham? Where the f*** is that?

There have been plenty of years when Leeds United have regularly travelled to old something-or-other, Highbury, Anfield, Goodison Park and the like, but Whaddon Road?

No, surely this was not happening. Sinking to the depths of the old Third Division was something that anybody who was around in the 1970s would have laughed their heads off at, thinking you must be off your rocker. Super Leeds in the Third Division? Don't be daft.

Cheltenham Town versus Leeds United – you really are off your rocker. Sadly in 2007 this fixture became a fact. Cheltenham? Don't they do stuff with four-legged creatures that jump over fences? They don't play football do they?

The first meeting between the two clubs, in November 2007, ended with an astonishing outcome.

It wasn't that spectacular. The fixture was moved to Sunday because of a far more important event taking place on the Saturday. It was the big switch-on of the Christmas lights in the town centre and fearful of infiltration from thousands of Leeds fans (God only knows why they would think that), the game was moved. Apparently the lights weren't that spectacular either.

The match itself was a sell-out and as I looked around the ground I couldn't help thinking that I had been shrunk and I was at a Subbuteo match in a Subbuteo ground. The Leeds fans were all massed down one side and the rest of the crowd looked like it was painted on. Nobody moved. They all looked absolutely petrified as they just stared at the visiting supporters throughout.

Leeds knocked the ball around and it looked as though it was just a matter of time before they would score, but time passed and as the game entered the last few minutes the score was still 0-0. The Leeds fans roared as the strike force of Jermaine Beckford and Tresor Kandol surged forward, awaiting a cross from Seb Carole out wide. But the Cheltenham full-back robbed Carole and in a bid to waste precious time booted the ball forward.

There was no imminent danger as reserve keeper David Lucas (standing in for the injured Casper Ankergren) raced out of his box to launch the ball back up to the attack. But he messed up the clearance and the ball struck Cheltenham's Steven Gillespie who was as surprised as anybody as he tapped it into an empty net.

I wouldn't say Whaddon Road erupted, but some of the home fans did appear to move. Welcome to League 1.

As if that wasn't bad enough Cheltenham came to Elland Road the following March and beat us 2-1. The cheeky beggars! They became the first team to do the double over us in League 1. How embarrassing is that? That 1-0 win of Cheltenham's is officially regarded as 'the club's most famous victory'.

But fear not dear reader, the following season we stopped those pesky Cheltenham-ers in their tracks and we did the double over them. Becchio scored at Whaddon Road for a 1-0 victory and in February we rubbed their noses in it with a 2-0 triumph at Elland Road. That'll teach 'em. 'You're not singing anymore...' Oh, sorry, they weren't singing anyway.

I took a fair bit of stick over those two defeats in 2007/08. Cheltenham's captain was John Finnigan – who comes from my village of Kippax.

In recent years it has to be said that Huddersfield Town have been a bit of a thorn in United's side but there are two results that gave me great pleasure.

The first was a victory over Town at Elland Road in November 2007. This win was particularly satisfying due to the fact that earlier that morning, a few Huddersfield fans had crept up to Elland Road when no one was about and sprayed blue paint all over the statue of Billy Bremner. This understandably upset everyone connected to Leeds United, none more so than the players who went out that afternoon and pulverised Huddersfield to the tune of 4-0. Fast forward five seasons to find out about a very satisfying second result.

Since that emphatic 6-2 victory over Hartlepool United back in 1979 Leeds embarked on a bizarre rollercoaster of a ride over the next 30 years, which saw them relegated, promoted, win the league and then get relegated twice more before we met Hartlepool again, this time though in the depths of League 1 on Boxing Day 2007.

Even more bizarre was that the manager was now Dennis Wise. He was a bitter enemy of Leeds and their fans for many years. Now, though, he was one of us, but I don't mind admitting that it never really felt right. However, the 15-point penalty created a siege mentality of 'us and them' within the closed ranks, which overshadowed any bitterness towards Wise and his assistant Gus Poyet (although Poyet was always popular with the fans and regarded as the 'brains' of the operation) and it was all hands to the pump to try and avoid yet another drop, this time into the basement division, League 2.

Leeds though, got off to a blistering start and by the time Hartlepool arrived at Elland Road on 8 September the Whites had taken maximum points in their previous four games and victory against the north-easterners would give them 15 points and they would then be on 'nil'. After a somewhat edgy start Leeds finally overcame a plucky Hartlepool side 2-0 and could now start to climb the table, which indeed they did.

By the time Leeds visited the Victoria Ground for only my second game there we were racing up the table and a Jermaine Beckford goal earned a 1-1 draw and another priceless point in the quest to defy all the odds and in doing so stick two fingers up to the Football League.

It is of course illegal to drink alcohol on the coach to away games, but we tend to have drank up and cleared the bus of any empties by the time we pull up at a pub, usually about ten miles outside of the place we are playing at.

However the police in the north have a different policy to that of their colleagues in the south and whether it be Hartlepool, Darlington, Newcastle, Middlesbrough or Sunderland, as we trundle up the A1 we persistently encounter a crafty ambush laid on by the police in an attempt to catch us with alcohol on board.

We have, over the years, grown wise to this and can usually predict, thanks to mobile phones, where they lie in wait and can dispose of any incriminating evidence beforehand. However, when we next visited in April 2009, a carelessly-overlooked bottle top found by an over-zealous female officer once caused a right inquest. Eventually they believed our driver's story that the coach had been used for a stag party the previous night and the bottle top 'must have been left by them'.

On that occasion we were allowed to proceed on to Hartlepool and a few hours later we were returning south with three very welcome points thanks to another goal from Beckford.

After Beckford's goal to earn a point we looked towards 2008, a year that would see Hatters, Cobblers and Glovers on my agenda.

Also in 2008 a massive earthquake hit China, killing over 69,000 people. London's Heathrow airport opened Terminal 5 but many problems saw over 500 flights cancelled and elsewhere in London, construction work began on the Olympic Stadium for the 2012 Olympics.

Britain's Lewis Hamilton became the youngest ever Formula One world champion at the age of 23, Arsenal equalled the record Champions League score with a 7-0 triumph over Slavia Prague at The Emirates and a month later Liverpool stole the record with an 8-0 thrashing of Besiktas at Anfield.

In January 2008 we picked up a 1-1 draw at Luton Town in our last game there to date as they disastrously, aided by various points deductions due to 'financial irregularities', went on to fall through the divisions to the Conference Premier, where they began life in the 2009/10 season having been in the Championship as recently as 2006/07.

They eventually returned to the Football League as Conference champions in 2014.

I never had the privilege of visiting Northampton Town's previous home, the County Ground, when Leeds had played there in 1966 but a 2-1 victory to the Cobblers is still talked about in certain quarters of their faithful today.

It was Northampton's only season in the top flight after having got there from the Fourth Division in just five seasons. Unfortunately Town returned to the bottom tier in four consecutive seasons.

These days Northampton play at the Sixfields Stadium, a ground cleverly built on a retail park that has a lot to offer, though not necessarily on the football front. During the first half of my first visit to this well-hidden delight in February 2008, Jonny Howson put Leeds ahead, but disappointingly Northampton managed to salvage a point in the second half against a United team now managed by Gary McAllister following the January departure of Dennis Wise.

No alcohol is allowed in this stadium, not for away fans anyway, so we had to endure a particularly boring affair without the assistance of a beer or two. Because Sixfields is on a retail park the ground is in very close proximity to establishments such as Frankie & Benny's, TGI Friday's, Bella Italia and many more culinary hostelries. But these were off limits to Leeds fans, except if you needed to use the toilet, which of course we did.

The thing is, once you've used the toilet you need to replenish, and as the bar was out of sight of the friendly doormen who had let you in it would have been plain silly to leave without having a drink, or two. We discovered that the bowling alley was the easiest access route to a beer, but it is slightly puzzling how hundreds of Leeds fans, including myself, found ourselves loitering at the bar close to the lanes without so much as a bowling shoe between us.

For many years Somerset was never a place that Leeds United fans would be descending on in their thousands. There simply were no clubs to play against in the league. Somerset has always been somewhere far more associated with music, with Glastonbury taking centre stage all over the world during most summers.

Yeovil turned professional way back in 1921 but became the first Somerset outfit to enter into the Football League some 82 years later at the start of the 2003/04 campaign. It would be another four seasons before Leeds would be travelling to this part of the world for their debut visit, which took place on 25 April 2008.

'Where the F*** is Yeovil?'

That was the slogan emblazoned on the t-shirts of thousands of Leeds fans as we started the long journey south for our first trip to Yeovil and 272 miles later we were at Huish Park. By the end of the 2013/14 season we had only played there four times and on each occasion the police made it extremely difficult for Leeds fans.

By their own admission, police ordered evening kick-offs to deter Leeds fans from travelling to this sleepy little hamlet. Of course it didn't prevent large numbers of travellers. The capacity at Huish Park is 9,665 and the record attendance there was the 9,527 against Leeds in 2008. But even then, despite a record crowd, the Avon and Somerset Constabulary issued the following statement, 'Home supporters became disgruntled due to the fact that large numbers of Leeds United supporters gained entry into home areas of the stadium. There were no arrests or ejections for home supporters, but a Leeds fan was ejected for poor behaviour.'

This 'ejection' was the only recorded incident in three visits by Leeds fans. Our supporters have openly mixed with the Yeovil faithful at Huish Park without the slightest hint of trouble except for the odd good Samaritan pointing out Leeds fans for 'ejection', only to be met by a wry smile and a shake of the head by a policeman.

The Yeovil Town CEO, Martyn Starnes, called for an inquiry into how Leeds fans got tickets for the home end. One supporter posted on the Leeds forum 365, 'I can save the Yeovil CEO the bother of an inquiry. Leeds United have been a "big club" for nearly five decades and during that time we have garnered supporters from all over the country, including Somerset! Many of the Leeds fans in the home end were there because they bought tickets in their home town – Yeovil! And Martyn, how about a thank you, on the record, for the extra £85,000 in your club's bank account from all the Leeds fans that made it a record-breaking night for you, despite the best efforts of the Yeovil Town board and the Avon and Somerset Police?'

Yeovil supporter Steve Howden wrote in the *Somerset County Gazette*, 'Leeds are one of the best supported away sides in the country and if you give their fans half a chance to get hold of a ticket, they will do, in their droves. They are certainly the most vociferous and best behaved fans I have come across.'

The match itself saw Leeds win 1-0 thanks to an early Dougie Freedman goal that was enough to confirm a place in the play-offs.

In 2008 we locked horns with Carlisle United in the unfamiliar surroundings of League 1. After sharing the spoils in our two league games we met the Cumbrians in the semi-final of the play-offs. It proved to be one of the most memorable encounters in Leeds's recent history.

The first leg at Elland Road saw Carlisle take a 2-0 lead just after half-time in front of a crowd of over 36,000. Carlisle had travelled down with an octopus as a goalkeeper. It seemed like Keiren Westwood had gloves on eight arms as he thwarted Leeds time after time, but in the dying seconds Dougie Freedman pulled a goal back which would prove priceless in the second leg at Carlisle.

Jonny Howson levelled the aggregate score at Brunton Park but when the fourth official unbelievably signalled just one minute of additional time (despite several players from both sides receiving treatment), it looked all over for Leeds. Lovely one-touch football then resulted in Howson getting an amazing goal to send us to Wembley and send the Leeds fans home delirious.

%%%%%

Things improved greatly for Doncaster 13 years after that infamous fire when they gained back-to-back promotions to climb into the Championship. Unfortunately they beat Leeds in the play-off final at Wembley to take that last step into the league's second tier.

It was estimated that Leeds had close to 40,000 fans inside Wembley, many occupying areas designated for Rovers fans, who numbered around 7,000. In the days up to the final, Doncaster had to suspend ticket sales after Leeds supporters travelled to the Keepmoat Stadium to buy the unsold tickets with their allocation of 36,000 having sold out in less than 24 hours.

The club feared, however, that some Leeds fans had already purchased tickets for the Doncaster areas of Wembley. Doncaster chairman John Ryan was happy to send 12,000 unsold tickets to Elland Road, even offering to drive them there himself, but the Football League refused to give Leeds any more tickets.

Ryan has always moaned about the lack of support that his club receives and once said, 'If I could move my club on wheels to Sheffield it might do quite well, but in reality most people in Doncaster support Leeds United.'

I had agreed before the final with Doncaster to be interviewed afterwards by BBC Radio 5 Live whatever the result. I was obviously disappointed at the result and when they rang, I was in a north London off-licence. 'Hello there Gary,' said the interviewer, 'you must be feeling pretty upset right now, what are your thoughts?' I decided that I just couldn't continue with the interview and, very unprofessionally I replied, 'My only thoughts at this moment in time mate are concentrated on finding a large bottle of wine with a screw top, because I haven't got a corkscrew with me.' And I pressed the off button.

28

Pain In The Rain
At Histon

FOLLOWING friendlies in Galway, Bray and Dublin in 2008, we called in at Barnet where Leeds were about to play their next pre-season game. We had one or two light ales in the town before making our way to the ground on our coach. On board was a good lad by the name of Stu. Stu is a regular with us and is disabled after a bad car crash in the mid-1970s in which one of the lads died.

The game itself was a dismal affair to be honest, and for the record Leeds won 2-0, but things brightened up afterwards as we stood around the Leeds buses chatting. Jeff usually takes Stu into the ground with his wheelchair when Stu's brother Rob is not present and before this encounter, Stu and Jeff were in a different part of the ground from the rest of the Leeds fans after they had stumbled across a cosy little bar in the opposite side.

As we waited and waited at the coaches, there was only one lad missing – Stu. Jeff was pissed out of his head and had inadvertently forgotten to bring Stu back. It was a steep zig-zag path up to the coaches from the ground and then all of a sudden, we spied two of Leeds's regular travellers from London, Stew and Steve Heasman, and they were pushing Stu up this path, puffing and panting as they did so.

'I believe he belongs to you,' said Stew, drawing huge breaths of air. Stu was sat in his wheelchair with his baseball cap askew and a silly grin on his face, and a bent fag in his hand. One of the tyres had come off the chair, making it even more difficult for the Heasmans to negotiate. One of the small wheels at the front was so badly damaged it wouldn't turn. Everyone was falling about laughing. My sides were hurting so bad that I had to walk away.

The Don Valley Stadium, better known as an athletics venue, was the home of Rotherham United by the next time we visited them in October 2008 for the second round of the prestigious Johnstone's Paint Trophy Northern Section.

The crowd of just over 4,500 was made up almost entirely of Leeds fans. The atmosphere was surreal to say the least and the players, surrounded by a running track, were miles away from the spectators.

It was a terrible and wholly forgettable night for Leeds, who despite goals from Jonny Howson and our new scoring 'sensation' Enoch Showaddywaddy, lost 4-2.

We have yet to grace Rotherham's new home, the New York Stadium, which was opened in July 2012. We will be doing so in the 2014/15 season with Rotherham promoted back to the Championship and I for one can't wait!

Later that month we found ourselves back at Northampton Town for an FA Cup tie, which we won 5-2. But just a week later we returned to Sixfields and were beaten 2-1 in a disappointing league match.

Sixfields, though, does create quite a good atmosphere from Town fans, and despite being in predominantly a rugby union town the Cobblers are relatively well supported. This is despite huge numbers of football fans supporting other clubs such as Leeds (Wellingborough is one of Leeds's oldest and most established supporters' clubs) among others.

With Leeds residing in League 1, travelling to non-league Histon for the FA Cup second round at the end of November didn't appear on the face of it to present any great problems for the Whites.

But many Leeds fans were clearly not feeling confident and were uneasy about this trip deep into Cambridgeshire. Their fears were well founded as Histon became the first (and so far only) non-league opposition to knock Leeds out of the FA Cup.

It was raining hard as we arrived at Histon's quite impressive supporters' club bar and after a few pints we progressed into the scruffy little Bridge Road ground that was dripping rain on Leeds fans' heads everywhere through leaky roofs.

It was a dreary feeling all over and despite a good start by Leeds on a very heavy pitch, things just didn't feel right. Shortly before half-time Histon took the lead and that's how it stayed.

Leeds boss Gary McAllister was full of flu and was basically non-existent as he slumped on the bench throughout. It was left to ITV to provide the only bright spots for Leeds fans. Whites were all over the ground and many were very close to the pitch. So close in fact that some of them commandeered an ITV microphone situated at the side of the pitch and proceeded to give their rendition of 'ITV is fucking shit!' that was heard by millions of television viewers watching it live. Eventually, ITV did manage to cut the sound but it was too late.

Later ITV said, 'Unfortunately during the live broadcast of the FA Cup match one of the pitchside microphones was removed from its position by some fans and taken into the crowd where it picked up some swearing.'

Then ITV dropped another clanger when they showed, again on live TV, one of the Histon players fully naked in the dressing room afterwards. *The Sun* quoted one viewer who said, 'I couldn't believe it. When Histon's name came out of the hat they went live to see the players' reaction to the third-round draw. One of them was stood there with absolutely nothing on. It was hilarious. Not at all what you expect to see on telly on a Sunday afternoon.'

We left wet Histon and stopped off at Barnsley to drown our sorrows. We did slightly overdo it and Jeff, who you may recall left Stu behind in his wheelchair at Barnet, was so drunk that he arrived home minus his jeans.

In June 2009 I was surfing the waves to New York on the *Queen Mary II*. I was travelling economy class of course, but that didn't dilute the pleasure of the trip in any way whatsoever. There were a dozen or so bars on board and it was while I was stood in one of these one afternoon that I got chatting to a Stockport County fan.

We had played at Stockport just after Christmas in 2008 and this County fan told me that he had been absolutely 'blown away' by the huge following that Leeds took. Leeds fans had filled all one end of the ground and one entire side stand.

It was in this side stand that I found myself almost level with the Whites' upcoming young superstar Fabian Delph. He was only yards into their half and about a yard in from the touchline when he looked up and seeing the County keeper off his line, launched a sublime lob that fell majestically into the net, gaining huge appreciation even from the home fans during our 3-1 win.

Sadly, as I sailed across the Atlantic on *QMII*, Leeds were cashing in on this exceptional youngster, a trait that has unfortunately become a regular occurrence from our beloved club.

In 2009 the Yorkshire Ripper, Peter Sutcliffe, was released from Broadmoor Hospital for a life sentence after doctors claimed he had been treated for schizophrenia. He murdered 13 women and attempted to kill a further seven. Great Train Robber Ronnie Biggs was granted release from prison on compassionate grounds due to being gravely ill.

At the Academy Awards, British film *Slumdog Millionaire*, directed by Danny Boyle, won eight prizes. Jonathan Ross returned to the BBC after serving a three-month ban for prank calls to Andrew Sachs, who played the brilliant Manuel in the classic comedy *Fawlty Towers*. Comic Relief raised over £57m, surpassing the previous record in 2007 by over £17m.

Our next visit to Hereford United, after those FA Cup matches in 2007/08, came in February 2009 and it was far worse than our first, though in many ways it turned out to be something of a watershed for the club.

We had started the 2008/09 season fairly brightly under Gary McAllister and according to the bookies were favourites for promotion to the Championship but a severe dip in form saw us drop out of the play-off places as we travelled to Hereford. Leeds had replaced McAllister with Simon Grayson at Christmas and our fans, as usual, had snapped up their allocation of just 2,000 out of a capacity of 7,700.

As the players took to the field the fans crammed into the Blackfriar Street End, chanting their team's name. Leeds, under Grayson, had been doing OK, but that was about it. I was down the side of the ground at the Blackfriars end with several hundred other Leeds fans in the world-famous Floors 2 Go Stand.

United weren't particularly impressive and there was an obvious lack of commitment from certain players. Leeds supporters are loyal to the end but on that evening on a freezing cold February night, they began to grow restless.

Then things looked up briefly as we were awarded a penalty. Lee Trundle put the ball on the spot and casually strode up to take the kick in front of the visiting fans. It was a pathetic attempt that even if it had got past the goalkeeper, which was nigh-on impossible, it would have needed the new goal-line technology to establish whether or not the ball had crossed the line.

The Leeds fans were incensed, quite rightly, but worse was to come. From the keeper's clearance, Hereford scored at the other end just seconds later. Then, after the home side added a second goal, with the Leeds players seemingly just walking around chasing shadows, the unthinkable happened.

Our supporters turned on their team. I've never booed Leeds in my life and never will, but I've been at Elland Road when the supporters have turned. I have not, however, witnessed it at any away game. This was a first. And you could tell by the players' reactions that they were completely shocked.

The game gradually ended and the players trudged off down the tunnel with the chants of, 'We're shit and we're sick of it!' from their own fans ringing loudly in their ears.

Even Grayson, who had stepped a couple of yards on to the pitch to thank the travelling support, which has always been customary, thought better of it and he too disappeared down the tunnel, ashen-faced.

In a statement afterwards Grayson said, 'When you hear your own fans singing things like that, then the players should be hurting. We've got to use tonight as an example of inspiration between now and the end of the season. One or two players might not play for this club again.'

Despite a lot of bickering I've enjoyed my few visits to Yeovil, and the team certainly have too. Luciano Becchio (replacing Enoch Showaddywaddy) made his full league debut on our second visit there in August 2008 and repaid manager Gary McAllister with a goal after just 25 seconds. However this was the only blemish on our record so far against the Glovers. Leeds drew that game 1-1, while they have won in the other five meetings between the two clubs. One of those fixtures was a 4-0 victory at Elland Road in March 2009 under Simon Grayson.

I was in the Spencers pub in the city centre when one Yeovil fan decked from head to foot in green and white walked in. He was immediately made welcome as a pint of cider was thrust into his hands. You could tell from his face that he expected a good hiding any time soon but that never came.

It was a somewhat interesting atmosphere in Spencers that Saturday afternoon. As well as hundreds of Leeds fans and this Yeovil supporter there were about 100 skinheads from many different cities across Britain, including Birmingham, Luton, Newcastle, Bolton, Salford, Liverpool and many others.

They weren't there for the football though. Just around the corner in City Square was a march held by the English Defence League. The pub was like a smouldering powder keg to begin with and the police, who kept coming in and out, were shitting themselves. To the relief of everyone, none more so than the landlord (himself a former member of the notorious Leeds Service Crew), there wasn't a single spark of trouble as everyone mingled and drank together before leaving in different directions.

To Leeds's credit they did kick on from the Hereford defeat back in February and went on a great run of form including ten successive home wins, the club's best run since the Revie era, and reached the play-offs for the second season in a row. Unfortunately we lost to Millwall over two legs in the semi-finals.

29

Old Trafford In
The FA Cup

W E have met Darlington a couple of times in the prestigious Johnstone's Paint Trophy and our paths crossed again in the first round of the 2009/10 League Cup, a game we won 1-0.

To date, Darlington have never beaten Leeds but they don't need to. They have a truly colourful existence all of their own. Their chairman in 1999 was a chap called George Reynolds. Once in the top 112 richest people in the country, he promised the fans that he would take the club to the Premier League and he built the team a new £20m stadium, which of course he named after himself.

However, five years later and with the club still in the basement division, Reynolds took the club into administration, and days after the brand new 25,000-seat stadium was unveiled he buggered off, never to be seen again.

Reynolds made former Leeds chairman Peter Ridsdale look like a Samaritan. He has been jailed no less than six times since the 1960s, his latest incarceration being in 2007. His offences included safe-cracking, handling explosives, burglary and theft, and in 2004 he was jailed for three years for tax evasion when police stopped his car with £500,000 in cash in the boot. Reynolds is currently involved in retail.

In 2010, the Darlington mascot Darlo Dog was captured and ejected from the ground after jumping on to an advertising hoarding in front of the television cameras. He was forced into retirement and replaced by a panda.

Darlington currently reside in Division One North of the Evo-Stik Northern Premier League under the new name of Darlington 1883. But in the words of my father-in-law Harry's boat, 'One Day...'

Four days after that trip to Darlington we were on the road again to Wycombe Wanderers and we were like half a dozen giggling schoolkids as we entered a pub close to the ground.

Hours of preparation had taken place on our lengthy coach trip down and now we were to put that painstaking rehearsal to the test. In we walked. 'Hi, Wycombe!' we announced. In hindsight it wasn't really worth all the effort. Luckily our team's preparations were put to much better use and Luciano Becchio scored the only goal of the game to give us our second win from two matches to start the season. We went on to notch up six straight wins from the off.

Later that season, as Leeds headed for promotion, Wycombe arrived at Elland Road in January and ground out an impressive goalless draw in front of an appreciative 25,000 crowd.

Wycombe had first arrived on the Football League scene back in 1993 under the expert guidance of manager Martin O'Neill, who had already orchestrated two FA Trophy wins in 1991 and 93. In their first season as a Football League club they won promotion again to go straight up to the Second Division. O'Neill moved on to Norwich City in 1995 and Wycombe have remained in the bottom two divisions since joining the Football League but in 2001 they reached the semi-finals of the FA Cup as a third-tier club, taking Liverpool right to the wire before going down 2-1 at Villa Park.

The break-up of Wimbledon Football Club in 2004 became a bitter wrangle among the supporters. In a nutshell and without any concern for their existing fans whatsoever, Wimbledon packed up and headed 60 miles north to set up a new base at Milton Keynes. Consequently a totally new manufactured club was formed and became Milton Keynes Dons.

The vast majority of fans stayed behind in London and subsequently AFC Wimbledon became the focus of their attention and gradually emerged from non-league into the Football League, just as their forefathers had done over 20 years ago.

It has to be said that the Dons' ground, *stadium*mk, is impressive, boasting luxurious leather seats – even in the away end. Understandably though, MK Dons don't have a massive fanbase, which is shown by their regular low attendances.

We lost on our first visit there just before Christmas in 2008, but returned with a vengeance in September 2009 with an emphatic 1-0 victory thanks to a solo effort from Robert Snodgrass.

A month later, before a 4-0 away win at Bristol Rovers, we were having a drink with what turned out to be Bristol City fans in a pub near to the Memorial Stadium.

The City fans despised Rovers so much and one of them was telling us, while his mates nodded in approval, that his brother was convicted of arson against Rovers in 1990. Apparently, when Rovers played City at Twerton Park, City fans set fire to the Main Stand causing damage worth more than £800,000. This lad's brother was one of seven City fans who were convicted and jailed for the arson attack.

In November 2009, Leeds very nearly came a cropper at the hands of Kettering Town in the second round of the FA Cup in 2009 at Nene Park.

Leeds had been the better side almost throughout the game with Tony Capaldi providing many chances with his dazzling wing play. But it was Kettering who drew first blood and there were only 12 minutes left when Jermaine Beckford latched on to a Snodgrass cross to equalise.

The replay at Elland Road finished 5-1 to Leeds but the game was by no means a walkover. In fact it went to extra time when late on Kettering's Anthony Elder cancelled out a strike from Luciano Becchio to add another half an hour to the tie. Then, in the closing stages of extra time and with the score still standing at 1-1, Leeds sent on Mike Grella who scored twice. Tresor Kandol and Beckford then added one each to give the scoreline a distorted look.

But there was further action to come, this time off the field as Kettering's player-manager Lee Harper, a former Arsenal goalkeeper, gave his post-match interview. His assistant John Deehan had been sacked in the wake of the defeat and Harper was furious, threatening to quit and claiming, 'Some things have been said to my assistant manager that he is not to come back to the club. It's a strange way to go about things. We have just made the club £200,000.

'I'm considering my own future now and have told the players who have said that they are fully behind me. Everyone is disgusted at what has gone on. I am not going to name names, but he is high up.'

Leeds, in the meantime, quietly dropped into the hat for the next round.

As a kid, the only time I had heard the name Brentford was on a TV advert. A well-known BBC disc jockey and TV personality at the time, Alan 'Fluff' Freeman, used to advertise Brentford Nylons, where you could get an absolute bargain on your next nylon bed sheets, or get polyester cotton sheets at unbelievable prices.

Leeds and Brentford had some real tussles during the 1930s (when the Bees were a top First Division side), 40s and 50s but our only meeting at the home of the west London club in recent times was on a cold December afternoon in 2009.

I looked forward to my first visit to Griffin Park, mostly because I had heard that there was a pub on every corner of the ground – in fact the only venue in the country to have this luxury. I wasn't disappointed either, it creates a great atmosphere and one of the pubs, The Griffin, was actually used in the cult football hooligan film *Green Street*.

Unfortunately, the game itself *was* a disappointment. A goalless draw that was no good whatsoever to either side and with so many yawns occurring around the ground, it looked more like an advert for bedspreads. But with Alan Freeman and Brentford Nylons long gone I couldn't even nip out and buy a couple of nice pillowcases for the wife.

When our daughter Vicky emigrated to Australia in 2006 with husband Ste I looked on it as not so much losing a daughter but gaining free accommodation in Brisbane.

When they made their first return to Blighty for Christmas in 2009, we arranged to pick them up at Heathrow. They were due to land early so we had to stay in London the night before to meet them. By pure chance, Leeds were playing at Orient that evening so it couldn't have been arranged any better if we had tried, and it was at Brisbane Road – perfect.

That is except for one thing. It snowed like I had not seen for a long time and postponed every game in and around London. I remember thinking that the snow had been pre-ordered by the Metropolitan Police because that night Leeds were not the only away fans who would have been in the capital. Our friends from Old Trafford, Everton, Portsmouth, Swansea and Cardiff were all due in the Smoke that night, as well as a derby game between Tottenham and Chelsea.

We eventually played Orient two months later, a 1-1 draw, but by then Vicky and Ste had long since returned to sunny Australia.

Three days after Christmas came an away game at Stockport County. We arrived about 20 minutes before kick-off and Jeff, Basher and I snuck into the back door of a pub near the ground. We hadn't noticed this little gem on our previous visit, and apparently neither had any other Leeds fans.

It was well hidden off the beaten track but only a few minutes from the ground. The three of us demolished three rounds of cider in just over ten minutes. The landlady couldn't believe it. 'Are you coming back in after the game?' she asked eagerly.

After the match, in which Leigh Bromby scored his only Leeds goal in a 4-2 win, we did manage to nip in for a quick couple more as we waited for the coaches to be allowed to move on by the police. Sadly we've not had the opportunity to return to that lovely little nugget since that day.

In 2010, the General Election resulted in a coalition government made up of the Conservatives and the Liberal Democrats. A police manhunt for Raoul Moat, who shot dead three people in the north-east, came to a halt after a six-hour stand-off with officers ended with Moat shooting himself. Ed Miliband became the new leader of the Labour party.

In sport, Chester City Football Club went out of business after 125 years, Brazil won the World Blind Football Championship at the Royal National College for the Blind in Hereford, beating Spain 2-0 in the final. England's bid to host the 2018 World Cup failed with just two votes and FIFA announced that the host nation would be Russia. Spain became world champions for the first time by beating the Netherlands 1-0 in the final in South Africa.

As for my own world, I really could not believe the start of 2010. It was simply magical.

Possibly the most popular song at Leeds these days begins with these words, 'January the third, remember the date.' This was the day that God returned from wherever he has been to once again shine upon us at Old Trafford.

It was in the FA Cup third round. The sun was bright and around 9,000 visiting fans arrived at Old Trafford in buoyant mood. Leeds were in the third tier but were on course for promotion with the supporters singing proudly, 'Nah nah nah nah nah nah nah nah nah, Leeds are going up, going up, Leeds are going up, nah nah nah.'

Leeds were more than holding their own against the Premier League champions and then in the first half, Jermaine Beckford, who had been linked heavily with a move to Newcastle, scored the opening goal. 'Jermaine Beckford, scores a fuckin' great goal, in the scum shit ole, in the scum shit ole, Jermaine Beckford,' sang the jubilant fans.

We were in heaven and no one could believe it. And we certainly couldn't believe it when the final whistle went and Leeds had beaten manchester united 1-0.

This is worth repeating:

'January the third, remember the date, we beat the team that we fuckin' hate. We knocked the scum out the FA Cup, we're Super Leeds and we're goin' up!'

Incidentally, throughout Alex Ferguson's long reign at Old Trafford this was the only time a club in the third tier of English football had knocked his side out of the FA Cup. When all the well-over-the-top coverage of his retirement, three years after this glorious event, was plastered all over the newspapers and the preposterous amount of TV coverage was afforded to him (even the Queen's speech took second fiddle on news bulletins – how ridiculous is that?), BBC's *Football Focus*, a well-respected programme, showed some footage of great FA Cup giant-killings as they previewed the 2013 FA Cup Final between moneybags Manchester City and soon-to-be-relegated Wigan Athletic.

They failed to show or indeed mention this tremendous effort from 'League 1' Leeds United. The 9,000 Leeds fans present that day will never forget it. Neither, I must add, will manchester united.

But just to illustrate the ups and downs of life with Leeds United – take a look at the next story from a visit to Exeter City.

In 2003 Exeter were struggling to stay in the Football League but they won their final game of the season. Cruelly, though, Swansea City beat Hull City on the same day to condemn Exeter to the Conference. As they entered non-league, Exeter were taken over by their own supporters. To this day the Exeter City Supporters' Trust owns the club – Ken Bates take note.

The next time we visited Exeter was for our League 1 clash at St James Park in mid-January 2010. It absolutely chucked down with hard rain (not that fine rain) throughout the game. It was probably the wettest and saddest I've ever felt at a Leeds match, perhaps with the exception of that brilliant Sunday afternoon out at Histon in the FA Cup. My leather jacket took over a week to dry out but that was the least of our problems.

The tiny venue, quite simply, could not cope with the vast away support from Leeds and consequently our fans ended up all around the ground. Then, just before kick-off, a loudspeaker announcement asked the supporters in the home sections of the ground to move to the away end or risk ejection.

Around 100 took up the offer and were escorted to the visitors' section. They then joined hundreds of other Leeds fans still queuing outside because the police had delayed them at various motorway service stations. Then, very early in the game, Exeter scored and the supporters still outside poured into the ground to see what was happening so absolute chaos ensued.

A huge bottleneck in the already overcrowded end caused some fans to spill out over the wall and hoardings and on to the track around the pitch. Police immediately attacked the supporters, provoking even more trouble. Thankfully the police soon realised the severity of the situation and with the assistance of the stewards and the trusty St John's Ambulance medics they began to assist the fallen and order was restored, luckily without serious injury.

In the days that followed our 2-0 defeat, the police and Exeter City blamed Leeds fans for the trouble because they arrived late. As a direct result of these accusations the Leeds United Supporters' Trust (LUST) and Leeds United Supporters' Club (LUSC) sought help and advice from the official Football Supporters' Federation (FSF).

A meeting was called which was attended by the FSF, LUST, LUSC, Exeter City FC and their safety officers and the Devon and Cornwall Police. Afterwards, the FSF issued a statement that totally exonerated Leeds fans of any blame whatsoever.

The police agreed to review their policy on matchdays and Exeter agreed to certain ground alterations such as extra turnstiles and promised to meet with Leeds fans' representatives prior to any future fixtures between the two clubs. Hopefully that won't be any time soon.

I honestly think that Exeter City are a lovely club, but unfortunately so too did Michael Jackson. Many football grounds host pop and rock concerts, seminars and other weird events such as Jehovah's Witness gatherings, but surely nothing could be quite as bizarre as events that unfolded at St James Park in 2002.

Well-known weirdo Uri Geller, who was co-chairman of Exeter at the time, tried to raise funds for his stricken club by enlisting the services of another weirdo and his friend, Michael Jackson. Jackson was made an honorary director and agreed to stage an event at St James Park. But in return he wanted Geller to agree to bring along some 'sick kids from hospitals' and give half the money raised to 'children with Aids'.

Geller agreed and a crowd of 10,000 gathered to watch Jackson, Geller, Patti Boulaye and David Blaine perform on a ramshackle old stage erected at the side of the pitch. If that wasn't strange enough, Jackson then told the crowd to, 'hold the hand of the person next to you and tell them you love them'. Brilliant!

The image of burly six-and-a-half-foot skinheads with tattoos and battle scars holding hands and saying to his mate that he 'loves' him will stay with me forever. Once they had all found their partners, these loveable thugs were then told by Jackson, 'Help the people of Africa find a solution against the spread of HIV. And malaria.'

I love you Jacko.

The reward for that FA Cup victory at manchester united was a fourth-round tie away to Tottenham Hotspur, which saw Leeds earn a well-deserved 2-2 draw before losing the replay at Elland Road.

Sadly, nothing has changed at White Hart Lane over the years and after the first cup game, once again Leeds supporters were attacked by the home fans as they left the ground. That said, I have to say that the view from the away end at Tottenham is probably the best in the country.

We also progressed to the Northern Area Final of the Johnstone's Paint Trophy and we witnessed some incredible scenes in the second leg at Brunton Park in February 2010.

With the tie level it went to penalties, and Carlisle eventually went through to Wembley but in very controversial circumstances indeed. Lasers were clearly seen to be shone in the eyes of Leeds players as they took their penalties and after the game, as hundreds of Carlisle fans invaded the pitch, three of our men were punched and kicked including captain Robert Snodgrass.

Unfortunately those obliging stewards we had witnessed back in 1985 were obviously no longer at the club as stewards and police did little to intervene in the appalling scenes while Leeds players dashed for the safety of the tunnel.

Despite overwhelming TV evidence showing the players being attacked, as well as the laser incidents, Carlisle, other than a ludicrously small fine, received no further punishment.

※ ※ ※ ※ ※

Late spring 2010. Leeds United had been running away with the league for almost the entire first half of the season, but after the satisfying FA Cup victory at Old Trafford on 3 January, the wheels on the bus were in serious danger of falling off.

A bad loss of form and four straight defeats in March had given rivals Norwich City the upper hand as they went top and left Leeds struggling and desperately trying to cling on to second place. Play-offs are certainly not United's strong point and it was imperative that we avoided the shoot-out.

As we headed into the final straight we were fighting off teams from all directions for that coveted second spot, but four wins out of six games put our destiny in our own hands as it went down to the final and extremely crucial game of the season – at home to Bristol Rovers on 8 May.

Norwich had been crowned champions the week before a sun-drenched crowd of over 38,000 watched the visit of Rovers nervously from all four sides of Elland Road. Norwich had become a real thorn in our side as we had turned into the New Year and beyond and now, as if to gain a psychological advantage, Bristol Rovers strode out on to the hallowed turf wearing the yellow and green colours associated with the Canaries.

Then, after about half an hour, Max Gradel saw red, literally. Jermaine Beckford scored for Leeds, but it was immediately disallowed for offside and as some players protested, tall Rovers defender Daniel Jones fell to the ground as though he had been shot by a sniper lurking in the South Stand.

In reality he had clashed with five-foot-tall Leeds winger Max Gradel and a lengthy melee between several players ensued, including Gradel and Jones. Then the referee sent Gradel off and gave Jones just a yellow card which understandably incensed Gradel, who began running around and even confronted the referee. He had to be escorted from the pitch by stewards.

Jones was loudly booed every time he touched the ball following this incident and the boos turned to outrage when he provided a cross early in the second half which was finished by Darryl Duffy who stabbed the ball home from close range to give Rovers the lead.

The crowd were incensed and went absolutely berserk before falling into a deathly silence...an awful heart- and gut-wrenching silence. The disappointment among the crowd was immense and I remember looking round at other Leeds fans and the despair was etched deep into their faces. It was awful.

Thankfully, Leeds were made of stern stuff and a stunning 20-yard strike and a close-range effort from Beckford in the space of a few minutes either side of the hour earned ten-man United a 2-1 victory that lifted the roof off a joyous Elland Road.

Automatic promotion had been seized and I'll never forget manager Simon Grayson dancing up and down the touchline like a demented schoolkid at the final whistle, pausing only to put on a serious face to shake hands with Rovers manager Paul Trollope before resuming his celebratory jig where he hugged everyone who came near him.

Hours later, as I soaked up the euphoria in my local pub, I felt that twinge again. The one I had as Leeds beat Bristol Rovers at Elland Road when I was just three weeks old.

30

Marching On Together

LEEDS UNITED'S trips to Bury in my lifespan have been quite rare. We last called there for a pre-season friendly ahead of the new 2010/11 campaign and got hammered 4-0.

It is interesting to note though, that the attendance that evening was just 2,769 and the official Leeds following numbered 1,739. Well, there was nothing else to bleat about.

Early on in that first season back in the Championship, Preston featured in one of the most bizarre games that I have ever seen at Elland Road.

Leeds were leading 4-1 at half-time in a midweek match. Then in the second half a catalogue of disastrous errors allowed Preston to overturn the deficit and cross the finish line with a 6-4 victory.

Our manager that evening was Simon Grayson who, at the time of writing, occupies the hotseat at Deepdale. Much more worrying for Preston fans must be that another former Leeds employee, Peter Ridsdale, occupies the chairman's office.

Sometimes it's interesting to have a pre-match drink 'behind enemy lines' as it were. I'd been at a Cleethorpes/Grimsby Whites function the night before Leeds were due at Scunthorpe United in October 2010 and the next morning Lesley and I drove to the outskirts of Scunthorpe and had some lunch in a country pub.

As it got nearer to kick-off the pub began filling up with Scunthorpe fans and it was fun to hear their views on the Whites. They had no idea I was a Leeds fan and at times I was straining my head to hear the gossip, so much so that Lesley slapped my hand more than once. To be honest most of the comments were favourable, though of course the odd 'I hate Leeds!' echoed above the general conversation now and again.

With about 20 minutes to go to kick-off we left the pub and Lesley dropped me off at the Frankie & Benny's restaurant just outside the ground and then drove back to Leeds. Frankie's was full to the brim with Leeds fans and there was even a bottle bar outside which was very well received by the thirsty travellers.

A lot of the talk in the Scunthorpe pub had predicted a win for their side but Leeds ran out easy 4-1 winners. Scunny Bunny, the Scunthorpe mascot, made his presence known at the Leeds end, but as the goals flew in for the Whites the hapless rabbit was getting some right stick from the away fans so he hopped to the other end and sat for the remainder of the game in front of the Scunthorpe fans with his sad long-eared face resting firmly cupped between his two front paws.

Afterwards, I jumped on our coach for the trip back to Leeds and we stopped at a lovely little pub near Selby on the way, capping a very pleasant couple of days indeed.

I have a bit of a soft spot for York. Our popular winger Albert Johanneson ended his playing career in the red shirt of York in the early 1970s and our reserve team played there for a couple of seasons in the 1980s, plus I have family in Strensall on the outskirts of the city.

Some of their fans tested the resolve of their illustrious neighbours while returning from a cup match at Rotherham in November 2010. About 50 of them got off their train in Leeds and headed in to the city centre towards the Spencers pub, well known as a regular haunt for Leeds fans. But on this particular day, Spencers was almost deserted with Leeds conveniently playing away at Coventry.

'The York fans began drinking,' said manager Ryan Jones. 'But then the place erupted with bottles, glasses, chairs and tables being thrown everywhere. Bar optics were destroyed and beer pumps ripped off.' Ryan rang his father Bob, who owned the pub, and told him that York fans were smashing the place. 'I thought he was winding me up,' said Bob. 'But they caused £2,500 of damage and almost the same again in lost earnings.'

Eventually four or five regular drinkers in the bar and a handful of Christmas shoppers forced the City fans to flee back to the train station.

Bob challenged the police afterwards and demanded to know why they hadn't prevented City fans from leaving the station, to which a British Transport Police statement said, 'They [City fans] could not be stopped from leaving the station because they were behaving lawfully at the time.'

That didn't explain why it took the police so long to arrive at Spencers when the trouble flared and also begs the question: Why is it that Leeds fans are often restrained from moving around freely from train stations up and down the country despite them too behaving lawfully?

Leeds have played several friendlies at Bootham Crescent and it's always a pleasant evening, except for the summer following the Spencers incident when our fans meted out certain forms of retribution to sections of the home crowd.

Moving into 2011, Prince William married Catherine Middleton at Westminster Abbey and Queen Elizabeth II became the second-longest-reigning monarch behind Queen Victoria.

The *News of the World* ceased publication after the newspaper was found to have hacked the mobile phones of celebrities, politicians and high-profile crime victims, while at the age of just 27, singer/songwriter Amy Winehouse was found dead in her London home.

Tragedy struck at the Bournemouth Air Festival when Red Arrows pilot Jon Egging crashed and died on the way back to the airport. He could have ejected but the plane would have hit houses. Instead he steered the plane into a field and sacrificed his own life.

In cricket, England won the Ashes with a 3-1 series victory in Australia. Sky Sports commentator Andy Gray was sacked for making sexist comments about a female official, and Rushden & Diamonds went out of business after 19 years of existence due to financial problems.

And early in the New Year, we had the famous blackout of 2011 down at Portsmouth. Pompey's increasing financial difficulties and subsequent administration were highlighted, perhaps not the best description, when the floodlights went out with five minutes to play of our 2-2 draw at Fratton Park.

I know Leeds supporters toot their own horn on occasions but that's only because no one else gives them the credit they deserve. We hear all the time about 'Scouse humour' and those 'loveable Geordies' but none are as original or funny as our fans. For decades they have been churning out spontaneous ad-lib chants for the moment. This was highlighted, sorry there's that word again, when those lights went out in late January 2011, plunging Fratton Park into total darkness.

Immediately, the Leeds masses sprung into action. 'Pay up Pompey!' was a classic. Then came, 'We can't see you sneaking out!' Pure genius. Portsmouth Football Club quickly moved to issue a statement that the switch-off was due to a power cut outside of the ground, but street lights could clearly be seen immediately beyond the stadium's walls.

A couple of weeks later we headed back down to the West Country for a visit to Bristol City. These days there is a roof over the away end and on this trip we certainly needed it. Snow and sleet fell on us as we left the coach park to make our way to the ground.

We turned into the street where there stands a block of multi-storey council flats. These are the very same flats that overlook the stadium, but more importantly they are also used at the start of each episode of *Only Fools and Horses* as the building where Del and Rodney live.

With a 2-0 win behind us we headed back up north as the snow continued to fall heavily. Eventually the motorway was reduced to one lane made by the cars in front and we were travelling at a snail's pace. Steve, our driver, said, 'I hope you've got your sleeping bags lads, there's no way we're gonna get through this tonight.'

We had more pressing things on our minds as we all checked our alcohol stash. But as we began making rationing arrangements, a big brown luxury coach drove alongside us and as if raised above the snow soared past us into the distance. It was the Leeds team bus and the driver drove past without a care.

Immediately, Steve pulled our coach in behind the team's bus, and although there was no way we could keep up with them, they had cleared a route for us to follow and we were on our way again. 'Marching on Together' indeed.

We ended our first season back in the Championship by finishing seventh, three points behind the play-off places.

Towards the end of May, once our fixtures were over, I was dog-sitting for my sister-in-law Gina in Huddersfield. It was a Saturday afternoon and I decided to take a stroll down into town to watch Huddersfield Town on the television at the Rope Walk pub right next to the Terriers' John Smith's Stadium. They were contesting the play-off final against Peterborough United at Wembley to see which of them would clinch the last league place to jump up into the Championship.

I have no affinity with either club and took my place standing at the bar as a neutral observer. The place was packed with Huddersfield Giants rugby fans who had returned from their game earlier that morning over in Hull, and a smattering of Town fans who I assumed couldn't get tickets for Wembley.

I have to admit that Huddersfield were by far the better side and optimism was rising around the pub, but it was Peterborough who took the lead against the run of play. I had been chewing over which of the two would benefit Leeds more from coming up, and by Leeds I mean our fans. Huddersfield, of course, is only ten miles down the road, while Peterborough is not exactly a million miles away down the east coast rail line, so I suppose the Edwards Pendulum wasn't swinging either way in particular.

I had a wicked notion in my head that it was quite satisfying to see Huddersfield scrapping and struggling to get out of League 1 because we ourselves had battled for three seasons to get out of the 'forgotten division', and there was certainly no love lost between our two clubs.

Just when the Edwards Pendulum began to move slowly in favour of Peterborough, the TV cameras zoomed in on their manager, Darren Ferguson, son of you-know-who, stood on the touchline. As I ordered another pint of Stella, the pendulum slowly creaked in the opposite direction, and because of my natural instinctive dislike of all things manchester united I suddenly found myself in the totally unnatural situation of sort of wanting Huddersfield to win. Or did I?

I had gone from an unassuming neutral to what can only be described as a 'Liberal Democrat voter'. I had no idea which side of the fence I was on! I had only come for a few pints and to watch a game but I found my mind in turmoil.

With just ten minutes remaining and with Huddersfield pressing hard for an equaliser, Peterborough broke clear and scored a second goal to make it 2-0 and in doing so clinch promotion. This was greeted by total silence except for a huge solitary shout of 'get in'. Everyone in the pub, including me, turned around to see who had shouted this clearly hurtful statement (tee hee!). It was the bar manager no less. I looked on in astonishment and with a warm sense of satisfaction inside as he stuck his chest out and bleated from behind the bar, 'Fuck you, you Third Division Huddersfield bastards!'

I fully expected the whole pub to get trashed but amazingly that didn't happen. I could not believe how this bloke, who wasn't the tallest in the world by any stretch of the imagination, hadn't been torn limb from limb. Apart from the odd bit of verbal abuse from some Town fans no one physically challenged him.

After the final whistle most people left disappointed and thinking what might have been. I decided to order another pint of Stella from the delighted boss. 'I take it you're a Leeds fan then?' I enquired as he handed me my pint. 'Too fucking right mate,' he said. 'I can't do with these knob-heads. I'm Leeds through and through,' and he gave me the Leeds Salute, which in real terms is the equivalent to the Masonic handshake. He was definitely one of us.

In the summer of 2011 I found myself thinking a lot about Plymouth Argyle. Their ground, Home Park, survived multiple hits from the Luftwaffe during the Second World War. Plymouth, home to the largest naval base in Western Europe, was seen by Hitler as a vital target and in April 1944 Home Park suffered substantial bombings leaving the club with a massive rebuilding project.

But the club overcame an even greater obstacle in July 2011 – Peter Ridsdale. After a highly controversial and much publicised exit from Elland Road and two more similar tenures at Barnsley and then Cardiff City, Ridsdale moved into Home Park as consultant with the club already in administration. He then became chairman before announcing his plans to buy Argyle for £1 with what he called an 'eminently sensible business plan'.

However 12 weeks later Ridsdale left Home Park with Plymouth at the foot of League 2 and homed in on poor old Preston North End, becoming chairman of football. Preston are currently in League 1.

As the 2011/12 season went on Leeds finally managed to banish the curse at Leicester City when a cracking long-range shot by Adam Clayton gave us our first win at their Walkers Stadium – by this point renamed the King Power Stadium under a sponsorship agreement – that November. But the month would have a tragic end.

It was a truly sad occasion when Gary Speed passed away. Gary had been an integral part of Howard Wilkinson's championship-winning side and was truly a legend in football, playing for Everton, Bolton, Newcastle and Sheffield United after Leeds.

United's first game after Gary's untimely death was at Nottingham Forest and arrangements had been made by supporters for their own tribute to the man himself, who proudly wore the number 11 shirt during his precious time at Elland Road.

Things also happened that night that had even the staunchest atheist believing in some form of afterlife. As planned, at exactly the 11th minute Leeds fans began chanting the name of Gary Speed for an uninterrupted 11 minutes. Then on the exact second that the chanting stopped, Robert Snodgrass opened the scoring with a left-footed drive.

Leeds later added to their tally with goals from Jonny Howson, Luciano Becchio and Adam Clayton without reply, and then Forest had Andy Reid sent off. He was their number 11.

The Telegraph reported afterwards, 'Leeds supporters may have their detractors, but they honoured one of their own in the East

Midlands with passion and good grace as their side obliged by romping to a conclusive victory over Nottingham Forest.'

The Guardian said, 'Four thousand Leeds fans packed into the Bridgford End layered with tiers of white scarves, reflecting a hostility inspired by diverse forces from Brian Clough to the miners' strike.'

℀ ℀ ℀ ℀ ℀

A tribute to Gary Speed
8 September 1969–27 November 2011

I met 'Speedo' on a number of occasions. He was always, without exception, a thoroughly nice bloke. Much more importantly, he was a superb footballer who was loved and admired by everyone who he came into contact with.

A product of the Leeds academy, Gary could head, shoot, pass and tackle with equal accomplishment and scored some priceless goals for the club, many with his sweet left foot. He was obviously a good-looking son of a gun, and was adored by the ladies, but he was also held in extremely high esteem by the male population of the Leeds fans, also for obvious reasons.

Although originally from Chester, he had a Yorkshire twang to his accent which always filled me with pride. Selfishly, my favourite memories of him are more on the social side. Gary went out of his way to talk to the fans and many a time he would buy generous amounts of beer for them. I have been in his company in bars and nightclubs in Japan, Germany, Sweden, Ireland and many more, including our very own Leeds city centre. He once bought so many drinks for us in a Cork nightspot that you literally couldn't see the top of the bar.

He once pulled up in a car driven by someone else while we were in Ireland also and he was standing half out of the sunroof as he handed me and a couple of the lads some cans of beer as we stood around outside a fast food joint. I have lost count of the whiskies he would buy and place in front of me and my mates.

But it wasn't just the fact that he was generous with his wallet, he genuinely talked to you about anything, and was certainly interested in what you had to say.

He had a wicked sense of humour too and he was like a schoolkid whenever you saw him out with his best buddy, David Batty. I have a special photograph of the Leeds team taken on the streets of Tokyo in 1991 and on it you can see the overwhelming friendship of Bats and Speedo.

I learned of his tragic death the morning after when a friend of mine, a Leeds fan from Liverpool, Jed Stone, telephoned me with the news. I couldn't believe it, and to be honest I still can't believe he's gone.

Football fans all over the world were magnificent with their many tributes – Leeds supporters in particular – and the send-off they gave to their hero at the game at Nottingham Forest just days after the tragedy is still talked about today.

United's manager at the time, Simon Grayson, who had roomed with Gary as a Leeds player, dedicated the 4-0 win to his friend's memory. He said after the match, 'It was incredible, the Leeds fans, the timing of the goal and Snodgrass scoring with his less-favoured left foot. The team and supporters did him proud tonight. Speedo was a true friend and a very, very popular man.'

Gary's captain at Leeds when we won the last First Division championship in 1992 was Gordon Strachan. He said simply, 'I was proud of Gary Speed every time I saw him play or train.'

As we left the ground after that 4-0 victory over Forest, you could almost hear the echo of that famous line of commentary from a game at Elland Road in 1990. With Speed bearing down on the opposition goal during a Leeds romp over Sheffield United the man with the microphone said, 'Go on Gary Speed, get one yourself son.'

※ ※ ※ ※ ※

In 2012, Queen Elizabeth II celebrated her Diamond Jubilee with 60 years on the throne. At the age of just 30, Claire Squires collapsed and died during the London Marathon. She had planned on raising £500 for The Samaritans but following her tragic death she raised almost £1m.

Tennis 'ace' Andy Murray got to the final of Wimbledon but lost to the multiple Grand Slam winner Roger Federer. Bradley Wiggins became the first British rider to win the Tour de France.

Oh, there was something happening in London in 2012. That's right, the London Olympics and Paralympics, in which Great Britain excelled tremendously. All the GB athletes were absolutely superb and Danny Boyle, the director who produced the opening and closing ceremonies, was perfection personified.

For me, part of 2012 was a very disappointing reception at a place I did have a soft spot for – Blackpool.

Simon Grayson remained in charge of Leeds until February and by the time of the April visit to Blackpool we had spent a couple of months under our new manager – Neil Warnock.

After that game between Leeds and Blackpool back in March 1971 the paths of both clubs took different directions. Blackpool were relegated and Leeds continued from strength to strength under Don Revie, winning another league title, the Fairs Cup for a second time and the FA Cup. Even long after Revie had left, Leeds would win the league title again and went on to compete quite successfully in Europe, reaching both the UEFA Cup and Champions League semi-finals.

But then Leeds took a nosedive of astronomic proportions, getting relegated from the Premier League and the Championship before coming to a shuddering halt in League 1. However, and this is quite true, I kept thinking that at least I would get to go to Blackpool again. I had always longed to play Blackpool again.

But as we were subsiding through the divisions we somehow avoided them. When we dropped into the Championship, Blackpool were in League 1. I couldn't believe it. After we got relegated to League 1 in 2007, I was totally distraught and I escaped to Brisbane in Australia for a few weeks to get away from football altogether. But I consoled myself a little with the fact that at least we would be playing Blackpool the following season.

Then, one lunchtime, I was in a hotel bar in the Surfers Paradise resort when I got a phone call from my mate Andy. 'Bad news mate, Blackpool have just won the play-offs, they've been promoted to the Championship,' he said.

We awoke from our coma in League 1 on 8 May 2010. Our final and crucial game was against Bristol Rovers, which we won 2-1 with ten men to clinch promotion to the Championship. On the same day, Blackpool were playing Bristol City *in* the Championship.

We'd had a great season for a change. We had knocked our old enemy out of the FA Cup in the third round at Old Trafford, and won promotion. But yet again those bloody Tangerines didn't read the script. A draw against Bristol City was enough to take them into the play-offs. They had finished sixth in the Championship, ironically their highest position in the league since that season when Leeds fans were tipping people out of their deckchairs in 1971. Then they beat Cardiff in the play-off final at Wembley to go into the Premier League. You couldn't make it up, could you?

They say you should be careful what you wish for and that was never truer than my wish for Leeds to play Blackpool again.

Despite being welcomed with open arms, many hotels and pubs were ordered to refuse any kind of service whatsoever to Leeds fans. We had this confirmed by a number of establishments. We drank in many pubs and even had lock-ins on the few nights we were there. There was no trouble of any kind anywhere.

One pub that was ordered to close was the venue for a Leeds on the Road event the night before the visit there in April 2012. This event was hosted by the Blackpool Whites with several Leeds players attending.

The police issued a statement saying that they did not want large groups of Leeds fans gathering in one place. It was only when the landlady pointed out that it was an official function sanctioned by Leeds United that the police relented. But they maintained a high, heavy and above all totally unnecessary presence outside the pub all evening.

Incidentally, the venue was only yards from the Mayfair Hotel. I knew that Charlie and Ivy would sadly have long since departed this earth but I had a quick look inside for nostalgic purposes. Like most things these days it had changed beyond all recognition. Even the famous Pleasure Beach was ordered to close for the few days that Leeds fans were in town and for our entire stay the tide stayed out!

I can reveal exclusively that I no longer have a soft spot for Blackpool Football Club.

31

A Note Of Genius

EARLY in the 2012/13 season I was at London Road once again watching Peterborough face up to Leeds. Darren Ferguson was again stood on the touchline barking out orders to his charges.

Despite it initially being sunny, the heavens opened and absolutely drenched Ferguson in his expensive suit and although he tried really hard to look as though he wasn't bothered, he quite clearly wasn't enjoying the weather as much as the thousands of away supporters directly behind him. Neither did Ferguson enjoy the final score of 2-1 to Leeds.

Right outside the ground there was a conveniently situated beer festival taking place, so naturally Leeds fans set about chucking funds into the Peterborough economy by pouring copious amounts of beer down their throats before boarding several buses and heading home via several different directions up and down the country.

The League Cup had yet another corporate name during the 2012/13 season, the Capital One Cup. Our opponents in the third round were Everton, who had among their number a big Belgian by the name of Marouane Fellaini. With his distinctive big black hair, Fellaini looked more like a member of the 1970s pop group The Stylistics than a brilliant footballer.

Fellaini was just one of a star-studded Everton team that arrived at Elland Road that wet September evening. With Everton sitting third in the Premier League and Leeds lying 12th in the Championship the Toffees were the bookies' overwhelming favourites.

Christian Crowther of Betfair proclaimed, 'The Toffees will not come unstuck at Elland Road. Everton will have the bit firmly between their teeth after a blistering start to the season. Everton's exciting brand of football has seen them rack up goals galore, with at least two to four goals in their last six games. Leeds, on the other hand, have conceded an average of more than two goals a game, which should mean that Everton will find a way past their defence more than once. And unfortunately for Leeds fans, Everton are taking this competition very seriously this season.'

On the night, Aidan White opened the scoring for Leeds very early on and Everton were completely outplayed for most of the match as Rodolph Austin added a second with 20 minutes remaining. Everton pulled one back with less than ten minutes left but both parties agreed that the 2-1 scoreline at the end had greatly flattered Everton.

One thing that united both Leeds and Everton and their supporters was the memory of the outstanding Gary Speed, who took his own life less than a year earlier. This was the first meeting between the two clubs he served so well since his tragic passing.

Sadly, on 31 October 2012, Alan Osborne – more commonly known as Geezer – passed away. Gary was a West Ham fan and also a great friend of mine so I travelled to London along with several other Leeds supporters for his funeral on 9 November.

When Geezer's son and daughter read from the Bible there wasn't a dry eye in the house. The funeral was organised by the Salvation Army and they complimented how Leeds and West Ham fans had come together for a mutual friend. RIP Geezer.

Back on the pitch:

Leeds have not had much luck six miles west along the A62 since Huddersfield's Leeds Road home was demolished in 1994 and Town set up camp at a new stadium only yards away from the original site. That changed on 1 December.

As you approach the newly-named John Smith's Stadium you could be forgiven for thinking that you had arrived at some amusement theme park, such is the huge white steelwork that dominates its appearance, but for once the fun belonged to the Whites as they dominated Huddersfield, now managed by former Leeds manager Simon Grayson, and won 4-2, which by Grayson's own admission flattered Town's performance somewhat.

The New Year quickly came around and in 2013 North Korea conducted its third underground nuclear test, former British Prime Minister Margaret Thatcher passed away following a stroke and a tornado hit Hayling Island in Hampshire and damaged around 100 homes.

In sport, David Moyes, although a good manager during his days at Everton without winning any silverware, replaced Alex

Ferguson as manager of manchester united. Andy Murray finally won Wimbledon following a period of 77 years without a British champion – Fred Perry in 1936 being the last Brit to claim the prize. Murray beat his good friend Novak Djokovic in straight sets to win a final that produced some incredible rallies. The Rugby League World Cup took place in Britain with England bowing out in the semi-finals before Australia thrashed bitter rivals New Zealand 34-2 in the final.

Early in 2013 our FA Cup campaign began as we inflicted further cup damage on Birmingham City in the third round.

After a dull and disappointing 1-1 draw at Elland Road we travelled to St Andrew's for the replay and thousands of fans endured the freezing conditions, then matters weren't helped when we fell behind after half an hour's play.

Things improved greatly in the second period though and some truly brilliant football from the Whites produced a fine 2-1 win. Goals from Ross McCormack and a cheeky penalty from El-Hadji Diouf, who tricked the keeper into diving to his right before chipping a soft ball straight down the middle into the net, were enough to send Leeds into the fourth round of the FA Cup for the first time since winning at Old Trafford three years earlier.

We would reach the fifth round where we lost 4-0 at Manchester City but the Championship form was to prove inconsistent.

On 30 March 2013 Leeds United were beaten 3-0 at struggling Ipswich Town after having Tom Lees sent off with the scoreline at the time goalless. Two days later it was Easter Monday and April Fool's Day. In front of the Sky Sports cameras, Leeds suffered another Easter defeat as they went down 2-1 at home to Derby County.

Manager Neil Warnock felt the full wrath of the home faithful and just a couple of hours after the game it was announced that he had departed the club.

Many supporters were optimistic that Warnock could achieve his eighth promotion in his career and more importantly get Leeds back to the top flight but, following these two defeats, we were now languishing in 12th place, nine points off the play-offs with just six games to go. Worryingly we were also only five points clear of the bottom three.

A week later I undertook something very strange on my trip to Charlton. I actually drove there. My wife Lesley had an operation the day before the match so I said I would drive to London in order to be home fairly early Saturday evening to look after my little wounded angel. So on a bright sunny morning I pulled out of my street in the Jeep and was soon ambling down the A1 with Baz, Jeff and Neil in tow.

Despite losing 2-1 after a Charlton goal seconds from time, plunging us perilously close to the dogfight going on just beneath us, our journey home wasn't too bad. With all sports reports from the radio banished, the lads tucked into lashings of cider as we all crooned to the sounds of the mighty Dean Martin and Dusty Springfield from the 'easy listening' section of my CDs.

As the sun fell slowly in the distance I decided to up the tempo slightly and the 'little old wine drinker' was replaced by Black Sabbath, and then The Doors and we entered our home city to the splendours of Led Zeppelin. By then, although completely sober, I had forgotten all about the match.

In March 2013 Reading sacked their manager Brian McDermott and he was replaced by Nigel Adkins, who had been sacked by Southampton. Leeds had also sacked their manager Neil Warnock and Adkins was on the shortlist. In a weird twist of fate that it was hoped would benefit Leeds United, Brian McDermott became manager of the Whites.

McDermott took over on Thursday 11 April and replaced Warnock. Less than 48 hours after McDermott's arrival the new boss was in the dugout for his first match in charge. It couldn't have been much more high-profile than the visit of Yorkshire rivals Sheffield Wednesday.

At first it was all looking like his tenure at Elland Road was going to begin with a disappointing defeat after Jermaine Johnson had given the Owls a 27th-minute lead. Two second-half goals from Luke Varney then turned the match in Leeds's favour and a much-needed victory was wrapped up.

The three points were vital given Leeds were only five points clear of the relegation places. With the way United were playing under Warnock we were in real danger of slipping out of the Championship via the wrong exit. McDermott's first win though, not only provided the points but a display of vastly improved proportions gave the whole club a huge lift. The fans were singing, 'We're Leeds and we pass the ball.'

Our season ended on 4 May when our fans did get a morsel of revenge over Watford and their supporters for the play-off final defeat of 2006.

United halted the premature celebrations from the home faithful and knocked Watford out of their automatic place for promotion to the Premier League and dumped them into the play-offs. 'We're only here to spoil your party!' sneered the Leeds fans, many in fancy dress including 50 convicts from South Leeds, as Ross McCormack chipped the Watford goalkeeper in the dying seconds to earn a memorable 2-1 victory.

McCormack's goal proved to be a crushing blow to Watford as they went on to reach the play-off final only to lose 1-0 after extra time against Crystal Palace, with 39-year-old Kevin Phillips scoring from the penalty spot.

The Championship Play-Off Final is the richest game of football on the planet, reputedly worth in the region of £120 million to the winners. I repeat, McCormack's goal was a crushing blow to Watford!

Although it resulted in only a win and two defeats, the 2013 pre-season tour in Slovenia had been a very pleasant one for the travelling Whites fans. Brian McDermott even handed over a 50 euro note towards a round of drinks for supporters during the first game against FC Domzale. The recipient, Dan Lambert, however, didn't spend it. Instead he bought the drinks out of his own money, choosing to get McDermott to sign the note and then he kept it.

Sun and lashings of cheap beer were aplenty as we discovered the delights of the capital Ljubljana and Murska Sobota in the northeast of the country before getting down to business for the opening game of the season at home to Brighton.

The sun was still shining as Leeds came from a goal behind to clinch it 2-1 with the winning goal coming from new signing Luke Murphy in the 94th minute. Although there were shades of handball by the youngster from Crewe before he prodded the ball home in front of the Kop, the crowd of 33,432 erupted as Leeds put down their marker for the nine months ahead.

Unfortunately, it was to be a very long nine months as an indifferent start to the season saw an inconsistent Leeds struggle to keep within touching distance of the early leaders.

Despite not being in particularly good form, Leeds were featured on television more times than Clare Balding and one of those games was at home to Birmingham City in mid-October. Jamaican international midfielder Rodolph Austin put in by far his best performance in a Leeds shirt, even grabbing a goal as we cruised to a 4-0 victory.

Sadly for the club and fans however, this type of performance would be very few and far between. That said, Leeds still managed to keep a hold on the coat-tails of the lower clubs in play-off positions and suffered only one defeat throughout December.

In 2014, the Winter Olympics took place in Sochi, Russia. Great Britain won one gold, one silver and two bronze medals, which represented the best outcome at a Winter Games since 1924. Britain also won six medals in the Winter Paralympics.

Following a dismal reign as manager of manchester united, David Moyes was sacked after just ten months. The FIFA World Cup, held in Brazil, introduced goal-line technology for the first time. England bowed out after just two group games, as did defending champions Spain.

In the world of news, publicist Max Clifford was convicted of eight indecent assaults on women and girls.

Leeds's good form in December was reversed though as we went through the month of January without winning a single match as well as crashing out of the FA Cup in the third round at Rochdale.

All of this took place amid the backdrop of a proposed takeover of the club by Italian billionaire Massimo Cellino, as well as discovering that the owners GFH (Gulf Finance House) weren't the saviour the club and the fans thought they would be. In fact they were far from it.

This takeover would dictate the whole season. Cellino is controversial to say the least and when his bid was delayed by the Football League because of a pending court case it looked in serious doubt.

Subsequently when Cellino was found guilty of not paying import duties on a yacht called *Nelie*, the Football League disqualified him under its owners and directors test. Cellino's lawyers argued successfully that the case, under Italian law, could not prevent him from buying Leeds United at this stage, and an independent QC overturned the League's decision, allowing Cellino to proceed with his 75 per cent buy-out of Leeds United.

Leeds fans usually fear the final day of the football transfer window as this is traditionally a time when the club offloads its best players at knockdown prices without the merest hint of replacing them. But what happened on the last day of January would put the writer of any soap opera firmly in the shade.

It seemed like any ordinary transfer deadline day on 31 January 2014. Our prized asset Ross McCormack was being sought by a number of Premier League clubs and once again Leeds fans feared the worst. Cellino had promised to inject transfer funds into the club, but because of the uncertainty surrounding his takeover he was, quite understandably, reluctant to do so. Therefore it was down to the normal nailbiting end of January.

I sat in my local pub as snippets began coming in from different mobile phones that West Ham had enquired about McCormack and Cardiff City had put in an offer for the Scot. Another story said that McCormack wanted to stay at Leeds and repay Brian McDermott's faith in him. Another newsflash revealed that Cardiff had improved their offer to £4m.

My local is a Samuel Smith pub, which basically, because of the owner's stance of choosing not to pay the television/music tax, means there are no televisions or jukeboxes in any of their pubs. Even the fruit machines are on mute. I kid you not. So I decided to watch events unfurl at home.

I opened a bottle of wine and turned on Sky Sports. At 8pm, the presenters discussed the McCormack saga as Cardiff increased their bid by £500,000, then, just as I poured myself a glass, the drama really began, and it proceeded to take over the entire show.

'Breaking News. Brian McDermott has been sacked as manager of Leeds United.' I couldn't believe it. Where the hell did that come from? As the presenters tried to digest the incoming news, Ross McCormack appeared on TV and gave what I personally thought was an ill-advised interview given that the sacking had only just taken place, in which he seemed to give the impression that he would now be prepared to leave the club.

Almost immediately, Cardiff's bid rose to £5m. I felt like putting my boot through the screen as the female presenter kept on saying, 'So what would it take now for clubs to buy McCormack?' I was screaming at the TV as she then said, 'Surely this could start a bidding war for him, other clubs are interested, they could now bid for him couldn't they?'

She was then given a reality check by a colleague who said, 'Hang on, news just in, McCormack now says he wants to stay at Leeds and help get them up into the Premier League.'

A last-gasp bid by Cardiff of £6m, minutes before the deadline passed at midnight, was promptly turned down by Leeds, but the high drama was far from over as attention remained focused on Elland Road and there was more 'Breaking News'.

McDermott had just had a torrid week at Elland Road as Cellino, although not yet officially instated as the new owner, began to make changes.

One of these was to put Gianluca Festa, also with no ties to the club but a friend of Cellino's, in the dugout alongside McDermott for a home game with Ipswich Town, a move that the manager, quite rightly in my opinion, refused to let happen.

Admittedly, Leeds had just endured a poor run of results, but no one seriously thought that at the time McDermott's job was on the line. Regarding the recent goings-on, including the on-off takeover bid as well as the Festa situation, McDermott would only say, hinting heavily at interference with his preparations for games, 'This has been one of the most difficult periods I've had as a manager, especially the last few days. Some of the stuff that's gone on has not been pleasant and it doesn't belong in football in my opinion.'

Meanwhile, following the sacking of McDermott, the 'Breaking News' at the end of deadline day was now on the main TV news with the story unfolding, 'Leeds fans descend on Elland Road in protest over sacking of Brian McDermott.'

Just after midnight a large group of supporters, who had been communicating on Facebook and Twitter, arrived at Elland Road and prevented the taxi sent to collect Massimo Cellino from entering the West Stand car park. The taxi kept circling the stadium but was unable to pick Cellino up before eventually being allowed in the car park by the fans. Then it was prevented from leaving with Cellino, prompting a comical statement on Twitter by the taxi firm in question, saying, 'Leeds fans, please let our taxi come home.'

Order was restored soon afterwards with West Yorkshire Police confirming, 'A number of fans went to protest at Elland Road against the sacking of the manager, wanting to speak to the possible new owner of the club. A small number of officers were on hand and no arrests were made.'

Protests continued the following day as Leeds took on neighbours Huddersfield Town at Elland Road and the 31,000 crowd chanted McDermott's name throughout the game, which saw United slaughter Huddersfield 5-1 with McCormack fittingly grabbing a hat-trick.

Then, in a further bizarre twist, rumours were circulating fast that McDermott had been reinstated. News had obviously reached the players too and afterwards a delighted McCormack gave this statement, 'That was the team that the gaffer [McDermott] picked. Nigel Gibbs and Neil Redfearn [assistant managers] took care of us and on behalf of the players I want to thank them because they were brilliant in difficult circumstances. You could see in Gibbo's face that it was hurting him. He's obviously close to the gaffer. I felt on Friday night that it was up to me to speak on behalf of the players as club captain. It's been a surreal 24 hours, now hopefully, we can start and build this club again, starting with the gaffer taking training on Monday.'

Leeds United and Brian McDermott tried to resume business as usual but it was obvious to everyone concerned that difficulties still remained. Heavy home defeats to Bolton and Reading put further pressure on McDermott. A run of three consecutive losses was halted briefly by a 2-1 victory over Millwall, which is always good, before four reverses in a row dragged United seriously close to the relegation zone.

When Leeds met Blackpool at Bloomfield Road on Boxing Day, both teams had aspirations of promotion, but when the teams next met at Elland Road in the middle of April it was during a potential relegation fight. Thankfully Leeds won 2-0 and the following week put a long-standing hoodoo to bed by beating Barnsley at Oakwell for the first time since a rainy day in November 1997. Our win also contributed to Barnsley's eventual relegation.

A 3-1 victory at St Andrew's over Birmingham, who were still in relegation trouble themselves, dragged Leeds well out of the quicksand and well away from danger, leaving a home draw against Derby on the final day purely irrelevant. Derby, incidentally, went on to the play-offs, but would be lining up against Leeds in the 2014/15 Championship after losing at Wembley to QPR.

Sadly, Leeds United would be lining up without Brian McDermott. At 11.30pm on 30 May the club's official website declared, 'Brian McDermott has left the club by mutual consent.'

To be perfectly honest, it looked inevitable that McDermott would lose his job, but equally it has to be said that he was an absolute gentleman throughout and remains one of the best managers in the game today. There is absolutely no doubt that his hands were tied and that he was thrust into a no-win situation.

Cellino said, 'Brian has been very understanding of my wish to implement a new structure. He is a great manager and a great guy. He has been unfortunate to work in such difficult circumstances. I did not realise the mess he had to work in, and the broken promises he had to deal with. He has been a gentleman to deal with in our discussions and has been very understanding of my wish to build a new structure. His main concern and priority at all times has been the welfare and protection of Leeds United.

'I wish him well for the future where I am sure he will continue to have more success and thank him for his efforts in being a stabilising and unifying figure behind the scenes in very difficult circumstances. His honest efforts to guide us to the safety of mid-table when faced with many difficulties is appreciated by us all. He will always be a friend of Leeds United.'

McDermott added, 'Massimo wants to bring a new energy to the club so that we can return to where we belong as a healthy football club. To my players for their efforts I say a big thank-you. To all the staff I am especially grateful for their support. Finally, to the incredible force that is the Leeds United supporters, I offer my heartfelt thanks. I urge everyone to get behind the team and the new owner next season to get us back to where we need to be, fighting for trophies and competing at the top table of English and European football.'

I would like to say a heartfelt thank-you to Brian McDermott. And I am sure that Dan Lambert's decision to keep his 50 Euro note signed by Brian from the Slovenia tour was one of pure genius.

Epilogue

SO there you have it. One man with one mission, one passion and one goal – never to miss a Leeds United match. It's been an incredible journey thus far. Countless grounds, cities, counties and countries have been on Gary's itinerary since January 1968 and his dedication has determined that, even though sometimes it seemed impossible he would be able to watch his beloved Leeds, somehow he found a way.

On one such occasion he even discharged himself from hospital after a rather violent nosebleed suggested he should remain under care. He ended up on the terraces as usual. After all, it was only a violent nosebleed!

I hope you've enjoyed Gary's story and, if there is anyone out there, throughout the world, who can top a record of 46 years without missing a single competitive match and only one friendly (through no fault of his own) of their beloved club I will eat next door's cat. Don't worry Snowy, that isn't going to happen!

Gary's total of consecutive matches seen up to the end of the 2013/14 season, not including friendlies, stands at an amazing 2,419.

In that time he has seen 1,063 Leeds wins, 731 defeats and 625 draws. Leeds have scored 3,486 goals with a further 2,773 conceded to give an impressive goal difference of +713.

Next chapter – the Premier League. Marching on Together!

Andy Starmore

Bibliography

Leeds United – The Complete Record, by Martin Jarred and Malcolm Macdonald, published by The Derby Books Publishing Company Limited, 3 The Parker Centre, Derby, DE21 4SZ.

Website: www.leedsunited.com

We Are Leeds! by Andy Starmore, published by The Derby Books Publishing Company Limited, 3 The Parker Centre, Derby, DE21 4SZ.

Website: www.leedsunited-mad.co.uk

Other books by Andy Starmore and Gary Edwards:

We Are Leeds! by Andy Starmore, as mentioned above.

Paint It White, by Gary Edwards.

Leeds United, The Second Coat.

No Glossing Over It, How Football Cheated Leeds United.

All three of Gary Edwards's books published by Mainstream Publishing Company (Edinburgh) Ltd, 7 Albany Street, Edinburgh, EH1 3UG.

More to come in the future from Gary and Andy.